INSTITUTE FOR AFRICAN STUDIES
RUSSIAN ACADEMY OF SCIENCES

I0085562

AFRICA'S GROWING ROLE IN WORLD POLITICS

MEABOOKS Inc.
Lac-Beauport, Quebec
2016

Editors:

Tatiana DEYCH
Alexander ZHUKOV
Olga KULKOVA
Evgeny KORENDYASOV

All papers referred by external peer review.

The views expressed in articles are the authors' own and do not necessarily reflect the publisher's editorial policy.

Originally published by Institute for African Studies of the Russian Academy of Sciences in 2014.

This reprint edition by Meabooks Inc., Africana publishers and booksellers.

MEABOOKS
34 CH. DU BOISE

CONTENTS

PREFACE

We have witnessed an unprecedented growth of the African countries' role in the international relations and world policy. The Africa of nowadays is on the upsurge. We see the process that used to be called "African Renaissance". Although the differentiation between African countries takes place, some countries experience robust economic growth: seven from ten most quickly developing countries of the world are from Africa. There is much to debate about political and economic processes in Africa and about its current and probably future orientation.

Earlier Africa was largely oriented towards former colonial countries in the continent as well as towards the USA. The latest global financial crisis, that had a heavy impact on Europe and North America, motivated the countries of the continent to "look at East" and to forge closer ties with Asia and Latin America. The emergence of BRICS as a new global entity has marked some of the large-scale changes in the landscape of the world economy, and Africa has become more involved in its orbit. As some experts argue, Africa's growth was influenced greatly by its relationship with BRICS. But, for African countries, their relations with the West are not less important and still draw major attention to themselves because of growing competition between 'old' and 'new' actors in the political and economic arenas of the African continent.

This volume, titled "Africa's Growing Role in World Politics," includes a selection of papers dedicated to the problems of the contemporary international relations and foreign policies of the African states. Most of these papers were presented at the panels, held within the framework of the 13th International Conference of Africanists "Society and Politics in Africa: Traditional, Transitional and New" (Moscow, Russia, May 27–30, 2014): Panel IV-7 "Russia and Africa in the Context of North-South Relations and in the Framework of BRICS", Panel IV-1 "Africa and the EU: Past, Present, Future" and Panel VII-2 "External Agency in the Greater Horn of Africa: A Comparative Analysis of Non-Regional Powers Engagement from the Cold War to Present". The reader will find below a collective work aimed at analyzing various aspects of the present-day political and economic situations in the African continent and around it. The volume also seeks to contribute to the study of the African countries' growing roles in the global international relations of the 21st century.

The book contains many articles devoted to the Western countries' policies in Africa. On the background of the ongoing competition between Washington and Beijing, the US Administration has recently increased the amount of attention it pays to the continent. European Union is also actively developing its strategic partnership with Africa. The authors analyze the peculiarities of economic and political relations in the EU-Africa framework, the changing aid paradigm, the European countries' engagement in conflicts resolution in Africa. Some of the problems that are in the focus of researchers' attention are the growing African migration to Europe and the challenges related to this process.

African policies of emerging powers, first of all, of the BRICS countries, which are now effectively competing in Africa with the USA and former colonial powers, is another subject of major attention in the contemporary African Studies. The authors analyze thoroughly the ongoing cooperation between African states and a great "emerging donor" and investor – China. They particularly address the question about possible implications of China's African policy for the countries of the continent. Another subject of their analyses is the Russia-Africa relations. Several articles are devoted to African policies of such BRICS countries, as India and Brazil. The foreign policy of BRICS newcomer – South Africa – has also attracted considerable interest of the researchers, participating in this book. They argue, for example, that South Africa's priorities in international relations include its advocating for the consolidation of global powers' Africa Agendas. South Africa has also positioned itself as an arbiter in the African continent. The volume also sheds light on the policies of other emerging Asian powers, such as South Korea. These states are currently enhancing their engagement with the countries in the African continent. In particular, over the last years, they have been expanding the technical, economic, trade and cultural ties with Africa.

The book also includes articles devoted to the global problems, pertaining to the African states and to their regional issues, particularly to their relations with the world, and to their regional problems related to the questions of security and conflict resolution. The authors pay major attention, in particular, to Sudan and South Sudan. One of the urgent problems addressed by this book is the situation with African IDPs and refugees, their life conditions in camps and the measures for their transition to normal life.

Authors of the presented articles are researchers, working in African Studies and representing different scientific schools of the world. Among them are PhD holders, professors and post-graduate students. Many of them represent institutions affiliated with Russian Academy of Sciences, primarily the Moscow-based Institute for African Studies and Institute for Oriental Studies. Some researchers represent Peoples' Friendship University of Russia, other Russian universities and non-educational research centers. The selection also includes a number of papers written by scholars from the USA, France, Canada, Algeria, South Africa, and Kazakhstan.

6

I. AFRICA: GLOBAL, REGIONAL AND LOCAL DIMENSIONS

Evgeny Korendyasov,
PhD (Economy)
Institute for African Studies RAS

AFRICAN STATES' FOREIGN POLICIES
IN THE 21st CENTURY:
NEW OPPORTUNITIES AND CHALLENGES

In two last decades the foreign policy concepts of African states have undergone significant and large-scale changes. The essence of these changes is in the increasing independence of African foreign policies and in the growing role of the African continent as a dynamic actor in global politics and economy.

Today African states have more opportunities than ever before to determine their own future, to build the architecture of inter-continental and external relations independently. The driving force of the current changes generated by the energy of global transformations, by the acceleration of the economic development and modernization processes on the continent, by the shift of the main axis of the global economic development to the East, and also by the emerging challenges and threats of globalization. These same changes contributed to the collapse of the bipolar model of international relations, to the extinction of rigid confrontation between the opposing groups, to the fall of the Soviet Union, and the end of the Cold War. The system of international relations, which formed in the second half of the 20th century, has come into sharp collision with the new realities.

The search for the new world order adequate for the new challenges and threats the humankind faces has taken a stormy, often conflicting character.

The African continent has found itself in an extremely difficult position. It has become a stepdaughter of globalization. It seemed that the 21st century would not promise it any change for the better. However, such predictions soon disproved. A British magazine with worldwide reputation, *The Economist*, in 2000 described Africa as a "hopeless" continent. However, in 2011 the same magazine pictured Africa as "rising", while in March 2011 – as "hopeful".

The Africans themselves are optimistic about their future. The former chairperson of the Commission of African Union, Jean Ping, stated that Africa would soon shed the reputation of a "hopeless continent". It would join the ranks of the key players of the global politics. Jean Ping believed that Africa was going to be in the centre of the struggle between the great powers for the control over the energy resources, that Africa would take an active part in the reformation of the "outdated system of global governance"[1].

When the 21st century came, the processes of structural re-formatting of global political space and of creating the new world order based on the principles of the primacy of the international law, democracy and justice have intensified.

African governments started to re-consider their foreign policy priorities, their close attachment to the national interests and to the aim of overcoming their economic backwardness, keeping in mind the new realities generated by the deepening interdependence and the need to consider the interests of all regions and peoples.

Beginning a new attack on the foreign policy front, the Africans are relying on their improved economic positions. The economic growth of African countries in the past two decades has been an average of 4–6%. In twenty oil not-producing countries of sub-Saharan Africa the annual growth rate from 1998 to 2008 was 4% and above[2].

Africa's GDP grew (according to purchasing power parity, PPP) from $1.9 trillion in 2000 to $3 trillion – in 2014, i.e. by 70%. In terms of per capita, GDP in 2014 reached $3 thousand (by PPP)[3]. Africa occupies the second or third place in terms of the attractiveness for foreign direct investment. From 2000 to 2012, its value increased fourfold (from $154 billion to $630 billion)[4].

The drivers of the "African boom", in our opinion, are long-term.

These include:

– the wealth of natural resources, which are of critical importance to the global economy;

– the demographic trends: by 2040 the continent will account for 90% of the growth of the world population and for 65% of labour force growth[5];

– the growing consumer demand (by 2020 the Africans' consumption expenditures will amount to $1.4 trillion, whereas today they are at the level of $800 billion)[6].

The development of positive trends in the economy of the continent gave grounds to Jean Ping to declare, "In the context when the evolution of production and the possession of natural resources predetermine the international relations, the whole world realized that it would be more and more difficult and even impossible to continue to systematically ignore the whole continent..."[7].

In these circumstances, the foreign policy of African states underlines new energy and persistence in defending their national interests.

Today there are four strategic factors shaping the main foreign policy priorities of the African states: Pan-Africanism, inter-African bilateral state relations, the priority of the partnership with the emerging countries, and "resource diplomacy".

In 2002, the African Union was created, succeeding the Organization of African Unity, which fulfilled its main mission – the eradication of colonialism and apartheid in the continent. The African Union designed to make the processes of development and integration of the continent irreversible and to base them upon the "common African identity", giving the Africans themselves the decisive role in solving their own problems[8].

The founding documents of the AU reflected the liberal concepts of democracy and of the open market economy, and highlighted the commitment to "respect democratic principles, human rights, good governance and the rule of law".

In the foreign policy sphere the AU right to intervene (subject to certain procedures) in cases of war crimes, genocide, crimes against humanity, mass human rights violations was proclaimed. The AU condemns the unconstitutional methods of regime change, including coup-d'états. It is envisaged, that the country in which regime change is effected by the coup and other military actions, is temporarily excluded from the AU. Thus, the most important prerequisite for the legitimacy of power is the observance of the rights and freedoms of the individual, the creation of the relevant institutions and mechanisms of social-political and state structure.

However, following these rules is not easy. African ruling elites are reluctant to part with the inviolability of national sovereignty and non-interference in internal affairs. They challenge the decisions of international institutions taken over their heads and against their opinion.

It is indicative in this respect that Africans actively supported Brazil's proposal to change the UN General Assembly resolution "On the responsibility to protect". This resolution sanctions the intervention of the international community in the internal affairs of a state if it does not provide adequate protection for its population against genocide and crimes against humanity. Brazil and African states suggested re-naming that resolution "Responsibility during the operations of protection".

Problems of security and conflict resolution occupy the central place in the activities of the African Union. "African peace and security architecture" was created. Its core structures include the Peace and Security Council of the African Union, the continental early-warning system, the African Standby Force, and regional mechanisms meant to prevent and resolve conflicts.

During the AU existence, there has been a significant relaxation of tensions on the continent. From 1963 to 2014, there were in total almost 70 coups on the continent, including 11 between 2003 and 2014. It should be emphasized (in order to clarify the extent of instability on the continent) that 54% of coups in 1963–2014 took place in seven countries – Benin, Burkina Faso, Burundi, Ghana, Mauritania, Nigeria, Central African Republic, in each of which 5-6 coups happened.

The African Union has taken part in seven peacekeeping operations and in numerous mediation missions. Nigeria, Sierra Leone, Liberia and South Africa are most active in the AU peacekeeping efforts (in Burundi, Comoros, DRC, Cote d'Ivoire, Rwanda, Sudan, mediation efforts in Zimbabwe and Swaziland). According to the former President of the CAR F. Bozizé, there was signed an agreement on defence between South Africa and the Central African Republic in 2007. In 2012, it extended. On January 2013, 300 the South African military was sent to the CAR at the disposal of the President of the Central African Republic[9].

However, the role of the AU and its institutions in these generally positive developments can hardly considered decisive. Declared solutions and peace plans remain largely on paper. The African Standby Force still has not properly formed. The African Union failed to implement its proposals for overcoming the political crises in Gabon, Togo, and Côte d'Ivoire. Its attempts to achieve peaceful resolution of the Libyan crisis were unsuccessful. African countries had different positions on this problem, and those differences not settled. South Africa, Gabon and Nigeria voted in the Security Council for the resolution 1973, against the advice of the AU high-level mediation team on the Libyan situation, consisting of the presidents of Mali, the Republic of Congo, Uganda and South Africa. The Libyan opposition rejected suggestions of the AU regarding peace settlement. Even before the AU leadership made a decision, African countries have recognized the Libyan transitional government, which seized the power with the decisive support of NATO. French troops have played the leading role in the peacekeeping efforts in Mali and the Central African Republic.

AU peacekeeping activities continue to depend critically upon the Western powers. The Union's budget for 2014 is $308 million; the contributions from the participating countries amount to 46% ($138 million), while the assistance of foreign partners – to 54% ($170 million). More than 60% of the budget intended for peacekeeping operations.

It should be borne in mind that 66% of contributions to the budget of the African Union are the contributions of just five countries: Algeria, Libya, Egypt, Tunisia, and South Africa[10].

The UN and the European Union continue to play a major role in peacekeeping efforts in Africa both in the financial/material and conceptual aspects. The UN has deployed about 100 000 soldiers in Africa in the framework of its peacekeeping missions; its expenses for these purposes reached $7 billion per year[11].

Currently, seven UN operations are continuing on the continent (FISNUA, MINUL, MINURSO, MINUSCA, MINUSMA, MONUSCO, MINUAD, MINUSS, ONUCI). The largest of them is a "hybrid" (with AU participation) operation in Darfur. As part of this operation, a contingent of 22.4 thousand people was deployed (as of April 30, 2014), including 16.2 thousand of military personnel. The budget for the period from 1 July 2013 to 30 June 2014 was $1.3 billion.

The European Union demonstrates particular activity in Africa. It indicates that the distance between Europe and Africa is only 12 kilometres, thus proclaiming North Africa its southern border. Since 2004, the EU has assigned $740 million for peacekeeping aims[12]. In addition, France, the United States, and the European Union finance the work of several African training centres preparing soldiers-peacekeepers.

France has implemented a training program for peacekeeping forces – RECAMP (Reinforcement of African Peacekeeping Capabilities Programme). Americans in the framework of the program ACRI (African Crisis Response Initiative) prepared 9000 African peacekeepers during 1997–2002, allocating for this purpose about $20 million dollars per year. Then, instead of ACRI, a new programme, ASOTA (African Contingency Operations Training and Assistance), has been developed, with a budget of $50 million per year[13].

Therefore, the African Union has no discretion to seek settlement of the conflicts, according to its desired scenarios. On May 27, 2013 the program "African Capacity for Immediate Response to Crises" (Capacité Africaine de Réponse Immediate aux Crises – CARIC) adopted at the initiative of South Africa. The new initiative launched in connection with the postponement of the creation of the African Standby Force. It provided for the immediate creation of collective response forces on a voluntary basis and mostly at the expense of the participating countries in case of conflict. The aim was to create the conditions for an independent, self-reliant policy of the African Union. Speaking at the mini-summit of CARIC in Pretoria on November 5, 2013, South African President Jacob Zama told: "Africa has means to act quickly and decisively"[14]. There are grounds for such a statement. Suffice it to recall that military expenditures of African states exceed $39 billion (in 2012), among which sub-Saharan Africa accounts for 22 billion[15].

However, the new programme has met a mixed reaction. It supported by only ten countries: Algeria, Angola, Guinea, Niger, Uganda, Tanzania, Chad, Sudan, Ethiopia, and South Africa.

The executive bodies of the AU find it increasingly harder to achieve a coordinated position, "one common voice" of African states in many cases. The AU failures in Libya, Côte d'Ivoire, Mali, and the Central African Republic have caused considerable damage to its prestige. At the same time, the image of the regional integration groupings on the continent is improving. In our opinion, it is premature to argue that the African Union (in the form in which it appears in its constituent documents and ambitions) is accomplished, and it is hard to predict when and in what form it will accomplished.

The ideals of Pan-Africanism, which formed by the middle of the 20th century, were transformed and significantly faded. The cohesion of the continent, based on the commonality of the colonial past, the need for solidarity in the struggle for the complete decolonization of the continent, the similarity of the problems of nation-building, have significantly weakened due to various reasons. However, the key role of the pan-African ideology as one of the building blocks of the foreign policy of African states remains unchanged.

Today the concerns related to the development of bilateral relations between the African countries themselves come to the forefront. The scope of disagreements and even confrontations inside the space of intra-African, intercontinental inland relations in these conditions is expanding. Such a situation emerged largely due to the growing uneven socioeconomic development of African countries.

The UNECA data show that between 1995–2009, the GDP of some countries grew by 500% and above (in Angola – 1200%, in Mozambique – by 590%, in Tanzania – 520%, in Ethiopia by 493%), while in others – by 100 – 200% (in the DRC – 90% in Tunisia – 116%, Gabon – 150%, Zambia – 200%)[16]. The group of nineteen oil-producing countries stands out, followed by the states where the extraction and processing of minerals and metals gather pace. The countries whose economies mainly linked with the development of agriculture or forestry resources are falling behind.

Moreover, we may see the destructive tendencies associated with different orientations of individual African regions to emerging global development poles. North African countries are coming closer to the Mediterranean pole, African East coast states – to the countries of the Indian Ocean; Southern Cone countries – to the emerging Latin American and Indian poles. Against this background, there is a competition and a struggle for leadership at the regional and continental levels.

All this makes it difficult to develop a consensus approach of the African countries towards common international problems, weakens the positions of the continent in the international arena, forces African diplomacy to search agreements with the neighbours in order to create local zones of good-neighbourliness and mutual security.

The new strategic priority of the foreign policy of African countries has become a comprehensive development of political and economic partnership with the emerging countries – the BRICS, Turkey, Mexico, Indonesia, Vietnam, etc.

The economic strength of this group of countries is becoming a key factor in the evolution of the world economy and world economic relations. Only BRICS countries now account for over 43% of the world population, 20% of world GDP, 20% of world trade, more than 20% of foreign direct investment[17].

Over the recent years, there has taken place a significant reorientation of foreign policy and economic priorities of African countries towards emerging countries. As a result, the traditional monopoly positions of the Euro-Atlantic partners have been significantly undermined. If at the end of the 1980s, Europe accounted for 60% of African foreign economic relations, then in early 2010s – for 30%. The foreign trade turnover of the BRICS states with the countries of the continent exceeds $200 billion; it projected to increase to 530 billion by 2015. The share of the emerging countries in African foreign trade will increase from 20% in 2010 to 33% in 2015[18]. BRICS countries invested more than $70 billion in the countries of the continent during 2003–2012, ranking fourth after Europe, the USA and the Middle East[19]. In 2012, foreign direct investment of the emerging countries amounted to 25% of the total inflow (19% in 2003)[20].

The partnership with emerging countries expands the foreign policy geography of African countries, strengthens its multi-vector character, and ensures the access for Africans to new sources of financing for development and to the latest technologies.

The so-called resource diplomacy becomes the separate and essential component of the foreign policy of African states. Today, when structural changes in the global markets of energy and other natural resources have a direct and decisive impact on the pace of global economic growth and on the reformatting of the system of international relations as a whole, Africa gets a real chance to accelerate its development and expand its influence in the global system of international relations.

In developed countries, and in close proximity to them, the exhaustion of fuel and mineral resources has reached the critical level. At the same time, the demand for them has increased – 27 times more for solid minerals in the 20th century, and 5 times for oil from 1960 until the beginning of the 21st century (from 6 billion to 30 billion barrels)[21].

Meanwhile, it is known that Africa plays a key role in the production of many minerals. It accounts for 74% of the world production of platinum-group metals (PGM), 62% – of cobalt, 54% – diamonds, 42% – chromites, 30% – manganese, 26% – phosphates, etc. The PGM production is projected to increase by 33%, cobalt – by 87%, copper – by 86%, iron ore – by 466% by

2017[22]. In the depths of Africa, there are 33% of world uranium resources, 12% of oil, 8–10% of gas[23].

In the new situation, the competition in world commodity markets has escalated. "Resource wars" have broken out. Balance of power between the countries producing and consuming raw materials has changed drastically. Resource-rich countries have got the chance to force consumers to consider their conditions of access to raw materials and their sales. Africans thus get a chance to redistribute resource rents, which today are often the main source of replenishment of investment resources. For ten oil-producing countries, for example, the resource rent is on average 39%[24].

Africa's "resource diplomacy" has to lead to finding the optimal solutions for the twofold task: saving sovereign rights over natural resources and ensuring favourable conditions for partnership with consumer countries in terms of sustainable development of the mining sector and the successful sales of products on the world markets. Meanwhile, in the new battles for control over the natural resources of the continent, multinational companies do not hesitate to seek the support of separatists in regions rich in energy and other critically important raw materials. They do so in order to weaken the jurisdiction of the central authorities and to establish their complete control and ensure the continuous supply of raw materials.

African states have become the key actors of the resource diplomacy. They actively support the adoption of multilateral international agreements governing the exploration, production and marketing of natural resources.

In the past two decades, African foreign policy concepts have undergone significant and dramatic changes. Africa is gradually moving away from the Euro centrism in its foreign policy. Cooperative relations have become more equitable and balanced. Nevertheless, this vector remains dominant and for many countries, dependence on traditional partners retains critical importance. All the more so because in recent years Western countries have been revising their assessments of the role and place of Africa in the future global system of relations and have been vigorously increasing the scale of their ties with the continent. The United States is actively "returning" to Africa, especially in the area of military cooperation. France, which has undertaken military operations in four African countries in the last three years (in Libya, Côte d'Ivoire, the military intervention in Mali and the Central African Republic), demonstrates its desire not to relax its efforts on the African direction. The European Union is implementing a multifaceted expansion programme in Africa.

The overall positions of Africa in the world remain precarious, while new tendencies are paving their way with difficulty. It is so because, first, the entire system of international relations remains unbalanced. Omni directional, contradictory, fickle trends of its evolution are preserved and even enhanced. More or less certain and stable consensus parameters and principles of the future world order have not yet been clearly defined.

[1] Jean Ping. La place de l'Afrique dans les relations internationals aujourd'hui; http://appablog.wordpress.com/2011/03/25/la-place-de-l'Afrique-dans-les-relations-...

[2] Foreign Affairs. May – June 2013; http://foreignaffairs.com

[3] www.africaneconomicoutlook.org/data-statistics.2013.

[4] UNCTAD. World Investment Report 2013; http://www.africaneconomi coutlook.org/data-statistics

[5] БРИКС – Африка: партнерство и взаимодействие. Отв. ред. Е.Н. Корендясов, Т.Л. Дейч. М. 2013. С.28. BRICS–Africa. Partnership and Interaction. Editors: E.Korendyasov, T.Deych. M.2013. P. 28.

[6] Оценки Всемирного Банка. Data of World Bank.

[7] Jean Ping. Op. cit.

[8] Act Constitutif de l'Union Africaine.

[9] Nguembock S. Le Caric. Thinking Africa. Note d'analyse politique, N 15, février 2014. P.3. www. Thinkingafrica.org. Institut de Recherche et d'Enseignement sur la Paix. Paris.

[10] Ken A. L'Union Africaine doit s'autosuffir financièrement. PA – Union.com. 29 janvier 2014.

[11] Williams Paul D. The Africa Center for Strategic Studies USA. Les operations de paix en Afrique depuis 2000. http://www.Africacenter.org

[12] Исследовательский центр «Международные программы мира и безопасности» Университета Лаваля (Франция).Issledovatelskij centre "Mejdunarodnije programmy mira I bezopasnosti Universiteta Lavalle (France). Bulletin N 58 septembre – octobre 2012. Sécurité mondiale. P.6. http://www.psi.ulaval.ca/publications/sécurite mondiale/

[13] Bulletin du maintien de la paix № 97. Janvier 2010. Ministére de la defense nationale du Canada (http://www.cepes.uqam.ca)

[14] Nguemboc S. La CARIC. Enjeux politiques et défis de la mise en oeuvre. Note d'analyse politique № 15 – janvier 2014. P. 4.

[15] SIPRI. Yearbook 2013. Summary. P. 6.

[16] http://www.nouvelle-dynamique.org/article-union-africaine

[17] БРИКС – Африка: партнерство и взаимодействие. Отв. ред. Е.Н. Корендясов, Т.Л. Дейч. М. 2013.Cc. 49-50. BRICS –Africa: Partnership and interaction.Editors: E.Korendyasov, T.Deych. Moscow, 2013. Pp. 49-50.

[18] Gaunt J. Building BRICS in Africa. http://blogs/reuter.com. Macroscope 2010/11/23

[19] Подсчитано на основе публикаций Африканского банка развития, ЮНКТАД, ЭКА ООН, МВФ. Podschitano na osnove publicatsij AfDB, UNCTAD, UNECA, IMF.

[20] UNCTAD. World Investment Report 2013.

[21] Лоран Э. Нефтяные магнаты. М., 2010. С. 318. Loran E. Neftijanye magnaty. M. 2010.

[22] AfDB, OECD, UNDP, ECA. African Economic Outlook 2013. P. 140.

[23] AfDB, OECD, UNDP, ECA. African Economic Outlook 2013. P. 140.

[24] British Petroleum Statistical Review. World Energy. June 2013. P.10; Hugon Ph. Des solutions africaines face aux nouveaux enjeux internationaux. Paris, 2013. P. 5.

Anatoly Khazanov, Prof., Dr.Sc.
Institute for Oriental Studies,
Russian Academy of Sciences

WHY ANTI-AMERICAN FEVER IS SHAKING ARAB WORLD?

This paper describes an original concept that, in our opinion, helps explain the present-day turbulent events in the Arab world and other Muslim countries. It also seeks to answer the question used for the headline. I have called it the concept of 'valves for a steam boiler'.

It is no secret that the majority of the population in many Muslim countries still lives below the poverty line. For this reason, power holders in these countries always face a major task to find an appropriate valve. By opening the valve, they would release the steam of social protest and lower the internal pressure of «steam boiler». During the colonialism, ruling elites found such a 'valve' in the slogans of nationalism, in the Soviet-backed ideology of anti-colonialism. At that time, nationalism in Asia and Africa was synonymous with anti-colonialism. According to Francis Fukuyama, nationalism has often played a leading role in the struggle of suppressed nations for their freedom and democracy...

The same happened in Europe, argues Fukuyama, which had to pass through the stage of nationalism, so that, nowadays, European nations may peacefully coexist in the European Union. After African and Asian nations had obtained their independence, the slogans of nationalism exhausted their potential. In order to «release the steam of social protest», yet another «valve» was badly needed and the political elites bet on the once popular slogans of Socialism and Socialist orientation. However, the Soviet invasion of Afghanistan in 1979, under a very strange pretext of «international assistance», and lack of understanding in Muslim countries for what it was, did much to discredit Socialism in that part of the world. Ruling classes and societies in general interpreted this as «declaring war on Islam». When the Socialist model of development clearly lost public appeal in the Islamic world, a number of Middle and Near Eastern leaders (Qaddafi, Khomeini et al.) turned to various doctrines of the so-called «Third Way». However, when this also failed to bring major positive changes to people's lives, a new «valve» became necessary in order «to lower the steam pressure». It was at this point when societies started voicing protests against dictatorial regimes, which eventually lead to the Arab Spring.

Another important factor is that in all Arab countries youth makes up the majority of the population (which is very different from the situation in Europe where the population is aging). Due to high birth rates in Muslim countries, Muslims have now become the fastest growing religious community in the world. In the recent years, the Middle Eastern population was growing faster than the population of any other region. With an average growth rate of 2.7%, the Middle East has left behind Asia (1.6%) and Latin America (1.7%).

Similar processes are going on in a number of predominantly Muslim countries that form a 'belt' alongside the southern borders of Russia. Their joint population totals 300 million people now. It is likely that by 2025 this will grow to at least 450 million people. Unresolved social problems, especially the unemployment, hit the youth more heavily than any other part of the society. In addition, the youth forms a clear majority in Arab countries. Lack of work, lack of social lifts and grim prospects in life make sure that the youth is striving for revolution like no other part of the society. This is a heady brew, which feeds the revolutionary fire.

Many young people do not have families, have few duties and bear no responsibility other than for themselves. They have nothing to lose and little to risk.

Another specific feature of the Arab youth is that it is generally very politically minded. Young Arabs (including those not so well educated) like to discuss politics. All of them are relatively well aware of what is happening in the world. Largely, it is the result of the fact, that the percentage of Internet users is very high in the Arab world. It is higher than, say, in Russia.

Information from all over the world became available to the broad masses of the population in Tunisia, Libya, Bahrain, Oman, Yemen and other Arab states which have recently experienced revolutionary events. What people in these countries learn about the life abroad enables them to compare their own conditions and standards of life with those of the so-called 'golden billion'. Besides, Egypt, Tunisia and other countries are popular tourist destinations, and international tourists are yet another source of information. There are millions of migrants from North Africa living and working in Europe. What they tell their relatives about living conditions in the EU produces certain reactions too. Thus, we consider the globalization and unresolved controversy between traditional Islamic values and Western values to be the most important factors of revolutionary movements in the Arab world. The globalization exposed once 'dormant' minds to the destabilizing influence of this controversy.

People of North Africa would like to have living standards of Western Europeans and continue with their lifestyle of Northern Africans. For several reasons, it is impossible. Nevertheless, they start asking questions: where are billions of dollars earned by oil exports? Moreover, if thousands of barrels of oil are daily transported through the Suez Canal, then where are billions of dollars that pour into the country in the form of transit fees?

Searching for answers to these questions inevitably leads Arab intellectuals to a conclusion that the present-day political elites of their countries have wallowed in corruption and moral decay. The first generation of Arab leaders that led independence movements in their respective countries is long gone (Nasser, Sadat, Ben Bella, King Abdullah I of Jordan, Arafat *et al.*). New times give way to new names. Romanticized heroes replaced by pragmatic and, in certain cases, corrupted politicians, some of whom neglect their people even to the point of despising them.

It is the Westernized and liberally minded youths that initiated revolutionary processes in the Arab world, which came to be known as the Arab Spring. Many of these young people are frequent Internet users, and adopted a number of Western values. Before the breathtaking spread of the Internet, broad masses of the population in the Arab world were only slightly familiar with the Western system of values. The internet is a bridge, which hosted an encounter between the Arab society and the contemporary West, with its moral and legal principles. The Internet, with its huge power based on modern information technologies, played a decisive role in the revolutionary uprisings in Tunisia, Egypt and Libya. The American magazine *Foreign Policy* even applied a term «WikiLeaks revolution» to the uprising in Tunisia, although later this changed for «Jasmine Revolution». The explanation is simple: the exposes published on the WikiLeaks website caused popular indignation in Tunisia and, thus, became the catalyst for a revolutionary situation in this country. Leaked dispatches and cables written by American diplomats and exposed to the widest audience by this website shed light on horrific corruption in the country. It became clear to everybody that the surrounding of President Ben Ali had transformed itself into a mafia clan. Broad-based anti-governmental demonstrations in Egypt, which began on 25 January 2011, were organized and manipulated with the help of various Internet resources.

A Russian historian Klyuchevsky who lived and worked in the 19th century, once wrote that «the Time of Troubles[1] became the first time ever to shake somnolent minds [of Russians]] ». Paraphrasing this conclusion, we may argue «the globalization and Internet were the first to shake somnolent Arab minds» and motivated people for the revolutionary uprisings. These people started asking questions: where do billions of petrodollars go? The Suez Canal used to transport 1.5 billion dollars per day earns billions of dollars. Where are these revenues? A search for answers to these «cursed questions» has lead young Arab intellectuals to a conclusion that the dictatorial regimes in their respective countries have wallowed in corruption and moral decay. In addition, as it stated above, the young and educated proponents of

Western values that succeeded in the revolutionary uprisings of the Arab Spring rose in favor of democratic elections. However, unlike these young intellectuals, the majority of voters in Muslim countries (where 85% of the population live in poverty and an average illiteracy rate amounts to 60%) favor 'traditional Islamic' values. No wonder that the elections have been won by Islamists on the political stage. Thus, a historical paradox has emerged: revolutions in the Arab world have been driven by those advocating for the Western values, whereas the fruits of their victories are being used by proponents of the Islamic values.

Thus, Westernized liberal forces had enough capacity only to launch the process, which later became dominated by their opponents, those who favor traditional values. The cases of the *Islamic Front of Salvation* in Algeria and *Hamas* in the Palestinian Autonomy, both of which succeeded in elections in their respective countries, show, that democracy and, in particular, democratic elections, create more favourable conditions for the Islamists to come to power. Nowadays, the *Muslim Brotherhood* is striving for power in Egypt. They are waging an information war in the Internet, betting on the following argument: «We have tried Socialism under Nasser, tried Capitalism under Sadat and Mubarak. None of this has brought us any good. Let us now try the Islamic model». The economic situation in Egypt has deteriorated much nowadays. Since 2011, when the civil unrest began, the country has been losing about 310 million dollars per day. Already by February 2011, the budget deficit in Egypt has climbed to 8% of the GDP. In other North African states, where local dictators were toppled, people's lives have not changed for the better either. As a result, the pressure of «parasocial progress» in these countries came close to the critical level. There, at that point, the above-mentioned 'Innocence of Muslims' movie rendered some very helpful services to the new Arab regimes.

Once again, a new "valve" has been found that enabled to «lower the steam pressure» of social protest. Thinking about possible historical analogies, this situation reminds us of the so-called 'Beilis Affair' in Russia at the beginning of the 20th century. By giving much publicity to this trial, the czarist government of Russia managed to redirect the popular discontent to the bed of primitive anti-Semitism.

Going back to nowadays and to the Arab countries, the scandalous movie provoked anti-American demonstrations, which swept the entire Muslim world. Furious crowds stormed the U.S. embassies in Afghanistan, Egypt, Yemen, Iraq, Jordan, and Libya and even in Bangladesh. Protest demonstrations spread throughout the Arab world as a fire in a bush. It was a video, uploaded on the YouTube website, that sparked this fire. More than a million of Internet users watched the 'Innocence of Muslims' from YouTube.

On 11 September 2012 (a date not to be forgotten in the United States), the American ambassador in Libya was killed in Tripoli. According to V. Naumkin, Director of the Institute for Oriental Studies in Russia, a wave of anti-Americanism not only prevents the US from taking military action against Iran, but also eases the tensions between Shi'as and Sunnis: such moments usually bring about a motion towards consolidation of all Muslims. This creates a situation that Israel and the United States need to take into account. According to Naumkin, this situation may well serve the interests of radical Salafis that seek to discredit those in power, in particular more moderate Islamists and pro-Western political forces that strengthened themselves: "this film was popularized by apologetics of global Jihad who used it as a tool to mobilize the street".

For the first time since 1979, an ambassador of the United States was killed while on duty in foreign lands. A response from Washington was predictable and manifested itself in a clear demonstration of power. Two boat destroyers were promptly sent with a mission to the Libyan coast. They were carrying U.S. marines assigned to safeguard the country's embassy in Tripoli.

There is no doubt that the above mentioned movie strengthened the positions of President Obama's rivals in the United States and radical Islamists in the Arab world. The latter received yet another chance to portray themselves as the only and consecutive defenders of Islam in Arab countries. They also managed to direct the flow of people's indignation into a predictable bed of anti-Americanism.

---

[1] A period in the history of Russia marked by severe internal strife and devastating foreign invasions of late 16th – early 17th centuries.

Natalia Sepeleva
Institute for African Studies

ANALYSIS OF THE HUMANITARIAN SITUATION
IN AFRICA SOUTH OF SAHARA
(The case of the Great African Lakes)

In the contemporary world, the world of the 21 century, instability within some of the world regions, given their growing mutual dependence, creates most serious challenges to global stability. As for Africa, it considered one of the least stable regions in the world. Starting from its independence, the continent has suffered a lot from armed clashes, endless coups d'état', numerous civilian deaths, etc. Negative consequences of African states' internal conflicts affect not only their immediate neighbors, but also the countries situated far from their borders too.

This paper offers a brief analysis of the humanitarian situation in the Great Lakes region, which may be called an «African pearl», and has a potential to become the moving force of the continent's growth. However, today it is a typical example of a region overwhelmed by violent conflicts.

The Great Lakes region is enormously rich in natural and human resources. It is one of the densest African regions and includes the territory of six states: Burundi, the DRC, Kenya, Rwanda, Tanzania and Uganda. The total number of population in the region equals 110 million people, of which 70 million people (as of 2009) live in the DRC[1]. The population density varies from 30 (DRC) to 400 (Rwanda) people per sq. km^2. The region has its main natural wealth in 15 large lakes with huge deposits of sweet water. Seven of these lakes (the Victoria, the Tanganyika, the Malawi, the Turkana, the Albert, the Kiwu and the Edward) are among the largest in the world. For example, the Lake Tanganyika is the world's second largest deposit of sweet water (after the Baikal). Overall, the Great African Lakes store 25% of sweet water in the world[3]. Moreover, the Great Lakes region has rich deposits of minerals: gold, platinum, silver, diamonds, tantalites and columbites, stannum, nickel, bauxites, tungsten, copper, zinc, uranium, limestone, timber of precious tropical species, etc.

Deposits of tantalites have so far discovered in Germany, Sweden, Greenland and the USA, but 80% of all deposits in the world are in Africa, 80% of which are in the DRC.

However, it is a matter of fact that the resource bonanza of the DRC (gold, diamonds[4], uranium, copper, tantal-coltan (At present, 1 kg coltan

22

costs $450 in the world market), cobalt, tungsten, manganese, zinc, silver and lead) has brought about yet another 'resource curse' of an African state. The main deposits of tantalites situated in the eastern provinces of the DRC. These provinces have long controlled by gangsters and rebel groups supported by the neighbouring Rwanda and Uganda such as the *March 23 Movement* (M23).

It would not be an exaggeration to say that almost every government or armed group participating in the Congolese conflict starts plundering the country's natural resources as soon as they grab some part of its territory. For example, Rwanda alone earns up to 240 million USD by illicit extraction of tantalites, whereas the total revenues from diamond production in the country is just 2.4 million USD per annum[5].

Some of the senior governmental officials and local entrepreneurs are often involved in making astronomic sums out of the mining business. Exploitation and exports (both legal and illicit) of the country's natural bonanza are taking place under participation of many large transnational corporations and foreign companies from Belgium, the Netherlands, the UK, Germany, Switzerland and some other countries. According to Elliot Green, an expert in this field, 95% of violent conflicts in the Great Lakes region have been provoked, in this or that way, by land grabbing or competition over natural resources[6]. However, for some reasons, this competition or struggle takes a shape of an evident ethno political conflict (e.g., civil war in the DRC and the 1994 genocide in Rwanda) which may also lead to an unprecedented environmental catastrophe.

The 20 years of civil war in the DRC has resulted in almost one million people in the country becoming homeless and about a quarter million women and girls becoming victims of sexual violence. The region still suffers from the consequences of the most disastrous military conflict after WW2, which claimed, according to different estimates, from four to 5.4 million lives. These were mostly civilians who lost their lives primarily to famine, violence or epidemics.

What gives a more eloquent picture of the humanitarian situation in the region and of its lack of socioeconomic development, are the countries' figures for GDP per capita. On average, this does not exceed 900 USD. The figures for Burundi and the DRC are particularly low: just 544 and 319 USD accordingly. Most of these people live on 1-1.5 USD per day. The region shows extremely low figures in terms of average life expectancy and average duration of education. At present, average life expectancy in the Great Lakes region comprises 54.9 years (70.1 in the world), whereas the region's average duration of education doesn't exceed 4.7 years (7.5 in the world).

The scale of the socioeconomic plight of the region is particularly large in the DRC. There are 16 million people, who are starving every day, thousands of people die of malaria and other infectious diseases and almost 5 million people live with HIV.

The situation with infant mortality is particularly alarming: according to statistics, two out of five infants die during their first year of life. Forty percent of children do not go to school. There are also 10 thousand former child-soldiers in the country[7].

Many experts see the rapid population growth in the region (including the growth caused by migration) as one of the root causes of such a low level of socioeconomic development of the region. The current growth of population by far and large exceeds the region's ability to adapt to constantly changing political, economic and social realities. The population growth in the region in general is one of the highest in the world, as well as the growth in particular countries of the region, especially the DRC. According to various estimates, by 2025, the number of population in the DRC will grow by 2.5 times compared to 1995. Beside the growing birth rates, the socioeconomic situation in the region is affected by uncontrollable flows of migrants within the region, in particular in the DRC, Burundi and Uganda. According to the UN, by mid-2013, the total number of forced migrants in the region, including IDPs, refugees and asylum seekers, has exceeded 3.5 million people (2 million in 2010).

Intra-regional forced migration (as of mid-2013)

Country	Fled from	Fled into	IDPs
Burundi	73.143	44.034	78.948
DRC	490.095	183.244	2.607.407
Rwanda	172.450	72.856	0
Tanzania	1.142	10.946	0

UNHRC Statistical Snapshot 2013 – http://www.unhcr.org/pages/49e45abc6.html

The DRC continues to be one of the leading «suppliers» of refugees and internally displaced persons (IDPs) in the world. In mid-2013, the UNHRC reported of 490 thousand Congolese refugees in the neighboring countries (5th place in the world). At the same time, there were 2.6 million IDPs inside the country (3rd place in the world).

By the beginning of 2014, the number of IDPs in the DRC exceeded 2.96 million people, 90% of whom are concentrated in four provinces – North and South Kivu (1.12 million and 580 thousand accordingly), Orientale (550 thousand) and Katanga (402 thousand). As in previous years, in 2013, the humanitarian crisis in the country remained centered on its North Kivu Province.

The UNHRC, UNICEF and World Food Program resumed aid supplies to Congolese refugees and IDPs. In particular, aid agencies work 24 hours a day to support 140 thousand IDPs in 12 camps around Goma. In North Kivu, there are 31 camps, supported by agencies, INGOs and local NGOs, which may host up to 159 thousand people, but, still, this capacity is not enough. The province has 37 spontaneous IDP camps (239 thousand people more), that also receive humanitarian aid. There are other IDPs whose location is unknown. Some of them may be staying with their relatives. Access to these people is constrained.

Some international experts believe that successful military operations against M23, which before the end of 2013 controlled much of North Kivu, have slowed down the growth of number of IDPs. However, the IDPs may not return to the areas liberated from M23, because their houses destroyed or burnt down and the transport and social infrastructure are practically missing. Another negative factor is activation of other armed groups after the defeat of M23. In Katanga, a recent growth of rebel activities has led to increased numbers of IDPs. By February 2014, the number of IDPs in this province has reached half million people.

Against this background, the situation with refugees from the DRC considered slightly better. By the end of 2013, their number has fallen to 430 thousand people (of which 153 thousand remain in Uganda, 72 thousand in Rwanda, 64 thousand in Tanzania). One of the factors that contributed to this positive dynamic has been the voluntary repatriation of 62.5 thousand refugees from the Republic of Congo to the DRC, which supported by the UNHRC.

The situation in the Equatorial Province, one of the poorest regions of the DRC, has deteriorated. From January 2013 to February 2014, the DRC received around 60 thousand refugees from the Central African Republic, mostly women and children without means of subsistence, 53 thousand of which arrived in the Equatorial Province.

The UNHRC and other international donors of aid assist almost every refugee from the CAR in the Equatorial Province. The refugees are supplied with food, water, tents, medicine and other necessities of life (50% of refugees live in camps, the rest is hosted by families). The major constraints are absence of roads and lack of funding from the center. For these reasons, many of the refugees in urgent need of aid cannot receive it. For 2014, the UNHRC office in Kinshasa (capital of the DRC) asked 175 million USD for its humanitarian programs. This means that, despite the growth in numbers of foreign refugees in the DRC (more than 200 thousand people not including those from the CAR); the UNHRC country office has lowered the budget figures when compared to the previous year (183.2 million USD in 2013). It may signal that the UNHRC seeks to optimize part of its programs in the region to reduce expenses. If so, this cannot but affect the living conditions of refugees and IDPs. According to the UN, in 2014 the DRC will remain one of the world leaders as for the number of refugees.

On 28 March 2013, the UNSC adopted Resolution 2098, which authorized the deployment of an intervention brigade within MONUSCO. This is a one-of-its-kind unit within a UN peacekeeping mission, which includes three infantry battalions, one artillery battery and one special task force company. Its declared aim is to help 'reducing the threat posed by armed groups to State authority and civilian security in eastern DRC' and 'to make space for stabilization activities'. The intervention brigade is authorized to «carry out targeted offensive operations», either on its own or in cooperation with the DRC national armed forces. No other UN mission has a structural unit of this kind that would also have a similar mandate.

Russia has supported the deployment of the intervention brigade by stating that this should help achieve a 'qualitative breakthrough' in the struggle against the anti-governmental groups that resumed hostilities in the DRC.

In order to stop ultimately violence in the Great Lakes region in a quickest way possible, it is necessary to regulate the extraction and sales of mineral resources, as well as to expand the regional cooperation. This should help solve many of the region's political and economic problems, as well as improve the catastrophic humanitarian situation of nowadays.

---

1 http://www.newworldencyclopedia.org

[2] Guy Aundu Matsanza. Congolese Crisis and Demographic Problems in the African Lakes. Kuenga Amani. 2013. P. 23-46.

[3] UNECA. The IEGLR Regional Initiative against the illegal Exploitation of Natural Resources(RINR) and other Certification Mechanisms in the Great Lakes Region (Special report) – http:/www.uneca.org/publications/special.report. 2005.

[4] 85% diamonds from the DRC are exported illegally.

[5] Blood minerals.The criminalization of the Mining Industry in East DRC. Pole Institute (Goma), 2010. August. P.8-27.

[6] Elliott Green. The Political Demography of Conflict in Modern Africa. Department of International Development. London School of Economics. L.2009. P. 35-60.

[7] Sara Uso, Alphonso Maindo. New Perspective of the Conflict at the Great Lakes Region: The demographic and social factors. UNISCI Discussion Papers. May 2005. P. 26.

Alexander Zhukov, PhD
Institute for African Studies
Russian Academy of Sciences

ERITREA'S ROLE IN THE HORN
OF AFRICA REGIONAL POLITICS:
BACKGROUND, STATUS QUO, AND PROSPECTS

Eritrea is the name given in 1889 by the former Italian colonial administration to a strip of land on the Red Sea coast of Africa from the southeastern border of what was then Anglo-Egyptian Sudan and almost to the southern rim of the Bab el Mandeb strait. Over millennia, the people, inhabiting this land, has maintained close historical and cultural links with their southern and southwestern neighbours, the people of modern-day Ethiopia, to whom many of them are related closely. However, these historically strong ties suffered a lot, sometimes even to the point of disappearance, during the Italian colonization of Eritrea in late 19th – first half of the 20th cent.

Following the end of WW2, the successful anti-colonialism movement all across Africa did not bypass the Horn region, and the Italian rule in Eritrea officially ended. However, despite many pro-independence voices in Eritrea, the country was not granted independence. It was incorporated instead into the state of Ethiopia, which resulted in a short-lived period of regional autonomy in Eritrea. In 1960s, after the autonomy was abandoned by the Ethiopian Emperor Haile Selassie I, those forces in Eritrea that favoured independence reacted by starting an insurgency. This led to a thirty-year guerilla war against two successive Ethiopian regimes. Eventually, by the time a coalition of rebel forces from different regions of Ethiopia toppled the country's dictator Mengistu Haile Mariam (1991), the pro-independence Eritrean People's Liberation Front (EPLF) managed to establish its control over most of the territory of the former autonomous region. At the same time, an allied insurgent group, the Tigrean Peoples Liberation Front (TPLF), took over power in the Ethiopian capital, Addis Ababa, which paved the way to a historical compromise that gave Eritrea a right for self-determination. After being part of Ethiopia for forty years, the people of Eritrea held a UN-supported referendum in April 1993 and voted to secede from Ethiopia. Between 1993 and 1998, the governments of Eritrea and Ethiopia, headed by the EPLF and TPLF, enjoyed good, almost excellent, relations. The two countries share not only common history, but also a vast common border, and their very geographic position in relation to each other prompts them to seek

27

to maintain good bilateral relations, which is especially important for Eritrea, the less populated and less abundant in resources out of the two countries. In 1993–1997 Eritrea had a common economic system that gave Ethiopia access to the Eritrean Red Sea ports and provided a stable of budget revenues for what at that time was Africa's youngest state. The relationship started to cool in 1997 when Eritrea created its own currency. The Ethiopian government announced that it would not accept cross-border trade operations in other currencies than US Dollars, which resulted in a financial setback for Eritrea because of its limited access to hard currencies. As a result, Eritrea's national currency, the *Nakfa*, tremendously devaluated. Bitter contradictions between the neighbors over trade and financial issues have radicalized their stances in an unresolved border dispute over small areas of land with arguably little value for either of the neighbours. In 1998, a series of violent cross-border accidents and mutual accusations lead to a massive Ethiopian invasion in Eritrea. This unleashed a disastrous war that lasted two years and caused approximately 100,000 lives on both sides. Under the Algerian mediation, a cease-fire was accomplished in 2000. This paved the road for the attempts to resolve the border dispute between the two countries. An international arbitration followed the cease-fire, but the resolution that it produced was never implemented in full volume, with both sides blaming the deadlock situation on each other.

This total stalemate in the bilateral relationship has continued until the present, which means that both governments are still reluctant to seek actively for a compromise. Due to this reason, the border has remained heavily armed on both sides. This situation has caused particular hardship to Eritrea. Because of the country's small population, young men conscripted into the armed forces to patrol the long border have had to serve for indefinite periods without clear prospects of returning to civil life.

A complete breakdown of economic and business cooperation with Ethiopia was also followed by major crises in Eritrea's relations with the country's other immediate neighbors, Yemen and Djibouti. It has produced an effect of a 'besieged state', a state with a degrading national economy, a state that is hostile to almost all of its neighbors and overlooked by most of the international investors active in the region. It also remains almost entirely closed to major macroeconomic processes that nowadays shape the economic development of other countries in northeastern Africa. This has resulted in the overwhelming and still worsening poverty in Eritrea and in a loss of economic prospects for most of the country's population. The country has an extremely authoritarian regime, with a highly repressive politico-military apparatus, with no legal political opposition, no free elections and, since recent times, no institutions of higher education. It is not for nothing that Eritrea is ranked 173 out of 177 countries listed in the "2014 Index of

Economic Freedom"[1], while the 2013 Mo Ibrahim Index of African Governance ranked Eritrea 50 out of the 52 indexed countries[2].

In short, although in the first years after the country's independence there was much hope vested in this young Horn of Africa nation, the postwar Eritrea brought neither peace nor prosperity to the population under its control.

Eritrea remains, at present, one of the world's main sources of refugees. According to the UN, in 2000-2013 around 300,000 Eritrean refugees have fled the country, and roughly 4,000 still flee each month[3]. The majority of Eritrean refugees nowadays reside in Sudan (109,600), Ethiopia (84,400) and European countries (65,300).[4] Israel, Egypt and Arab countries of the Persian Gulf host other major groups of Eritrean refugees. However, these official figures are based on rather humble estimates, and the real numbers may be significantly higher. They could have been still higher, had not the Eritrean government put its hurdles on the migrants' way out of the country trying to curb what it perceives as 'illegal emigration'. In any case, given the country's small population, the suggested figures, however precise, make up a very significant percentage of Eritrea's population. Worst of all, these are young Eritrean women and men, a could-be driving force of the country's future economic resurrection, that yearly flee the country in thousands to seek asylum abroad. The outflow of migrants, has reached the scale of an exodus, a national disaster. Nevertheless, despite a very high level of youth emigration and even despite a recent series of defections from the Eritrean army, the country's regime seems to still control most of its military force and the security apparatus, whereas the country's clandestine opposition groups remain weak and disjoint. Besides, most of the latter operate from abroad and have no stronghold inside the country.

The given overview enables us to conclude that the very nature of Eritrea's incumbent regime and the legacy of its bitter and unresolved conflict with its closest (and more powerful) neighbor have determined not only the regime's internal policies, mobilizationist and repressive, but also its conduct in he regional and international arena. To a large extent, the foreign policies of Eritrea in the past fifteen years have been based on the premises, that (a) the country is and will remain 'besieged', and (b) most, if not all states and inter-state bodies in Africa and the outer world are 'biased' against Eritrea, because they assumingly favor the richer and more influential out of the two neighbour-foes, Ethiopia.

It is now necessary that we begin an analysis of Eritrea's role in the regional political arena and, in particular, its conduct towards other countries in the region, with an overview of its relations with Ethiopia in the postwar era. The 1998–2000 war between Ethiopia and Eritrea has not produced a momentum for reconciliation, but has rather transformed itself into a long-running frozen conflict. This resulted in the creation of yet another source of instability and tension in the Horn of Africa regional politics, which over the following years has contributed a lot to the general deterioration of security situation in the region. The two countries' relations have ever since been characterized by lack of dialogue, mutual accusations and animosity. This has repeatedly produced situations of the so-called 'proxy war' waged by both states across their common border and in third countries, most importantly in Somalia. Addis Ababa and Asmara have long accused each other of providing material, organizational and other kinds of support to members of the armed opposition groups in Eritrea and Ethiopia accordingly. In particular, there have been numerous accusations by Ethiopian officials of continued Eritrean assistance to ONLF and OLF, regional Ethiopian groups fighting the country's governmental forces. Ethiopia has also been repeatedly accused of maintaining links with Eritrean rebels.[5] Up to nowadays, Addis Ababa and Asmara reportedly provide financial, operational and other kinds of support (incl. weaponry and training) to members of armed opposition in Eritrea and Ethiopia accordingly. In the international arena, Asmara also openly realigned toward countries hostile to Addis Ababa (and in some cases hostile also to Ethiopia's Western allies), in particular to Qaddafi's Libya, Iran, Egypt (under Mubarak) and Qatar. There have been reports, based on leaked intelligence data, about Iranian military bases in Eritrea, but it still lacks solid evidence.

Just like in the case of Eritrea's conflict with Ethiopia, Asmara's troubled relationship with Djibouti, the smallest and least populated country in the Horn of Africa, resulted from the two country's failure to resolve their bilateral disputes, including those resulting from territorial claims, by the means of negotiation. Although the level of animosity between Eritrea and Djibouti has generally been much however than that of the Ethno-Eritrean relations, the border between Eritrea and Djibouti, a narrow strip of land stretching from the Red Sea coast, has seen a series of tensions over the past two decades. The two countries tittered on the brink of a military conflict in 1996, following a border accident. During the Ethio-Eritrean border war, Eritrea accused Djibouti of siding with Ethiopia and providing its port facilities for Addis Ababa to receive supplies for the Ethiopian military. The two countries then restored relations in 2001, but in June 2008 new fighting broke out along their border. The hostilities erupted over an old border dispute centered on two areas, Ras Doumeira and Doumeira Island, which are under the Djiboutian jurisdiction and claimed by Eritrea. The outbreak of violence was, probably, provoked by Eritrea alone, which dramatically increased the concentration of its military forces close to the Djiboutian borders in early 2008. The United Nations condemned Eritrea's violent actions[6] and called on the two countries to reach a ceasefire and withdraw their troops from the border area.

It is well-known that the main reason of Eritrea's general animosity towards Djibouti are not the territorial claims, but the existing strong ties between Djibouti and Ethiopia (after Eritrea had closed its port facilities for Ethiopia, the port of Djibouti became Ethiopia's 'new sea gate', to a deep disappointment by Asmara). However, Eritrea, quite naturally, dismissed any argument that it had attacked its neighbor's territory and, at the early stage of the border conflict, rejected all mediation proposals. The border clashes did not result in any major invasion by either side into each other's territory (some of the main reasons for this are probably, the presense of French omilitary bases in Djibouti and the operational support given by the French troops to the Djiboutian forces to retaliate Eritrea's military activities in the border zone). Although the international mediators eventually stepped in, and a ceasefire agreement, sponsored by Qatar, was signed in 2010, some Western countries, particularly the U.S.A. and France, later on expressed their concerns over slow implementation of the agreement, in particular over allegations that Eritrea had delayed the withdrawal of its troops from certain areas inside Djibouti. As for Djibouti itself, it still remains suspicious of Eritrea's further intentions and apparently perceives its northwestern neighbor as a major threat to its security, which motivates the small Horn of Africa nation to spend considerable sums on maintaining strong military presense along the troubled border.

Another of Eritrea's immediate neighbors, with whom it has had very strained relationship, is Yemen. In the past, Eritrea and Yemen waged a short war over disputed insular territories in the Red Sea. Eritrea is apparently dissatisfied by the outcome of the conflict, given that it lost control over the islands, but, since then, the animosity between Yemen and Eritrea has decreased or become less visible. The Yemeni leadership still perceives Eritrea as a threat, given the recent reports about training camps in Eritrea for the Yemeni armed opposition. But the level of internal pressure that the government in Sana'a is facing nowadays is so huge, that it is apparently not in a position to take strong action against Asmara.

Eritrea's relations with the present-day Federal Government of Somalia, which, on its turn, is very vulnerable and fully dependent on foreign military presence, have never been warm. The Somali government, as well as other governments in the region and beyond, have long accused Eritrea of providing support for extremist groups in Somalia that oppose the governmental forces and the foreign troops stationed in the county. But, as a matter of fact, to target the central government of Somalia was never the real aim of Eritrea. Whatever Eritrea has done in Somalia, it did with the purpose to counter and contend the policies of its arch-foe, Ethiopia, since Somalia has effectively become a terrain for 'proxy war' between Eritrea against Ethiopia.

In December 2006, Ethiopia's army entered Somalia to oust Islamist militia, the Union of Islamic Courts (UIC), from the country. Ethiopia's Prime Minister Meles stated that his government reacted to a direct threat to Ethiopia's border. This happened after Ethiopia had received a direct request by Somali Transitional Federal Government (TFG) President Abdullahi Yusuf to intervene. Following the Ethiopian military operation against the ICU, Eritrea attempted to counter Ethiopia's interests in Somalia by assisting those Somali groups that proved ready to offer armed resistance to the Ethiopian military. Some (not all) of those who received support from Eritrea would later become associated with the notorious *Al-Shabaab al-Mujahidin* movement. Eritrea seized upon Ethiopia's move into Somalia to put pressure on Addis Ababa. Eritrea supported extremist groups in Somalia, including one of the successor groups to the UIC, al-Shabaab, which opposed the Ethiopian intervention and wanted to establish an Islamic caliphate.

Although this is denied vehemently by Asmara nowadays, there was strong evidence that Eritrea even allowed, for some limited time, training camps for Al-Shabaab on its territory. Although some experts believe that those camps did not exist on the Eritrean soil for long and the relations between Asmara and the leadership of *Al-Shabaab* soon became very strained, what may be called a '*short romance*' with the terrorist group from Somalia became a political disaster and diplomatic curse for Asmara for years to go. Besides, it is widely believed that the Eritrean government did not accommodate *Al-Shabaab* in Eritrea without substantial financial support from abroad. Many fingers point at the state of Qatar[7], which, of course, has never admitted this. In any case, allegations of the Qatari involment in that '*Eritrea-Shabaab-gate*' appear to be well founded, if one takes into consideration that in 2008 Ethiopia went as far as to break relations with Qatar, following a series of third parties' statements accusing Qatar of supporting *Al-Shabaab* through Eritrea[8].

In 2009, Ethiopia successfully lobbied for U.N. sanctions against Eritrea by pointing to its support for armed movements in Somalia. The African Union, an ardent supporter of the Somali government, also called on the U.N. Security Council to impose the sanctions, which motivated Eritrea to withdraw from the African Union in protest. As a result, in December 2009, the United Nations Security Council adopted its Resolution 1907 that imposed heavy sanctions on Eritrea including arms embargo, travel bans on its leaders, and an assets freeze on individuals (some of the country's top political and military officials).[9]

The 2011 UN report even alleged that Eritrea was behind a failed plot early in 2011 to bomb targets in Addis Ababa to coincide with the 16th Ordinary Session of the Assembly of the African Union. The report added that Eritrea was involved in smuggling weapons through Sudan and Egypt.

Another UN report, released in July 2012, concluded that the level of cooperation between Eritrea and armed groups in Somalia appeared to have declined. The Monitoring Group found no evidence that Eritrea continued to supply al-Shabaab with arms and ammunition, but it also stated in its report that Asmara maintained relations with known arms dealers in Somalia and violated the international arms embargo for this country.

In general, Eritrea's policies towards Djibouti and Somalia caused further deterioration in Asmara's already strained relations with the Western powers, especially the United States and France, both having military presence in Djibouti. There is almost no dialogue between the United States and Eritrea today or it is minimal[10].

The general direction and contents of Eritrea's relations with the main regional inter-state body in Africa – the African Union – since its foundation in 2002 has been determined mostly by the grievances of African governments resulting from Eritrea's conduct towards its immediate neighbors and other states in northeastern Africa, such as Somalia. For this reason and given the continued complaints of the governments of Somalia, Djibouti and Ethiopia about Eritrea's destabilizing policies in the region, the relationship between Asmara and the African Union has been troubled from the very beginning of the AU. It is also true that the AU has more often than not supported Ethiopia's initiatives aimed at contending Eritrean policies in the region, which, to some extent, may be explained by a traditionally significant role and place of Ethiopia in the pan-African organizations, both the AU and its predecessor, the Organization of African Unity (OAU).

Following the outbreak of war between Ethiopia and Eritrea in 1998 and the closure of the Eritrean embassy in Addis Ababa, Eritrea no longer had a representative to interact with the political structures of the OAU in Addis Ababa. The last Eritrean ambassador to Ethiopia and to the first pan-African inter-state body left in 1998. This lead to the country's growing political isolation in Africa and the outer world, which only exacerbated in the following years. The location of the OAU (and, since 2002, the AU) headquarters may not have been the single reason of Eritrea's lack of motivation to maintain strong relations with the main regional body in Africa. Asmara has also long considered the African Union as a mere tool of Ethiopia's foreign policy and has rarely camouflaged its lack of trust or respect for the AU. In 2007 Eritrea took a further move towards its international isolation by pulling out of the Intergovernmental Authority on Development (IGAD) – the key subregional bloc in northeastern Africa, after IGAD backed Ethiopia's military intervention in Somalia. IGAD subsequently called for tough sanctions against Eritrea for its alleged links to extremist groups in Somalia and its continued hostile steps against its neighbors, particularly Djibouti.

However, starting from 2010, the Eritrean government has sent some signals that could be interpreted as its will to end the international isolation. In particular, it made some efforts to improve relations with the largest inter-state body in Africa. In July 2010, Eritrea sent a high-level observer delegation to an AU summit in Kampala. In January 2011, Asmara finally reopened its mission to the AU in Addis Ababa and assigned as its ambassador to the African Union an experienced diplomat with good knowledge of the political establishment in the U.S.A. and other Western countries.[11] This may have been the beginning of Asmara's opening to the fact that it has only few alternatives in the international arena. These are, essentially, to counter its regional diplomatic isolation and, thus, make a first step towards improving the appalling international image of the country's regime – or face further diplomatic isolation and, consequently, see the cost of its failure to achieve a strong international position rising.

As a part of its slow and timid returning to the political arena of the region and Africa in general, Eritrea also sought, in 2011–2012, to improve its damaged ties to Uganda, Kenya and some other African countries. In particular, in 2011–2012 presidents of Eritrea and Uganda exchanged state visits to each other's countries, which resulted in the signing of a number of bilateral agreements. There has been less positive dynamics in Eritrea's bilateral relations with Kenya, which maintains military presence in Somalia, is challenged by the extremists from this country and perceives as a threat a possibly still existing link between Eritrea and militant groups in Somalia. In accordance with the same foreign political strategy and in the same period of time, president Afwerki made several efforts to strengthen his government's ties to the leadership of Sudan. Eritrea and Sudan, both struggling with diplomatic isolation and international sanctions, share common interests. Both governments strongly condemn the existing practices by the International Criminal Court to open cases against incumbent African leaders and other senior state officials in Africa. Moreover, up to separation of Sudan in July 2011, Eritrea voiced strong support for the unity of this country, which did not fail to find a grateful response in Khartoum. President Bashir visited Eritrea several times in 2011 and 2012. Eritrea and Sudan plan to enhance economic cooperation and have recently moved forward in the construction of transport communications between the two countries. After July 2011, Eritrea also made it clear that it leaves the door open for the development of fruitful bilateral relations with Sudan, but the level of cooperation between these two countries is currently much lower than between Eritrea and Sudan.

Those clear, albeit incomplete, attempts by the government of Eritrea to engage more with the countries of the region (except for Ethiopia and Djibouti) might have been accelerated by the outcome of the 2011 civil war in Libya. When the Gaddaffi regime, one of the few remaining external backers of Afwerki's government, was toppled in late 2011, not only did it mean for Eritrea that the once significant inflow of money from Tripoli had then ceased for good. It also became a clear indicator of major geopolitical shifts in the whole Middle East and Northern Africa (MENA) region, – the shifts that could bring about more revolutionary movements not only in the Mediterranean Arab countries, but also, quite possibly, in the closest vicinity of the Arab world – the Horn of Africa.

In mid-2011, Eritrea made a formal application to rejoin IGAD. However, IGAD is not at all in a hurry to accept it. Although the positions of the IGAD member-states differ much when it comes to their attitude towards the Eritrean regime, all members of the regional body more or less agree that Eritrea has yet to make more meaningful steps towards the improvement of its image in the region and has yet to demonstrate more willingness to seek compromises with the neighbors. Thus, rejoining the IGAD is still an open question for Eritrea, and as long as it will remain open, Asmara's role and place in the regional political arena will remind those of a 'pariah state'.

As for Eritrea's relations with Western countries, particularly France and the United States, another issue that caused their critique was Asmara's approach to resolving its border conflict with Djibouti. Although some progress was achieved in the peace talks in in 2010–2011 (Eritrea agreed to the interposition of Qatari peacekeeping units on the border and pulled its troops of Ras Doumeira and Doumeira Island)[12], the Western powers unilaterally favored Djibouti's stance in the conflict and blamed the unresolved issues solely on Asmara. They were particularly displeased with Eritrea delaying the handover of prisoners of war to Djibouti, and held Asmara responsible for lack of progress in the border-demarcation proce.[13]

It may be argued, that Eritrea remains considerably isolated from the regional politics, especially in terms of public diplomacy. At the same time, the Eritrean government may be not interested to ease tensions in the relations with its neighbours, since this enables the regime to further exploit the image of 'enemy' and try to strengthen its positions domestically. This has become even more the case in the past two years – due to the recent cases of defection from the Eritrean army. The regime fears that, in the situation when citizens cannot bring about political change by voting, more and more people will decide to "vote" by fleeing the country. For these two reasons, Asmara's conduct in the region, therefore, has become less predictable. It would not be an exaggeration to say that the lack of dialogue between the Eritrean government and the international community poses a serious threat to the regional security in the Horn of Africa, but, first of all, to Eritreans themselves and to their immediate neighbors – people who live next to the borders of this troubled nation.

It is widely believed that the present-day Eritrean regime is hardly able or willing to transform itself into a less authoritarian one, the one that would conduct a more predictable and non-aggressive policy in the region, at least without major interference from abroad. The political prospects for Eritrea, therefore, do not offer much ground for optimism. However, this does not mean that the country is very unattractive to foreign investors and that Eritrea's leadership is not able to secure investments from abroad for purely commercial, civil projects that would not have anything to do with military buildup or enhancing political violence in the region. On the contrary, the country has some lucrative opportunities to offer to foreign businesses, most of which are linked to its growing mining sector.

Over the past few years, the government in Asmara has managed to attract some business groups from Anglo-Saxon countries into the country, in order to develop tits gold deposits. This was namely not encouraged by the governments of Western countries, but, still, there are private investors who are willing to do business in Eritrea, despite its alarming indicators of economic liberty and very negative image of its political regime in the international media. Despite certain restrictions stipulated by the international sanctions, these do not go that far as to prohibit foreign investment in Eritrea, although, in 2011, the United Nations Security Council adopted Resolution 2023, which called upon UN member states 'to be vigilant' that profits earned through mining activities in Eritrea will not be used to sponsor terrorist groups. And even if any major force in the international arena decides to increase pressure on the Eritrean regime, there is no easy way for the UNSC to agree on *any* further sanctions against Asmara, given the existing acute contradictions between the UNSC permanent members. It is also clear that, as long as the Eritrean regime controls most of its military and security apparatus, it will still be able to secure a certain (albeit very modest) level of direct foreign investment in the country's mineral sector, even in the case of further international isolation.

To sum it up, we may argue that at present there is no political recipe in view that could facilitate non-violent transformation of the political regime in Eritrea. A scenario similar to any of those from the 'Arab Spring' also remains unlikely, at least in the nearest future. The only foreign actor, which has enough motivation to facilitate a violent change of political regime in Eritrea, is its closest neighbour Ethiopia. But Ethiopia, on its turn, is unlikely to attempt a new intervention in its arch foe's terrain without an international mandate or, at least, without major military backup from AMISOM and the Pentagon. Neither of this is in view, since Eritrea is not on the top of the foreign policy agenda of the United States, as far as the U.S. perception of major challenges to international security is concerned. There exist neither economic nor security-related incentives for the United States and/or their

Western European allies to intervene in Eritrea directly (the 'Libyan scenario' could be mentioned here as one of the available options) or use the Ethiopian military as a "proxy force" to do the same.

At the same time, there is very little, if any, chance for reconciliation between Ethiopia and Eritrea in the forseeable future – for as long as the incumbent Eritrean president remains in power. This means that the bitter Ethio-Eritrean rivalry will remain a pivotal factor of regional instability in the Horn of Africa, most probably, for years, if not decades, to go.

1 The 2014 Index of Economic Freedom. – The Heritage Institute. 2014. – http://www.heritage.org/index/ranking

2 The 2013 Mo Ibrahim Index of African Governance. – The Mo Ibrahim Foundation. 2013 – http://www.moibrahimfoundation.org/downloads/ 2013/2013-IIAG-summary-report.pdf

3 Assefa Bariagaber. Globalization, Imitation Behavior, and Refugees from Eritrea, Africa Today, vol. 60, no. 2 (winter 2013), p. 7; Nearly 4,000 Eritreans flee each month, says UN. Agence France-Presse, 19 June 2014.

4 UNHCR Global Trends 2013: War's Global Cost", UN High Commissioner for Refugees, 20 June 2014, p. 16.

5 Jason McLure, "Ethiopia Plans to Increase Support to Eritrean Rebel Groups, Ministry Says", Bloomberg, 15 April 2011; Abdiqani Baynah and Mohamed Gulaid, "Somaliland: Eritrea trained ONLF rebels", Somalilandpress, 13 September 2010; William Lloyd George, "The Ogaden problem: Will an old insurgency tip the balance in East Africa?" Time, 7 November 2012.

6 UN Security Council, "Statement by the President of the Security Council", 12 June 2008, S/PRST/2008/20 – http://www.geneva-academy.ch/RULAC/pdf_state/ SC-Statement.pdf

7 Bystrov A. Eritreya: problemy s sosedyami. – Institut Bliznego Vostoka (Institute for Middle Eastern Studies). 20.11.2012. – http://www.iimes.ru/ ?p=13834

8 Ethiopia-Qatar Relations // The Official Blog of Amb. David H. Shinn. – Entry from Nomevber 7, 2012 – http://davidshinn.blogspot.ru/2012/11/ ethiopia-qatar-relations.html

9 United Nations Security Council Resolution 1907 (2009) adopted by the Security Council at its 6254th meeting. 23 December 2009 – http://www.un.org/ga/ search/view_doc.asp?symbol=S/RES/1907(2009)

10 David H. Shinn. U.S. Policy in the Horn of Africa. – Paper presented at the 13th International Conference of Africanists in Moscow, Russia on 30 May 2014. – Unpublished.

11 http://www.voanews.com/content/eritrea-reopens-african-union-missi-on-114212594/157253.html

12 http://hornofafricanews.blogspot.ru/2012/10/djibouti-eritrea-border-dis-pute.html

13 David Shinn. Time to Bring Eritrea in from the Cold (But It's Harder than It Sounds). African Arguments Discussion Blog. – January 13, 2014 –

http://africanarguments.org/2014/01/13/time-to-bring-eritrea-in-from-the-cold-but-its-harder-than-it-sounds-by-david-shinn/

Sergey Kostelyanets,
Phd (Political Science)
Institute for African Studies
Russian Academy of Sciences

SUDAN AFTER THE DIVISION WITH SOUTH SUDAN: ECONOMIC CRISIS AND POLITICAL INSTABILITY

The political context in the Republic of the Sudan characterized by political instability, continuing civil wars and complex relations with its southern neighbor – the Republic of South Sudan. At the same time, the country is experiencing a severe economic crisis, which is mainly a result of the loss of oil revenue after the secession of its southern regions.

The division of the country, which officially proclaimed on 9 July 2011, left its northern part with just about 25% of oil reserves. This puts an end to the oil era of fast economic growth, which had started when Sudan entered world oil markets as a major exporter in 2000 (in 2008 the oil exports reached the peak of $12 billion). In 2012, the country exported only $2 billion worth of oil. The loss of oil production translated into a large fiscal and balance-of-payments shock, involving the loss of almost 60 percent of total fiscal revenues and two-thirds of current account payment capacity[1].

In 2011, Sudan's GDP fell by 3.3%; in 2012, it fell by 10.1%[2]. Sudan was forced to monetize its fiscal deficit, leading to high inflation, which peaked at nearly 50% in April 2013. This could not but affect currency exchange rates. The latest devaluation took place in September 2013, when official rate brought down from 4.4 pounds to 5.7 for one US dollar. However, the black market rate has currently reached 9.3 pounds per dollar. The huge gap between the official and parallel market exchange rates indicates the level of uncertainty in Sudan's economy and its trade imbalances[3]. Given that Sudan imports most of its food, food prices have been especially affected.

Another blow to the economy served by the decision by banks of Saudi Arabia, Egypt and some other countries to suspend most dealings with Sudanese banks within the framework of anti-money laundering laws and US sanctions against Khartoum. These countries not only are among the largest Sudan's trading partners, but also are important sources of remittances from Sudanese working abroad. Over 500,000 Sudanese are working in Saudi Arabia alone[4].While Sudan's authorities promised to resolve the situation quickly; the ban has remained in force since February 2014.

The move is especially worrisome in view of Sudan's huge external debt. According to the IMF, in 2013 the country owed almost $45 billion, or 88%

of GDP and 800% of annual exports. For decades, the external debt only partially been serviced. Eighty-five percent of the debt is currently in arrears[5]. The latter fact cuts off the country from access to most external financing sources, including IMF resources. Sudan's strained relations with the West and even some rich oil Arab Gulf states make it seem very difficult to achieve debt relief. It should be noted however, that some of the debt should be apportioned to South Sudan, but the countries have-not yet been able to split the debt.

Lastly, it should be mentioned, that Sudan's crisis is aggravated by rampant corruption. In 2013, the Corruption Perceptions Index by Transparency International put Sudan in 174th place out of 175 (higher numbers indicating greater corruption), just below South Sudan and above only Somalia, North Korea and Afghanistan, which share the last place[6]. The problem has become so glaring amidst growing poverty among the population that some members of parliament have recently openly accused several ministries of engaging in corruption schemes. In response, pro-government MPs have accused opposition parties of working with Transparency International against the national interest by supplying them information about corruption[7].

In mid-2012, the government adopted an anti-crisis program, which focuses on generating new sources of revenues, primarily from gold mining and agriculture, and reducing imports and government spending. In addition, it passed a series of austerity measures, including the abolishment of food and fuel subsidies, and raised a number of taxes. The government also established an Inter-Ministerial Committee to monitor implementation of policies and coordinate fiscal and monetary policies. These steps have somewhat stabilized the economy, but their overall success has been rather limited.

In 2013, the economy grew 2.9% and is expected approximately the same result in 2014. In the first quarter of 2014, inflation decreased to 35%, and the fiscal deficit has fallen. However, in March 2014 Sudan's finance minister acknowledged stagnation in all non-oil exports except for gold[8].

As a measure to stabilize the Forex market, the Central Bank has prohibited foreign firms in Sudan to repatriate their profits abroad. It has also limited sale of foreign currency to individuals, who are now required to prove that they need currency for going abroad. Businesses and individuals who are unable to buy dollars from official venues resort to the black market. While the measure saves the country's Forex reserves, it greatly limits its attractiveness for foreign investors.

For example, because of the monetary policy, fewer international air carriers are now flying to Khartoum, refusing to be reimbursed in devalued Sudanese Pounds. The last European carrier providing service to Khartoum, Lufthansa, has stopped flights this year. There are reports that a number of airlines from the Gulf region are also planning to suspend flights to Sudan[9].

The government still hopes to rebuild its oil production and take advantage of the existing oil infrastructure. In May 2014, Sudan's oil minister announced a plan to increase oil production greatly in the coming years[10]. The IMF expects Sudan's oil exports to reach $3.5 billion by 2016, which is still only 30% of the 2008 result but $1 billion above the 2013 level. Following South Sudan's secession, several foreign companies, including Saudi and Canadian, started exploring for oil in previously untapped regions of the country, including in eastern Sudan and near the border with Libya[11].

However, Sudan's oil industry faces serious challenges that block its potential. High on the list is the security and political instability in Southern Kordofan and Darfur regions where fields with great potential are located. The fighting with the Sudan Revolutionary Front, the largest armed opposition movement, is one factor, in addition to the general deterioration in security conditions. Even more serious is the growing demand by local communities to have their share of the oil wealth pumped out of their land. It became a normal practice to force companies stop work until some community demands were met in terms of providing some services or job opportunities. The result of this environment is that operating companies are less enthusiastic to put in more investment.

While the boost in gold exports has been a Sudan's greatest economic success since 2011, this sector is not likely to become the engine of Sudan's growth as oil used to be. In 2012 gold briefly became Sudan's most important export earner (in 2013 it was overtaken by oil, which reclaimed the usual first place), while Sudan is now Africa's third largest gold producer behind South Africa and Ghana. The figures are quite impressive: in 2008, Sudan exported $112 million worth of gold; in 2010 – $1 billion; in 2012, the figure reached $2.2 billion. Yet the World Bank and IMF predict that exports will level off at $2 billion over the next 5 years and thus will not hold the key to Sudan's long-term growth[12]. In addition, the sector experiences serious logistical and security risks because main extraction facilities are located in Darfur, a region engulfed in the insurgency.

Another source of hard currency is an oil transit from South Sudan. In 2012 and 2013, Khartoum proved to be a hard negotiator and gained rather favorable terms of transit, but the ongoing conflict in South Sudan threatens the stability of oil supply. Sudan expected to receive over $1.4 billion from Juba in transit fees in 2014, but some of the oil fields in South Sudan are at present controlled by the rebels. South Sudan's oil output has already fallen to half the pre-conflict level. While in the short term the source of revenue is unreliable, in the long term situation is even more bleak because South Sudan plans to build a pipeline either to the Kenyan Port of Lamu or to the Port of Djibouti via Ethiopia and consequently reroute all of its oil exports.

The government has also been active in attracting foreign capital into the agricultural sector. While the sector holds much promise, some of the government policies in this sphere question the sector's ability to improve the country's economic situation in the short or medium term. For instance, foreign investment in agriculture enjoys up to 10 years in tax exemptions, duty-free exports of produce, and the freedom to employ workers from abroad. As a result, local populations reap little benefit from such enterprises, but rather may face food shortages (as a rule, foreign investors export 100% of their production) and unemployment. There has been a number of popular protests against sell-offs of farmland to foreign investors, most of them dispersed by force. However, if the government were able to attract investors on fairer terms, agro-industry could be the choice path of development.

In Sudan, the intrusion of politics into the field of economics is raised to an extreme. The conflicts in the region are certainly the main reason for poor economic performance. The war with the South led to the secession and the economic crisis, but it is finding a solution to the conflicts in Darfur, South Kordofan and Blue Nile that holds the key to the future development of the country. 70% of Sudan's budget goes to security- and defense-related spending. In March 2014 the chairperson of the parliament's subcommittee on economic affairs, said that if Sudan did not stop the war, it would not reach a stable economic situation and would not solve its problems. He noted that the anti-crisis program failed to achieve its objectives because the conflicts diverted millions of dollars to war efforts. What was not said is that finding a solution to the conflicts largely depends on carrying out comprehensive political and economic reforms in Khartoum.

While Sudan's government clearly understands the demand for change, its steps have so far been inconsistent. On the one hand, President Omer al-Bashir has initiated the national dialogue process, in which he has been able to involve the two largest opposition parties – Umma and Popular Congress Party. The declared objectives of the dialogue include stopping the war, reestablishing political freedoms, combating poverty and revitalizing national identity. There has even been some talk of establishing a coalition government to prepare the country for a new democratic era. In this regard, the leader of Umma party Sadik al-Mahdi said the regime had two options only: either face a popular uprising or engage in national dialogue that would lead to dismantling it.

The reconciliation process has already suffered some setbacks. To begin with, Khartoum has proved unable to draw any armed rebel movements in the dialogue. Consequently, army officials now speak of preparing a full-blown offensive to crush the rebels. Given Sudan's limited financial resources, the country's security agencies are putting greater focus on arming and training the paramilitary group called the Rapid Support Forces (RSF).

The RSF has been formed on the base of infamous Janjaweed militias accused of perpetrating crimes against humanity in Darfur.

In May 2014, Sadik al-Mahdi claimed that the RSF had already committed serious abuses in conflict zones in Darfur and Kordofan including rape as well as looting and burning villages[13]. In response to these accusations, the government arrested al-Mahdi and charged him with undermining the constitutional order. Accordingly, the Umma party suspended its participation in the national dialogue[14].

It should be noted, that violence continues or even escalates, both in the periphery and in the center. UN officials describe the situation in Darfur as severely deteriorating, the number of refugees quickly rising[15]. Student protests against censorship, war in Darfur, and economic hardship take place in the capital and other major cities almost every month, resulting in clashes with riot police and mass arrests[16]. The bloodiest protests so far took place last year following the abolishment of fuel subsidies. Hundreds of protesters are said to have been killed.

In another unwelcome development, the ruling party has declared that nothing prevents al-Bashir from running in 2015 presidential elections. In 2013, al-Bashir vowed that he would not run for president again, the move being a part of promised democratic transition in the country[17].

As a step towards political freedom, President al-Bashir has lifted the ban on public rallies and meetings. On the other hand, the new decree requires political parties to obtain authorization prior to any public activities. Such a half-measure has drawn much criticism from the opposition[18].

All of this demonstrates that the ruling party is divided over the best course of action and has so far been unable to formulate a consistent policy. The government appears to be waiting for an economic miracle to avoid having to democratize the country. The miracle is, however impossible without substantial external resources, the access to which appears contingent on solving a great many political conundrums, including reaching a political compromise among main political parties, ending violence in Darfur and other areas through demarginalization and political inclusion, implementing a comprehensive institutional reform, and conducting a more cautious foreign policy.

However, the longer the ruling party waits, the more likely it lose control of the democratization process it has initiated, with all the unpredictability it entails.

---

[1] International Monetary Fund. Sudan. Selected Issues – http://www.imf.org/external/pubs/ft/scr/2013/cr13320.pdf
[2] World Bank – http://www.worldbank.org/en/country/sudan

[3] International Monetary Fund. 09.05.2014 – http://www.imf.org/external/np /sec/ pr/2014/pr14214.htm

[4] Sudan Tribune. 10.05.2014 – http://www.sudantribune.com/spip.php?article 50950

[5] International Monetary Fund. Sudan. Selected Issues...

[6] Transparency International. Corruption Perceptions Index 2013 – http://cpi. transparency.org/cpi2013/results

[7] Sudan Tribune. 29.04.2014 – http://www.sudantribune.com/spip.php?article50824

[8] Sudan Tribune. 07.05.2014 – http://www.sudantribune.com/spip.php?article50925

[9] Reeves E. Khartoum: A Criminal Regime in Its Death Throes Lashes Out With More Violence – http://sudanreeves.org/2014/03/14/khartoum-a-criminal-regime-in-its-death-throes-lashes-out-with-more-violence

[10] Sudan Tribune. 12.05.2014 – http://www.sudantribune.com/spip.php?article50979

[11] Sudan Tribune. 23.04.2014 – http://www.sudantribune.com/spip.php?article50756

[12] International Monetary Fund. Sudan. Selected Issues...

[13] Al Jazeera. 19.05.2014 – http://www.aljazeera.com/news/middleeast/ 2014/05/ sudan-arrest-threat-national-dialogue-20145195454298127 4.html

[14] Gulf Times. 19.05.2014 – http://www.gulf-times.com/region/216/details /392623/

[15] United Nations. 25.04.2014 – http://www.un.org/apps/news/story.asp?NewsID =47429#.U51qsfl_uUU

[16] Sudan Tribune. 04.04.2014 – http://www.sudantribune.com/spip.php?article50539

[17] Sudan Safari. 25.04.2014 – http://english.sudansafari.net/index.php?option=com_content&view=article&id=5856

[18] Africa Review. 16.04.2014 – http://www.africareview.com/News/Sudan-opposition-rejects-presidential-decree-on-meetings/-/979180/2282164/-/15eu570z/-/index.html

Sergey Seregichev, PhD (History)
The Russian State University
for the Humanities

AN 'ARAB SPRING' SCENARIO IN THE REPUBLIC OF SUDAN: STILL REALISTIC OR YET UNREALISTIC?

In 2010–2012, the dramatic events of the "Arab Spring" swept away the political regimes in Tunisia, Egypt, Libya and Yemen, all of which had previously seemed to be stable. These regimes collapsed despite the fact that they had enjoyed the support of powerful allies both within and outside their countries (these was the army, police, security services and pro-government media in each of the countries and Western world led by the United States outside).

Now Libya stepped back in its development for many centuries, returning to the era of feudal fragmentation, when warlords were true decision-makers, not the parties or individuals in public politics. Egypt, on its turn, is teetering on the brink of civil war between the army and radical armed Islamists, members of the *Muslim Brotherhood* movement. In Syria, the forces loyal to the country's incumbent president Bashar Assad are still fighting a number of rebel movements and groups, which results in a disastrous civil war claiming thousands of lives.

However, among all these states, we do not find the Republic of Sudan (ROS), even though it is true that the latter faces too many challenges both in its internal politics and in its relations with the outer world. Sudan has even qualified as a "failed state". Nevertheless, the state power in Khartoum is still in the hands of President Omar Hassan al-Bashir and his team. So, what keeps the current Sudanese regime afloat in such turbulent surroundings? What makes it succeed? Why the Arab Spring" has bypassed the streets of Khartoum on its 'victorious' march across Northern Africa and the Middle East? This article will attempt to bring these crucial questions further toward their possible answers.

The secession of South Sudan (July 2011) forced the government of Sudan to start looking for ways to effect the transformation of its oil-dependent economy to other, more diverse models of economic development. The economic difficulties have been further exacerbated by foreign political challenges, since the relations with the newborn Republic of South Sudan (ROSS) have become tense from the very beginning of South Sudan's independence. These relations remain strained up to now, due to a large number of unsolved disputes between the two countries (over incomplete border demarcation, over oil transit and the exports of mineral resources, etc.).

An acute conflict between the ROS and ROSS, caused by the two countries' inability to agree on terms of oil transit from the ROSS through the territory of ROS, has led to a drastic reduction of Sudan's revenues in hard currency. For this reason, the government was forced to stop subsidizing its nationals on petroleum products. This has caused a sharp rise in prices for staples and other goods, which, on its turn, has led to the September 2013 riots in Khartoum and other Sudanese cities. In order to prevent similar events in future, Khartoum needs to normalize its relations with Juba and reach an agreement over oil transit.

The Sudanese government, due to lack of funds, could not prevent the growth of rebel activities in Darfur, the Nuba Mountains, and Blue Nile, which resulted in a weakening of Khartoum positions in those regions. The government of South Sudan, on its turn, also faced serious financial problems and had to cut its support for the rebel groups in Sudan. Things got worse for the government of South Sudan, when a civil war broke out in the country between the forces loyal to the president Salva Kiir and those favouring his former vice-president Riek Machar.

The socio-political dynamics in both Sudans has a large impact on the situation in the Northeast Africa in general. This is due to geopolitical position of the two countries, which together serve as a bridge from the Sub-Saharan Africa to the northern part of the continent. In the situation when South Sudan is being torn apart by an acute internal conflict, destabilization of the Republic of Sudan can cause destabilization of the entire region. That is why it is important to examine the probability of any of the "Arab Spring" scenarios in Sudan. Are these scenarios possible in the country? Why? Why not?

Let us start with the arguments on why an "Arab Spring" is still feasible in Sudan:

• Firstly, due to the poor socio-economic conditions of the majority of the country's population, which is especially noticeable in big cities (46.5% of the Sudanese are below the poverty line; poverty takes more acute forms for the urban population, and 26.5% of the Sudanese live in urban areas[1]). This increases the risks of popular unrest similar to that of Egypt in 2011 and of Sudan in 1985, when the April revolution lead to the collapse of the Nimeiri regime, which had been existing for sixteen years, but was demolished in two weeks;

• Secondly, due to the lack of sufficient financial means to solve problems in the economy, or at least mitigate the negative impact of the economic crisis on low-income groups of the population;

• Thirdly, due to the armed conflicts in Darfur, Abyei, the Nuba Mountains, and Blue Nile. Khartoum is not in the position to spend more money on social needs and economic reforms in the country, since it takes the "lion's share" of funds to supply the government troops and security forces. These conflicts also disrupt the economic activity and destroy the social infrastructure of the country, making it much more difficult to increase the economic growth and per capita income;

• Fourthly, due to the lack of an established and functioning mechanism of oil transit from South Sudan to the Red sea coast of Sudan. Revenues from this transit could improve the situation in the Sudanese economy and increase the overall budget revenues (before the partition of the country in 2011, oil exports earned at least 60% of the state budget revenues of the Sudan[2]);

• Fifthly, due to intentions of certain external actors, especially the U.S., to replace the incumbent government in Khartoum with a new and pro-Western one to ensure the realization of their commercial and political interests in Sudan;

• Sixthly, because of an active political position of those Sudanese that support democratization and liberalization of the country's political sphere along the Western models. Those are basically well-educated members of the upper middle class, including university professors, members of administration in institutions of higher education, etc., all of whom are dissatisfied with the current autocratic regime of al-Bashir;

• Finally, over the past half-century a large part of the Sudanese came to the conclusion that the situation in their country may change for the better only with a change of regime and of the country's political orientation.

Despite all that, there are other strong factors, that speak against the possibility of any "Arab Spring" scenario in Sudan. These are listed below:

• Firstly, since the separation of the former southern region the level of internal social protests in the Republic of Sudan has significantly decreased, given that the "Southern problem" has ceased to be an internal issue for Sudan. This problem remained unresolved for many decades and often became the cause of most violent clashes between the government and opposition. Some Egyptian journalists in the 1980s even dubbed Southern Sudan the "graveyard of the Sudanese governments";

• Secondly, the majority of the population fears a new full-scale civil war similar to the one that keeps destabilizing Syria;

• Thirdly, the Sudanese authorities have learned the lessons of Tunisia, Egypt, Libya, and Syria. They are now attempting to prevent the broad-based civil unrest by eliminating its possible triggers. In order to achieve this, the authorities have adjusted their foreign policies in a way to attract new loans and investments into the country;

• Fourthly, there is some stabilizing role played by the international Muslim Brotherhood movement, which acts under relative control of the Qatari government. The international Muslim Brotherhood and their patrons in Doha are interested in maintaining internal political stability in Sudan and in keeping the al-Bashir government in pace, since the latter is believed to represent the Sudanese branch of the Muslim Brotherhood;

• Fifthly, the military and technical assistance from the Islamic Republic of Iran enables Khartoum to keep its armed forces at a certain level of combat efficiency and prevent the rebel activities from growing out of its control;

• Sixthly, the Sudanese police service and intelligence (National Intelligence and Security Service, NISS) are very active in trying to prevent any attempt to repeat the "Tahrir scenario" in Khartoum, The governmental forces are ready to use firearms and, if necessary, heavy armored vehicles (tanks and armored vehicles) against the protesters;

• Seventhly, the Sudanese opposition still remains fragmented and has no real leadership who would be able to challenge al-Bashir. Sudan government is carrying conducting the policy of "divide and rule" towards the internal opposition.

In sum, we see that at present Sudan is facing a risk to submerge in a large-scale and dangerous unrest, which may also lead to a civil war, but has a chance to avoid all of this. Much will depend on success or failure of the socio-economic activities currently undertaken by the government of al-Bashir. Sudan needs to invest more in the development of industrial and social infrastructures, in particular to modernize and expand its motor– and railways, to revive its dated agricultural sector, etc.

It is also crucial to reduce the high level of youth unemployment in the country (23.8% in 2012[3]), especially among the university graduates[4]. The current number of unemployed young Sudanese, aged between 15 and 24, makes up 20% of the total population[5]. This makes the sociopolitical situation in Sudan extremely fragile. In these circumstances, any new whirl of economic crisis in the country could lead to mass protests and riots among the unemployed young people.

However, no real stabilization can be achieved until the country is removed from the U.S. list of "state sponsors of terrorism", which is a key condition for the Western countries to lift their sanctions against Sudan. The country has lived under Western sanctions (mainly in the financial sector) since late 1990s. Besides, it seems that Sudan cannot become a stable country without normalization of its relations with South Sudan. The political, diplomatic and economic confrontation between the ROS and the ROSS only fuels numerous armed conflicts inside Sudan and deprives its government of an opportunity to earn good money by offering the Sudanese territory for oil transit from South Sudan.

Another important and negative factor is worsening of the situation in South Sudan, where violent clashes between the Dinka and the Nuer ethnic groups have reached the scale of a civil war. This has virtually destroyed the fragile political balance, which existed in South Sudan within a short period after its independence. Given this situation, the vast region along the southern border of Sudan is becoming even less secure than it was before the outbreak of internal conflict in South Sudan.

It is likely that in the case of an imminent threat of a so-called "democratic revolution" in Khartoum, the army elite will react by staging a coup, overthrowing al-Bashir and replacing him with another, a "more appropriate", military officer. Otherwise, Sudan may see yet another experiment with a civil democratic government, if a coalition of popular politicians manages to come to power. This has repeatedly happened in the past, and one cannot rule out such a scenario in the near future. However, what we have learnt from the recent Sudanese history is that a civil cabinet has little chance to survive in long term, and will be most likely replaced by a military regime shortly after its formation.

---

[1] Sudan: Country Brief – 2012–2014. African Development Bank Group. Regional Department, East II (OREB). October 2012. P. 4.

[2] Country Analysis Brief: Sudan and South Sudan. U.S. Energy Information Administration. Last Updated: September 3, 2014. P. 1.

[3] The World Bank: http://data.worldbank.org/indicator/SL.UEM.1524.ZS

[4] Samia Satti Osman Mohamed Nour. Structure of labour market and unemployment in Sudan // UNU-MERIT Working Paper Series. Maastricht Economic and social Research institute on Innovation and Technology (UNU-MERIT). #2014-016. P. 17.

[5] 5th Sudan Population and Housing Census – 2008. P. 3.

II. OECD COUNTRIES AS AFRICA'S TRADITIONAL PARTNERS

Andrey Urnov, Dr.Sc.,
Institute for African Studies
Russian Academy of Sciences

B. OBAMA ADMINISTRATION POLICY IN AFRICA

Let us start with a very short retrospective review. At the beginning of the 90s, when Africa ceased to be an object of confrontation in the "cold war", the US geopolitical and strategic interests in Africa lost their acuity. But not for long. The US turn back towards Africa began in the middle of the 90s under President Clinton. President Bush made his African policy more active and diversified. Under George W. Bush, the US African policy was characterized by growth of activity and serious innovations. It also inherited much from the policy of President's Bush predecessor. On the economic part, innovations included the Africa Growth and Opportunity Act (AGOA). Passed in 2001, it, up to now, remains one of the main instruments of the US policy on the continent. The stronger part of this policy represented by its humanitarian and health assistance component, which included, in particular, President Bush's Emergency Plan for AIDS Relief (PEPFAR).

The military sphere of the US policy saw some serious shifts under George Bush Jr. In 2002, a new military base was established at Fort Lemonier in Djibouti, which came to host the U.S. *Joint Task Force – Horn of Africa*. In October 2008, the U.S. Africa Command (AFRICOM) was created, which became the Sixth U.S. Regional Command in the world. This step equated, at least formally, military and strategic importance of Africa to that of the Near and Middle East and other regions of the Third World.

President Obama generally followed the course of his predecessors, while increasing the efforts aimed to strengthen political, economic, military, and other links with African states. This done for three major reasons:

1) Geopolitical and strategic in the context of proclaimed once and for all US goal for global leadership.

2) Economic – due to US interest in natural resources and markets of Africa, for which it has to compete with other world actors, China, first of all, while China is taking the upper hand.

3) Specifically African: numerous conflicts, instability, uncontrolled borders and territories, favoring terrorist and transnational crime activities on the continent. This not only deprives the US of some sought for political and economic dividends, but imparts to the continent the potential to become a generator of world calamities that Washington considers to be a threat to America's security.

When referring to the African policy of the Obama administration, its members prefer to speak about the 'pillars' that support its foundation, a term coined by former Secretary of State Hilary R. Clinton. In general and official terms, the basic program settings of the US policy towards Africa are as follows:

1. strengthening democratic institutions;
2. stimulating economic growth, trade and investment;
3. contributing to capacity building and development;
4. enforcing peace and security, conflict resolution.

The Obama administration presents its policy to Africans in a tempting propaganda-like package. It is emphasized, that Africa is now an equal partner and the full-fledged subject of world politics. For Washington this thesis is quite compatible with the above-mentioned goal of the U.S. world leadership.

In June 2012, a new «U.S. Strategy for Africa South of the Sahara» adopted in accordance with a president's decree. All four principal «pillars» of the U.S. policy were retained. «Promoting Peace and Security» moved from the fourth to the third place[1]. For the first time ever, the Sub-Saharan region became an object of the U.S. political strategy.

The year 2013 saw the intensification of the U.S. diplomacy in the direction of Africa. In June and July, Obama traveled to the continent, for the first time since 2010, where he stopped in Senegal, South Africa and Tanzania. In December 2013, he participated in the funerals of Nelson Mandela in South Africa. At home, in the United States, Obama received the visiting presidents of Somalia, Nigeria, Malawi, Senegal, Sierra Leone, the king of Morocco and prime-ministers of Libya and Cape Verde.

Similar to President Obama, U.S. Secretary of State John Kerry has also paid considerable attention to Africa in his official service. His participation in the events held in Addis Ababa in May 2013 and dedicated to the 50th Anniversary of the OAU/AU received much publicity and caused a considerable outcry throughout the continent. In March and November 2013, Kerry visited Egypt.

To summarize it, backbones of the U.S. policy remained the same. Most recent changes affected not the fundamental principles, but the actual contents of this policy. Addressing the audience in Cape Town, President Obama stated that Africa is «on the rise», and this enabled the U.S. «to proceed from mere aid supply to a new model of partnership between Africa and Amer-

51

ica». According to Obama, the U.S. involvement in African affairs had to upgrade itself to a «completely different level» and embrace the issues of security, economics, social support and education[2]. «I am proud to announce that next year I'm going to invite heads of states from across sub-Saharan Africa to a summit in the United States to help launch a new chapter in the U.S. – Africa relations», said the U.S. President.

There were two major reasons behind the U.S. intention to launch a 'new chapter' in their relations with Africa. The evident positive shifts in Africa's development opened a new opportunity before the United States to use them for the sake of their own development and the overcoming of difficulties faced by the American economy. However, America's further economic involvement with Africa became challenged by competition offered by other international actors, first of all China. «Russia, Brazil, China, Japan and others – are investing and moving to take advantage of the economic possibilities of growth and development in Africa. The United States has been behind on that, and we need to change that», said J. Kerry during his trip to Ethiopia[3].

The fact that, in 2010, President Obama launched a 'Young African Leaders Initiative' (YALI) leads to the conclusion, that the United States had long-term goals in respect of the continent. In Africa, where people below 35 years comprise around 60% of the total population, the ruling elite will see a next generation change in the nearest future[4]. Bearing this in mind, Washington started to engage directly with the African youth. The above-mentioned initiative aims at selecting most able and enterprising young Africans and drawing them in the American sphere of influence by holding political conversations and discussions with young Africans, helping them find opportunities for higher education and vocational training, creating and developing business opportunities, offering work placements and internships in American companies, etc. According to a reference paper published by the White House press service, «engagement with young African leaders has become a key focus of the U.S. engagement in sub-Saharan Africa and priority for our embassies and USAID». In 2013, twenty-five US embassies in Africa had youth councils[5]. In principle, this implies that the U.S. attempt to create an 'American pillar' across the continent, which is expected to become a U.S.-oriented ruling class in Africa.

On 29 June 2013, the US President officially launched a new program called 'Washington Fellowship for Young African Leaders'. It is planned that, starting from 2014, the U.S. universities and colleges will admit at least 500 Africans annually. Within the first five years, this figure will grow to 1000. According to the plan, education and professional training would focus on «three vital spheres: business and entrepreneurship; civic leadership; and public administration»[6]. Obama announced that, following the intergovernmental U.S.-Africa summit, he would hold another summit with young African leaders[7].

The U.S. President and his team did not miss a chance to stress that Africans, and nobody else, must define the future of the continent. «We trust your judgment», stated Obama in Cape Town[8]. But, it went without saying that, in order to earn the «trust» of Washington; a decision must first of all coincide with the U.S. vision of Africa's future. «Some in Africa», continued Obama with a touch of reprimand, including «those in power», criticize the U.S. for their «interference» and «export» of Western values. But, according to the U.S. President, such arguments are only used by those "trying to distract people from their own abuses"[9]. What is implied here, is that those «meddling» about the U.S. policy and those who openly disagree with it have been included in a sort of «blacklist». And not only that. The U.S. continued to appropriate the right to interfere in African states' internal affairs under the pretext of defending democracy.

Another initiative announced by B. Obama during his trip to the continent, was called «Trade Africa». At the first stage, in its focus was the East African Community (EAC). The initiative aimed at doubling the amount of regional trade and increasing the EAC countries' exports to the U.S. by 40%. Washington also promised to contribute to the regional integration[10]. It was stated, that the realization of this initiative depended on what the U.S. are going to decide on the extension of AGOA, which expires in 2015. B. Obama stands not just for extension of the Act, but also for its «renewal», for making AGOA «more efficient»[11]. In Cape Town, U.S. President specified that this implied «breaking down barriers to trade»[12]. It is generally accepted in the U.S., that the AGOA Act needs to be extended. What remains an issue on debate are the future contents of a renewed program.

The U.S. imports from Africa South of the Sahara amounted to $49.7 billion in 2012, their exports to $22.5 billion accordingly[13]. In the first quarter of 2013, the U.S. exports to 48 countries in Africa South of the Sahara grew from $5 to 6.4 billion if compared with the same period in 2012, whereas their imports from Africa fell from $12.4 to 10 billion. In the list of the biggest U.S. trade partners in Africa, the top three places were kept by the same states: South Africa, Nigeria and Angola[14]. Direct U.S. investments in Africa comprised to $61.4 billion in 2012, or approx. 1% of the country's overall investment abroad[15].

The third initiative announced by President Obama during his trip to the continent is called «Power Africa». The aim of it is «to double access to electricity» of the people living in Africa South of the Sahara. It is planned, that within the next five years $7 billion from governmental funds will be allocated for realization of the initiative. On its turn, the private sector in the U.S. committed to invest $9 billion to the project[16].

The U.S. continued to implement the programs «Feed the Future» and «New Alliance for Food Security and Nutrition». The former was targeting 19 African countries. The latter entered partnership with 10 countries[17]. Within the framework of «Global Health» program, the U.S. provided $4.6 billion to 27 countries of Africa South of the Sahara and four regional blocs in the financial year 2013[18]. As for Development Assistance, in 2013 the United States allocated $1.187 billion for 20 states in Africa South of the Sahara and for Morocco[19]. Economic Support Fund alone provided $595.8 to the nine African states, regional organizations and foundations in 2013[20].

The military cooperation with African states was being developed on the basis of both bilateral and multilateral partnership agreements and in accordance with different programs, from the global ones to those designed specifically for Africa («African Contingency Operations Training and Assistance» (ACOTA), «Trans-Sahara Counterterrorism Partnership» (TSCTP) etc.). In particular, the Seychelles and Niger hosted bases for American drone aircrafts.

The military activity of the U.S. in Africa, their cooperation with African states in this sphere were referred to as an indispensable, but not the principal element of the U.S. Africa policy. «A lot of talk of America's military presence in Africa», – stated Obama in Cape Town, but the United States, according to him, "are only putting muscles behind African efforts"[21].

Independent or self-sustained military operations were allowed. However, its "core mission" is understood as "assisting African states and regional organizations to strengthen their defense capabilities", [which] "better enables Africans to address their security threads and to reduce threads to the U.S. interests"[22].

It remains a matter of fact that the American military presence in the continent and, therefore, direct U.S. influence on African states' military policies and armed forces were constantly on the rise. Although American military experts cooperated with their African partners in the past, as well, the recent change, brought about by AFRICOM, is explained by the fact that over the past five years this cooperation became «more engaged, more direct, more coordinated, more strategic, than it has been in the past», – said L. Thomas-Greenfield, Assistant Secretary of State and Head of the Bureau of African Affairs of the Department of State in October 2013[23]. Critical observers noted that, despite official statements, the U.S. were undertaking «stealthy militarization of Africa».

«The Pentagon has begun a burst of spending in Africa», The Los Angeles Times wrote in 2013. According to the paper, in September 2013 the U.S. allocated 200 million for expanding the military base at Fort Lemonier. By that time, the base already hosted 4 thousand members of military and civil personnel, including a combat crew for special operations. It was planned that, within the next 25 years, the U.S. will invest 1.2 billion in further expansion and reinforcement of Fort Lemonier. The total area of the military base will be increased from 20 to 600 acres[24]. In October 2013 General David Rodriguez was appointed new chief commander of AFRICOM When it comes to the relationship between AFRICOM and African military specialists, «partnership is a key word», General Rodriguez told journalists at his press conference on 23 October 2013. «Our focus continues to be on strengthening the African defense capabilities so the Africans can solve this problem themselves», – continued Rodriguez[25].

In 2013, the U.S. allocated 1.5 billion for eight UN missions in Africa, including the hybrid UN-AU mission in Darfur[26]. 334 million dollars spent on other peacekeeping operations, including the emergent ones that took place in seven states and regions of Africa[27]. Most of these expenses went to Darfur (400 million), the DRC (339 million), South Sudan (303 million) and Somalia (229 million). 106.6 million dollars were provided to 12 African states and regional blocs within the program called 'International Narcotics Control and Law Enforcement'[28].

«Foreign Military Assistance» was another program that made part of the U.S.-Africa military cooperation: Egypt alone received from the U.S. 1.2 billion allocated for the needs of this program only[29]. Besides, representatives of 44 African states were enrolled in the United States as trainees in programs of International Military Education and Training. To summarize it, the total amount of money provided by the U.S. to African states in this sphere of cooperation amounted to 19.3 billion in 2013[30].

In October 2013, Washington, D.C., hosted the eighth Annual Conference of TSCTP. «The stakes for TSCTP have never been higher than they are today". This partnership cannot serve as a solution to all problems, but it "brings together all the best tools of diplomacy, development and defense», said L. Thomas-Greenfield who addressed the conference participants[31].

The intention of the Obama administration to convene the first U.S.-Africa summit ever implied that it wanted the year 2014 to become the «Year of Africa» for the U.S. Administration.

On 21 January 2014, the White House spokesperson announced that the summit would take place on 5-6 August and that its aim was «to strengthen [the United States'] ties with one of the world's most dynamic and fastest growing regions»[32].

Invitations to attend the summit were sent to heads of 47 North African and Sub-Saharan states, and to N. Dlamini-Zuma, Chair of the Commission of the AU. The list of invited persons did not include heads of the states which «were not in good standing with the U.S.» and also those, whose membership in the AU had been suspended. These were Egypt, Guinea Bissau, Zimbabwe, Madagascar, Sudan, the CAR, Eritrea and Western Sahara.

At the same time, the governments of Libya and South Sudan did receive the invitation, which means that these states did not lose their 'good standing' in the eyes of Washington, despite all the violence and crisis of state that were going on there at that time[33].

In 2014, the activity of the U.S. Department of State towards Africa began with the participation of a high-level American delegation headed by the U.S. Deputy Secretary of State W. Burns in the AU summit in Addis Ababa (January). It continued with the trips by J.Kerry to Tunisia (February), then to Algeria and Morocco (March).

But the most important surge of activity by the U.S. Secretary of State in Africa took place in late April-early May. On 29 April, Kerry held talks with the Egyptian foreign minister N.Fahmi in Washington, D.C. On 1 May, he arrived in Addis Ababa to take part in a «high-level dialogue» between the U.S. and the AU. In Ethiopia, he met that country's Prime Minister H. Desalegn and minister of foreign affairs, and also spoke to foreign ministers of Kenya and Uganda. On 3 May, Kerry was already in Kinshasa where he met the DRC leader J. Kabila. The day after, he moved to Luanda, Angola, to meet the country's President J.E. dos Santos. In addition to talks about conflict resolution in Africa, the May trip of the U.S. Secretary of State was focused on preparing for the U.S.-Africa summit.

The keynote of Kerry's speeches in Africa was confined in the following: the U.S. are friends with Africa, and they are doing and will always do their best to help the continent[34]. Besides, the headlines, under which two statements by J.Kerry timed to his Africa trip were posted, speak for themselves: «Africa is on the Rise and We Need to Help Make Sure it Continues»[35]. And a brief one – «Commitment to Africa»[36]. «President wants African leaders to «come and join us in Washington», said J.Kerry[37].

The summit's central theme was formulated as «Investing in the Next Generation»[38]. The U.S. Secretary of State said little new about his country's African policy. He broadly mentioned the same «pillars» that have defined the U.S. strategy in Africa for years. However, this time it was 'peace and security' that was mentioned before other «pillars», the reason for which could be a considerable deterioration of the situation in South Sudan and the CAR[39].

Some passages from Kerry's speeches clearly resembled preaching. What needs to be done in order to overcome the challenges faced by Africa was «crystal clear», according to Kerry[40]. One needs to «set aside sectarian and religious differences»[41], one needs to move «towards reforms and not retribution; towards peace and prosperity, not revenge and resentment»[42], preached to African leaders the U.S. Secretary of State[43]. J.Kerry listed the aid programs implemented by America in Africa and said that the U.S. officially started to review the future of AGOA. According to J. Kerry, President Obama himself was looking to a «seamless renewal of AGOA»[44].

The Secretary of State did not doubt in the efficiency of the U.S. assistance, since «U.S. is blessed to be the world's epicenter of innovations»[45]. «Africa can be a beacon for the world», prophesied J. Kerry[46].

As for the policies towards individual African states, Washington was paying more attention to «African heavy-weights» – South Africa, Nigeria, Egypt, Ethiopia – and to the countries rich in mineral resources (Angola, Gabon, etc.). Special attention was paid also to the countries that represent high military-strategic interest for the U.S., in particular due to their geographical position (Djibouti, Niger, Mauritania, the Seychelles, etc.). When the Department of State evaluates policies of different African states and speaks about their pros and cons, it, first of all, takes into account the existing level and nature of these states' bilateral relations with Washington, the level of their readiness to cooperate with the U.S. or, better, support the U.S. policies in Africa and the global arena.

The U.S. Policy towards South Africa is rather flexible and based on long-term vision. Since the U.S. has practically no chances to turn South Africa to its obedient satellite, Washington pursues the goal of strengthening ties to Pretoria, making it one of the most confident and reliable partners of the U.S. in the 'Third World'. America demonstrates tolerance when Pretoria takes a stance, which does not coincide with the American one.

The U.S. relations with Nigeria and Ethiopia were constructive and avoided major tensions. At the same time, the American policy towards Libya was an actual fiasco. The US diplomacy faces complex tasks in South Sudan. The relations with Egypt, after the latest general elections in this country, will be working, but, in our opinion, not particularly close. Zimbabwe's president R. Mugabe remains 'enemy number one' of the United States.

On 27 March 2014, The UN General Assembly voted on the anti-Russian A/RES/68/262 on Crimea. The US were particularly insistent in pushing for the resolution. The very geographic representation of the votes submitted 'in favor' of this document draws, in our opinion, a very clear picture of the U.S. influence in the continent, of their ability to manipulate the foreign political steps of those states in accordance with the U.S. global interests. Out of 54 African members of the UN, two voted against the resolution, namely the antagonist opponents of the US in Africa – Zimbabwe and Sudan. Nineteen states voted in favor of it. We will not argue that all of them did so because of their dependence on the U.S. or due to any external pressure. However, in some cases, particularly in the cases of the DRC, Libya, Niger, the Seychelles and Somalia, the situation is clear. At the same time, as far as Nigeria is concerned, we believe that it would be extremely hard for this state to vote in a different way, taking into account its bitter experience with the 'Biafra' project and the existence of other separatist projects in Nigeria that take their origin in the country's colonial past. Other states that voted 'in favor' could also have done so according to their own interests and understanding of the problem.

Twenty-seven states abstained from vote. These included South Africa, Angola, Algeria, Egypt, Ethiopia, Senegal, Kenya, Tanzania, Uganda, Zambia, Mozambique, Namibia and even Djibouti, Mali and South Sudan. Six states, including such rather close partners of the U.S. as Ghana and Morocco, preferred not to attend the voting. It is a disappointing picture for the United States. Africa clearly demonstrated to Washington its readiness to act independently.

---

[1] U.S. Strategy Toward Sub-Saharan Africa – www.whitehouse.gov/sites/default/files/docs/africa_strategy_2.pdf.

[2] Remarks by President Obama at the University of Cape Town. June 30, 2013; http://www.whitehouse.gov/the-press-office/2013/06/30/remarks-presi-dent-obama-university-cape-town.

[3] John Kerry. Remarks with Ethiopian Minister Tedros Adhamon after their meeting. May 25, 2013 – http://www.state.gov/secretary/remarks/ 2013/05/209963.htm

[4] Fact Sheet:The President's Young African Leaders Initiative. June 29, 2013. The White House Office of the Press Secretary – http://www.whitehouse.gov/the-press-office/2013/06/29/fact-sheet-president-young-african-leaders-initiative

[5] Ibid.

[6] Ibid.

[7] Remarks by President Obama at the University of Cape Town. Op. cit.

[8] Ibid.

[9] Ibid.

[10] Fact Sheet: Trade Africa. July 1, 2013; http://www.whitehouse.gov/the-press-office/2013/07/01/fact-sheet-trade-africa

[11] Remarks by President Obama at Business Leaders Forum, Dar es Salam, July 1, 2013 – http://www.whitehouse.gov/the-press-office/2013/07/01/remarks-president-obama-business-leaders-forum

[12] Remarks by President Obama at the University of Cape Town, Juny 30, 2013. Op. cit.

[13] http://www.ustr.gov/countries-regions/africa

[14] U.S. Department of Commerce, Bureau of Census – www.trade.gov/agoa/pdf/Jan-Mar2013-us-ssa-trade.pdf.

[15] U.S. Direct Investment Abroad – Trends and Current Issues. James K.Jackson. December 11, 2013. P.4. Congressional Research Service. 7-5500 – www.fas.org/sgp/crs/misc/RS21118.pdf

[16] Remarks by President Obama at Business Leaders Forum....

[17] Fact Sheet: Food Security in Sub-Saharan Africa. The White House. Office of the Press Secretary. Juny 28, 2013 – http://www.whitehouse.gov/the-press-office/2013/06/28/fact-sheet-sub-saharan-africa

[18] Congressional Budget justification. Department of State. Foreign Operations and Related Programs. Fiscal Years 2015. March 4, 2014. p. 154, 156 – http://www.state.gov/documents/organization/222898.pdf

[19] Ibid. P. 156.
[20] Ibid. P. 160, 161
[21] Remarks by President Obama at the University of Cape Town, July 30, 2013. Op. cit.
[22] Fact Sheet: United States Africa Command. U.S. Africom Public Affairs Office – http://www.africom.mil/get/article.asp?art=1644&blog=all
[23] Live A State: U.S. Foreign policy and Secretary Cooperation in Sub-Saharan Africa Remarks Linda Thomas Greenfield, General David M. Rodriguez. October 23, 2013 – http://www.state.gov/r/pa/ime/215819.htm
[24] U.S. Military investing heavily in Africa, October 20, 2013 – http://www.latimes.com/world/la-fg-upmilitary-africa-20131020,0,4805969.story #axzz2ud466Dt9
[25] Live A State: U.S. Foreign policy and Secretary Cooperation in Sub-Saharan Africa Remarks Linda Thomas Greenfield, General David M.Rodriguez. October 23, 2013. Op. cit.
[26] Congressional Budget Justification. Department of State. Fiscal Year 2015. Op. cit. P.48-49.
[27] Ibid. P.169.
[28] Ibid. P. 165, 166.
[29] Ibid. P. 174, 175.
[30] Ibid. P. 170, 172.
[31] Eighth Annual Trans-Sahara Counterterrorism Partnership Conference. Washington. October 30, 2013; www.state.gov/p/af/rls/rm/2013/216028.htm
[32] White House on U.S. – Africa Leaders Summit by Office of the Press Secretary, January 21, 2014 – http://allafrica.com/stories/20140122001.html
[33] Ibid.
[34] Africa is on the Rise and We Need to Help Make Sure it Continiues, John Kerry. The Washington Post. May 2, 2014 – www.state.gov/secretary/remarks/2014/05/225572.htm
[35] Ibid.
[36] Commitment to Africa. John Kerry, Addis Ababa, May 3, 2014; www.state.gov/secretary/remarks/2014/05/225571.htm
[37] Remarks at the US-African Union High Level Dialogue. John Kerry. May 1, 2014, Addis Ababa – www.state.gov/secretary/remarks/2014/05/ 225469.htm
[38] Commitment to Africa. John Kerry. Op. cit.
[39] Ibid.
[40] Africa is on the Rise and We Need to Help Make Shure it Continiues, John Kerry. Op. cit.
[41] Ibid.
[42] Commitment to Africa. John Kerry. Op. cit.
[43] Africa is on the Rise and We Need to Help Make Shure it Continiues, John Kerry. Op. cit.
[44] Commitment to Africa. Op. cit.
[45] Ibid.
[46] Africa is on the Rise. Op. cit.

Olga Kulkova, PhD (History),
Institute for African Studies
Russian Academy of Sciences

AFRICA AND THE EU: DRIFTING TOGETHER OR RUNNING COUNTER? KEY PROBLEMS OF THE DIALOGUE AT THE PRESENT STAGE

Africa and the EU have a long story of the relationship, which interlaces with the colonial legacy. The EU remains the main international, aid and trade partner for African states at least in medium-term. However, there are many challenges in the relations between two continents. Some of them are of decisive importance. If not properly addressed, they can lead to the continents' loosening political dialogue and lack of understanding and common achievements. In this paper, some "bones of contention" in the Euro-African relations will be highlighted and their possible consequences will be analyzed.

EU-African relations often tend to be bilateral relations between individual countries. The EU still has to build up its common policies towards Africa. Different EU members often have contradicting visions of cooperation with Africa.

Still, since 2000, the EU tries to build up its own collective policy towards the African continent. The potential to do so increased when the Lisbon Treaty was adopted in 2007. It reformed the EU internal structure, and one of the novelties was the establishment of European External Action Service acting as the EU Foreign Office and the network of the EU Delegations has expanded in African countries.

Since 2000 the summits EU – Africa started. The first one was in Cairo, the succeeding one – in Lisbon in 2007, then in Tripoli in 2010, and the latest one, though retarded – in Brussels in April 2014. In 2005, the EU adopted a strategy towards Africa and then in 2007 it became a basis for the adoption of the Joint African-European Strategy (JAES)[1].

JAES and the strategic partnership based on it pursued two main aims from the start – to overcome the "donor – recipient" paradigm in Euro-African relations and to tackle the challenges posed for the EU by the active engagement of China and Africa with the continent. Even the timing for concluding JAES was indicative because in November 2006, a major Sino-African summit took place in which 48 African heads of countries and governments participated, and soon afterwards, in April 2008 the first Summit India-Africa was convened.

JAES meant to be an overall framework for co-operation between the EU and Africa in eight spheres called "partnerships". They included the following:

1. Peace and Security
2. Democratic Governance and Human Rights
3. Regional Economic Integration, Trade, and Infrastructure
4. Millennium Development Goals
5. Climate Change and Environment
6. Energy
7. Migration, Mobility and Employment
8. Science, Information Society and Space.

By now two Action Plans (2008–2010) and (2011–2013) on fulfilling the Strategy have been enforced. They have brought fruit: in a July 2012, a mid-term review of the key deliverables of the second plan was issued. These results included progress in the implementation of African Peace and Security Architecture, fostering political dialogue on pressing political problems of co-operation, implementation of the Africa-EU Renewable Energy Cooperation Programme and a range of other important achievements and initiatives in the above-mentioned spheres of co-operation. Besides, the EU financed the African Union Support Programme (€55 million), forged peace and security on the African continent through the financing of the African Peace Facility since 2004. The European Commission also supported financially the African Peer Review Mechanism, helped in the implementation of the Comprehensive Africa Agriculture Development Programme at continental, regional and national levels. The EU – Africa Partnership on Infrastructure is very significant. European Commission and separate EU Member states contributed about €392.7 million to it[2]. The EU supports the continental initiative, Climate for Development in Africa together with UNECA in order to prepare the African population to the consequences of the ongoing climate change.

Nevertheless, there is a great deal of difficulties in political and economic relations between the two continents. In addition, the implementation of the JAES was not without problems: some aims were not realized fully. One of the examples is the Partnership on Migration, Mobility and Employment (PMME). The problem of migration is one of the most sensitive and divisive issues in the intercontinental relations. In addition, within this problem the issue of mobility is quite emblematic of the current state of affairs. As researcher Jack Mangala points out,

"Although the concept of mobility figures prominently in the PMME, the general framework of mobility agreement has never been the subject of any open and frank political discussion between the EU and Africa. ... As indicative of this state of affairs... as recently as 2010 – three years into the partnership – the two sides had yet to agree on visa issues related to the mobility of AU officials that frequently travel to the EU. ... It exposes a rift between stated goals and the reality of the partnership, a rift that might – if left unaddressed – call into question the relevance and legitimacy of the whole edifice"[3].

The European approach to migration up to 2005 was mainly self-defensive, it was security-centered and this caused a lot of tension between the EU and Africa. Since 2005, things have started to change and gradually migration started to be viewed not only as a threat, but also as an opportunity in the migration – development nexus. Nevertheless, the EU is still often perceived as a "fortress Europe".

However, two interesting tendencies of the EU – Africa relations can be shown on the example of migration issues. The first is that the European population is ageing while in Africa, the majority of the population is young and jobless and birth rate is very high[4]. The EU has already realized the necessity to attract young skilled (and even unskilled) workers to support its social dependency ratio and level of life. For example, the EU Blue Card Scheme has been developed to this end since 2009.

The second point is that for the last few years, Europe has been in economic crisis and there is a high unemployment rate among its own population. African migration to the EU states in such conditions can be again perceived as a threat. Moreover, young, educated Europeans now try to find the job outside the EU – some in the US, some in emerging economies, some, mainly, the Spanish and the Portuguese – in their former colonies[5]. This means that the problem of migration is very challenging and has many aspects to be addressed and re-assessed. Both African states and the EU may benefit from the properly managed migration.

Economic relations between the continents are a huge theme with its own undercurrents. Today the Cotonou Agreement regulates the EU relations with the African, Caribbean and Pacific (ACP) group of countries. Signed in 2000, it presupposed the complete change of paradigm of the trade relations. Instead of continuing to support the African economies with one-way trade preferences, the EU wants to build a system based on reciprocal preferences. The Cotonou Agreement supposed that by the beginning of 2008 all African countries and their regional economic communities will have concluded Economic Partnership Agreements (EPAs) with the EU but many African countries protested and not without a reason. Many Africans believed that the new trade system would bring more benefit to the Europeans. Besides EPAs implied that African countries should agree to a number of clauses some of which were not in the interests of Africans, but were meant to help the EU in the competition with the emerging economies on the continent (like the most-favoured nation clause). There were many other clauses related to trade in services, product standards, intellectual property rights and "Singapore Issues" which meant liberalization of government procurement, health and services, competition policies and investment. The EU has seen all these things as central to the EPAs while African countries strongly objected to such nontariff liberalization measures because as Ian Taylor puts it, they threatened "to reify, if not extend, the domination of ACP economies by EU corporations and any liberalization of such 'new generation' issues will be mostly unidirectional in the EU's favour"[6] . The EU has put a lot of pressure on African governments to agree to the EPAs and achieved some results, though not very inspiring: by September 2013, only 16 out of 48 Sub-Saharan African countries had signed or initialed the EPAs[7]. The EU decided to set a deadline by which African countries will have to either ratify the interim EPAs or sign the permanent ones and start fulfilling them or they will have to export their products to the EU countries, according to a much less profitable scheme – GSP[8]. Such a pressure can lead to a long-term deterioration of relations between the continents. EPAs pose a problem, not merely economic but political. Pushed by the deadline – 1 October 2014, the ECOWAS has initialed its EPA with the European Commission on 30 June 2014[9] and so did a group of states-members of SADC on 15 July 2014[10].

Overall, economic relations between the continents also pose some questions. While official EU statistics state that between the 2000 and 2009, the trade turnover between the two continents doubled[11], other experts are not so sure. In 2012, the company "Renaissance Capital" has published a report, in which stated: SSA's exposure to the EU is at its lowest. ... In 1960, when colonialism was ending, two-thirds of SSA's trade was with the EU. Over the next four decades, the EU's importance as SSA's trade partner declined. ... In 1989, the EU accounted for 50% of SSA's total trade. A decade later, this share had dropped to 38% and it fell further in the 2000s. In 2011, 25% of SSA's trade was with the EU, the same proportion as with developing Asia. This is a significant reduction in SSA's exposure to the EU in the course of two decades, which implies that the region's exposure to an EU recession is lower than it used to be"[12].

Today, many countries in Africa demonstrate high rates of economic growth – in Sub-Saharan Africa in 2013 GDP growth equaled to 5,7% and even higher in oil-exporting countries, while in the rest of the world it was only 3,3%[13]. In 2013, the multinational professional services firm "Ernst and Young" provided the results of the "Africa Attractiveness Survey", which showed that the investors were very keen to collaborate with Africa and that there was a big competition among them. Experts from the company also pointed out that during the last few years the investments from the developed countries in Africa have decreased while investment from the emerging and developing ones have been stable[14]. Now investment in Africa goes is not only in the energy sector, but also in infrastructure projects, agriculture and services.

China is a major competitor for the EU in the African countries and its policy really worries the EU authorities. In fact, even the adoption of the Joint Strategy to some degree was a response to a Chinese initiative, FOCAC. The EU and China offer Africa two different models of development. The EU puts emphasis on the promotion of good governance, human rights protection, and economic liberalization and for this aims it has always included a degree of political conditionality in all its programmes in Africa. Africans tend to view such actions as often denying their ownership even of the programmes meant to be "joint" ones and as interference in their domestic affairs (gay rights infringements in Nigeria and Uganda and a harsh European reaction to it are recent examples).

Meanwhile, China has become not only a major economic and investment partner for Africa. Now it is a new and important donor and it strives to promote its "soft power" and values on the continent through Confucius Institutes and many other initiatives. China positions itself as a developing country, which can understand and share all the hopes of African countries and finance their dreams without unnecessary interference into their internal policies. This appeal reaches its aims in Africa.

In these conditions the EU has to re-consider its approaches to the political dialogue with the continent. Emerging countries like China, Brazil and India show less appreciation of the EU on the global stage. The data of opinion surveys by the Pew Research Center in 2011[15] and some of the concerted political actions of these countries support this claim. They (and African countries often too) tend to perceive the EU as a neocolonial power because of its subsidies for its own producers and its behavior reminiscent of the colonial past.

Building peace and security on the African continent is a crucial task for both sides of the dialogue. Africans understand that peace is a pre-requisite for growth and prosperity. Europeans believe that instability and conflicts in Africa directly deteriorate their own security situation due to the geographical proximity of the continents and the transnational character of criminal activities and terrorism in the global world. Moreover, conflict situations in Africa often generate flows of refugees forced to migrate and many of them want to find shelter within the EU borders.

In the last two decades, the EU has contributed a lot of efforts and financial resources to stabilize the situation in a range of African countries.

Currently, as of May 2014, the EU has a range of missions deployed in Africa. They include EU Training Mission in Mali, EUCAP Nestor (Horn of Africa), EUCAP Sahel Niger, EU Training Mission Somalia, EU Naval Force Somalia – Atlanta, EU Police DR Congo, EU Security DR Congo, EU

Border Assistance Mission in Libya. The EU force in Central African Republic is going to be deployed[16].

The direct military interventions in African conflicts also performed by some member states of the EU – recently we have seen this in Mali and Central African Republic. The EU also participated in the UN peacekeeping missions in Africa.

One important trend has been the increasing number of operations that involve collaboration among two or more international institutions, most notably involving the UN, AU, EU, and various bilateral partners. Such "partnership peacekeeping" has become the new norm in Africa whereby African states provide the majority of the personnel, but other actors provide significant forms of assistance in terms of funding, training, logistics, and planning[17].

The EU supports the African Peace and Security Architecture and the African Stand-by forces through the African Peace Facility, which is a fund to finance those initiatives. Moreover, all these efforts of the EU authorities as well as initiatives of other international actors have led to the fact that the number of conflicts in Africa has decreased by a half since 1990s[18]. One cannot say that efforts to bring peace to Africa were in vain.

Despite this, there are still many factors that can trigger conflict in African states – struggle for resources and power, ethnic and religious contradictions, climate change, poverty, etc. However, there are also factors enabling to hope for the best – high rates of economic growth, more stable political systems in a range of countries.

Africans speak a lot about their agency and the ownership in solving the problems of the continent, but the realities may be different. For example, although the AU provides peacekeepers for joint missions in recent years, the AU Commission Chairperson Ms. Dlamini Zuma when asked about the crisis in Mali during the interview to the Russian newspaper in 2013 said that the foremost responsibility for peace and security in Africa belongs to the UN Security Council. She pointed out that the international community has means to solve such problems, whereas Africa does not and it is not even the aim[19]. However, she added that without African participation, any external mission will be doomed and she offered the example of Somalia, where the situation has started to change only when Africans themselves started to act – AMISOM mission.

At present stage, Africa is still in need of international assistance to bring peace to its conflict-affected countries. The EU is ready to do so, but what price must be paid? It again presupposes help with a certain degree of political conditionality. Besides, such dependence on external assistance means, that African opinions will not always be taken seriously and that African countries will not be in a position to take important decisions. The example of Libya fits in well in the argument. In the course of the Libyan crisis in 2011, the African

Union offered its own strategy of diplomatic solution – it suggested negotiations. However, NATO countries opted for military intervention. To African voices were not listened. Now when Gaddafi is gone Libya stopped being one of the motors and major donors of the African Union, which leaves Africa more dependent on European help[20]. Dependence even strengthens dependence in the future – it appears to be a vicious circle. So what is really behind the African agency and how it could be strengthen?

It seems that for Africans the answer is in the increasing diversification of external ties in all policy spheres including aid. Now the EU admits that during the last decade the aid landscape has changed dramatically. There emerged new donors – for example, China now offers economic cooperation to its African partners, donors are multiple and include private institutions and philanthropists.

The EU is still the largest donor for Africa (according to the OECD data, in 2011 the EU has provided €25,3 bn as official ODA which is more than a half of all amount of international ODA to Africa)[21]. However, at the current stage the EU has to re-think its development aid strategies for the continent. The EU was very committed to helping Africa achieve the Millennium Development Goals. Most of them however have not reached. Although the EU helped to lift millions people out of poverty this plague was not eradicated. Now the EU authorities think about the change of paradigm after 2015 – the year by which it was planned to reach the MDGs. New priorities the EU wants to put in the post-2015 agenda are as follows:

– An emphasis on sustainable development, more inclusive growth, higher impact of aid;

– Need to increase the Policy Coherence for Development;

– More emphasis on the consequences of climate change for development;

– More usage of aid to promote the EU "soft power in Africa" – accent on promotion of values, institutions and practices, which comply with the European principles, developing the civil society.

These priorities have been indicated in such policy documents as 2005 "European Consensus on Development", 2012 Green Paper and "Agenda for Change" that set the route for the renewed EU development policy. Negotiations on the future of the EU multiannual financial framework and development cooperation instruments for 2014–2020 continue.

The current 11th EDF may be the last one before budgetisation, which means that EDF will no longer be financed by member states individually, but from the single EU budget. Budgetisation must start since 2020, which is also the year when the Cotonou Agreement expires. It may lead to an eventual decrease in financing the EDF. There are several major problems and perspectives with the EU aid to Africa.

First, both the EU and Africa understand that aid dependency should be reduced. Development can be fostered through trade, investments, public-private partnerships, exchange of technologies. Some African experts criticize the practice of European aid like Zambian analyst Dambisa Moyo in her book *"Dead Aid*: Why Aid Is Not Working and How There Is a Better Way for Africa".

Secondly, the EU is currently undergoing the serious financial crisis. Current EDF (€29 089 bn) is only slightly bigger than the 10th EDF (by 0,2%) if we consider the difference in the duration and inflation[22]. If we look at aid amounts as a percentage of the common GNI of Member States, we can see that since 2002 until 2010 it was always increasing, in 2011–2012 when the crisis happened it decreased. However, the EU still has not reached its aim set in 2002 – to give 0,7% of GNI as aid[23]. "Even though the ODA to SSA nominally grew at 13 percent for the period 2008-2010, it would drop to barely 1 percent for 2011–2013"[24].

Europeans started to be more attentive to the funds spent for development, although they still support the idea of ODA. However, it can be argued that it costs not so much – only 2 euros a month for each European citizen[25]. Some experts point out that the European aid will more than pay its way by 2020. The report "The effects of EU aid on receiving and sending countries. A modeling approach" (12 November 2012) prepared by the British charity "One", Overseas Development Institute and National Institute of Economic and Social Research, made the point, that €51 bn of the EU aid to the poorest countries from 2014–2020 (21 bn will go to SSA) "under certain plausible assumptions… can lead to positive net effects on the growth in the EU. We estimate a 20 per cent return on the investment in the developing countries, if aid will channeled effectively. By 2020, this €51 bn aid investment will lead to an almost 0.1 per cent boost in European GDP, a 0.2 per cent boost to global GDP and global gains in employment which are expected to fall within the range of 600,000 – 3,000,000. The net cost to the EU citizen of this investment would be zero, and the boost in growth will mean the positive net gain for the EU, as well as for the recipient countries"[26].

However, one should take into consideration that the EU's aid always implied political conditionality – African countries could only receive it in exchange for certain political concessions, if they satisfied the European demands. This is also the case at the current stage. Many African leaders do not like it; they see in it the old paternalistic approach going back to colonial epoch. South Africa's president Jacob Zuma sent the Western countries a strong message in 2013 urging them to end their "colonial approach" to investment, saying, "They still sought to negotiate from positions of strength from where they could "make the rules". Mr. Zuma said financial institutions had "squeezed Africa" and, referring to China, "now we are dealing with a new partner who is not putting all these strings attached"[27].

Of course, Chinese and anybody else's aid to Africa is also conditioned, but their conditions can be more agreeable for Africans.

To sum up – which way the EU – African relations go? Are the two continents drifting together or running counter? It can be supposed that despite the crisis and many internal problems the EU will strive to enhance its cooperation with Africa as new actors actively engage in the process, which can be called "the new struggle for Africa". To slow down now may mean a strategic failure with long-term consequences for the EU. As for the African countries, despite their strengthening cooperation with the emerging powers, they continue to appreciate the European aid; they want to trade more with Europe and have access to the European knowledge and expertise, education and lifestyle. The EU provides them with a working model of regional integration project from which they can learn.

However, now African states want to develop their agency, find a new place in international relations and economy and they are eager to explore all the opportunities they have. Africans see the EU approach in some cases as neocolonial, authoritative, not taking into account their countries' specific, culture, their own ideas. Africa wants help in fulfilling its own dreams and hopes, but not those of external players – anymore.

This is an important challenge and if the EU – African relations are to continue developing, the EU leadership will have to re-imagine its policy towards the continent, in the middle and especially the long-term aspect – after 2020. In the quest to enforce the European values on Africans, the EU authorities should not forget that the values should speak for themselves; they should attract and not be directly imposed. The EU should not make Africa choose either European or Chinese model of development because this makes the strategic partnership with Africa very problematic.

---

[1] The Africa – EU Strategic Partnership. A Joint Africa-EU Strategy. Lisbon, 9 December 2007 – http://www.consilium.europa.eu/uedocs/cms_data/ docs/pressdata/ en/er/97496.pdf (Accessed 15 April, 2014).

[2] Key facts about the strategic partnership between EU and Africa. South African Foreign Policy Initiative. 25 January 2013 – http://www.safpi.org/news/article/2013/ key-facts-about-strategic-partnership-between-eu-and-africa (Accessed 15 April, 2014).

[3] Mangala, J. Africa – EU Partnership on Migration, Mobility and Employment. Chapter in "Africa and the European Union. A Strategic Partnership". New York, 2013. Pp. 214, 216.

[4] Abramova, I. Afrikanskaya Migratsya: Opyt sistemnogo analiza (African Migration: experience of system analysis). In Russian. Moscow, Institute for African Studies, 2009. Pp.61-68.

[5] Entin, M. Po-nastoyaschemu bol'shie problemi ES. (The Truly Great Problems of the EU). Internet-magazine "Vsya Evropa" ("All Europe"), № 4 (86), 2014. Editorial article. In Russian. http://www.alleuropa.ru/po-nastoyaschemu-boljshie-problemies (Accessed 15 May, 2014).

[6] Taylor, I. The Empire (s) Strike Back? The European Union and Africa. Chapter in "The International Relations of Sub-Saharan Africa". New York, London, Continuum, 2010. P. 106.

[7] The African, Caribbean, and Pacific Group (ACP) and the European Union (EU). Centre for Conflict Resolution, Policy Research Seminar Report, Cape Town, January 2014. P.18.

[8] Mackie J., Rosengren A., Roquefeuil de, Q., Tissi N. The Road to the 2014 Summit. Challenges for Africa – EU Relations in 2013. By Policy and Management Insights. № 4. December 2012. ECPDM. P. 7 – http://www.ecdpm.org/WebECDPM/Web/Content/Download.nsf/0/E460D4ECD9AF0D2AC1257AD40046423F/$FILE/11-PMI04-challenges%20final.pdf (Accessed 15 April, 2014).

[9] West African leaders back Economic Partnership Agreement with EU. European Commission press release. Brussels, 11 July 2014 – http://trade.ec.europa.eu/doclib/press/index.cfm?id=1123

[10] Southern African region and the EU complete negotiations for an Economic Partnership Agreement. European Commission press release. Brussels, 22 July 2014 – http://trade.ec.europa.eu/doclib/press/index.cfm?id=1135

[11] Znaete li Vy? Fakty I tsifry o Evropeiskom Soyuze I "Gruppe Dvadzati. (Do you know? Facts and figures about the European Union and G20.). Prepared by the European Commission. Saint-Petersburg, 2013. P. 21 – http://eeas.europa.eu/delegations/russia/documents/news/faq_g20_ru.pdf (Accessed 15 April, 2014).

[12] Renaissance Capital on SSA's Changing Export Patterns. 2 November 2012. http://www.ratio-magazine.com/201211024175/Africa-Agenda/ Renaissance-Capital-on-SSAs-Changing-Export-Patterns.html

[13] Regional Economic Outlook. Sub-Saharan Africa. Building Momentum in a Multi-Speed World. International Monetary Fund, Washington, 2013. P. 2 – https://www.imf.org/external/pubs/ft/reo/2013/afr/eng/sreo0513. pdf (Accessed 15 April, 2014).

[14] Ernst and Young press release. Dolya Afriki v obschemirovom ob'eme pryamyh inostrannyh investitsiy uvelichilas' za poslednie pyat let (Africa's Share in Global FDI has increased over the last five years). London, Johannesburg, 16 May 2013 г. – http://www.ey.com/RU/ru/Newsroom/News-releases/Press-Release---2013-05-16 (Accessed 15 April, 2014).

[15] China Seen Overtaking U.S. as Global Superpower. 23-Nation Pew Global Attitudes Survey. Chapter 8. Rating Countries and Institutions. European Union. PEW Research Center – http://www.pewglobal.org/2011/07/13/chapter-8-rating-countries-and-institutions/ (Accessed 15 April, 2014).

[16] CSDP Note. Overview Ongoing CSDP Missions. ISIS. May 2014. Pp. 1-4 – http://www.isis-europe.eu/sites/default/files/publications-downloads/CSDP%20Over view%20May%202014.pdf (Accessed 15 May, 2014).

[17] Williams, Paul. Peace Operations in Africa: Lessons Learned Since 2000. Africa Security Brief № 25. July 2013. P. 2 – http://reliefweb.int/sites/reliefweb.int/ files/resources/Africa%20Security%20Brief%20N25.pdf (Accessed 15 April, 2014).

[18] Cilliers, J., Schuenemann, J. The future of intra-state conflict in Africa. Institute for Security Studies official website. 23 May 2013 – http://www.issafrica.org/iss-today/the-future-of-intra-state-conflict-in-africa (Accessed 15 April, 2014).

[19] Interview with N. Dlamini-Zuma. Rossiyskaya gazeta. 10 May 2013 – http://www.rg.ru/2013/05/10/afr-site.html (Accessed 15 April, 2014).

[20] Martinelli M. The IV EU – Africa Summit: an intercontinental strategy adrift? AfricaEU2014 Blog. 20 March 2014 – http://africaeu 2014.blogspot.ru/2014/03/the-iv-eu-africa-summit.html (Accessed 15 April, 2014).

[21] EU funding in Africa. European Council official website – http://www.european-council.europa.eu/eu-africa-summit-2014/eu-africa-relations (Accessed 15 April, 2014).

[22] CONCORD Briefing Paper (Cotonou Working Group). The 11th European Development Fund. ACP – EU Joint Parliamentary Assembly. 25th Session. Brussels. 15-19 June 2013. P. 1.

[23] Giovannetti, G. The EU Development Policy. Lecture at Iversity MOOC platform. Course "The European Union in Global Governance". 2014 – https://iversity. org/my/courses/the-european-union-in-global-governance/lessonunits/16523 (Accessed 15 April, 2014).

[24] Babarinde, O., Wright, S. Africa – EU Partnership on the Millennium Development Goals. Chapter in "Africa and the European Union. A Strategic Partnership". New York, 2013. P. 132.

[25] Giovannetti, G. Op.cit.

[26] Holland, D., te Velde, D.W. The effects of EU aid on receiving and sending countries. A modelling approach. London. 12 November 2012 – http://one.org.s3. amazonaws.com/pdfs/The_effects_of_EU_aid_on_receiving_and_sending_countries_ Report.pd (Accessed 15 April, 2014).

[27] Gernetzky, K. Zuma challenges West to 'end colonial approach' to investment. 4 March 2013. Business Day Live – http://www.bdlive. co.za/national/2013/03/04/ zuma-challenges-west-to-end-colonial-approach-to-investment (Accessed 15 April, 2014).

Claudia Mularoni, Piero Scarpellini,
Pragmata Institute
(Dogana, Republic of San Marino)

EU PROCEDURES RELATED TO AFRICA SUPPORT PROGRAMS: A TRANSPARENCY TOOL OR AN INCOMPREHENSIBLE BARRIER?

1. What does Africa represent today and what will it represent in the next 50 years.

The future of the African continent has been probed and outlined in a series of top-level strategic analysis documents.

We quote here *Post-2015 Development Agenda* drawn up by the UN Secretary-General's High-Level Panel, which outlines a clear roadmap to uproot poverty, by means of economic changes able to improve living standards by strengthening innovation, technological development, diversification of domestic economies, strengthening of social inclusion, above all as regards the younger generations, and greater consumption and sustainable production.

We quote the endorsement which the African Heads of State and Governments recently addressed to the African Union regarding *"Transformation Vision 2063"*, where the key dimensions of the vision are the structural transformation of Africa's production capacities, of intra-trade, the strengthening of infrastructures and human resources, and the modernization of the African scientific and technological system.

We quote the African Development Bank's long-term strategy named *"At the Center of Africa's Transformation"* which aims at establishing Africa as the next global emerging market.

We quote the Economic Commission for Africa's 2013 economic report, *"Making the most of Africa's commodities: industrializing for growth, jobs and economic transformation"*, detailing what is needed to promote competitiveness, reduce dependence on primary commodity exports, and emerge as a new global growth pole.

We quote the important African Transformation Report, published on 18 March in Brussels by the ACET – African Center for Economic Transformation, entitled *"Growth with Depth"*, which starts with the concept that, more than growth, the African economies require growth with **DEPTH**, where **DEPTH** means **D**iversify their production; make their **E**xports competitive; increase the **P**roductivity of farms, firms and government offices; upgrade the **T**echnology they use throughout the economy; all to improve **H**uman well-being.

This latter report, in particular, codifies an African Transition Index which assesses the performance of countries, showing policy makers, business people, media and public how their economies are transforming and where they stand in relation to their peers, a fundamental starting point for national dialogue on key areas for launching long-term transformation drives and processes.

Africa is a continent of great importance in terms of potential and development over the next 50 years, a continent that has begun a strong process of reflection and internal renovation keyed to the stabilization of national systems, regional cooperation and a continental vision to acquire all the tools needed for sustainable and long-lasting growth.

2. Which players are moving in support of the development of the African continent.

And while Africa is interrogating itself about future scenarios, reflecting on the opportunities in the offing, and implementing programs of its own, the international players continue to plan programs and measures in support of the continent and its five macro regions.

To briefly sum up all the parties currently operating in favor of the continent, we can list the following groups:

➢ *Multilateral Financial Institutions (MFIs)*: this category includes the European Commission, the European Development Bank, the Islamic Development Bank, the Nordic Development Fund and Nordic Investment Bank and the OPEC Fund for International Development. These institutions provide financial backing and professional advice for social and economic development.

➢ *Multilateral Development Banks (MDBs)*: this category includes the African Development Bank and the Asian Development Bank. These institutions provide Long-term and Very Long-term Loans in support of development projects, and sometimes grants for technical assistance, advisory services or project preparation.

➢ *Bilateral Aid Organizations* : these are national aid programs covering various sectors and different types of support models. Major ones are USAID, GTX now rebranding to GIZ, Italian Development Cooperation.

➢ *Multilateral AID*: this category includes the United Nations which, through its programs and funds, supports numerous initiatives.

➢ *World Bank Group*: it is specialized in reducing poverty in middle-income and creditworthy poorer countries promoting sustainable development through loans, guarantees, risk management products, and analytical and advisory services. Its work is complemented by that of the International Financial Corporation (IFC), Multilateral Investment Guarantee Agency (MIGA) and International Centre for the Settlement of Investment Disputes (ICSID). IFC fosters sustainable economic growth by financing the private sector investment, mobilizing capital in the International financial markets and providing advisory services to businesses and governments. MIGA provides political risk insurance (guarantees) to the private sector, guarantees to protect investors against risks of transfer restrictions, expropriation, war and civil disturbance, breach of contract, non-honoring of sovereign financial obligations.

➤ *Trust Funds*: the Trust Funds are more specific to a purpose, cause or country and more flexible tools. The major fund managers are World Bank and European Union. An example could be the EU-Africa Infrastructure Trust Fund.

All the above-mentioned institutes represent a highly important growth instrument for the African continent, capable of freeing funds and expertise in support of local players and creating crucial development levers.

3. The role of the European Union in Africa

Of all the entities indicated in the previous chapter, the European Union remains Africa's major donor. The European Union has a long history in terms of support of the ACP – Africa, Caribbean and Pacific – countries, especially the African continent.

The philosophy which drives the EU's development support in favor of Africa is based on the consideration that creating growth opportunities and jobs in Africa is crucial because in this continent, as in other developing regions, job and income opportunities are lacking and the younger population is rapidly expanding. In many developing countries, the expansion of the private sector represents the main source of employment and fuels economic growth. The private sector provides 90% of existing jobs! An essential element in the struggle against poverty. Its expansion is hindered in many ways: widespread red tape, a "median void" as regards the size of companies and lack of vertical mobility, slack ties between companies, lack of export competitiveness, lack of innovation capacity, complicated procedures and corporate taxation, lack of infrastructures, difficulties as regards energy supplies, limited credit access and corruption.

The European Union aims at sustaining the growth of the private sector in Africa using various instruments:

✓ Improvement of the business climate, by upgrading the efficacy of national investments, making direct foreign investments more attractive and upping productivity;

✓ Cutting red tape for entrepreneurs (technical assistance to competent ministries for trade exchange and regulatory revision of applicable policies);

✓ Support in favor of businesses (training, consultancy, information) with the aim of increasing technical, management expertise and supporting the transfer of specialist and technological skills.

✓ Promotion of direct foreign investments and cooperation between companies, and access to financial markets.

The European Union's support programs in favor of Africa fall within the context of Joint Africa-EU Strategy (JAES). Development Cooperation Instrument (DCI), Instrument for Stability (IFS), but the most important of these is the European Development Fund (EDF).

The EDF has now reached its 11th cycle. It was first launched in 1959 as a fund not falling within the EU budget, but financed by the member states with its own financial rules. The 11th EDF will be the last and will make it possible to realize projects for the 2014–2020 period with a budget of over 35 billion euro to be used for service, work and supply activities in favor of nearly all the African countries. Increasingly greater attention is also being given to regional programs.

EDF finances have grown from one cycle to another and passed from the 23 billion euro of the 10th cycle to the approx. 35 billion euro of the 11th.

A closer look at how the 11th EDF's finances will be used shows how the European Union is trying to learn from its past mistakes in implementing its funding programs.

• In the new EDF, in fact, each beneficiary country has been called upon to indicate just 4 goal sectors towards which to direct the EU funds, instead of spreading the funds themselves over 10–12 theme areas of intervention. This should prevent the numerous allocated funds from not reaching the minimum critical mass for creating visible and incisive projects as regards individual national economic systems. This should also enable the ministerial departments involved to acquire, during the 7-year period, enough expertise to optimize the exploitation of the funds themselves, and avoid leaving them unused, as has often occurred in the past.

• It should in fact be remembered, that, except for the odd virtuous case (Mozambique, Ghana, Uganda, ...) of countries, that have achieved a high degree of exploitation of the allocated funds (up to 80–90%), many beneficiary country have failed to exceed 40%, thereby creating a negative impact not only for the country itself, which failed to benefit from the funds, which could have produced important effects on development, but also for the entity providing the funds (European Union) which, following the non-use of the funds, was forced to admit wrong intervention and budget planning with subsequent cuts in available amounts.

• In the new EDF, measures of an infrastructural nature have lost their prominence in terms of funds in favor of sectors such as "Democracy, Human Rights, Rule of law", "Development and Security nexus", "Natural resources/Environment", "Energy", "Education".

To the positive factor relating to the large budget dedicated to Africa corresponds the fact that activation procedures exist that are far from easy and not always immediately understandable.

For reasons of transparency as regards the use of funds, provided by European taxpayers, the European Union in fact, with the aim of using the procedures as an exercise in the correct management of dossiers and the implementation of projects, has created a system which to most people appears complicated and confusing, both as regards the activation of projects and their implementation.

The complexity of the procedures and the long time required to activate the funds represent the main conditioning factors, which often translate into a scanty use of the funds themselves.

The complex aspects can be summed up as follows:

❖ The community language: the definition of the context of the funding programs, the definition of priorities and objectives and operating method identification comply with the specific dynamics of the European institutions, which have become, over the years, extremely bureaucratic and compartmental. The European fund beneficiary party, whether national or regional institution, often finds it hard to understand the community language and the true objectives of the launched programs.

❖ The approach of the European officials competent for the beneficiary companies: since the last reform of European institutions, now only one third of those who head the European delegations in third countries come from European institutions. The other two thirds are appointed by the member states of the European Union and therefore come from the ministries of the European States, and are themselves often poorly acquainted with European procedures.

❖ The dialogue between the beneficiaries and those in charge of decentralized cooperation of the European Union is often not easy due to the difference existing between the expectations and the objectives of the two parties involved, donor and beneficiary.

❖ The beneficiary parties often do not know that it is up to the beneficiary to activate procedures for unlocking European funds in support of strategic projects, according to specific procedures. This is not the responsibility of the European Union offices, which, on the other hand, after receiving the beneficiary's application, must assess consistency with the priority plan negotiated with the European Union and launch tenders and/or calls for proposals to assign, according to precise schedules, appointments for services, works or supplies to candidates having the requisites indicated by European public procurement. The result of this lack of awareness is that, on the one hand, the beneficiary expects the European Union, which has allocated the funds, to activate them under its own initiative, something that cannot happen, and, on the other, that the European Union is unable to use planned funds because it does not receive applications and/or receives them with nonconforming objectives and procedures, with the result that such non-use produces, in future budget cuts for the non-virtuous countries.

❖ The short circuit produced by language differences and lack of acquaintance with procedures results in the ineffectiveness of European planning, the inability for beneficiaries to correctly exploit available financial opportunities and the impossibility of producing positive repercussions in the area consistent with expected financial potential.

Over and above aspects concerning the application of procedures to programs already authorized by the European institutions, with respect to which there is a clear need to support the beneficiaries and enable them to correctly understand the various steps to be followed for a correct and virtuous use of funds, a further aspect, that undermines the ability of the beneficiaries to optimize relations with the EU, is also the lack of understanding of the dynamics regulating relations between the various European institutions – European Parliament, European Commission, European Council.

It is vital that the profiles and responsibilities of the various European institutions be understood in order to usefully relate with them to define an intervention strategy, which is best in conformity with the expectations of the beneficiary parties.

Political relations intended to condition strategies and priorities, which go on to affect the definition of budgets, must be directed towards the Council and Parliament and not the European Commission. The diplomatic representations of the beneficiary states and the delegations of the states and/or of the regional bodies all too often focus relations on the competent desk of the European Commission. This occurs without considering that the Commission is an executive body of the European Union, entrusted with preliminary, management and reporting duties, but which only acts within the limits of the appointments received from the Council and Parliament.

A well-constructed, constant and targeted action of relations with the competent commissions of the European Parliament and with the Council represents the foundation on which to build up a relationship with the European Union focused more on priorities and contents than on fund activation procedures.

In this direction as well, an urgent need is felt to assist the institutions of the beneficiaries to work out lobbying activities which are productive and successful, not only in their interest but also in that of the European institutions.

4. Africa: role of the beneficiary country players.

The parties, which can be strongly involved in this procedure for the virtuous exploitation of the potential of European funds and which can play a major role in eliminating the barriers created by the difficulty in understanding the decisional mechanisms of the European institutions and the operating procedures for the assignment of funds, are varied and diversified.

First of all, the African Union, which to an increasing extent plays a key role in relations with the European Union in defining continental strategies and in directing focus towards priorities of African interest. The African Union also has the advantage of being able to coordinate, on its own account, the programs and funds coming not only from the European Union but also from other multilateral organizations and from bilateral cooperation, testing the different use and approach procedures. Finally, the African Union, in a reasonably short space of time, will address the pressing issue of originating forms of financial independence with respect to the funds of international donors, starting a reflection on the combination of different ways of supporting continental development programs (internal contribution, PPP projects, integration of various donors, etc).

Alongside the African Union are numerous African regional bodies, each of which covers the interests of territorial areas with defined intervention priorities, in some cases with overlapping responsibilities for territorial and topic areas. Among the many, we can mention CEN_SAD (Community of Sahel-Saharan States), COMESA (Common Market for Eastern and Southern Africa), EAC (East African Community). ECCAS (Economic Community of Central African States), ECOWAS (Economic Community of West African States), IGAD (Intergovernmental Authority on Development), SADC (Southern African Development Community), AMU (Arab Maghreb Union). The regional Groups play an increasingly more important role in the context of development programs, considering the donors' intention to support projects with enough critical mass to create concrete system effects and to be replicable. Hence, the conviction that valid support in favor of regional bodies, in their capacity to optimize the opportunities provided by international funds, in particular in relations with the European Union, can represent an exponential and sustainable growth factor.

Finally come, the individual beneficiary countries, each with its own characteristics, its speeds, its operating priorities, its strategies and its international positioning and exposure problems. As regards these individual countries, the provision of extensive support and technical assistance targeted at providing instruments for approaching the contact persons of public authorities and international financial organizations with skill and expertise would represent a turning point for boosting development.

If we take a look in fact at the classification of African countries, which have most benefited from European funds in past years (first and foremost Mozambique), we see, that the distinguishing factors that have made possible this performance are precisely the managerial capacity of the national institutions charged with looking after relations with European institutions and not only; the vocation to create a department capable of coordinating measures and international aid and funds in support of the country's development plans; lack of red tape; the fight against corruption; the vocation to support public-private partnership projects. All these objectives can also be achieved thanks to the European funds, which support technical assistance and the training of public managers.

5 . The solution to the complexity of procedures.

The complexity of procedures, programs, organization charts of institutions involved in decisional processes and also in the mid-term assessments of long-term programs, the origins of which stem, as we have already said, from the need for transparency in using funds and also from excess bureaucracy, can be managed thanks to knowledge.

The providing of support to the political and administrative representatives of the beneficiary parties, along a path which is first of all of a relational and then technical expertise nature, can represent the key to providing the beneficiaries themselves with the skills and elements needed for the increasingly more independent and successful management of international aid dynamics.

Such process is even more useful in a perspective of change of the concept of international aid which is already under way and which will lead to the gradual reduction of grants in favor of developing countries, replacing them with PPP programs and subsidized loans in support of sustainable and profitable projects. These very projects will in fact make direct foreign and local investment capacity easier and produce truly sustainable domestic growth.

Such process, furthermore, would represent a departure point for the application of another truly valuable operating model, that of the integration around priority projects of a number of compatible financial instruments. By way of example, we quote the case of an infrastructural intervention in the water sector, for which 20% public funding was envisaged, with the remaining 80% coming from private sources. The private party could only free 20% of its share and seek a loan for the outstanding amount. This project found a solution in an integrated financial engineering model thus formulated:

➢ 60% loan granted by European Investment Bank over 35 years at 6%. The condition required by the EIB was however a triple-A rated guarantee on the national economic system, an impossible guarantee.

➢ Intervention of the European Commission which, considering the operation socially useful, guaranteed the project thus allowing the EIB to authorize the loan. The Commission also contributed by lowering the interest rate from 6 to 2% and shouldering itself the outstanding part.

➢ Intervention of the African Development Bank with a grant in favor of the country benefiting from the work for the feasibility study and executive project.

➢ Intervention of MIGA to insure the private investor against country risk.

The operation proved highly successful as regards the protection of public and private interests.

This just goes to show that an increasingly more complex, articulated and innovative approach is also necessary in the world of aid and funds in support of development in favor of both the public and private sectors.

6. Training, a key to success

Training therefore remains a key to success because of its capacity to transfer to the cadres appointed to manage complex projects the expertise required to address never completely codified and increasingly more articulate dynamics, the complexity of which stems from the complexity of the reference bodies and from the necessary integration of several players in order to ensure the sustainability and the success of any project.

The bodies that intend presenting themselves as trainers in favor of the contact persons of the countries benefiting from development programs must also appreciate the potential which their training efforts represent for the country of origin, for its institutional interlocutors and for the local business community. The training periods can and must become an opportunity for building more trustworthy relations with professional figures who, duly educated, have the chance to cover, in a short space of time, key roles in the countries of origin, thus becoming a privileged relational source, while always of course maintaining the transparency and correctness of the relationship, in favor of the interlocutors of the country where training occurred. The maintaining of continuative, post-training relations with such figures can represent a highly effective instrument of penetration into the country of reference.

Sergey Poruchikov,
Tambov State University

COOPERATION BETWEEN AFRICAN STATES AND EUROPEAN UNION IN THE SPHERE OF INTELLECTUAL MIGRATION

As the process of global integration strengthens, the problem of international intellectual migration becomes very important. The term "intellectual migration" means the circulation of qualified specialists in various professions, scientists, students and post-graduate students between different countries and regions of the world, which is caused by political, economic, social and other reasons.

Rapid growth of the population, mass poverty, connected with the uneven distribution of income among people, poor infrastructure, low levels of education and health care, social and political instability (including the lack of guarantees of key rights and freedoms and reduced number of workplaces) in Africa and other less developed regions of the world, force a huge part of skilled workforce to look for the more favourable prospects for self-realization outside their motherlands.

Qualified professionals constitute the large part of potential immigrants. According to the official statistics, in such states as Liberia, Sierra Leone, Somalia and Mozambique, about 50% of total skilled workers prefer to emigrate. The outflow of skilled workers causes the destructive consequences for main public sectors: healthcare, education and engineering industry.

As practice shows, the European Union is one of the biggest geopolitical centers, which many Africans prefer to emigrate to as it offers them a wide range of employment and educational opportunities. It is also important to note that the decrease in the birth rate and the increase of the median age of European citizens provide more vacancies in various working spheres, which can be successfully filled by the foreign experts.

Traditionally the flows of migrants come to the EU from Algeria, Morocco, Tunisia, Libya, Cameroon, Ivory Coast, Senegal, Mali, Ghana, Nigeria, Eritrea, Somalia, Burkina Faso, Rwanda, Congo, Cape Verde, Angola, Guinea, Tanzania and Sao Tome. The recipient countries include France, Germany, Great Britain, Italy, Spain, Portugal, Belgium, Switzerland, Norway, Sweden and others[1].

On the one hand, those Africans who were educated in the West are more successful with employment in emigration and are better adapted to the Westernized lifestyle than their counterparts who studied at home. However, entering the European society, they inevitably lose some features of their national identities.

On the other hand, the choice of emigration destination by migrants certainly depends on the traditions of the relationship between the metropolitan powers and their former colonies. Former colonial ties also left their impact upon the systems of education in many African countries, which are still in the vein of the European (French, British, German, etc.) educational traditions[2].

Generally, the variety of donor and recipient countries provides sufficient differences in the types and levels of training among the African specialists on the move.

In particular, according to the British Medical Journal, the large number of medical personnel from the poor African states regularly migrates to the Great Britain in search of well-paid jobs and professional development. Despite certain expenses, a lot of African doctors and nurses actively cooperate with their European colleagues in the numerous programmes, which aim to fight dangerous diseases[3].

Therefore, it means that the partner relations between Europe and Africa in a context of the full-fledged exchange of professional experience and providing employment have a good potential.

Interaction at the political level

The European-African cooperation enjoys a high-level political support. One of the forms of that cooperation is represented by regular summits at which the leaders of the European and African states and governments try to solve the actual problems of bilateral relationship. The intercontinental migration takes an important place on their agendas.

The first meeting in such a format was held in 2000 in Cairo (Egypt). It became an important starting point in establishing the strategic partnership between the EU and Africa in the XXI century. In December 2007, the second summit took place in Lisbon (Portugal), at which the "Joint Africa-EU Strategy" (JAES) adopted. This document defined the prospects of the long-term European-African policy, outlined the common political and economic interests and created the framework of the eight main areas of strategic partnership. One of these areas deals with the promotion of bilateral migration, mobility and employment between the sides.

The third Africa – EU summit, which brought together the leaders from more than 70 states, took place in November 2010 in Tripoli (Libya). It resulted in the acceptance of the second "Joint Africa-EU Strategy Action Plan" which was implemented from 2011 to 2013. This plan provided further steps meant to deepen the understanding of the root causes of African migration to solve the problems of seasonal and circular migration and to prevent the negative effects of the "brain drain" in Africa. It also included measures to fight illegal migration, to protect the rights of all categories of workers and to increase the intercontinental mobility through visa facilitation[4].

The fourth meeting of the European and African leaders was held in Brussels (Belgium) in April 2014 under the motto: "Investing in People, Prosperity and Peace". The participants discussed, among others, the problem of coordination in pursuing common goals in the sphere of migratory cooperation between the regions in 2014–2017, joint programmes for professional training of young people and women from Africa to increase their competitiveness on the global labour market[5].

The politicians agreed to continue the collaboration, according to the "Africa-EU Migration, Mobility and Employment Partnership" (PMME) of the JAES, "Migration Policy Framework for Africa" and the "Global Approach to Migration and Mobility" (GAMM)[6]. Let us consider these initiatives in more detail to understand their main principles.

"The Africa-EU Migration, Mobility and Employment Partnership" (PMME) aims at developing the concrete solutions of the problems, connected to migration and employment, by overcoming the bureaucratic barriers in order to facilitate the employment of foreign nationals in the European Union and to promote the creation of the new workplaces for Africans on their own continent[7].

"The Global Approach to Migration and Mobility" (GAMM) originated in 2005 for conducting migratory dialogue with the non-European countries. Since November 2011, the updated project has become an important link in the EU foreign policy in the area of humanization of the international migration and assistance to development in Africa. The project is based on the achievements of the "Rabat Process" (2006) and the provisions of the "Dakar Strategy" (2011).

"The Rabat Process" originates from a first meeting of African and European ministers in Rabat (Morocco) in 2006 devoted to creating a framework for mutual dialogue and consultation by implementing practical initiatives as a new vision of migration issues characterized by a global, balanced and concrete approach to managing these issues.

Through this process, the EU provides the political and economic support for the countries of Central and Western Africa within the European-African Dialogue on Migration and Development. The Process unites more than 50 states based on preliminary consultations and practical implementation of joint initiatives for the rational management of migration flows in the Western and the Central African regions[8].

Two years later, the Second Euro-African Conference on Migration and Development, organized in Paris in 2008, confirmed the vitality of the process and resulted in the adoption of an ambitious three-year cooperation programme resulting from the preliminary work done at three thematic meetings on legal migration, irregular migration and migration and development[9].

"The Dakar Strategy" was signed during the Third Euro-African Ministerial Conference on Migration and Development in the capital of Senegal in November 2011 as a further development of the Rabat arrangements for 2012–2014.

This Strategy based on the gradual achievement of 10 priority goals by providing the international exchanges, respecting the rights of migrants, and giving grants for African national organizations and establishments, which involved the integration of effective tools and new opportunities in the sphere of migration. It was meant that all relevant policies should ensure close coordination and the promotion of synergies within the Africa-EU Partnership on Migration, Mobility and Employment and other migration dialogue processes. Among them were the Global Forum on Migration and Development, the EU-ACP dialogue on migration and development and the regional and sub-regional action and cooperation frameworks, as well as the multilateral instruments, involving migration matters, such as the "5+5" process, the European Neighbourhood Policy, the Union for the Mediterranean, and the Dialogue on Mediterranean Transit Migration[10].

The last meeting of the officials to control the progress on the previous steps took place in 2012 in Madrid. During the summit, the "Road Map" was adopted for monitoring and planning the further actions for the 2013-2015.

To sum up, it is necessary to say that the European Commission implements the so-called "Blue Card Scheme", which makes it easier for the qualified specialists, who are third country nationals, and for their families to enter the European Union legally with the purpose of employment.

This initiative is based on the European Commission Directive of 25 May 2009, according to which legal migrants have a residence permit and the right to work on the territory of the particular European country, except the Great Britain, Ireland and Denmark, which have not signed such an agreement.

Along with the above-mentioned projects, there are many other steps for facilitating the workflow, namely the adoption of the common rules governing the stay of the welcomed highly qualified foreigners on the territories of all the EU-member states. This, undoubtedly, benefits each participating side[11].

Cooperation in the sphere of scientific and educational migration

The European Union fully supports the educational migration between two continents with allocating significant funds to support African science and educational mobility.

For example, the African Studies Center in 2012-2016, with the support of investors from the Netherlands, France and the Great Britain, has organized a competition of research projects among the graduates of African universities concerning the development of effective measures to improve the quality of life in Sub-Saharan Africa. The offered rewards were money prizes ranging from one to three thousand euros[12].

Earlier, in 2008–2010, the programme "Access to Success: Fostering Trust and Exchange between Europe and Africa" was implemented with the financial support of the European Union. It helped to establish the working relations between the university associations and political organizations on both continents, which supposed a mutual exchange of teachers, students and postgraduate students, guaranteed the advantages in the further scientific career, and increased the prestige of state universities in the Europe and Africa[13].

Now there are many interconnected programmes of academic mobility: "Nyerere Programme", "Intra-ACP University Mobility Programme", "Tempus Programme" and some others directed at the exchange of academic staff and students between the universities in Europe and Africa and at the development of other forms of educational cooperation between them. More than 2000 participants from 63 universities and 13 other high-priority projects are involved in various thematic directions of cooperation and that number is increasing.

"The Mwalimu Nyerere Programme" – a programme aimed to support the intra-African academic mobility for prevention of the massive "brain drain". The African students, scientists and teachers have an opportunity to get the European grants for work in five research directions and to increase their own level of professional qualification. By February 2013, about 67 partnership associations from 29 African states were involved in the programme.

"The African Higher Education Harmonization and Tuning Initiative" aimed at strengthening the cooperation between the EU and Africa by ensuring the availability and improving the quality of professional education of teachers, doctors, industry and agricultural workers, including the integration of higher education institutions in Africa into united network – the Pan-African University. This association implies an intercollegiate study in five research areas: 1) Science, Technology and Innovation; 2) Water and Energy; 3) Life and Earth Sciences; 4) Space Sciences; 5) Governance and related issues. In addition, each geographical region has its thematic area: North Africa – medical research, South Africa – teacher training, West Africa – improvement of agriculture, Central Africa – engineering projects, East Africa – building the civil society.

To participate in the 18-month pilot project launched in September 2011, about a hundred applications from six African universities were received. By

January 2013, there were sixty participants. It is expected, that in the second phase, launched in 2014, the number of involved partners would increase several times.

"The Intra-ACP academic mobility scheme" – a project financed by the European Development Fund and managed by the Education, Audiovisual and Culture Executive Agency of European Union (EACEA), the African Union Commission (AUC) and the Africa, Caribbean and Pacific Group of States (ACP) which provides support to the universities of Africa, the Caribbean and the Pacific. In the medium-term, this initiative provides selected students, post-graduate students and faculties from countries in Africa, the Caribbean and the Pacific regions with an opportunity for establishing scientific, economic, political and cultural links during migration between ACP-countries and Europe. In particular, by 2013, the project included 79 partners, from Benin, Morocco, Nigeria, Egypt, Tanzania, Togo, Zambia and other African countries[14].

"The Tempus Programme" is a programme for the reform, modernization and unification of the higher education systems in Europe and neighbouring regions, including Africa. It encourages the inter-university cooperation in the sphere of developing new educational programmes, teaching and management techniques by providing an interaction with the academic community and civil society.

The aim of this programme is to solve the problem of academic staff circulation between the EU-member states and their foreign partners. The project has been developed for many years during the four stages. The final stage (Tempus IV) lasted from 2007 to 2013. Over the past years there were realized more than 171 thematic projects in four geographic regions, from which 26 – in partnership with the Maghreb countries (Tunisia, Libya, Algeria, Morocco), and 16 – with Egypt[15].

The key ideas were to develop the programmes of lifelong education for different age categories, to ensure the professional development of industrial workers and to define the standards for the accreditation of the African universities according to the European model[16].

In 2014, the "Tempus Programme" was replaced by the two new programmes of student exchange – the "Erasmus +" and the "Erasmus Mundus".

"The Erasmus +" – an educational programme of the EU, which was designed for the foreign youth. The first time it was introduced at the summit of the European Commission on November 23, 2011, and was finally approved by the end of 2013. The action period: 2014-2020.

The programme reaches out to organizations and individuals from 28 Member States of the European Union, Macedonia, Iceland, Liechtenstein, Norway, Switzerland and Turkey. The representatives of non-European countries from the North African states, Ethiopia, Nigeria, Kenya, Cameroon, Sierra Leone, Ghana, South Africa and other countries can also participate in this programme, if they conclude the agreements with the EU partners.

Since 2014, the project unites all international educational programmes of the European Union excluding their duplications. It provides a direct benefit for foreign specialists through the simplified scheme of receiving the scientific grants[17].

"The Erasmus Mundus" – is the system of thematic sub-programmes of student exchanges, which was established in order to increase the student mobility and to improve the quality of higher education by financing the co-operation between the academic institutions in Europe and the other world. The main advantage of this programme is in providing access for non-European participants to the EU educational opportunities.

In particular, the regional programme "Erasmus Mundus – Al Idrisi II Programme" involves citizens from the North Africa: Algeria, Egypt, Libya, Morocco and Tunisia. It includes the organization of studies and providing grants covering a tuition fee, monthly expenses on transport and medical insurance for bachelors, masters, post-graduate students, doctoral candidates and the persons with a scientific degree temporarily moving to the European Union. The programme is meant to strengthen the educational and business relations between the Europe and the North Africa.

This project concentrates on training the demanded specialists in joint master and doctoral programmes and on the increasing the attractiveness of higher education by fostering a close partnership between the European and African universities.

The purposes of this programme include providing equal opportunities for the socially vulnerable groups from developing states and for the students from poor families to receive a quality education, ensuring a full-fledged exchange of innovative experience and the establishment of the new friendly and professional contacts[18].

For the recent years, the EU has provided millions euro to support the students and universities from North and Sub-Saharan Africa. Hundreds of African students and scientists received educational and research grants under the "Erasmus +" and the "Erasmus Mundus"[19].

In the following years, in the framework of the new project "Horizon 2020", EU plans to provide about 25 research grants to thousands of African students and 2,750 researchers. This can significantly increase the prestige of the higher education and research in Africa.[20]

It is necessary to mention the activity of the African Diaspora Policy Centre (ADPC), with headquarters in Hague (Netherlands), which serves as an important link in the context of the EU-Africa migration policy.

The representatives of the Centre, including African politicians, scientists and businesspersons, are extremely interested in social, economic, cultural, information and technical development of their continent. They facilitate it by actively participating in the solution of professional cooperation questions between Europe and Africa. They see their mission in ensuring the transfer of the necessary knowledge and experience for the Africans living in different parts of the world, thus, connecting migration and development.

ADPC's work focuses on four main interlinked areas:
• Mobilizing African Diaspora in Europe for the development of Africa,
• Influencing and advising migration and development policy makers in the host countries,
• Strengthening the knowledge, network and policymaking capacity of African governments in the field of migration and development,
• Fostering viable partnerships between African Diaspora organizations in Europe and civil society institutions in Africa[21].

In the modern society, the understanding grows that skilled migrants have a significant impact on the development of their own countries. In many cases, after training in Europe, they tend to return to the home countries, and they use their financial, informational, technological and intellectual resources in practice to improve the life-level of people in Africa.

Noticing that, the African Diaspora Policy Centre promotes the interregional cooperation through joint African-European research, publications, conferences and seminars within four integrated projects.

1) "Strengthening Policy-Making Capacities of Emerging Diaspora Ministries in Africa" (SEDIMA) – this programme aims to contribute to strengthening the policy-making capacity of the newly formed Diaspora Ministries, which means the creation of the departments of diasporas in the governments of African states to interact with the nation's emigrants and expatriates in other states.[22]

The objective of this programme is twofold: to develop the new knowledge in the field of migration and development tailored to the specific policy-making needs of the Diaspora representatives and to provide the capacity-building training that will enable these newly appointed policy-makers to gain access to the up-to-date information.

2) "The Civil Society Migration and Development Network" (MADE) aims is to connect with civil society networks and thematic groups around the world. Its goal is to increase these organizations' cooperating capacities and ability to speak in one voice. Existing networks include the Global Coalition on Migration, Migrants Rights International and The Pan African Network in Defense of Migrants' Rights. The project builds further on civil society groups' recommendations made by European officials for the Global Forum on Migration and Development, 2011, and on the Action Plan pro-

posed during the UN High Level Dialogue on Migration and Development (HLD), 2013.

3) "European-wide African Diaspora Platform for Development" (EADPD), 2011–2013. This project, funded by the European Commission, was initiated to foster the creation of a solid and viable network that considerably increases the contribution of the African Diaspora in all 28 EU Member States, Switzerland, Norway, and in the 5 African regions to the overall development of Africa.

4) "African Consultative Forum on Migration and Development" (AFCMD) – the objective of this programme is to facilitate the establishment of the Consultative Forum on Migration and Development, which will stimulate the regular exchange of best practices among African policy-makers dealing with the Diaspora and development related issues. By now, with the common activities of Angola, Benin, Botswana, Burkina Faso, Burundi, Cameroon, Cape Verde, Chad, Democratic Republic of Congo, Ethiopia, Ghana, Kenya, Liberia, Madagascar, Malawi, Mali, Mauritius, Mozambique, Namibia, Niger, Nigeria, Rwanda, Senegal, Sierra Leone, South Africa, Southern Sudan, Tanzania, Togo, Uganda and Zambia, the establishment of this Forum is almost finished[23].

Therefore, the cooperation of the European Union and Africa in the sphere of intellectual migration presents the indisputable advantages for each involved part because it affects the main aspects of political and socioeconomic life.

Today, by watching for the acceleration of globalization and the increasing interdependence of states, the majority of scientists and politicians call for the long-needed elimination of various migratory and integration barriers for legal migrants all over the world and for the transforming the "brain drain" into the "brain gain". There are some results in this direction, however, quite modest.

The combination of long-term European experience in the area of research, education and academic and professional mobility with the African sense of purpose and huge human potential can provide a stable development and prosperity for countries and people on both continents.

---

[1] The European Union and the African Union: A Statistical Portrait [Internet resource] // Eurostat Statistical Books. 2011–2013 Edition. Luxembourg, 2011–2013; http://epp.eurostat.ec.europa.eu/cache/ITY_OFFPUB/KS-30-11-244/EN/KS-30-11-244-EN.PDF (Date of access: 03.09.2014); http://epp.eurostat.ec.europa.eu/cache/ITY_OFFPUB/KS-31-12-239/EN/KS-31-12-239-EN.PDF (Date of access:

03.09.2014); http://epp.eurostat.ec.europa.eu/cache/ITY_OFFPUB/KS-SB-13-001 /EN/KS-SB-13-001-EN.PDF (Date of access: 03.09.2014)

[2] Kohnert D. African Migration to Europe: Obscured Responsibilities and Common Misconceptions [Internet resource] // GIGA Working Papers, № 49. May, 2007. http://edoc.vifapol.de/opus/volltexte/2009/1609/pdf/wp49_ kohnert.pdf (Date of access: 03.09.2014)

Domingo Valls A., Vono de Vilhena D. Africans in the Southern countries: Italy, Spain and Portugal [Internet resource] // Development, institutional and policy aspects of international migration between Africa, Europe and Latin America and the Caribbean: Project document. http://www.cepal.org/publicaciones/xml/8/46188/ winternationalmig_final.pdf (Date of access: 03.09.2014)

[3] The financial cost of doctors emigrating from sub-Saharan Africa: human capital analysis [Internet resource] // The British Medical Journal, 2011. http://www.bmj.com/content/343/bmj.d7031 (Date of access: 03.09.2014)

[4] Joint Africa-EU Strategy Action Plan 2011-2013 [Internet resource]. http://www.africa-eu-partnership.org/sites/default/files/documents/03-jeas_action plan_en.pdf (Date of access: 03.09.2014)

[5] 4th EU-Africa summit background note. Brussels, 2014 [Internet resource] // General Secretariat of the Council – Press Office. http://www.european-council.europa.eu/media/1329122/140217_summit_ background_note.pdf (Date of access: 03.09.2014)

Issues of the Africa-Europe Summit on April 2014: A Critical Look at the Africa-Europe Partnership [Internet resource] // AGI Policy Brief. № 6, 2014. http://www.westafricagateway.org/files/Policy-Brief-N-6-Issue-Summit-Africa-Europe.pdf (Date of access: 03.09.2014)

The Fourth EU-Africa Summit Declaration [Internet resource] // EU-Africa Summit. Brussels, 2014. http://www.consilium.europa.eu/uedocs/cms_data/docs/pressdata/en/ec/142096.pdf (Date of access: 03.09.2014)

[6] MME senior officials meeting [Internet resource] // The Africa-EU Partnership [website]. [2014]. http://www.africa-eu-partnership. org/newsroom/ events/mme-senior-officials-meeting (Date of access: 03.09.2014)

4th EU-Africa Summit (2014) [Internet resource] // The Africa-EU Partnership [website]. [2014]. http://www.africa-eu-partnership.org/4th-africa-eu-summit (Date of access: 03.09.2014)

[7] AU-COMMIT Campaign: EU Representative Presents Africa-European Union Partnership on Migration, Mobility and Employment (MME) at the Djibouti Consultative Workshop for the IGAD/EAC Regions [Internet resource] // The Africa-EU Partnership [website]. [2010]. http://www.africa-eu-partnership.org/newsroom/all-news/au-commit-campaign-eu-representative-presents-africa-european-union-partnership (Date of access: 03.09.2014)

Africa-EU Partnership. Achievements and Milestones [Internet resource] // The Africa-EU Partnership [website]. [2014]. http://www.africa-eu-partnership.org/areas-cooperation/migration-mobility-and-employment/achievements-and-milestones-0 (Date of access: 03.09.2014)

[8] Communication from the Commission to the European Parliament, the Council, the European Economic and Social Committee and the Committee of the regions [Internet resource] // The Global Approach to Migration and Mobility. Brussels, 2011. http://ec.europa.eu/dgs/home-affairs/news/intro/docs/1_en_act_part1_v9.pdf (Date of access: 03.09.2014)

[9] Introduction to the Rabat Process [Internet resource] // Euro-African Dialogue on Migration and Development [website]. [2014]. http://process-usderabat.net/web/index.php/process (Date of access: 03.09.2014)

[10] Third Euro-African Ministerial Conference on Migration and Development [Internet resource]. http://www.dialogueuroafricainmd.net/web/ uploads/cms/Dakar-strategy_-Ministerial-declaration-migration-and-development_-EN.pdf (Date of access: 03.09.2014)

[11] MEPs support the European "Blue Card" proposal for highly-skilled immigrants [Internet resource] // European Parliament [website]. [2008]. http://www.europarl. europa.eu/sides/getDoc.do?type=IM-PRESS& reference=20081107FCS41562&format= XML&language=EN (Date of access: 03.09.2014)

[12] Research Masters African Studies [Internet resource] // African Studies Centre [website]. [2014]. http://www.ascleiden.nl/?q=content/research-masters (Date of access: 03.09.2014)

Visiting Fellowship Programme [Internet resource] // African Studies Centre [website]. [2014]. http://www.ascleiden.nl/?q=content/visiting-fellowship-programme (Date of access: 03.09.2014)

[13] Africa-Europe higher education cooperation for development: meeting regional and global challenges. White paper [Internet resource] // European University Association. http://www.eua.be/Libraries/Publications_homepage_list/Africa-Europe_Higher_Education_Cooperation_White_Paper_EN.sflb. ashx (Date of access: 03.09.2014)

[14] About the intra-ACP academic mobility scheme [Internet resource] // Education, Audiovisual and Culture Executive Agency of The European Commission [website]. [2014]. http://eacea.ec.europa.eu/intra_acp_mobility/programme/about_acp_mobili-ty en.php (Date of access: 03.09.2014)

General statistics – Intra-ACP Call for proposals EACEA/45/12. Country involvement in selected partnerships [Internet resource] // Education, Audiovisual and Culture Executive Agency of The European Commission [website]. [2014]. http://eeas.europa.eu/delegations/ghana/documents/press_ corner/ annex_2_general_statistics_selection_2013_en.pdf (Date of access: 03.09.2014)

[15] Accepted Projects – Tempus IV – 2013. Breakdown of projects by partner country, region and type of project [Internet resource] // Education, Audiovisual and Culture Executive Agency of The European Commission [website]. [2014]. http://eacea.ec.europa.eu/tempus/results_compendia/ documents/statistics-tempus-iv-2013-accepted-a.pdf (Date of access: 03.09.2014)

[16] Tempus IV (2007-2013): Overview of the Programme [Internet resource] // Education, Audiovisual and Culture Executive Agency of The European Commission [website]. [2014]. http://eacea.ec.europa.eu/ tempus/programme/about_tempus_en. php (Date of access: 03.09.2014)

[17] The future of the Tempus programme as of 01/01/2014 [Internet resource] // Education, Audiovisual and Culture Executive Agency of The European Commission [website]. [2014]. http://eacea.ec.europa.eu/ tempus/programme/new_tempus_ programme_en.php (Date of access: 03.09.2014)

[18] North African students invited to apply for Erasmus Mundus scholarships [Internet resource] // EU Neighbourhood Info Centre [website]. [2013]. http://www.enpi-info.eu/medportal/news/latest/35685/North-African-students-invited-to-apply-for-Erasmus-Mundus-scholarships (Date of access: 03.09.2014)

Scholarships in Europe for North African students open to nationals from Algeria, Egypt, Libya, Morocco and Tunisia [Internet resource] // ANSAmed [website.] [2014]. https://www.ansa.it/ansamed/en/news/nations/egypt/2014/01/09/Scholar-ships-Europe-North-African-students-open_9872416.html (Date of access: 03.09.2014)

About Erasmus Mundus – Al Idrisi II Exchange Scheme [Internet resource] // Erasmus Mundus [website]. [2014]. http://www.al-idrisi.eu/index. php/en/al-idrisi/the-project.html (Date of access: 03.09.2014)

[19] Erasmus Mundus Masters Courses [Internet resource] // Education, Audiovisual and Culture Executive Agency of The European Commission [website]. [2014]. http://eacea.ec.europa.eu/erasmus_mun-dus/resultscom-pendia/documents/statistics/ 2013/statistics_by_nationality_erasmus_mundus masters_students_selected_for_the_ academic_year_2013-2014_(category_ a). pdf (Date of access: 03.09.2014)

[20] Vassiliou A. Horizon 2020 and Erasmus+ boost African research and education [Internet resource] // Horizon-2020 Projects [website]. [2014]. http://horizon2020 projects.com/es-marie-sklodowska-curie-actions/ horizon-2020-and-erasmus-boost-african-research-and-education/ (Date of access: 03.09.2014)

[21] What We Do [Internet resource] // African Diaspora Policy Centre [website]. [2014]. http://www.diaspora-centre.org/home/what-we-do/ (Date of access: 03.09.2014); Policy and practice [Internet resource] // African Diaspora Policy Centre [website]. [2014]. http://www.diaspora-centre.org/policy-and-practice/ (Date of access: 03.09.2014)

[22] Strengthening Policymaking Capacities of Emerging African Diaspora Ministries in Migration and Development [Internet resource] // African Institute for Economic Development and Planning African Diaspora Policy Centre (IDEP/ADPC). Senegal, 2013. http://www.uneca.org/sites/defaultfiles/idep/announcementspc 2013_v.2_eng.pdf (Date of access: 03.09.2014).

[23] Projects [Internet resource] // African Diaspora Policy Centre [website]. [2014]. http://www.diaspora-centre.org/home/projects/ (Date of access: 03.09.2014)

Grigory Karpov, PhD (History),
Institute for African Studies
Russian Academy of Sciences

TRENDS OF AFRICAN DIASPORAS' DEVELOPMENT IN UK AND EU IN THE 2000S

The African Diasporas within the EU and the UK represents today one of the most active communities making up a society. Its quantity in 2011 was approximately 8 million people in the EU (in the United Kingdom about 1 million) and it is growing rapidly.

The largest communities of established immigrants are made up of migrants from Tunisia, Algeria, Morocco, South Africa, Nigeria, Kenya, Zimbabwe, Somalia, Ghana, Ethiopia, and Uganda. Immigrants from Sub-Saharan countries dominate in UK; migrants from North Africa prevail in the EU.

Africans take part in the daily life of European society; they are visible in politics, economy, social sphere, sports. In virtually all countries of the West with a notable presence of migrants from Africa, there is a small layer of Africans, who have succeeded in their new homelands. These successful people called the «new Africans». As a rule, these are big businesspersons, show business stars, scientists, musicians and teachers.

The EU has become a major world centre for labour immigration. Immigrants are mainly involved in the construction, automotive and road works. The problem of illegal migration remains very topical in the EU, particularly after the wave of Arab revolutions, when European countries (Italy, primarily) have seen an influx of refugees from North Africa. The problem of controlling and restricting migration is urgent for the EU countries.

Current EU estimates put the number of illegal, or irregular – African migrants in the EU-25 at about 8 million. This increase in irregular migration is largely resulting from a labour market demand, because in many EU countries the cheap and flexible workforce provided by irregular migrants has become a structural necessity. More precisely, irregular migration has been enabled by the past decades' neoliberal transformations of the EU's social relations and political economy. At first sight, there is a glaring contradiction between the EU's stated objective of fighting illegal migration on the one side, and its neo-liberal economic objectives on the other. That is to say, the latter objectives' translation into more flexible labour markets, which often rely on a steady increase of cheap and casual migrant labour, has acted to offset the former objective. In the early 1990s, research started to attend to this condition and was able to demonstrate that many EU governments that claimed to be fighting illegal immigration were actually quite aware of and even content with the fact that their economies were profiting from the cheap labour performed by illegal or irregular migrants[1].

According to various EU estimates, around half a million illegal immigrants still enter the European Union annually, even after years of measures that have included policing, detention, and repatriation. To achieve a widespread and lasting change, the European Union must address the reasons why many illegal immigrants leave their homes in Africa for what they perceive as a better life in Europe. In recent talks with their counterparts from African nations, EU ministers have now offered substantial development aid as part of a package to curb illegal immigration. In July 2006, EU Ministers and African leaders met at the Ministerial Euro-African Conference on Migration and Development held in Rabat, Morocco. European ministers adopted an action plan that included development aid, to dissuade illegal migrants who wanted to leave Africa. The European Union pledged 18 billion euros (approximately US$23 billion) to African source and transit countries over a seven-year period. This money will used to institute development and poverty-alleviation measures. The ministers also discussed creating avenues for legal migration[2].

The demographic situation in the EU has changed because of migration. This can be seen in many countries of the EU, including Britain. Another example is Spain, where migrants from Gambia have higher fertility rates than the Spanish citizens[3]. Besides other reasons, this achieved by the replacement of older wives by younger ones from Africa in the Gambian diaspora in Spain. Therefore, high rates of reproduction in short periods rely also upon a circulating pool of young women[4].

The issue of how do African elites and Africans at large perceive the European Union and what is the image of the EU in Africa remains open and highly topical. There are African perceptions of three key areas of the EU policy towards Africa: The EU's promotion of democracy and human rights, the EU's role in trade relations and the EU's policy in the field of peace and security. The EU is neither fully viewed as a soft power nor as a neo-colonialist power. The EU's self-ascribed role is not accepted fully in Sub-Saharan Africa[5]. This issue is particularly relevant due to the increasing influence of China in Africa[6].

In 2010-2011, the leading European politicians (David Cameron, Nicolas Sarkozy, and Angela Merkel) highlighted the shortcomings of multiculturalism in their respective countries. This tendency alongside with the growth of the right-wing sentiment in Europe leaves the question of the future of migrants and their descendants in the EU and the UK open.

African migrants represent one of groups of the UK population with the highest percentage of young people. One third of them are under age of 16, age range from 20 to 44 years accounts for 64%. A significant increase in the quantity of this group observed from the end of the twentieth century due to a high birth rate among those who had already settled in the country. The tradition of having many children in the families of descendants of migrants from Africa continues – 16% of their households consist of five or more members. Three-quarters of Africans are married, among the British the respective figure is 47%. In the religious context, there are more Christians among the African migrants – about 65%, a considerable proportion of them are Muslims – 20%[7].

Eighty-three percent of Africans live in large and port cities – London, Leeds, Liverpool and Cardiff. Of these, 80% came from different parts of London. 83% of migrants from Ghana (27 thousand people) and 77% from Nigeria (36 thousand people) live in the UK capital.

An open competition «100 Great Black Britons» has become one of the powerful tools to promote the role of Africans in British history and modern life, reflecting the presence of eminent British citizens of African descent in almost all spheres of life of the British society – sports, business, politics, art and social life[8].

The list includes Daley Thompson – a two-time Olympic champion (1980 and 1984) in the decathlon; boxer Lennox Lewis; a well-known music producer and DJ Trevor Beresford Romeo, better known by his stage name Jazzie B; Lenny Henry – famous writer, comedian; one of the leaders of the British labor movement William Manuel Morris; Baron Morris of Handsworth, who headed Britain's biggest trade union "The Transport and General Workers' Union" in 1992 to 2003; Eleanor Smith – the first female African head of the largest union in the UK public sector workers; Margaret Busby – the founder of one of the leading publishing houses of Great Britain «Allison & Busby», as well as many other figures of British history.

The foreign policy of the British authorities regarding the African countries greatly influences the status of the African Diaspora UK, as well as the influx of new migrants. On the one hand, Great Britain is interested in the collaboration with the African countries as the sources of natural resources (oil, primarily) and as rapidly developing markets. On the other hand, the UK is one of the leading creditors of the African governments, a major aid provider and a force capable of humanitarian interventions[9].

Britain remains one of the largest arms exporters in the world. Major buyers of British arms are African countries – Angola, Rwanda, Uganda, Zimbabwe, and Namibia. Britain also supplied weapons to both warring parties in conflict in the Congo. In 2000, 30 of the 40 most authoritarian regimes on the planet received British arms[10].

UK and African countries have retained strong cultural ties, mainly due to the use of the English language as a lingua franca for many nations of Africa. Africa remains an area of strategic interest for Great Britain. Forms and ways of projecting the British influence upon the political situation in different African countries have undergone significant changes since the colonial period. This becomes especially noticeable with the growth of the African Diaspora in the UK, which already affects the public rhetoric regarding the colonial past and the postcolonial present. However, British main strategic objective in pursuing its African policy is to preserve and protect British interests in Africa remains intact.

Multiculturalism allows separate ethnic groups to maintain their cultural norms and traditions. Because of this, some Africans and their descendants in the UK to the 2000s formed identity that partially or fully coincides with the identity of the majority.

Identity of African migrants and their descendants has certain specific in the UK. First, it should be noted, that migrants from Africa fall in the statistical category of «Black African». However, this is a very vague term, which does not reflect the ethnic, linguistic, religious and cultural diversity of immigrants from Sub-Saharan Africa, as indicated, in particular, by well-known researchers Peter Aspinall and Martha Chinouya[11].

Ethnic-based categorization of colors used in the UK since the XIX century («Black», «Yellow», «Color»), has now ceased to be relevant and is almost never used by official agencies. Migrants from Africa and the West Indies are one of the few exceptions; in relation to them official statistics continue to apply the outdated term – «Black». Some British public and academic associations dealing with the identity of Africans and African migrants in the UK, has been fighting with this state of affairs, for example, the organization «Ligali»[12].

In January 2013, a study was published, concerning the development prospects for the identities of ethnic minorities in the UK over the next 10 years. The British scientist Lucinda Platt from the Institute of Education conducted it. The report noted that the identity of African migrants has a characteristic emphasis on the religious component (Christianity, Islam), although to a lesser extent than among the groups, where the religion is predominant (Islam among Pakistanis and Bangladeshis). Among British Africans, the dual identity prevails. They identify themselves both as ethnic immigrants from Africa connecting themselves with their respective country of origin, and by citizenship defining themselves as British citizens. Africans are more likely than, for instance the South Asian group, to establish contacts with the members of other ethnic minorities, often establish friendships and business relationships outside their diasporas, they are not prone to separation on the basis of the country of origin or religious affiliation[13].

An interesting example in this context is Valerie Amos, who considers herself British even though she was not born in the territory of the metropolis. Immigrant origin has not prevented her from getting a quality education, to become an active member of the Labour Party and make a brilliant political career, becoming a member of the House of Lords.

African new religious movements, representing different strands of Christianity, have a huge impact on the identity of African migrants in the EU and the UK. The most active are the Churches of Nigeria and Ghana. One of the largest Nigerian churches is the church «Aladura». In addition to «Aladura», «African initiated church» also enjoys considerable influence among African migrants. African churches practice a unique switching, or exchange of pulpits, when the leader of one community is invited to a series of speeches and sermons in other communities, regardless of the views and doctrinal differences[14].

The question of whether migrants from Africa and their descendants have lost the African identity if they can at all be called Africans being born outside Africa, having received the citizenship of another country, and indeed had never been to Africa, remains an open one and highly controversial.

The above-mentioned dual identity phenomenon is very important, which is demonstrated by the following example. Nigerian Liquefied Natural Gas Company established a literary award for African writers in February 2004 with the big sum of prize money (20,000 pounds). However, the rules of the contest did not specify that only writers residing in Nigeria could take part in it. When the results were announced, they caused very mixed reactions and controversy about the identity of not only Nigerian writers living outside Nigeria, but among African writers from other countries[15].

The study, conducted by the Institute for Public Policy Research in 2007, revealed an interesting pattern when Africans more often associated themselves with the identity of "British" than the native population itself. Fifty-one percent of Africans have stated that they are "British", while among the indigenous population only 29% have indicated that they were "British". More than the half of respondents from local people associated themselves with the English, the Scots, the Welsh, and the Irish. This confirms the thesis of British identity crisis[16].

Migrants from African countries, besides the common features of identity outlined above, have peculiar and significant differences, determined by the specificity of their countries of origin.

Somalis, for example, tend to identify with either Islam or a shared African culture («wider black culture»), while maintaining a very strong clan ties and being very close in communicating with other African communities. The main flow of refugees from Somalia to the UK occurred in the late 1980s-early 1990s, when the Somali civil war took place. Great Britain for many

Somalis was a temporary shelter. Some representatives of the Somali community have not settled firmly in their new homeland, remaining, so to say, «nomads» like before.

Linguistic diversity also affects the identification of migrants from Africa. Migrants experiencing the minimum difficulties in speaking English – Nigerians, Zimbabweans – are the most likely to associate themselves with the British. Somalis and Ghanaians face the language barrier more often. While at home, they use a wide range of African languages, thus preserving their identity. The most common languages of African migrants in Britain are Yoruba (ninth by popularity in Britain after the English language, it is spoken by about 1% of all children in primary and secondary schools), Somalia (about 1%), Akan (Fanti and Twi), Igbo, Swahili, Lingala[17].

The UK Francophone African community is quite visible in the life of British African Diaspora. The vast majority of Africans in the UK are using the English language, but there is also the large number of immigrants from the former French and Belgian colonies – Zaire (DRC), Cote d'Ivoire, Rwanda and Togo. Their migration was driven by conflicts in their home countries. According to the 2011 UK population census, about 20 000 natives of Zaire, 8 000 of Cote d'Ivoire, 6 000 ethnic Rwandans and 2000 Togo migrants settled in the UK[18].

Many Francophone Africans began arriving in the UK in the 1990s and in a short period at the beginning of the 2000s created a relatively stable community. The most numerous and influential are the Congolese who settled in the North and East London in areas Haringey and Newham. They have their own newspapers, magazines, restaurants. Several Pentecostal churches, where sermons conducted in French and Congolese languages, operate in these areas. Catholic Cathedral of Notre Dame in the late 1990s even devoted a special time for the Francophone Africans to assemble and pray.

Until the mid-1970s, Africans in the UK quite often faced discrimination in education and were rarely on equal terms to qualify for a good education and highly skilled and well-paid jobs.

Since the beginning of the 1980s in British schools the curricula focused on ethnic minorities has been actively implemented; local and central authorities organized cultural programs aimed at supporting and developing cultural traditions of migrants, created language centers, financed the construction of religious buildings. Particular attention paid to the education of the younger generation in the spirit of tolerance towards otherness, familiarity with the culture and traditions of migrants. The government document «Education for All» (1985), recognized the principles of multiculturalism in education.

Educational projects of the later period – the late 1990s – early 2000s – continued to develop and strengthen the identity of ethnic and religious minorities, as a guarantee of social cohesion. «... [Projects] based on an approach deflecting simple assimilation: argues that social unity is possible only when the differences are recognized and appreciated»[19].

With regard to access to education for ethnic and religious minorities, by the beginning of the twenty-first century in the UK the situation is very beneficial. . In the 1990s, the British authorities have set a goal to improve the educational level of the population, by ensuring that at least 50% of young people by 30 years had a higher education. As a result, among the British population in 2001–2002 the quantity of people with higher education reached only 38%, and among minorities ranged from 39% to 49% for Bangladeshis and Pakistanis, to 71% and 73% for Africans and Indians, respectively. In the 2000s, every sixth British student belonged to a particular ethnic minority. Several researchers pointed out that in the modern education system in the UK the children and grandchildren of migrants are often more successful than their peers from the native population[20].

In the 2000s, the African Diaspora was leading in terms of enrollment in lifelong education. About 84% of Africans adults (age from 16 to 64 years) received education in one form or another, even more than the national average (78%), and 94% of Africans occupying the highly skilled and managerial positions continued their education in some form.

This may indicate two things. First, that in the UK the truly favourable conditions in education for all were created. Second, that also the African Diaspora members actively seek to join the British public, business, intellectual and cultural life through education in order to express their civic position more fully and to make their voices heard.

However, there are still notable difficulties for Africans obtaining education – it especially concerns schooling. Level of probability of exclusion from school for African teenagers is three times higher than the national average. In deprived urban areas, this figure could be six times higher. This situation has been more characteristic of families recently re-settled from Africa.

The life of African communities in Britain is regulated besides general laws by the laws designed to protect ethnic minorities against discrimination in public life, in education and at work. During the period from 1967 to 2010, more than two dozen laws, ensuring the equal rights and opportunities for migrants from Africa, have been adopted.

To sum up, it can be said that some African migrants' need to preserve and transmit to the younger generation the norms and traditions of their historical homeland cannot be realized fully for objective reasons although many possibilities to do so are well available under the current UK legislation.

British authorities do not create special obstacles in setting the African churches, in teaching African languages, in education and employment, or in the preservation of identities of Africans and their descendants.

Therefore, the identity of African migrants and their descendants retains certain linguistic and religious features. Migrants from Africa in most cases do not have trouble in obtaining a quality education because of to their religious or ethnic backgrounds. Bad English or other factors can also act as barriers.

Employment issues are directly related to the willingness of migrants to accept the values and norms of British society, or at least not to criticize them openly and not to oppose them. Thus, we observe the situation in which the greatest prospects in the labour market naturally have those representatives of the African diaspora, who are likely to accept the norms of British society at least in their public lives.

Migration from Africa to the EU has become one of the key events of the 20th century. Africans changed national and religious composition of the European states. However, at the same time the identity of Africans themselves in the EU has also undergone changes. The number of Africans in the EU is increasing constantly. These reciprocal processes have serious and permanent impact on the internal and external policies of the EU. If these trends continue, European countries should expect large-scale socioeconomic and political changes in this century.

---

[1] Hansen P. More Barbwire or More Immigration, or Both? EU Migration Policy in the Nexus of Border Security Management and Neoliberal Economic Growth // Seton Hall Journal of Diplomacy and International Relations, Vol. 11, No. 1.

[2] Addo A. Porous Policies: Illegal Immigration in Europe // Harvard International Review, Vol. 28, No. 3.

[3] Bledsoe C., Houle R., Sow P. High Fertility Gambians in Low Fertility Spain: The Dynamics of Child Accumulation across Transnational Space // Demographic Research, Vol. 16.

[4] Bledsoe C., Houle R., Sow P. High Fertility Gambians in Low Fertility Spain: The Dynamics of Child Accumulation across Transnational Space // Demographic Research, Vol. 16.

[5] Schmidt S. Soft Power or Neo-Colonialist Power? – African Perceptions of the EU // Review of European Studies, Vol. 4, No. 3.

[6] Sautman B., Hairong Y. Friends and Interests: China's Distinctive Links with Africa // African Studies Review, Vol. 50, No. 3.

[7] Ethnic minorities in Great Britain // Commission for Racial Equality. London, 2007. P.1 .

[8] Winner of 100 Great Black Britons. http://web.archive.org/web/20060428070751/http://rastaites.com/news/hearticals/100greatest.htm

[9] Africa in contemporary international relations. Moscow, 2011. P. 103-128.

[10] Watson M. How immigration in the UK is linked to corrupt British foreign policy overseas // Minority Perspective, 29 March 2010.

[11] Aspinall, P.J., Chinouya, M. Is the standardised term «Black African» useful in demographic and health research in the UK // Ethnicity and Health. 2008. № 13(3). P. 1-20.

[12] http://www.ligali.org

[13] Platt L. Future Identities: Changing identities in the UK – the next 10 years. London, 2013. P. 1-27.

[14] Adogame A. Betwixt Identity and Security: African New Religious Movements (ANRMs) and the Politics of Religious Networking in Europe. Center for Studies on New Religions, 2001. http://www.cesnur. org/2001/london2001/adogame.htm

[15] Aloh E. Writing the New African: Migration and Modern African Literary Identity // 4 August 2012. http://www.africanwriter.com/writing-the-new-african-migration-and-modern-african-literary-identity/

[16] Gill Ch. Ethnic Minorities Feel More British Than the Whites // Daily Mail (London), 19 February, 2007.

[17] New African Diasporas. London, New York, 2003. P. 19.

[18] Population by Country of Birth and Nationality Datasheets January 2011 to December 2011 // Office for National Statistics (ONS). http://www.ons. gov.uk/ons/search/index.html?newquery=Population+by+Country+of+ Birth+and+Nationality+ Datasheets+January+2011+to+December+2011

[19] Lall M., Gillborn D. Beyond a Colour Blind Approach: Addressing Black & Minority Ethnic Inclusion in the Education Strand of New Deal for Communities // Institute of Education, University of London. Research Report 49. November 2004. P. 1.

[20] Dustmann C., Theodoropoulos N. Ethnic minority immigrants and their children in Britain // Oxford Economic Papers, New Series. – April 2010. Vol. 62. №.2. P. 209-233.

Ivan Lileev, PhD (Political Science)
Center for Global and Strategic Studies,
Institute for African Studies
Russian Academy of Sciences

EVOLUTION OF EU POLICIES TOWARDS AFRICA
AND NEW EUROPEAN APPROACHES
TO DEVELOPMENT AID

The ties between the united Europe and Africa have a history dating back centuries, or, perhaps, millennia. No exaggeration. According to Herodotus, merchants from Africa could be seen in the streets of Rome as early as the beginning of the first millennium. Trade and economic relations had been growing in the following centuries, and by the end of the 19th century, the European powers divided virtually the entire Africa into colonial possessions.

Modern political and economic relations between Europe and Africa go back to the post-WWII times. In 1957, the Rome Treaty was signed, laying foundation for the European Economic Union, or the so-called Common Market, the very name of which implied that its activities would focus on trade and economic objectives.

Initially, the founders of the organization were supposed to put an end to intra-European wars that waged for centuries.

One should subscribe to the opinion that the creation of the European Economic Community in postwar times was largely attributed to the desire of some former colonial powers to share the burden of responsibility for the destiny of African states (nations) with their European partners[1].

This was also the goal of the trade and economic Lome Conventions, which cannot be forgotten when speaking about the African-European relations. These Conventions were signed in 1975 (strictly speaking, the agreements were reached in general as early as 1962 at a meeting in Yaoundé). They contained an obligation to allow duty-free access for African tropical farming products to European markets, as well as some other trade and economic preferences. In their later 'versions' (up to Lome IV of 1989), these Conventions were further developed and eventually 'transformed' into the Cotonou Agreement of 2000 that provided for a more ramified system of ties between European and African states.

Along with the changes of the international political situation and the development of the union, its foreign policy strategies evolved as well. The *perestroika*, or reformation, in the Soviet Union made it possible to

101

reunify Germany. The new quality of this pan-European union was confirmed in the Maastricht Treaty of 1992 that supported the new status of the European Union. Later on, the European Union expanded again by admitting countries of Eastern Europe.

It is noteworthy that initially and until recent years the EU positioned itself as an economic organization. In its constituent documents, mentioned that 'force can be used only for peace-enforcement purposes but not for the benefit of one or several the EU member states'.

The present-day strategy of the European Union regarding Africa is formulated both based on years-long experience of interaction between the two continents and considering the requirements of practical implementation of specific principles enunciated by the united Europe as the general basis for its foreign policy practices. Among such principles are the struggle for human rights, reduction of poverty and fighting famine with all of these directly referring to the European-African relations. The same principles should be used to shape the foreign policy strategy of the European Union towards Africa. Such approach based on the perception of the fact that people of different nationalities have common basic principles and interests with the maintenance of peace being one of them. In addition, the struggle against poverty as a part of it is very important.

For Africa, three priority directions, where the participation of the European Union most requested, were outlined – peacekeeping efforts, economic aid and combating illegal migration.

As far as peacekeeping is concerned, the European Union has sufficient experience of peacekeeping operations, for example, the EU participation in a peacekeeping effort in the Congo. Today, the European Union has an opportunity to reaffirm its vitality through actual participation in peacekeeping activities together with the African Union and in anti-terrorist programs. It appears that in this very context, we should assess the EU forces' missions in Mali and its participation in combating piracy. In other words, the EU strategy arises from the principle that prior to economic aid and implementation of the development strategy on the continent, there must be peaceful life and security there first. That is why the EU peacekeeping contingents have not only to act as a shield or fence between the confronting parties, but also to provide assistance in the organization of peaceful life, the establishment of local authorities and delivery of humanitarian aid to the population worn out by suffering.

The EU support of the peacemaking efforts of the African Union includes, *inter alia,* financial aid for the African Standby Force, units consisting of both military personnel and civilians (doctors, rescue workers, policemen) and trained to be ready for immediate interference in case of emergency situations in the continent. This aid has also included the creation of an African training center for maintaining peace and security in Africa (*Amani Africa 2*).

The leaders of the European and African Unions have repeatedly confirmed the existence of joint strategic goals not limited to the maintenance of the state of peace and security in the continent, but also in the areas of democratic governance and defense of human rights in Africa. Furthermore, closer coordination between the European Union, the African Union and relevant structures of the UN may be considered a new aspect of the peacekeeping process in Africa. In certain cases, the UN peacemaking contingents have replaced the EU forces that were the first to arrive in the areas of armed conflict to prevent their escalation.

It should be also mentioned that nowadays there is a momentum for closer cooperation in the fields of peacekeeping and peace-building between the European Union on the one hand and the African Union and regional African organizations (ECOWAS, in particular) on the other hand.

The EU has adopted the African Peace Initiative, which stipulates the active participation in peacekeeping operations in Africa and, by 2013, has participated in the following operations:

1. The African Union's mission in Somalia (AMISOM).
2. The EU-led International mission in Mali (AFISMA, in cooperation with ECOWAS).
3. Peacekeeping mission in the Central African region.

Meanwhile, a number of researchers and analysts raise a question to what extent the EU capabilities are sufficient to achieve the set goals and whether the declared engagement of the EU in peacekeeping efforts is adequate. In this connection, it is fairly noted that everything depends on what political and military goal they serve, and what resources are available for implementation of these objectives. In this connection, it is noteworthy that the peacekeeping also played an important part in establishing structures of the African Union. Already in early 1990s at various summits, the idea was suggested of giving a new dimension to peacekeeping efforts of the African Union. The very commitment to create own armed forces, prevent and put an end to inter-African conflicts became one of the driving motives for the transformation of the Organization of African Unity into the more efficient African Union.

As for the implementation of economic collaboration programs, the key factor in this respect remains the fulfillment of the Cotonou Agreement[2].

Nowadays, the problem resides in a greater diversity of priorities of different African states. That is to say that the needs of the most economically developed states on the continent interested in raising the competitive capacity of their economies differ from the necessities of the least developed countries seeking to receive more free subventions, donations and humanitarian aid. It should be noted that it is a long time since the 'debt relief' policy and provision of numerous subsidies and grants became an integral part of the Euro-African relations.

Since the early 1990s, the 'development aid' priorities have been shifted. Now it is becoming one of the tools of the African community transformation. Both on the all-European and national levels it had confirmed that the 'development aid' would be provided in previously fixed volumes only to the states that have accomplished democratic reforms on a multi-party basis. In a short period, such reforms were implemented. However, the very process of democratic transformation and development of the African community proved to be work that is much more painstaking.

It is worth mentioning, that the importance of 'development aid' can hardly be underestimated. In many cases, these programs implemented, as a rule, at the national level became a part of national budgets and the ground on which the poverty reduction national programs were established. To a certain extent, that, of course, weakened the impetus for the African states to develop their own agricultural production. For many years, no attention was paid to another important aspect of the issue that is the control over the distribution of funds received.

Many researchers believe that the aid provision mechanism that existed in the recent decades now needs to be substantially redesigned. This concerns the allocation of rather big amounts. Sufficiently to say that only in 2007–2012 the African nations received from the European Union over €24 billion through Official Development Assistance. However, an effective tool of control over fund spending is virtually missing. Today, the challenge is to make sure that the money flows not simply 'come to the country' but reach the end-recipients, i.e. the poorest strata of the population. It is no coincidence that the anticorruption efforts, as well as the reforms of local governments today, also fall within the area of strategic collaboration between Europe and Africa[3].

The Cotonou Agreement contains a special section confirming the existence of the problem. It is also pointed out that 'grave instances of corruption' are being revealed not only in the distribution of financial aid provided through the European Development Fund but at a more strategic level as well. Especially for the anticorruption purposes, the European Union has been establishing contacts not only with governmental institutions but also with social entities.

In the statements of European politicians including national leaders, with ever-increasing frequency there appears the thought that no one is going to prejudice the African traditions. However, the aid will be provided to countries where responsibility of the rich for the destiny of the poor is practiced and the agreed 'rules of political behavior' are followed, among which the most sought for are the transparency of distribution funds and the observance of the basic rules of pursuing economic goals.

There is no doubt that while carrying out the aid programs in Africa the European Union also protects its own interests: the exodus of Africans to the successful and prosperous Europe is perceived as a disaster.

As far as the present state of affairs is concerned, as mentioned in the EU foreign policy strategy, the achievement of this essentially strategic goal is hampered by several factors. First, it is a result of the institutional uncertainty (absence of clear division of powers within the EU). Secondly, due to the tendency in some states to resolve all issues domestically but not at the European level; and thirdly, because of the budget cuts in the EU structural subdivisions including those responsible for aid to Africa[4].

It is clear, that the comprehensive strategy of enhancing security in Africa, implemented by the European Union, also aimed at prevention of exodus of Africans to Europe[5]. Only joint efforts of governmental, supranational and public organizations may help the poorest African nations to reach the set objective and to secure true progress and prosperity.

---

[1] Verheugen Günter. New European Identity // Internationale Politik. 2/2014. P. 12.

[2] Grimm Sven. Africa-ein Testfall fur die Instrumente europaischer Aussenpolitik in Globaler Aussenpolitik der Europaischen Union. Berlin. 2009 . S. 12.

[3] Gaigner Michael. Eine Strategie fur Africa in «Europas Aussenpolitik» Frankfurt, 2006. P. 94.

[4] Peter Gerlich. European policy paradoxes and Pittfalls in Leshek Jesien European Union policies in the Making. Tischler European University. Krakow. 2008. P. 3.

[5] Ziegmar Schmidt. Die Sicherheitspolitik gegenuber subsaharian Afrika/ in Gisella Muller-Brandeck – Boquet Die Africa Politik der Europaischen Union.

Dmitriy Kochetov,
Phd candidate,
Institute for African Studies
Russian Academy of Sciences

TRADE AND ECONOMIC RELATIONS BETWEEN ITALY AND NORTH AFRICA AFTER THE 'ARAB SPRING'

Traditionally Italy has very strong economic connections with North African countries, i.e. with Egypt, Morocco, Libya, Tunisia and Algeria. These countries had unchangeable rulers for many years before the Arab Spring. Each Italian government tried to maintain good relationship with them because political issues influenced economic relations. At the same time, Italian officials did not pay much attention to the personal qualities of even such a controversial politician as Muammar Gaddafi. The Italian Prime-Minister Silvio Berlusconi even kissed his hand in 2010 at the summit of the League of Arab states. In all of the above-mentioned countries, with the exception of Morocco and Algeria, previous rulers were deposed during the Arab Spring.

This dramatic political phenomenon has absolutely changed the political life in Egypt, Libya and Tunisia. That is why it is interesting to find out how these powerful political changes have influenced the economic connections of the North African countries with Italy.

For this purpose, statistics of the Italian Ministry of economic development is quite useful[1][2]. Before observing North Africa – Italy trade statistics, it is important to look at the statistics of Italian trade with the whole world. According to its figures[3], in 2010, directly before the Arab Spring, Italy's exports and imports grew after the crisis of 2008–2009.

The growth was rather fast. Total trade exchange increased by 19 per cent (from 589 bn in 2009 to 704 bn euro in 2010).

In 2011, growth of TTE slowed down. It increased by 10 per cent (from 704 bn in 2009 to 777 bn euro in 2010).

In 2010–2011, Italy managed to restore trade exchange with the world and even exceed the level of 2008[4]

In 2012, imports from all countries of the world to Italy decreased by 5 per cent (from 401 in 2011 to 380 bn euro in 2012). Exports to the world still increased, but only by about 4% (from 375 in 2011 to 390 bn euro in 2012). Total trade exchange stayed almost at the same level.

In 2013, exports did not change considerably, but imports decreased by 5%, which led to a decrease of the total trade exchange by 2.7%.

These figures changed differently than the figures of Italian trade exchange with North Africa. After the 2010 growth, in 2011 Italian imports and exports collapsed simultaneously. TTE fell down by 25% from 38 bn in 2010 to 28 bn euro in 2011.[5]

However, in 2012 TTE almost returned to the level of 2010, with insignificant difference. In the first three months of 2013, exports increased by 16%, as compared with the same period of the previous year (from 3 to 3.5 bn euro), but imports during the same period decreased by 6% (from 7 to 6.6 bn euro). That is why TTE remained largely unchanged.

For better understanding of situations, it is important to view each country separately.

Morocco is the simplest case, because the Arab Spring did not depose regime in that country. Its economic connections with Italy did not decrease in 2011, like in the cases of some other countries of the region.[6] Italian TTE with Morocco increased by 7%[7]. In 2012, TTE fell nearly to the level of 2010, but during the first eight months of 2013, it grew. Moreover, in June 2013, the journal *Milano Finanza* noticed that Italian exports to Morocco almost doubled over 12 years (from 2000 to 2012), and in first months of 2013 growth even sped up.[8] Italian businesspeople emphasized that the stability and predictability of Morocco's political and economic system is very attractive for them. Probably, they kept in mind the peaceful character of political changes in this country. In any case, the importance of Morocco is not enough to influence heavily the trade exchange between Italy and the whole North Africa.

In Algeria, the government managed to resist the Arab Spring too, but the President Abdelaziz Bouteflika had to declare wide political reforms, which were encouraged by Italy. In particular, the spokesperson of Italian Foreign Minister Franco Frattini, Maurizio Massari, said that Algerian government should fulfill the demands of people.[9] He also declared that Italy could support Algeria on its way to a more democratic society, for example, by conversion of 10 million of its debts and by helping it in realizing the programs of social development. Probably, this position has played its role, and in 2011 total trade exchange between the two countries[10] increased (by 3.6%, from 10.9 to 11.3 bn euro), although not so considerably as in 2010, when it increased by 26%. In 2012 TTE grew too, but in the first eight months of 2013 it decreased by 22% in comparison with the same period of 2012 due to the fall of imports to Italy by 34.3%.[11]

In Egypt and Tunisia, the Arab Spring swept away the previous regimes. In Tunisia, revolution finished in 2011, after street fights and resignation of Zine el-Abidine Ben Ali. Italy supported this revolution. Italian Minister of Foreign Affairs Franco Frattini said that he saw the reasons of Tunisian revolution in the oppression of democratic rights and the lack of alternation of generations (obviously, among the Tunisian political elite).[12] Frattini promised that the EU and Italy, in particular, would help Tunisia during the period of transition to democracy. He noticed that the more close integration with the EU and the struggle with the Islamist threat were very important for Tunisia after the revolution. Later Frattini even told that the EU could more actively render assistance to Tunisia. It is very important that a representative of Eni, Italian oil and gas production company with big state participation, declared that political changes could not affect ENI's projects in Tunisia.[13]

In Egypt, revolutionaries put an end to the regime of Hosni Mubarak, who had ruled Egypt for 30 years. It is important that Italy became the first European country to be visited by the new Egyptian president, Mohamed Morsi.

Before the revolution in Egypt, Italy was its very important partner. The new government did not forget about it and encouraged Italy to participate in new projects, including the reconstruction of railway system. At the same time, Italian entrepreneurs noticed that unpredictable changes in the new Egyptian government negatively affected the business atmosphere in the country.[14] In any case, this visit showed that the new president from the Muslim Brotherhood, absolutely different from the former Air Force officer Mubarak, made an important step to develop economic relations with Italy.

Moreover, this tendency continued after new bloody street fights and the military coup of 3 July 2013 took place. Led by the Egyptian army chief General Abdel Fattah el-Sisi, new Egyptian authorities deposed and arrested Mohammed Morsi and several other Muslim Brotherhood leaders. In addition, thousands of Muslim Brotherhood members were imprisoned, hundreds were sentenced to death, the organization itself was declared "terrorist group".[15] However, the new ruling circles just like their predecessors declared that Italy is the most important European commercial partner for Egypt.[16]

The trade exchange of Italy with Tunisia and Egypt has one common feature: after the growth in 2010, in 2011 imports decreased by nearly 10%, but exports still grew. In 2012, Italian exports to both countries decreased by nearly 10%, but imports began to increase. In 2013, total trade exchange with Tunisia grew[17] by 2.22 per cent (TTE in 2012 – 5.4 bn euro, in 2013 – 5.52 bn euro). Total trade exchange with Egypt in 2013 began to decrease[18] due to the fall of imports to Italy by 8.7%.[19]

The most interesting case is Libya, because in that country the Arab Spring has provoked a full-scale citizen war between the supporters and the opponents of the "Brotherly Leader and Guide of the Revolution" Muammar Gaddafi. The EU, the United States and their allies supported the Gaddafi's opponents by different means, including military intervention. Italy also took part in this intervention. In the beginning of

108

protests in Libya, Italy had rather a cautious position, in comparison with the positions of UK and France, because Berlusconi did not want to "jeopardize its privileged relationship with Qaddafi"[20]. Italian Prime Minister was also afraid that the influential "Northern League" party would leave the cabinet and provoke political crisis, because the "Northern League" was against military intervention. Moreover, only two and a half years before, in 2008 Italy and Socialist People's Libyan Arab Jamahiriya signed the Treaty on friendship, collaboration and cooperation[21], which made any step of Italy against Gaddafi at least ambiguous.

Nevertheless, later, after the armed attacks against Libyan protesters, Italy had to join its allies in the EU and NATO. Berlusconi said that Gaddafi had lost control over the situation, and Italy and Europe could not remain observers any more. Defense Minister Ignazio La Russa declared that the Treaty on Italo-Libian friendship was inhibited.[22] Italy took part in the operation "Unified Protector", which led to the fall of Jamahiriya.[23] After it, Italy, together with the EU and the USA, supported the National Transition Council and later – National Forces Alliance, the most liberal party in the General National Congress.[24]

However, even the revolution, war and bombings have not ruined oil and gas trade between Italy and Libya. ENI's official website proudly declared that the company was the first one to recommence activity in Libya after the war. It also invested millions of dollars in the Libyan health system.[25] Special interest of Italian business circles to Libya is confirmed by the fact that in August 2014 Italian embassy was still working[26] during street fights in Tripoli, unlike American[27] or Russian[28] ones, for example.

That is why the total trade exchange of Italy with Libya decreased in 2011, but restored very fast in 2012. After growth in 2010,[29] in 2011 it just fell more than by two-thirds, more precisely by 69%, from 15 bn to 4.5 bn euro. Such heavy losses have influenced the Italian trade exchange with North Africa in total. However, surprisingly enough, in 2012 the trade turnover returned nearly to the level of 2010. It happened because despite hostilities the pipeline system was not damaged greatly. Both sides tried to spare it because both wanted to use it in future after the victory. In 2013, TTE between Italy and Libya decreased by 28.35% due to the collapse of imports to Italy by 37%, while exports increased by 19.7%.[30]

The analysis of this information shows that in spite of the common features of political processes in the North African countries during the Arab Spring (the conflict between the old unchanging regimes and its opponents), the economic consequences for trade connections with Italy were not always the same. However, in each case, even if heavy losses were observed in 2011, in 2012 there was a restoration of trade exchange with Algeria or especially Libya. Moreover, it should be noticed, that economic losses of 2013 were usually connected with the decrease in Italian imports. It is a sign of significant internal problems of Italy.

For many years, Italy has been the recipient of economic support from the EU. In 2013, an internal political crisis, when Italy had no government for a few months, worsened the economic situation. Even the government of Enrico Letto, created with such difficulties, lasted for less than a year, and then was replaced by the government of Matteo Renzi. This political instability cannot be compared with the situation in Egypt, for example, but it still negatively influences the Italian economy. The grave condition of Italian economy is proved by the decreasing share of Italy in world exports and imports, which have not even grown during the post-crisis restoration[31]. It means that the Italian economy restored slower than the global one.

Italy remains one of the top 10 economies of the world, while none of the North African countries is even in the top 30. Consequently, even ordinary problems of the Italian economy harm its relationship with North Africa to a greater extent than serious upheavals in Libya or Egypt.

That is why we can conclude that the economic connections of Italy with the North African countries are strong and mutually beneficial and they have endured the dramatic political changes caused by the Arab Spring. Italy's internal problems, which are a more powerful factor, can influence this relationship just as negatively as the Arab revolutions.

---

[1] Statistics of Italian import and export with the world [Electronic resource]: Ministry of Economic Development of Italy: [site]. http://www.sviluppoeconomico. gov.it/index.php?option=com_content&view=article&viewType=1&id=2022949& idarea1=1579&idarea2=0&idarea3=0&idarea4=0&andor=AND&sectionid=2&andor cat=AND&partebassaType=0&idareaCalendario1=0&MvediT=1&showMenu=1&sh owCat=1&showArchiveNewsBotton=0&idmenu=3175&directionidUser=0 (date of access: 4 September 2014).

[2] Statistics of Italian import and export with Africa [Electronic resource]: Ministry of Economic Development of Italy: [site]. http://www.svilup-poeconomico.gov.it/index.php?option=com_content&view=article&viewType=1&id area1=1579&idarea2=1585&idarea3=0&idarea4=0&andor=AND&sectionid=0&and orcat=AND&partebassaType=0&idareaCalendario1=0&MvediT=1&showMenu= 1&showCat=1&idmenu=2161&showArchiveNewsBotton=0&id=2022487&direction idUser=0 (date of access: 4 September 2014).

[3] Statistics of Italian trade exchange with the world (2004-2013) [Electronic resource]: Ministry of Economic Development of Italy: [site]. http://www.svilup poeconomico.gov.it/images/stories/OsservatorioEconomico/statistiche_import_export /interscambio.pdf (date of access: 17 May 2014).

[4] Ibidem.

[5] Statistics of Italian trade exchange with the North Africa (2006 – March 2013) [Electronic resource]: Ministry of Economic Development of Italy: [site]. http://www.sviluppoeconomico.gov.it/images/stories/Osservatorio Economico/osservatorio_economico/africa/Nord_Africa_28_05_2013.pdf (date of access:use 17 May 2014).

[6] Statistics of Italian trade exchange with Morocco (2007 – April 2014) [Electronic resource]: Ministry of Economic Development of Italy: [site]. http://www.sviluppoeconomico.gov.it/images/stories/OsservatorioEconomico/osserva torio_economico/africa/Marocco_04_09_2014.pdf (date of access: 4 September 2014).

[7] Ibidem.

[8] Export italiano in Marocco: + 90% in 10 anni [Electronic resource] // Milano Finanza: [site]. [06/06/2013]. http://www.milanofinanza.it/news/export-italiano-in-marocco-90-in-10-anni-201306061619551535 (date of access: 7 July 2014).

[9] Focus-Libia – Ministro Frattini il 15 luglio al Gruppo di Contatto a Istanbul [Electronic resource]: Foreign Ministry of Italy [site]. [8 July 2011]. http://www.esteri.it/MAE/IT/Sala_Stampa/ArchivioNotizie/Approfon-dimenti/2011/07/20110708_fratist.htm (date of access: 7 July 2014).

[10] Statistics of Italian trade exchange with Algeria (2006 – January 2014) [Electronic resource]: Ministry of Economic Development of Italy: [site]. http://www.sviluppoeconomico.gov.it/images/stories/Osservatorio Economico/osservatorio_economico/africa/Algeria_16_05_2014.pdf (date of access: 4 September 2014).

[11] Ibidem.

[12] Tunisia: Frattini "l'Italia ha un ruolo chiave ma serve che Ue faccia la sua parte" [Electronic resource]: Foreign Ministry of Italy [site]. [20 January 2011]. http://www.esteri.it/MAE/IT/Sala_Stampa/ArchivioNotizie/Appro-fondimenti/ 2011/01/20110120_TunisiaFrattini.htm (date of access: 7 July 2014).

[13] Tunisia: Frattini "L'Europa faccia di piu per lo sviluppo" [Electronic resource]: Foreign Ministry of Italy [site]. [17 February 2011]. http://www.esteri.it/ MAE/IT/Sala_Stampa/ArchivioNotizie/Approfondimenti/2011/02/20110217Tavolo Tunisi. htm (date of access: 7 July 2014).

[14] Sally Khalifa Isaac. ""Italy – Egypt: Ever Closer Trade Partners?" // Italian Institute for International Political Studies [site]. [21 February 2013] http://www.ispionline.it/sites/default/files/pubblicazioni/commentaryisaac_ 21.02.2013.pdf (date of access: 7 July 2014)

[15] Egypt's Muslim Brotherhood declared "terrorist group" [Electronic resource] // British Broadcasting Corporation: [site]. [25.12.2013]. http://www.bbc.com/news/ world-middle-east-25515932 (date of access: 4 September 2014).

[16] Egitto – "Primi passi per progetto Maire Tecnimont ad Assuan" [Electronic resource]: Foreign Ministry of Italy [site]. [20 May 2014]. http://www.esteri. it/MAE/IT/Sala_Stampa/ArchivioNotizie/Approfondimenti/2014/05/20140520_Egitt o_progetto.htm (date of access: 7 July 2014).

[17] Statistics of Italian trade exchange with Tunisia (2006 – March 2014) [Electronic resource]: Ministry of Economic Development of Italy: [site].

http://www.sviluppoeconomico.gov.it/images/stories/Osservatorio Economico/ osservatorio_economico/africa/Tunisia_19_06_2014.pdf (date of access: 4 September 2014).

[18] Statistics of Italian trade exchange with Egypt (2006 – February 2014) [Electronic resource]: Ministry of Economic Development of Italy: [site]. http://www.sviluppoeconomico.gov.it/images/stories/OsservatorioEconomi-co/ osservatorio_economico/africa/Egitto_28_05_2014.pdf (date of access: 4 September 2014).

[19] Ibidem.

[20] Arturo Varvelli "Europe and the Libian crisis: a failed state in the backyard?" p. 2. // Italian Institute for International Political Studies [site]. [Analysis № 237, March 2014] http://www.ispionline.it/sites/default/files/pubblicazioni/analysis23720140.pdf (date of access: 7 July 2014).

[21] Threat of friendship, collaboration and cooperation between Italian Republic and the Great Socialist People's Libyan Arab Jamahiriya, maken in Benghazi on 30 August 2008 [Electronic resource]: Chamber of deputies of Italian Parliament: [site]. http://www.camera.it/_dati/leg6/lavori/schedela/apritelecomando_wai.asp?codice =16pdl0017390 (date of access: 4 September 2014).

[22] Treat Italy-Libya is inhibited [Electronic resource] // Corriere della sera: [site]. [26/02/2011]. http://www.corriere.it/politica/1_febbraio_26/ ibia-berlusconi-larussa-trattato-gheddafi_7acd0620-419b-11e0-b406-2da238c0fa39.shtml (date of access: 4 September 2014).

[23] Summary of operation Unified Protector [Electronic resource]: Ministry of Defence of Italy: [site]. http://www.difesa.it/OperazioniMilitari/op_int _concluse/Libia-UnifiedProtector/Pagine/default.aspx (date of access: 4 September 2014).

[24] Arturo Varvelli "Europe and the Libian crisis: a failed state in the backyard?" p. 3-7. // Italian Institute for International Political Studies [site]. [Analysis № 237, March 2014] http://www.ispionline.it/ites/default/files/ubblicazioni/analysis__ 23720140.pdf (date of access: 7 July 2014).

[25] Eni's response to the transition period in Libya [Electronic resource]: Eni: [site] http://www.eni.com/en_IT/sustainability/case-studies/2013/eni-response-libya.shtml (date of access:use 4 September 2014).

[26] Contacts of Italian Embassy in Tripoli [Electronic resource]: Italian Embassy in Tripoli: [site] http://www.ambtripoli.esteri.it/ambasciata tripoli (date of access: 4 September 2014).

[27] Temporary Stuff Relocation – Press Statement [Electronic resource]: U. S. Department of State: [site] http://www.state.gov/r/pa/rs/ps/2014/07/ 29805.htm (date of access: 4 September 2014).

[28] Communication for media – About temporary departure to Tunisia of the Russian Embassy in Tripoli [Electronic resource]: Ministry of Foreign Affairs of Russia [site] http://www.mid.ru/brp4.nsf/newsline/9C2D7AF668A829B44257D270050F6 C5 (date of access: 4 September 2014).

[29] Statistics of Italian trade exchange with Libya (2006 – February 2014) [Electronic resource]: Ministry of Economic Development of Italy: [site].

http://www.sviluppoeconomico.gov.it/images/stories/sservatorioEconomico/osservato
rio_economico/africa/Libia_04_06_2014.pdf (date of access: 4 September 2014).

[30] Ibidem.

[31] Share of Italian market in the world export and import [Electronic resource]:
Ministry of Economic Development of Italy: [site]. http://www.sviluppoeconomico.
gov.it/images/stories/OsservatorioEconomico/statistiche_import_export/quote.pdf
(date of access: 4 September 2014).

Anton Rodin, PhD candidate,
Institute for African Studies
Russian Academy of Science

JAPAN AND AFRICA IN THE BEGINNING OF THE 21st CENTURY

Despite the fact that in comparison with economic positions in Africa of such emerging powers as China, India and Brazil those of Japan look rather modest, we can expect that in the near future this situation will considerably change.

On June 1, 2013 Prime Minister Sinzo Abe announced that in the next five years Japan will invest in Africa up to approximately JPY 3.2 trillion or S32 billions of private and public capital. Almost half of this sum will be an Official Development Aid (hereinafter referred to as ODA). Over the last decades, Japan has ranked high on the list of ODA donor-countries and Africa's share in Japan's ODA tends to increase. In January of 2014 Sinzo Abe visited African countries (Cote d'Ivoire, Mozambique, and Ethiopia). African gets assistance from several non-governmental organizations and programs based in Japan. This fact shows that Africa is no less important for Japan than for China.

The government of Japan continues to consider Africa as one of the most promising directions for its foreign policy and economy. The proof, confirming this point of view, is the official position of Japan's Ministry of Foreign Affairs, who stated in Diplomatic Bluebook: «Africa is becoming increasingly important for Japan's foreign policy from the perspectives that (1) it is Japan's duty as a responsible member of the international community to earnestly work toward the resolution of the various problems facing Africa; (2) it is strategically important for Japan to strengthen the economic relationship with Africa, which is endowed with abundant natural resources and a growing population and therefore a potentially huge market with sustained high rates of economic growth; and (3) the cooperation with African countries is essential to further address global issues such as UN Security Council Reform and climate change. From this perspective, Japan continued to proactively advance its foreign policies toward Africa, focusing mainly on (1) contributions to peace and stability, (2) expansion of development assistance, and promotion of trade and investment, and (3) response to global issues»[1].

Another vital thing for understanding of Japan's contemporary stance and policy towards Africa and condition of nowadays Japan-Africa relations are the guideline and activity of the Tokyo International Conference on African Development (アフリカ開発会議, herein TICAD).

The conference has already been held every five years since 1993, and its scale and importance have grown noticeably. The Government of Japan is the co-organizer of the conference together with the United Nations, the United Nations Development Program (UNDP), the World Bank, and Global Coalition for Africa and since 2013 – African Union Commission (AUC).

The first conference conducted in 1993 may considered as an important milestone in Japan-Africa relations, starting a new chapter in these relations. Without totally replacing ODA, Japan's oldest instrument of foreign policy towards developing countries, TICAD conferences and its initiatives, have become the cornerstone of Japan's foreign policy toward Africa in the post-Cold War era. Since 1993, all ODA policies towards Africa are either directly or indirectly formulated and implemented through TICAD guidelines, yet not all ODA programs fit into the main concept of the conference.

The latest conference, TICAD V, which held on June 1-3, 2013 in Yokohama, attended by more than 4500 participants and appeared to be the largest international conference ever hosted by Japan, surpassing the scale of the previous TICAD summit.

The Prime Minister's statement mentioned herein above made in the course of this conference. The very existence of TICAD corroborates the suggestion that Africa is a key area for Japan's foreign policy nowadays. As stated on the official website, Tokyo International Conference on African Development is "more than a conference. TICAD has become a major global framework for Asia and Africa to collaborate in promoting Africa's development. The first Tokyo Conference was held in 1993 and ushered in a continuing process of support for Africa and consensus building around African development priorities. That process was bolstered with a second Tokyo conference in 1998"[2].

TICAD V attended by delegations from 51 African countries and representatives of 35 other partner countries, 74 international and regional organizations, both from Africa and Asia, the private sector and civil society. Among the guests of TICAD V were Mr. Ban Ki-moon, Secretary-General of the United Nations; Dr. Nkosazana Clarice Dlamini-Zuma, Chairperson of the African Union Commission, Dr. Jim Yong Kim, President of the World Bank; Miss. Helen Clark, Administrator of the United Nations Development Program and 39 heads of state level guests. The conference co-chaired by Sinzo Abe, Prime Minister of Japan, and Hailemariam Dasalegn, Prime Minister of Ethiopia and Chairperson of African Union. Mr. Yoshiro Mori, a former Prime Minister of Japan, who was the first Prime Minister of Japan to visit Africa, served as acting co-chairman of plenary sessions.

In keynote speeches at the Opening Session and Plenary Session, Prime Minister Abe announced the basic policy of Japan on assistance to Africa. It went along with an assistance package, comprising, apart from above-mentioned ODA and other financing, the capacity building for business and industry, including through "Africa Business Education Initiative for the Youth"; and development and humanitarian assistance to the Sahel region. TICAD V issued two outcome documents, "Yokohama Declaration 2013", which presents a future direction for African development, and "Yokohama Action Plan 2013-2017", a road map of specific measures to be taken under the TICAD Process over the next five years.

Under the basic concept of "Hand in hand with a more dynamic Africa", vehement discussions took place on the direction of African development in the line with the core themes of TICAD V, namely, "Robust and sustainable economy", "Inclusive and resilient society" and "Peace and stability".

Reflecting the importance of growth contributed by the private sector, a session called "The dialogue with the private sector" for the direct engagement between leaders of African countries and representatives of the Japanese private sector was held for the first time in a TICAD plenary session.

Besides the main sessions of the summit, TICAD also included nearly 50 official side events, a variety of seminars and symposiums. Among them were Special Conference on Somalia (during this meeting Prime Minister Abe predicated that Japan will restart direct assistance to Somalia), an international symposium on HIV/AIDS, Symposium on Human Security, concerning Millennium Development Goals, Japan-African Summit Meeting on United Nations Security Council Reform and many other official side events, that took place on the sidelines of TICAD V.

Furthermore, Prime Minister Abe held bilateral meetings with 56 participants – all of the 39 heads of state level, the Chairperson of the African Union Council, two Prime Minister's guests and the representatives of 14 international organizations, and hosted a dinner for African leaders. Fumio Kishida, Minister for Foreign Affairs of Japan, also held meetings with 32 participants, including bilateral meetings with 22 of them. These included heads of state level participants, Ministers of African countries and representatives of international organizations. The meetings in question covered a wide range of issues, such as African development, the regional situation and cooperation in international forums, accounting for high-level exchanges of an unprecedented scale in a short period.

Nevertheless, despite the positive tendencies in political relationships between Japan and African countries, economical connections of Japan and African countries are still not comparable to those of China, United States or European Union.

Japan's share in foreign trade of African countries can considered almost insignificant, as well as Africa's share in Japan's foreign trade. According to World Trade Organization's statistical data, in 2012-2013 the former was not more than 3% of the overall volume of Africa's trade while Africa as a region is at the bottom of Japan's both export and import structure. Nonetheless, Japan-Africa trade volume has been already comparable to the amount of Japan's trade with «Russia and Commonwealth of Independent States» group, being $27 billion and $34 billion respectively in 2011[3] (according to International Trade Centre statistics, $30 billion and $33.5 billion in 2011; $34 billion and $36.5 billion respectively in 2012)[4].

Certain recession in Japan-Africa trade in 2012–2013 (from $34 billion in 2012 to $30 billion in 2013)[5] could be explained with a general decline in industrial output and business activity of Japan, which was partly a consequence of the 2011 earthquake and Fukusima-1 nuclear power plant catastrophe.

Japanese direct foreign investment flows to African countries are still relatively low, tending to increase in some areas, focusing mainly on extractive industries in resource-rich regions. However, as mentioned above, according to the Yokohama Action Plan, an outcome document of TICAD V, the government of Japan intends to invest up to $32 billion in Africa's economy in the next five years. It means a significant and promising change in short-term outlook and promising perspective for a further cooperation.

It is emphasized in TICAD documents and press-releases that the government is not only going to augment the amount of investment, but also to stimulate investment from the private sector, especially in infrastructure development, HR-development and innovation, science and technology development. It also declares intention to finance projects focused on creating new jobs and opportunities, especially for women and youth, as well as projects aimed at environmental protection, low-carbon energy promotion, disaster risk reduction, deforestation, conservation and sustainable use of biodiversity, prevention of desertification and land degradation, etc.

The conference members recognized the priority of the integration of Africa into the multilateral trading system, so that the growth of Africa contributes to the prosperity of the global economy and vice versa. Nowadays Africa is the least economically integrated continent in the world, with low levels of intra-regional economic exchanges and the smallest share in global trade. Africa's share in global trade stands at only 3% and intra-regional trade is about 12%[6], which is also a scarce figure. It is considered that increasing intra-regional trade by developing growth corridors and supply chains will enable African countries to create larger markets, diversify their economies away from dependence on commodities, enhance economic competitiveness, reduce costs, improve productivity and reduce poverty. Such measures would especially facilitate trade for landlocked countries.

It is also planned to diversify private capital flows to the continent, which are now concentrated in extractive industries and resource-rich countries. The main aim is to attract investment into additional sectors, such as infrastructure, agriculture, manufacturing and tourism. These measures are forecasted to help boost employment and create opportunities for local countries as well as promote technology transfer.

According to the announcement of Prime Minister Abe, up to 6.5$ billion is to be spent as financial assistance for infrastructure through ODA and Japan Bank for International Cooperation loan. It is highly urgent because the African Union's Program for Infrastructure Development in Africa estimates that addressing Africa's continental infrastructure challenges from 2012 through 2020 will cost about 68$ billion or approximately 7.5$ billion annually for the next years, while the capital cost of long-term implementation through 2040 is currently estimated at more than 360$ billion[7]. That is why much higher levels of private investment is needed to close the continent's infrastructure gap, especially in energy and transport, which represents more than 90% of the total cost.

Among other important issues on the agenda of the conference were nutrition security, human resource development, science and technology development, education, tourism, health care, etc. Many new initiatives in these directions are about to be launched by TICAD participants. For example, the above-mentioned ABE initiative for the youth, that implies inviting one thousand competent African youths to study in Japan and join internship in Japanese firms, and building networks among the alumni to foster future leaders for business between Japan and Africa.

There are also plans of building TICAD human resource development centers for business and industry at 10 locations in 25 countries, support research institutes and universities, launch Japan-African Business Women Exchange Program, improving through financial and other assistance quality of primary and secondary education, etc.

Another important part of the agenda was supporting regional stability. Among planned measures for this purpose were capacity building of two thousand people and provision of equipment for counterterrorism in North Africa and the Sahel region; contributing 1$ billion in development and humanitarian assistance to Sahel region. It was also scheduled to ensure the maritime security off the coast of Somalia by implementing counter-piracy measures by Japan Maritime Self Defense Forces and Japan Coast Guard and capacity building of coast guards in neighboring countries of Somalia, including provision of patrol vessels. It was recognized as a very important step to support African initiatives in peace building and consolidation by financial assistance from funds of the African Union and Regional Economic Communities. Moreover, the government of Japan expressed intention to continue support of UN PKO activities and assist with capacity building of three thousand people engaged in peace building (supporting PKO training centers etc.).

Thus, all points considered witness to the fact that Japan is increasingly active in the region and becoming even more deeply involved in local and global processes through the TICAD initiatives. The sphere of economic collaboration between Japan and Africa is also widening. Classical scheme of import (raw materials and agricultural goods) and export (manufactured goods) is expanded, for instance, by export of services (education, including distance education through the internet, medical services, etc.) and diversifying the objects of investment.

The observers compare Japan's activity in Africa with China's one. In fact, as both of them are relatively new actors in Africa, their policies towards .African countries have a lot in common: both are highly interested in acquiring new partners among developing countries for profitable exchange of industrially manufactured goods to natural resources. In addition, their methods and strategies are often alike or even similar. For example, in 2000 the China-Africa Forum was organized. It takes place every three years and mainly deals with the same issues as the TICAD.

It is worth noting that Japan's efforts to strength its economic position on African continent meets a strong opposition from Chinese political leaders. One of the examples is the reaction to Japanese Prime Minister's visit to African countries, which took place at the beginning of 2014. Formally, the protest meetings organized in order to express public censure of the Prime Minister's visit to the Yasukuni shrine[8], which is considered as the memorial to the military criminals of World War II. However, it is clear, that this scandal also has an economic and political background.

Regardless of the fact that during the last decades, Japan is more or less experiencing economic stagnation, its tendencies in business in Africa or with African partners could be characterized as positive, and the significant role in this process of actualizing of Africa as a direction for Japan's foreign policy and business is attributed to TICAD and its initiatives. Thereby, we can resume that Japan has a good chance to succeed in becoming one of major economic partners for Africa in long-term outlook.

---

[1] Message from the Minister for Foreign Affairs // Diplomatic Bluebook 2013 Summary, Ministry of Foreign Affairs of Japan – http://www.mofa.go.jp/policy/other/bluebook/2013/html/chapter2/ssafrica.html

[2] http://www.ticad.net/ticad/index.html

[3] World Trade Organization, International Trade Statistics 2012 – http://www.wto.org/english/res_e/statis_e/its2012_e/its12_world_trade_dev_e.htm

[4] International Trade Centre – http://www.trademap.org/tradestat/Bilateral_TS.aspx

[5] Ibidem.

[6] Yokohama action plan 2013-2017. Ministry of Foreign Affairs of Japan, 03.06.2013 – http://www.mofa.go.jp/region/page3e_000054.html

[7] Ibidem.

[8] *Miseret Elias*. China condemns Japan leader on visit to Ethiopia // Yahoo News, January 15, 2014 – http://news.yahoo.com/china-condemns-japan-leader-visit-ethiopia-121823542.html

Murad Shamilov, M.A.
Kazakh Ablai Khan University
of International Relations and World Languages,
Almaty, Kazakhstan

SOUTH KOREAN INTERESTS IN AFRICA:
ANALYSIS AND PERSPECTIVES

This paper focuses on some aspects of relations between South Korea and Africa. The problem is relatively little studied in comparison, for example, with the vastly researched theme of Chinese impact on the region. Meanwhile, South Korea has become one of the top trade partners for Africa[1]. The collaborative advantages for Africa and the definition of the drivers of South Korean interests are the main issues considered in the article, which also provides an overview of future perspectives for the development of this cooperation.

When the former president of South Korea, Lee Myung-bak, went on a short-term trip to Africa on 1 July 2011, he visited South Africa, the Democratic Republic of Congo (DRC), and Ethiopia. As Korean media widely reported, the government believed that better ties with the African states could enhance opportunities for investment in infrastructure and for the greater exploitation of resources and the enlargement of export markets[2].

South Korea had much in common with the African countries. When the Republic of Ghana gained independence in 1957, its national income per capita was almost equivalent to such index for South Korea, namely a little less than $500. Nowadays, fifty-six years later, the economic characteristics of these two countries have become much more divergent. According to the World Bank, in 2009 Ghana's per capita income amounted to $1,530, while South Korea's one was $23,240[3].

Despite the availability of natural resources in Ghana, including gold, cacao, and recently discovered oil, and the presence of democratic institutions, it is clear that without reliable investment partners Ghana would need about three to four hundred years to overtake South Korea economically. Fortunately, in modern era, such countries as Ghana are in some sense on the verge of economic take-off, and South Korean companies have all the opportunities both to assist them and to benefit from this assistance.

The above-mentioned example is typical for many African countries. However, at the same time we are witnessing a growing interest of different countries, among them South Korea, in the region. The volumes of South Korea's cooperation with Africa are increasing, and it is happening due to the role of Korea's leading global companies.

Recently, Korean Air has launched a new route between Seoul/Incheon and Nairobi. With flights operating three days a week at a capacity of 253 passengers, Korean Air advertises itself as the first airline in East Asia to run *regular direct* services to an African destination[4]. This bold statement exemplifies Korea's recent 'African rush'. Yet, despite burgeoning economic and political ties between African countries and Korea, very few studies have touched upon this emerging relationship.

When the issue of Africa developing and emerging partners is discussed, China is being mentioned very often, usually as the most significant partner. Less known in this regard Asian countries are seeking the moment to make their own meaningful contribution to Africa's development. South Korea has a high potential, and has advanced its role of a marginal player to a full-right partner, because this could ensure its access to regional resources and enable it to export products and services to the African market.

The volume of South Korea's FDI in Africa increased quite rapidly from $24 million in the 1990s to $287 million in 2010. Moreover, bilateral trade indicator reached $25 billion in 2011 (in comparison with $6 billion in 2000), which became one of the fastest growth rates among African foreign partners according to the OECD estimations[5].

Despite that growth, Korea accounts only for 2.3 percent of Africa's trade with the world, with Africa accounting for just 2 percent of Korea's total trade[6]. Moreover, like other partners, Seoul's imports from the continent dominated by natural resources. That means that only a relatively narrow group of resource-rich countries is exporting to Korea. In 2009, more than 90 percent of exports to this country originated from 10 nations, led by South Africa and Equatorial Guinea, and including Algeria, Egypt, Zambia, Nigeria and Gabon[7]. However, it seems that South Korea is interested in something else. More than three quarters of Korean exports are composed of electronic equipment and electrical appliances, phones and transport equipment, versus 40 percent for this category in the case of China, pointing to the growing importance of the region as a market for Korea's manufactured goods.

There exist relatively few studies devoted to the role of South Korea in the African region. Considering mainly Korean and some Western researchers, we could point out that almost all authors agree on the key objectives and motivation of the South Korean policy in Africa that has emerged due to the situation after the Korean War. Three main factors are closely linked to how South Korea is positioning its national interests and understands the international situation and the sense of "global responsibility". The first factor, often quoted by Korean and international media, is economic interest. Secondly, it is important for South Korea to achieve political influence in Africa by diplomatic means. The third factor combines the first two and concerns the most recent issue – the role of new factors and new players in the development of cooperation, which based on the use of the so-called "soft power" along with the promotion of a diplomatic partnership.

To sum up, these three key factors have motivated Korea's Africa strategy: achieving resource security, gaining political influence through the UN voting system, and promoting soft power via contributive diplomacy. The early years of Korea's Africa diplomacy focused on securing formal support from African nations for Seoul's entry to the UN. This has changed drastically since the mid-2000s, as Africa became Seoul's battleground for conducting resource diplomacy and promoting soft power through the popularization of the Korean model of development. The renewed interest in Africa also provided a space to formalize and institutionalize hitherto limited Korea-Africa relations.

ODA data, trade and FDI flows suggest that African resources and markets are keys to Korea's strategy. These flows have increased sharply since the mid-2000s – and in favour of Korean exporters. In terms of trade, Korea imports mostly oil and gas, minerals and metals, and exports high-end capital goods like transport vessels, automobiles and mobile devices[8]. We could consider the nature of South Korean interests in the African region from two viewpoints. On the one hand, aid and investments provided to Africa by South Korea. On the other hand, we should also try to identify economic interests of South Korea itself.

Firstly, we should take into account several spheres in which South Korea invests and helps to facilitate development, including:

• Fostering agricultural revolution, which implies more sustainable development of this sector than as provided for by current Chinese involvement now. In November 2010, Rural Development Agency representatives signed a memorandum of understanding titled 'The Korea-Africa Food and Agricultural Cooperation Initiative (KAFACI).' The KAFACI emphasizes capacity-building in the mould of *Saemaul Undong* (as advocated by the Korea Saemaul Undong Centre (KSUC)), an agricultural movement in South Korea initiated by the South Korean government in the 1970s, which eventually led to the eradication of rural poverty in South Korea. Almost 20 countries, including Kenya, Ethiopia, and Uganda, participated in the event. The initiative could offer Africa several beneficial points, including so much needed new workplaces, the growth of national revenue and GDP, increasing food production with the new styles and techniques of farming, for example, in the rice production sphere;

• Construction of new training centres for industrial workers involving the creation of facilities and all necessary conditions;

- Projects in ecological sphere, such as construction of numerous solar energy plants in Mozambique;
- Funding of African Development Bank projects, for example, aid and modernization of Angola;
- The Korea Trade-Investment Promotion Agency (KOTRA) established several Korea Business Centres in Ethiopia, Ghana, and Cameroon in 2011, bringing the total of such centres to seven around the continent. These centres were established with the intention of easing Korean entry into African markets, and generally fostering trade and business relationships between two parties[9];
- South Korea has been actively participating in other arrangements for provision of peace and security. In 2013, the US government praised the role of South Korea in the global efforts for confrontation and prevention of maritime piracy in Somali waters. South Korea is one of more than 80 members of the Contact Group on Piracy off the coast of Somalia, a voluntary forum set up in 2009 under a UN Security Council resolution. South Korea leads the third sub-working group, "working closely with the shipping industry to ensure safe transit in the region," stated a U.S. State Department report on the contact group[10].

In addition, we should also think about the nature of South Korean economic interests in Africa. When considering that issue, several points could be point out, including:

- South Korean positive contribution to Africa has also been creating positive international image of South Korea in the region. Africans began trusting South Korean investors, which fosters the development of intercultural relations and business relations between the two parties;
- One of the main interests of South Korea, probably the most important one, is the issue of the export of technology to the African continent. Samsung and LG Electronics, two Korean giants, are leading the way with the spread of technology throughout the region. According to recent statements, Samsung will be expanding its 32-country footprint in Africa, soon establishing a physical presence in Gabon, DRC and Cameroon. It also plans to expand its local assembly plants, and boost job creation and the uptake of its technologies. Moreover, another Korean company, KT, which is the leading mobile operator of South Korea, is involved in installing information security systems throughout the region. The most recent successful examples of such cooperation include Rwanda, Morocco, DRC and Cameroon;
- Moreover, the issue of construction boom in the sub-Saharan region is also of high importance, fostering the development of infrastructure in Africa and offering lucrative contracts to South Korea. Additionally, we could mention Korean, mostly Samsung's, support of the Kenyan Electricity Company

and its power plant construction project in Kilifi. On the one hand, Korea is not really following China's state-led 'infrastructure for resources' model, but the government has been ramping up its commercial diplomacy;

• If proof needed that Seoul is serious about securing its share of the continent's growth story, it came when the government pledged $590m in aid and loans to African countries in October 2013. The package was small in comparison to the $20bn one that China offered to the continent in July, but it signalled the intent. In addition, Korea is also able to offer something more important than capital, argues Bahk Jae-wan, the country's finance minister – its developmental experience.

South Korea's population size matches that of many African nations, making its experience more applicable than the far bigger China's, some economists argue. Its progress relative to African counterparts has been astounding. Unsurprisingly, African governments are increasingly keen to learn from the country. That means that the Korean model is potentially becoming even more relevant for those who are looking to develop other sectors. "Koreans have gone through this development process and have learned real life lessons, necessary skill and technologies that are badly needed by African countries". Therefore, there is also an important process of learning and experience sharing.

One the one hand, there also could be pointed out several examples of how South Korea tries to contribute to the development of Africa and to benefit from it, including the promotion of business relations like PPP (Public Private Partnerships), trade balance, organizing 2011 Korean EXPO in Sandton, opening and developing new offices, facilities and research centers, etc. On the other hand, there are several negative moments in Korean policy in Africa. For example, the conduct of some Korean and Indian investors in acquiring agricultural land has produced local fallout and even contributed to the toppling of governments. Some African elites, like Mo Ibrahim, a Sudanese multimillionaire, have gone so far as to urge traditional powers like the US to stem their 'retreat from Africa'[11].

Therefore, we could consider the question of whether there is a furthering and strengthening of South Korean expansion of Africa. Some researchers believe that the time has come to turn to Africa. However, it seems that this influence and impact could not be called a full-scale expansion, because of South Korea's relatively low capabilities, yielding to not only Western countries, but also China and India. Nevertheless, at some point, given the support of South Korean government, a total expansion could begin, but currently there is still a long way to go. Moreover, investment in Africa is not risk-free as the region still faces many challenges in terms of market barriers and structural reforms. You can never predict the result and the effect of investment and business relations.

Thus, we could sum up, that South Korea has always been trying to enhance its diplomatic ties with Africa and to add new aspects to these relations. Despite the fact that it is hard to compare South Korea's influence in the African region with that of China or India, South Korea has a set of policies on Africa different of that of the aforementioned countries, and aims at fostering cooperation development based on strong economic and technological growth. Sustainable growth and strengthening of relations through cooperation and dialogue will create an excellent platform for the future partnership between South Korea and countries of Africa in different spheres of international relations and economic cooperation.

[1] Adapted from AfDB //Africa Economic Brief: Chief Economist Complex, July 2011, Volume 2, Issue 9.

[2] Jonsson G. 'Global Insider: South Korea-Africa Relations'// World Politics Review, 7 July 2011. http://www.worldpoliticsreview.com

[3] De Pontet Ph., Clifton J.F. Korea-Africa: Emerging Opportunities // Korean Economic Institute magazine, v. 27, 2011, pp. 59-67

[4] Korean Air, 'Korean Air to Introduce Direct Flights to Nairobi Starting June,' 2012. http://www.koreanair.com/local/kr/gd/eng/au/pr/20120314_ 85316.jsp.

[5] Whitehead E. South Korea: Africa's unsung Asian partner. // This is Africa: global perspective. Financial Times, 26 February 2013 – http://www.thisisafricaonline.com

[6] Kim Soyeun, Korea in Africa: A Missing Piece of the Puzzle? // LSE Ideas Library, Reports and publications from the center for the study of international affairs, 2012.

[7] Economic Development in Africa Report 2013, UNCTAD www.unctad. org/Africa/series

[8] Shelton G. Korea and South Africa: Building a strategic partnership // Institute for global dialogue. Occasional paper 61, July 2009

[9] 'Korean companies stepping up advances into Africa', The Dong-A Ilbo, 6 July 2011, http://english.donga.com.

[10] 'South Korea on prevention of Somalia piracy', 25 December 2013. http://www.ruskorinfo.ru/data/incidents/

[11] Chris Alden 'Africa without Europeans', in Chris Alden, Dan Large and Ricardo Soares de Oliveira, eds., China Returns to Africa – an emerging power and a continent embrace (London: Hurst 2008).

III. BRICS: ENTITY'S ROLE ON AFRICAN CONTINENT

Vladimir Yurtaev, Dr.Sc., Prof.
The Peoples' Friendship
University of Russia

BRICS: THE REGIONAL DIMENSIONS
OF ECONOMICS AND POLITICS

The focus of the article – the BRICS Group involvement in global-ization at the regional level as a basis for the formation of a new para-digm of global cooperation and the problem of the formation of global-ization portals (gates) with BRICS countries and features of their inter-action in the conjugate regions and with the partner countries.

Keywords: BRICS, regionalization, global cooperation paradigm, politi-cal guiding, gates of globalization, conjugate regions.

At the beginning of the XXI century, the whole system of reproduction of life on the planet is the focus of research. Thus, there is a constant expansion of the framework of sustainable development as a new paradigm of development – a product of increasingly globally oriented consciousness of new generations of people. In situation of global economic and financial crisis the emergence of the international concept of "BRICS" in fact was a response to the challenges of globalization. Delivered during the BRICS Summits problem of defining strategic dimension and the corresponding filling project of the Group showed the urgency of finding answers to the challenges of globalization in the para-digm of interdisciplinary research, wide format humanitarian and economic dialogue. In the process of globalization, one can witness the shaping and "soft" rising of the BRICS Group, which even now makes it possible to see the contours of the new world. In the early 21st century, the trade and economic space of the BRICS (Fig. 1, 2) ever more noticeably supplement the Eurasian and Pacific rings of cooperation as the two main spaces of the world market.

A new space of inter-regional partnership within the framework of the BRICS Group is emerging not only on a regional and country but also on a global level.

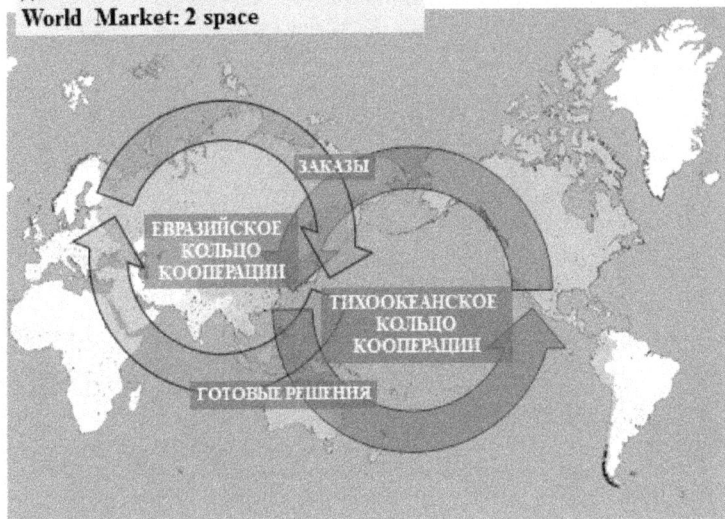

ДВА ПРОСТРАНСТВА МИРОВОГО РЫНКА
World Market: 2 space

BRICS

ЗАКАЗЫ

ЕВРАЗИЙСКОЕ
КОЛЬЦО
КООПЕРАЦИИ

ТИХООКЕАНСКОЕ
КОЛЬЦО
КООПЕРАЦИИ

ГОТОВЫЕ РЕШЕНИЯ

Fig. 1

Globality of BRICS. Analysis of strategic, demographic, technological and other indicators confirms the global potential of the BRICS Group arose and indicates its focus on overcoming the prevailing logic of the development within the center-periphery relations. BRICS countries have formed an independent trend in world politics, thanks to synergy methods in national foreign policies. In particular, in the field of political and economic governance BRICS seek polycentric world order in which they will occupy more important positions, matching their growing global and regional economic and political significance. Do not forget that BRICS includes countries, critically important to resolve global problems. Today we can say that ideology, objectives and principles of the BRICS went deep into the world community. The situation can be understood through the quintessential principle of "live drawing on each other".

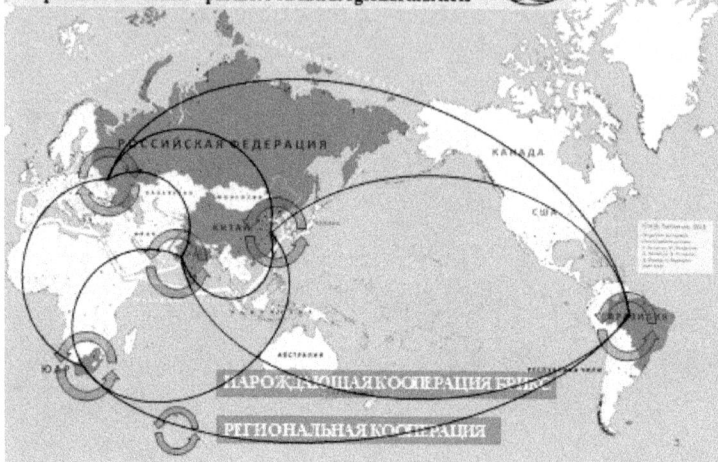

Fig. 2

Correlation: Policy and Economics. The problem of relating politics and economy, for the future format of interaction within the Group becomes a key for BRICS future. Critical value, it is obvious, given the current stage of social development of the world maintained the political will of the leaders of the Group and became the basis of origin and functioning of the BRICS – i.e. "Policy leads Economy".

The regional dimension of BRICS. However, each of the BRICS countries is an integral part of conjugate regional markets (East and South Asia, Africa, Latin America, North Eurasia) and geopolitical spaces. Global competition is most acute today in the regions and at the local level. Based on the foregoing (and without belittling the importance of the development of bilateral and multilateral relations between the countries – participants of the Group), we note that in the near– and medium-term focus of a global multilateral cooperation for all the BRICS countries, given their overlapping and intersecting interests and international participation in the globalization, more likely is to be directed to the regions. Therefore, integration of the regional dimension of interaction is becoming one of the prerequisites in developing strategies for economic and political cooperation within the BRICS (Fig 3).

GATES "R" – "C" : GROWTH POINTS AND ZONES   BRICS

Growth point: special economic zones, research towns, industrial parks, industrial clusters, ports, aviation hubs, multi- and intermodal logistics, financial centers, etc.
Growth zones: Transsiberian (Russia), airlines clusters, river navigation system

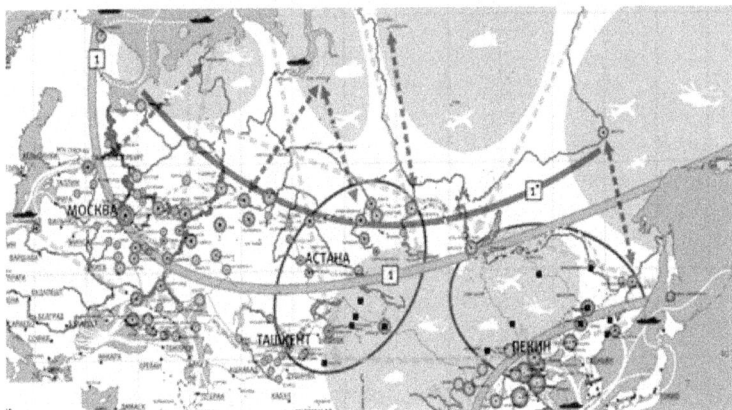

Fig. 3

In conjugate regions cooperation "five" as partners in intraregional markets should be different from the traditional level of bilateral cooperation and solve the problem of formation of trade, economic, financial, humanitarian and international infrastructure of regional cooperation that is to create the preconditions for interregional partnership. Regionalization in this case receives a triple dimension: global, regional and local, and becomes a working tool of globalization.

In this case, we can say about the new quality of relations within the Group and its external contacts, which is an expression of the principle of economic interaction network. Political appeal for third countries and for developing countries – in particular, arises from the Group's focus on overcoming the prevailing logic of the development within the center-periphery relations. We emphasize that the current format of the Group BRICS countries – it is not just "emerging markets» (emerging markets), but also the "big economy-regions." Therefore, the center-periphery relationship not for the BRICS countries – they gravitate to a network structure that arises with the arrival of these large nuclei in the conjugate regions. Hence updated ideas of self-reliance in the present situation of the growing importance of the domestic markets. Five BRICS countries have taken in their conjugate regions in 2010s the position similar to the five permanent members of the UN Security Council in the middle of the XX century. In general, we can say that the

BRICS Group acts as the five leaders for joining the globalization of independent subsystems of emerging new global labor organization ("think globally – act locally").

In international relations, a similar economic regionalism will be the key to good neighborly relations, defining logic of the new diplomacy ("economic base, political guiding").

In the economic sphere, it is important to see another dimension of the complementarity of the economies of the BRICS Group – in cooperation with its neighbors – small regional partners. BRICS countries are mindful of economic development in their respective regions. Each BRICS country is an integral part of its own regional markets and closely linked to other regions through trade, commerce and investment. Many of these associated regional economies represent a sizeable proportion of the world's fastest growing economies; Asia traditionally, and Africa recently, has seen significant economic growth in the past five years.

In the area of "Political and economic governance", BRICS countries seek to promote a more polycentric world order in which all BRICS countries assume an increasingly significant role concomitant with their growing global and regional economic and political importance.

Infrastructure. The main regional priorities include BRICS-Africa (Gates "B" – Brazil and "S" – South Africa). This does not mean that India, China and Russia will remain observers: they are taking an active part in the development of each adjacent region. The BRICS countries have already actively taken over part of the world community's mission to promote the revival of Africa. Notwithstanding favorable forecasts, it is indeed hard to expect sustainable economic development on the Black Continent in the conditions of continuing political turbulence and chronic instability of government. Under the unpredictable impact of the Arab Spring and the strengthening of the Islamic factor, the situation in the neighboring regions adjacent to Northern Africa is also aggravating. In this complicated situation, its southern region could become a locomotive for growth in Africa. This calls for a powerful start and political will.

In the eThekwini Declaration of the BRICS Summit (South Africa, 2013), a number of paragraphs focus on the issues of regional economic development on the African continent (for example, infrastructure development in Africa, para. 5; industrialization process, para. 5; regional integration for Africa's sustainable growth, development and poverty eradication, para. 4; multilateral agreements on infrastructure co-financing for Africa, para. 12). This may provide the basis for shaping an agenda for South Africa within the framework of the **BRICS Group** for adopting appropriate programs of multilateral cooperation.

Logistics. By virtue of the geography of its participants, air services between the **BRICS** countries should have particular significance. The new interregional logistics emerging between the **BRICS** portals probably implies the beginning of serious work on the issue of setting up a general trading company for the **BRICS** Group and developing a corresponding logistics system as the format for a future unified integrated global cargo transportation system.

The main factors determining the demand for transportation and logistics services: the dynamics of the world economy and the international exchange of goods, the dynamics of the Russian economy, the globalization of goods and the complication of delivery schemes, the need to optimize the costs of transportation, storage and distribution of goods.

By 2030 the economic growth will be achieved mainly by developing countries, especially China and India, which together will account for over a third of global growth and ensure: in 2010 – about 18%, and by 2030 – about 32% of world GDP.

It seems appropriate to initiate the creation of the Coordinating Committee on transport corridors BRICS to coordinate the development and project design Concept development of logistics infrastructure, located in places where the international transport corridors in the interaction of the BRICS.

In conclusion, should be noted the following. The process of globalization as "mainstream" development of human civilization more noticeable realized in world politics and economy through the transformation and the formation of new global development paradigms. Involvement of the "large economies" of Asia, Africa, CIS and Latin America defines the role and place of the participating countries and regions themselves in shaping the new world order. At the same time creatively destroyed the old division into "developed" and "underdeveloped" ("catch-up") the worlds. The ongoing development of a paradigm shift as the very core of the world economy and its periphery, are held hostage by limited financial resources are updated by the task of understanding the processes, especially with the participation of Brazil, Russia, India, China or the "large economies" looking for new formats for entry into world politics. Observed in the second decade of the XXI century activation of foreign policy activities of the Group integrates the BRICS in the world historical process of new projects. In the new conditions of globalization, the old recipes of the modern world are still used, but the world is changing rapidly. The process of regionalization (as the initial phase of the process of globalization), within whose framework the steady strengthening of the status of the **BRICS** countries as regional economic powers and actors of global politics is taking place, is gaining momentum.

Nina Tsvetkova, PhD (Economy)
Institute for Oriental Studies,
Russian Academy of Sciences.

TNC FROM ASIAN BRICS COUNTRIES IN THE ICT SPHERE IN AFRICA AND THE INTERESTS OF RUSSIA

In the 2000s, the role of Asian giants – China and India – in the international economy has increased. In 2012 China was second in the world by its gross national income (GNI) ($7731.3 bn , 10.8% of the world GNI) after the USA. Japan, the third, was far behind China with $6106.7 bn (8.5%). In terms of gross domestic product (GDP) calculated by purchasing power parity (PPP), the gap between China and USA is rapidly diminishing. In 2012, China's GDP by PPP equaled $14727.1 bn (15.2% of the world GPP by PPP), whereas that of the USA was $16514.2 bn (17.1%). China is expected to catch up with the USA by 2015. India, on its turn, was one of the top 10 economies by GNI in 2012 ($1913. 2 bn). India's GDP calculated by PPP totaled $6281.2 bn, leaving Japan ($4587.6 bn) behind[1].

At the microeconomics level, the number of companies and banks from China, India and Asian new industrial economies in international ratings has significantly increased. The Forbes list published in 2014 included 207 companies and banks from China (including Hong Kong), 54 from India, 59 from South Korea, 47 from Taiwan, and 17 companies and banks from Singapore.[2] Among the 500 Global companies rated by the Fortune in 2013, Chinese companies ranked second after the American ones.

The aim of the paper is to trace the presence of Chinese and Indian TNCs in the ICT sphere in African countries and to see how some African countries follow the Indian example by developing ICT services and business process outsourcing (BPO).

China and India have taken an active part in Information and Communication Revolution (ICR). It is possible to state that the involvement of these countries in ICR played a major role in their economic success. China has become the first world exporter of information and communication technology goods (ICT goods) that include telecommunications, audio and video, computer and related equipment; electronic components; and other information and communication technology goods (television sets, phones, etc.). In 2000 China ranked ninth by the volume of ICT goods exports. In 2012 71% of world exports of ICT goods originated from the developing countries, as compared to 43% in 2000. The share of Asian developing countries in the global ICT goods exports increased from 39% in 2000 to 67% in

2012, the share of China has risen from 4.4% to 31%. In 2012, Hong Kong became the second largest ICT goods exporter, Singapore the fourth, Taiwan the fifth and South Korea the sixth one. Former leaders in this list, the USA and Japan, moved to third and 7th places respectively.

Table 1. **Exports of ICT goods* ($ billion and %), 2000–2012**

	Exports of ICT goods ($ billions)		% of world exports	
	2000	**2012**	**2000**	**2012**
World	998.8	1800.2	100	100
Developed countries	568.7	522.6	56.9	39.0
Transition economies	0.9	3.6	0.1	0.2
Developing countries	429.2	1273.9	43.0	70.8
Africa	1.1	1.9	0.1	0.1
Latin America	38.9	66.7	3.9	3.7
Asia	389.2	1205.3	39.0	67.0
East Asia	216.8	957.4	21.7	53.2
South-East Asia	170.4	239.3	17.1	13.3
South Asia	0.9	5.8	0.1	0.3
West Asia	1.2	2.7	0.1	0.15
China	44.1	554.3	4.4	30.8
Hong Kong	50.3	207.9	5.0	11.5
South Korea	59.4	94.0	5.9	5.2
Taiwan	62.9	101.0	6.3	5.6
Singapore	75.6	116.0	7.6	6.4
Malaysia	51.7	63.5	5.2	3.5
Philippines	14.8	15.3		
USA	156.7	139.4	15.7	7.7
Japan	108.8	73.1	10.9	4.1
Germany	46.2	62.5		
Netherlands	38.2	56.6		

Source: World Development Indicators http://wdi.worldbank.org (13.04.2014).

ICT goods in Asian countries are produced by the affiliates of Western and Japanese transnationals. However, the significance of non-equity modes of international production (contract manufacturing, or original equipment manufacturing, original design manufacturing, etc.) is more important. An important share of electronic goods is produced by transnationals from Asian countries.

If we look at transnationals from Asian developing countries, one of their peculiarities is a great number of companies producing electronics and ICT goods and services in general. In 2008, the UNCTAD listed 100 major transnationals from developing countries and transitional economies, including 74 Asian TNCs, of which 20% were from the electronics industry. At the same time, the 93 transnationals from developed countries, also ranked by the UNCTAD, had only 8% share of companies working in the electronic industry. [3] Asian ICT-producing transnationals own well-known brands, such as Samsung Electronics (sales in 2013 $209 bn, 22th in the Forbes 2000 rating of 2013) and LG Electronics of South Korea, Flextronics of Singapore, Acer, Asus, Quanta, Compal, Wistron of Taiwan, Lenovo, ZTE, Huawei of China.

One of the biggest electronics companies is Hon Hai (with its Foxconn brand), which had the second largest sales volume in 2013 ($127 bn), after Samsung Electronics. But its brand is not particularly well-known as it is engaged mainly in contract manufacturing (one of non-equity modes of international production). According to the UNCTAD, non-equity modes of international production in electronics industry generate about ½ of the world exports of electronics[4]. Hon Hai had 1.2 million employees in 2012, mostly not in Taiwan, but in China, where its factories assembled iPhones and iPads for Apple Inc. The work conditions at Hon Hai factories in China were poor, the disciplinary requirements severe, conditions of life miserable, wages low, while iPods and iPads sold well in the international markets, and Apple enjoyed high profits. That situation caused workers' suicides and provoked strikes. For these reasons, the Hon Hai factories in China were called 'Nightmare'[5]. Hon Hai is also a subcontractor of Apple's main competitor – Samsung Electronics. And it works under contracts with HP, Microsoft, Intel, Dell, Sony-Ericsson and other TNCs. In the past, Samsung Electronics was one of Apple's subcontractors in the production of transistors.

Flextronics (160 000 workers in 2009, sales, $25 bn in 2013) ranks second among the leading contractors, and its main customers are Alcatel, HP, Microsoft, Intel, Dell, Sony-Ericsson, and two Chinese companies, Lenovo and Huawei.

Such Asian TNCs as Quanta, Compal, Wistron, Inventek are also among the main subcontractors working under the contract manufacturing system. Each subcontractor has more than a dozen of customers, and each customer – a TNC from USA, Europe or Asia – has more than a dozen of subcontractors that are not small companies serving one big contractor, but transnationals with the amount of sales exceeding $10bn. These subcontractors organize production units not in their home countries (Taiwan, South Korea, Singapore), but abroad, mostly in continental China, and also in Vietnam, Malaysia, Philippines, Czech Republic, Hungary, Poland, etc.

Therefore, these companies help to form and sustain global network systems, based on the relations of cooperation and competition and create global production chains, including chains of value added products. To find a place in such a chain is a good chance for a country or a company. There are new participants, but they are mostly in Asia.

Up to now, it is too early to say that African countries participate in such chains of value-added production in the electronics industry. There are few African enterprises, which assemble hardware and phones for local markets. However, the situation may change. The African countries' exports of ICT goods in 2012 were 0.1% of world exports, and in this respect, they were rivals of another group of countries – the transitional economies (0.2% of world ICT goods exports in 2012). Up to now, Asian electronics producers mostly act as suppliers for African markets and if they create a network of local affiliates (Huawei has affiliates in 20 African countries), it used for the promotion of sales and after-sale maintenance only.

A peculiar feature of Asian transnationals is that they introduce technology and business management innovations. Some technological innovations are called 'frugal' innovations, as they are aimed at producing affordable goods and services for low-income strata of the population. These 'frugal' innovations can be very suitable for African countries. For instance, they may enable production of cheap electrocardiographs that would cost about $800. This may lead to a revolution in the medical service not only in the poor developing countries of Asia and Africa, but also in other parts of the world. Indian companies, Tata Consultancy Services and Tata Chemical have developed a cheap water filter working on rice straw. Indian Godrej has developed a cheap refrigerator ($70) that can work on batteries. This may be compared to the Soviet meat-mincing manual devices of the past, which were once extremely popular in African markets, as they were cheap and could be used without electricity (which is not always supplied everywhere in Africa and is rather expensive). In general, Russian products based on intermediate technologies can be still in demand in African markets, due to their affordability.

As for India, it has found another niche in the global system. Since 2006, India is the first world exporter of computer services and outsourcing services for business processes. In 2012, the Indian exports of computer and information services (without BPO) amounted to $47 bn, 18.0% of the world total production. China was fifth with $14.5 bn (5.5%). In general, the volume of IT services produced in China is much higher than that of India, but the Chinese production intended for the internal market, as it embedded in ICT equipment produced in China.

Table 2. **Exports of computer and information services, 2000–2012**

	2000	2006	2006	2010	2010	2012	2012	2012
	$B	$B	%	Rank	$B	Rank	$B	%
India	4.0	21.4	16.7	1	40.2	1	47.3	18.0
Ireland	5.5	23.0		2	36.9	2	46.9	17.9
Germany	3.8	10.0		3	16.5	3	19.4	7.4
United States	6.9	5.6		4	14.0	4	15.5/ 2011/	
United Kingdom	4.3	12.4		5	13.5	6	14.4	
China	0.36	3.0		6	9.3	5	14.5	5.5
Russia	0.06	0.6		22	1.4	15	2.1	
Morocc	...	...			0.30		0.4	
South Africa	0.05	0.1			0.29		0.3	
Egypt	0.02	0.05			0.15		0.16	
Tunisia	0.02	0.02			0.04		0.041	
Uganda	0	0.02			0.04		0.06	
Senegal	0	0.003			0.006		...	
Developing countries	5.8	29.2	22.7		62.0		78.3	29.8
Transition economies	0.2	1.1			2.4		4.4	1.6
Developed countries	39.7						180	68.6
World	45.7	128.5	100		218.0		262.7	100

Source: http://unctadstat.unctad.org (14-04-2014)

BPO includes medical services (X-ray radiograms can made in the USA, whereas descriptions for them may come from India). Text can dictated in USA and typed in India. The main suppliers of ICT services in India are 'the big three' companies: Tata Consultancy Services (TCS), Infosys and Wipro. However, there are also other actors, such as Mahindra Tech (former Satyam), HCL and a lot of small and medium-scale businesses.

We can state that, since 2005, there occurred a revolution in the spread of new communication technologies in Africa. In particular, in 2005–2010 the number of mobile phones per 100 inhabitants in Africa increased significantly.

Table 3. **Cell phones (subscriptions) and Internet users per 100 inhabitants, 2005–2012**

Country, region	Cell phones (subscriptions) per 100 inhabitants		Internet users per 100 inhabitants	
	2005	**2012**	**2005**	**2012**
North Africa				
Algeria	42	**98**	6	15
Egypt	18	**101**	12	39
Morocco	41	**120**	15	55
Libya	35	**156**	4	14
Tunisia	57	**118**	10	41
Mauritania		**94**		5
Africa South of Sahara				
Congo, Republic of	16	**99**	1.5	6
Guinea-Bissau	7	**63**	2	3
Cape Verde	17	**86**	6	35
Senegal	16	**84**	5	19
Democratic Republic of Congo	5	**31**	0.3	2
Nigeria	13	**67**	4	33
Ethiopia	0.6	**22**	0.2	1.5
Benin		**85**		3.5
Burkina Faso		**45**		3.0
Burundi		**22**		1.0
Cameroon		**52**		5.0
Chad		**32**		1.9

Country, region	Cell phones (subscriptions) per 100 inhabitants		Internet users per 100 inhabitants	
	2005	**2012**	**2005**	**2012**
Cote d'Ivoire		**86**		2.2
Gabon		**117**		8.0
Gambia		**78**		11
Ghana		**85**		14
Guinea		**44**		1.3
Kenya		**68**		28
Lesotho		**56**		4
Madagascar		**41**		2
Mali		**68**		2
Mauritius		**99**		35
Namibia		**96**		
Rwanda		**41**		7
Sierra Leone		**36**		0.3
South African Republic		**127**		21
Tanzania		**56**		12
Zimbabwe		**72**		16
Asia				
China	30	81	19	42
Hong Kong (China)	125	229	57	73
North Korea	0	7	0	0
India	8	70	2	13
Qatar	87	127	25	88
South Korea	82	109	74	84
Other countries				
Russia	83	183	15	53
USA	69	95	68	81

Source: *Information Economy Report 2011, UNCTAD*. P. 120–125.http://data.worldbank.org/indicator/IT.NET.USER.P2 (14-4-14)

In 2005, the number of mobile phones per 100 African inhabitants was insignificant: 1 in Ethiopia, 5 in DRC, 7 in Guinea-Bissau, 16 in the Republic of Congo and Senegal. In North Africa, the situation was better: the figures ranged from 18 (Egypt) to 55 (Tunisia) mobile phones per 100 inhabitants. By 2012, the changes were quite significant: there were 20-40 mobile phones per 100 inhabitants in Ethiopia, Chad, DRC and Burundi; 40-60 in Guinea, Tanzania and Burkina Faso; 60-80 in Gambia, Guinea-Bissau and Mali; more than 80 per 100 persons in Senegal, Cape Verde, the Republic of Congo and Ghana (Table 3).

Supply of cheap cell phones, mostly from China and other Asian countries, became one of the driving factors of this 'mobile phone' revolution in Africa. In 2012, 13% of mobile phones sold in the continent were counterfeit. There is also a large second-hand market of mobile phones in Africa; for example, in Dakar there are large markets of second-hand goods from the US and Europe.

Chinese companies produce both mobile phones and equipment for mobile phone systems. Telecom companies represent a large share of Asian transnationals: Singtel, China Mobil, Eitilsaat, Zain. One of them, the Indian Bharti Airtel, has become an important mobile phone service provider in Africa. On March 2010, Bharti Airtel struck a deal with Kuwait's Zain to buy the assets running Zain's service operations in 15 African countries. It became the second biggest overseas acquisition by an Indian company after Tata Steel's $13bn purchase of Corus in 2007. Bharti Airtel has thereafter completed $9 bn acquisition, which made this company the fifth largest world's wireless operator. Moreover, Bharti Airtel is the world's second largest mobile telecommunications company by the number of subscribers, with over 275 million subscribers in 20 countries, as of July 2013. It is the largest mobile service provider in India, where it serves 192.22 million subscribers, as of August 2013. It is also the second largest in-country mobile operator worldwide, behind only China Mobile. Bharti Airtel has also pioneered in using a strategy, which stipulates outsourcing most of its business operations except marketing, sales, finance and several others. Several other operators have since copied this strategy. Ericsson and Nokia Networks service its network, whereas IBM provides the IT support, and transmission towers are maintained by another Indian company (Bharti Infratel Ltd.). An agreement with Ericsson enabled Airtel to provide low call rates (US$0. 02/minute) in India.

By the end of 2010, Bharti Airtel (sales $14.6 bn) had affiliates in 17 countries in Africa and another 3 in Asia (India, Sri Lanka, Bangladesh). In 2012, Bharti Airtel had 277 million subscribers, including 60 million in Africa: in Nigeria, Burkina Faso, Gabon, Chad, Kenya, Ghana, Sierra, Tanzania, Zambia, Malawi, Democratic Republic of Congo, Republic of Congo, and Rwanda. Airtel Congo is the market leader in the Republic of Congo with a 55% market share. Airtel Zambia is the market leader in Zambia with a 69% share, In Malawi, an Airtel-owned company, controls 72% of the mobile telecommunications market, in Niger its share is 68%. Besides, Bharti Airtel supports 20 schools in Africa and football team called 'Rising Stars'.

One of the main providers of ICT services for Bharti Airtel is Indian Infosys. Equipment providers for Bharti Airtel are Huawei (China), Samsung (Korea), and Nokia. Advertisement of Huawei smartphones dominates on Bharti Airtel websites in Africa. In Africa, there is a new supplementary service – money transferring from cell phone account. It has become popular and important, as 90% of customers in Africa are 'unbanked', they have no personal bank accounts.

The 'Big Three' Indian IT-service companies and other Indian IT companies have started making foreign direct investments (FDI). They invest in the USA and Europe in order to receive orders and promote their services. Their investment activities in Asian countries – Sri Lanka, Bangladesh, China – are called "near-shoring", as they offshore their operations to use lower wages, tax benefits and other advantages. They require additional language skills (knowledge of German) from the staff in their affiliates in Poland, Hungary, Czech Republic, which serve European markets.

Nowadays, the Indian IT services companies are moving to Africa. Wipro has already begun to offshore some of its contract work to Egypt. Ghana has emerged as a pole of attraction for graphic and web design, as well as data entry. AT Kearney offshore services location index includes such an indicator as wage costs, for which in 2009 Ghana received 7.12 points, India 6.86 points, USA 0.54 points. In 2011, the USA was ranked 18th and Ghana 27th in that index. At present, wages in Ghana constitute 25-30% of those in India.

In 2009, AT Kearney published an offshore services location index that rated countries' attractiveness as providers of offshore services. India was ranked first, followed by China, Malaysia, Thailand, Indonesia, Egypt (6th), Philippines, Chile, Jordan, Vietnam, USA (14th), Ghana (15th), Sri Lanka, Tunisia, Mauritius (25th), Senegal (26th), Morocco (30th), Czech Republic (32nd), Russia (33rd), South Africa (39th), etc. In total, 50 countries were ranked. There are three groups of indicators used for the rating: financial attractiveness – 1, personnel's skills and availability – 2, business environment – three.

Two years later, in 2011, AT Kearney offshore services locations index ranked India first, China – 2nd, Malaysia – 3rd, Egypt – 4th , Indonesia – 5th, Russia – 20th, Sri Lanka – 21st, Tunisia – 23d, Ghana – 27th, Senegal – 29th, Mauritius – 36th, Morocco – 37th, 38 – Ukraine – 38th and South Africa –

45th. According to this index, seven out of the 50 leading countries to host IT services were in Africa.

By people's skills and availability in 2011, the US was the first, India – 2nd, China – 3rd, Russia – 8th, Ireland – 9th, Egypt – 16th, Israel -17th.

African countries, especially Senegal, Ghana, Egypt, Tunisia, Morocco, possess substantial advantages in terms of low wage costs. By financial attractiveness in 2011, Vietnam was ranked 1st, Senegal – 3rd, Ghana – 5th, Egypt – 9th, Tunisia – 10th, Ukraine – 13th, Morocco – 15th, Russia -25th, Mauritius – 30th, South Africa – 34th.

The IT and BPO services are another industry that has recently demonstrated significant growth. Some producers – participants of this market – have managed to increase the added value of their products by offshoring, or transferring abroad, new types of services. At the same time, offshoring practices have expanded geographically to include a large number of countries 'specializing' in different services.

India, benefited from the skills and advantages of its companies, remains the unquestioned leader of the indexed countries – a half-point ahead of China and a full point ahead of Malaysia – and still keeps the lion's share of the IT services market. On top of that, India's IT services stalwarts are moving up the value chain. Companies such as Infosys and Wipro are enhancing their capacities for R&D and expanding well beyond their traditional roles of sellers.

Chinese companies began to offer specialized services not only in Chinese and English, but also in Korean and in Japanese. Their most attractive areas are high-end analytics and advanced IT, where they are alternatives to Russia and Eastern Europe, and BPO, where they compete with India. China is now developing R&D capacities as a necessary supplement to its manufacturing profile, which creates a strong foundation for knowledge process outsourcing, also called KPO services.

Indian IT services companies such as Infosys, Wipro and Tech Mahindra have long developed partnership with African universities, offering internship programmes to their students and expanding African countries' talent pool. Indian IT companies have been winning contracts with enterprises that focus on mobile technologies, e-governance, skills development and social media. Software services companies from India are expanding in Africa. Countries such as South Africa and Kenya are seen as next principal objects of commercial activity by Indian software outsourcers.

India's Wipro, the third largest software firm, declared that it would increase the intake of graduates for its India Gateway internship programme in South Africa. The programme, which enrolled 70 graduates in 2013, will admit 150 graduates in 2014. The internship, which offered to graduates specializing in Sciences and Mathematics, stipulates months of theoretical training, after which interns will interviewed. Successful trainees will be qualified and eventually absorbed in Wipro's operations in South Africa.

India's top software services companies are investing a lot in Africa and are eager to acquire new customers in the continent that is home to a large number of fast-growing enterprises, but also to under-developed infrastructure. "Lured by the growth potential of African economies and their burgeoning interest in technology, IT services growth in the African continent is being strongly driven by governmental expenditures on IT infrastructure and services", said Shailendra Singh, business director for Africa at Wipro.

While most technological companies have chosen South Africa as home to their 'African headquarters', many are also expanding into fast-growing economies such as Uganda, Kenya, Nigeria and Ethiopia. Indian IT-BPO firms won 25 large outsourcing contracts in Africa over the past four years. The IT market in Africa was evaluated $26.5 bn in 2014. HCL Tec is present in eight of the 54 African countries. Wipro, which has 1.100 employees in Africa, will hire 1.000 more at its three centers in South Africa. Tech Mahindra is betting high on Africa too[6].

In Africa, there are possibilities of developing not only BPO for external markets, but also ICT services for internal markets. World Economic Forum highlights the "success story" of Rwanda, describing its "road to knowledge-based economy". Rwanda, ranked 1st by competitiveness in Eastern Africa and 7th in the continent in general, has adopted a Strategy Vision 2020, for which a principle of knowledge-based economy is pivotal. "It is intended to use ICT for sustainable socioeconomic development (e-governance, health, education, small business promotion), to develop ICT infrastructure, data centers (cloud services), digital terrestrial television", etc. To achieve this, multi-task community telecommunication centers and information kiosks created; ICT buses provide ICT literacy trainings. Business incubators built, online tax calculators are used. Late starters sometimes have considerable advantages. Some tools prioritized by this strategy include E-Soko – mobile market information solution for farmers; Open MRS – medical records system; TRAC net – a system of centralized data management in clinical health care; Telemedicine facilities – advisors for hospitals in rural areas. A Technology Park created in Rwanda with the help of the Carnegie-Mellon University for BPO and cloud computing. MTN and Bharti Airtel (2.4% of Rwanda's market) help develop the mobile communications branch. ICT used in education. Knowledge labs created. Creation of national electronic distance education is in progress. The WEF experts admit that Rwanda faces some challenges – lack of electrical energy, of ICT qualified personnel, of broadband connections. Still, they state that Rwanda has chances to become a hub for BPO and financial services[7].

Russia, despite certain setbacks in its Africa policy, still has some chances to benefit from the continent's technological growth. Despite the fact that Russia's withdrawal from Africa cooled down the sincere sympathies of many Africans and loosened the old ties, Russia does possess competitive advantages in the ICT sphere (a number of technical universities, a number of experienced engineers in the country). The Soviet Union used to have an efficient system of rendering technical assistance to African countries. In Africa, there remain a significant number of graduates from Soviet institutions of higher education. We may argue that what is now the Russian, Ukrainian and Belorussian Diasporas in African countries used to be one diaspora, which was mostly comprised of Soviet-born women married to former African students in the USSR. Members of these diaspora may also contribute to the development of Russian-African relations.

Cooperation between Russia and African countries has rich potential not only in the raw materials field, but also in technological spheres. Russia still has some high-level technical universities and a considerable pool of engineers and technical specialists. There are of IT companies ("Kaspersky Lab", for example) that could expand their activity in Africa. Last, but not the least, Russia needs to develop cooperation with African countries, taking into consideration the newest geopolitical trends in the world.

---

[1] http://wdi.worldbank.org/table/1.1; http://wdi.worldbank.org/table/4.10 (23/05/2014).

[2] http://www.forbes.com/global2000 (10-05-2014).

[3] World Investment Report, 2010, UN. N.Y. Geneva. Ann., Table 26.

[4] World Investment Report, 2011, UN, N.Y. Geneva, 2011, p. 154.

[5] http//www.nytimes.com/2012/01/26/business/ieconomy-apples-ipad-and-the-human-costs-for-workers-in-china.html?_r=2 (2/6/12).

[6] http://economictimes.indiatimes.com/articleshow/34909633.cms?utm_ source= contentofinterest&utm_medium=text&utm_campaign=cppst

[7] Global Information Technologies Report 2013. World Economic Forum, Geneva, 2013, p. 122-125.

Justin van der Merwe, Dr. Phil.
Centre for Military Studies
(CEMIS)
Faculty of Military Science
Stellenbosch University,
South Africa

THE BRICS PUZZLE: RISE OF THE NON-WEST OR VEILED SUB-IMPERIALISM?

Abstract

This paper outlines the evolution of the concept of sub-imperialism and explores its suitability to describe the current rise of the non-West, as manifested through the BRICS alliance. Two trends suggest that the current multipolar global order presents a novel opportunity to investigate the phenomenon of sub-imperialism: the strong focus on non-Western rising powers in analyses at the regional scale and the recent inclusion of an *old* sub-imperial power, South Africa, into the BRICS alliance. Therefore, when viewed from a 'long' historical perspective, the recent rise of the BRICS alliance presents not only a good opportunity to reflect on the concept of sub-imperialism generally, but also as a reminder of the usefulness of the concept in describing the *modus operandi* of South Africa in its region, with the BRICS alliance being merely the next phase in this relationship.

History suggests that South Africa's involvements in such cycles of accumulation are the product of international elites engaging with local elites to solicit South Africa as a gateway into the region *vis-á-vis* BRICS as the new NEPAD. The fact that this drive is being led by a non-Western alignment does not exempt it from a neo-liberal version of its own that serves to leave weaker states in the region no better off whilst further skewing domestic and regional inequality. This paper suggests that a critical outlook towards the BRICS alliance should be adopted now before South Africa is swept away with unrealistic global ambitions, which do very little to ease poverty and underdevelopment.

Introduction

What if an American investment bank were to develop a term to describe a group of investor-friendly states based outside the West, and then these states were to use the term to develop a concentrated 'spatial fix' for investors to secure their markets, with limited intra-regional trade amongst themselves and their prospective regions, and the real beneficiaries were to be the Western countries once again? Does this sound like the latest in a series of crafty efforts by America to disguise the explicitness of imperial ambition? First, it was the 'American century', which was used to cloak territorial ambition. Then once territorial expansion was no longer necessary (or politically desirable), neo-liberalism was used to maintain control through privatization and consumption – whilst operating under the guise of globalisation. It seems that the next step would be to deny or usurp the non-West of its right to choose its development path and encourage a further growth of trade liberalisation within these territories.

Surely the real successes of a BRICS open model of trade should be the movement of capital, goods and people amongst their immediate regions, and to some extent, between the BRICS states themselves? The notion that the West is not a primary beneficiary of a BRICS-driven round of global capital accumulation should be closely interrogated.

The lack of a considered regional approach suggests that the BRICS alliance was not organically developed out of historical, political and economic struggles like most regional economic communities but rather, as is the case, born of an investment conception based on two decades of investor-friendly returns from several large non-Western countries. Its pretension to assume a shared experience in the non-West is in some respects equally flawed, and although having a certain logic to it, such pretensions could easily be thrust upon these states by others, and is not necessarily reflective of lived experiences within the non-West.

For example, the BRICS alliance has a tenuous geographical premise and could be construed as anti-geographical given the extremely diverse nature of the member states: the non-West is a very broad term, what about the complexities within the regions within which these states find themselves? Are China and Russia part of the developing world? The neat inclusion of a significant power from major regions within the non-West does not necessarily mean anything substantial other than a predilection to maximise markets. From a geostrategic point of view, it also certainly lends credence to the notion that these states are acting as sub-imperial gateways into their regions. Worryingly, there is no *real* consideration for the regional communities, of which the BRICS members are normally the most dominant. One would think that advancing the interests of weaker states and the general development of their regions would be a top priority of such an alliance. But rather, paradoxically, BRICS-driven rounds of capital accumulation may actually further skew regional inequalities and leave the more marginalised states worse off than before, especially those in Africa.

A closer inspection of South Africa's (SA's) inclusion into the formation may shed some light on these matters, particularly given its importance to the

146

sub-imperial debate (see below). Does SA's inclusion into the BRICS alliance lend credence to the notion that the BRICS states are fulfilling sub-imperial roles?

The analysis begins with a discussion of the geographical approach and why imperial geopolitics is still relevant today. This will be followed by a historiography of the concept sub-imperialism highlighting SA's centrality within the sub-imperial debate. The paper concludes by discussing the growing focus on non-Western rising powers in analyses at the regional scale.

Imperial geopolitics as an area of study

Modern geopolitical discourse is said to have started in the era of imperialist expansion between 1870 and 1945. During this period, opposing empires clashed and fought several wars, thereby actively changing the world political map. The dominant imperialist power of the age was the British Empire, which, despite its growing territorial size, was struggling to keep abreast of the transforming conditions of world power. The other imperial powers of the time were Russia, France, Italy, the United States, Germany and later Japan. These states were rivals of the British Empire and sought to benefit from its difficulties and relative decline. Each of these imperialist states produced their own leading intellectuals of statecraft and, on the basis of their own unique geopolitical cultures, developed various imperialist geopolitical discourses (Ó Tuathail, 2006: 17).

Imperialism has therefore not only been a subject of study for geographers, but political geographers in particular have played an instrumental role in actively promoting imperialism. Halford Mackinder was particularly prominent in the formation of imperialist geopolitical discourses for the British Empire. His well-known paper presented at a meeting of the Royal Geographical Society (RGS) at the beginning of the 20th century, 'The Geographical Pivot in History' (1904), was largely seen as an attempt to promote a decidedly Anglo-Saxon and European depiction of the globe. At that stage, the RGS was known for its role in promoting the British Empire through expeditions. The rising imperial aspirations of Germany in central Europe following the First World War were also driven by geographers such as Karl Haushofer and Friedrich Ratzel. Influenced by the work of these geographers, Adolf Hitler himself was instrumental in popularising the rationale for German state expansion through *Mein Kampf* (1942) and the concept of Lebensraum.

After the two major periods of decolonisation (in Asia immediately after the Second World War and in Africa from the late 1950s), some geographers emphasized the continuing political, economic and cultural legacies of imperialism (Gilmartin 2009: 117-118, referring to Berg et al. 2007 and Peters

1997; 1998). Hudson (1977) highlighted how the advancement of the discipline was based on its utilitarian value to the actual practice of imperialism. Late 20th century Western geographers continued to shine light on the complicity of geography and imperialism, particularly through what became known as 'critical geopolitics', after Ó Tuathail's now famous thesis by the same title. Crucially, critical geopolitics provided the necessary reflexive understanding behind the processes of imperialism and the constructed nature of geographical knowledge (Ó Tuathail and Agnew, 1992; Ó Tuathail, 1996; Ó Tuathail and Dalby, 1998).

However, parallel to the mainstream Western geopolitical discourse, other forms of geopolitical discourse were arising from the periphery of imperialism. Following the decolonisation processes in Asia, South America and Africa, the former colonial territories were to break up into independent states. Having struggled to attain independence, these territories sought to establish their sovereignty and assert their national and regional identities in response to the continuing inequities of colonialism. Typically such geopolitical discourses were driven by their own intellectuals of statecraft who developed according to their own distinctive geopolitical traditions steeped in a sense of resistance (Amin, 1977; Fanon, 1965; Said, 1978). These processes were also documented by Slater (2004). Throughout the second half of the 20th century, such geopolitical discourses made important intellectual contributions to understanding the impact of imperialism on recipient nations.

At the start of the 21st century, the post-September 11 global atmosphere had revived an interest in the analytical basis of the concept of imperialism. This was driven by a desire to make sense of America's interests in the Middle East and its 'war against terror'. Geographers in particular had taken up this mantle, placing American imperialism at the centre of their analyses (Gregory, 2004; De Zengotita, 2003; Hardt and Negri, 2001; Harvey 2005). They had managed to deal with the subject in a particularly nuanced way, and provided valuable critiques of the political economy and culture of imperialism. Of the recent post-September 11 geographical literature on the subject, Harvey's historical geographical materialist analysis of American imperialism in his book, *The New Imperialism* (2005), arguably provides the best set of tools to critically and systematically evaluate the ambitions and practices of imperialist powers in varying contexts and regions.

Despite the revived interest in imperialism and the rise of intellectuals of statecraft from outside the West, sub-imperialism was never really given serious consideration in geography or other disciplines. It was assumed to be a natural by-product of historical subjugation. Although there are studies which have treated sub-imperialism from a historical perspective and should be considered as important (see below), the phenomenon of sub-imperialism deserves re-examination and should not merely be understood as an unspecified by-product of historical conquest by Western colonial powers. What is unique about the modern state-capital relations forming at that level? How do they complement or challenge global processes of accumulation and neo-liberalism? What are the physical spaces and places where sub-imperialism arises? These questions are especially important given the current crisis facing Western-led global capitalism and the corresponding shifts in global power relations.

What we know about sub-imperialism

When Rosa Luxemborg was writing about the accumulation of capital at the beginning of the 20th century sub-imperialism did not really exist. It was only later in the 20th century when notable alternate centres of accumulation had started to develop within the former colonial world. The first attempt at developing a sustained critique of sub-imperialism was made by Ruy Marini in the 1960s and 1970s. In 1965 Marini, a Brazilian sociologist, drew from the work of German Marxist Ernst Talheimer (no reference given), describing how 'as a result of the influx of Northern American investments, [other industrialised states] became...centers of the export of capital and simultaneously extended their economic frontiers within the world-wide process of imperialist integration' (Marini, 1965: 12).

He did however concede that these processes were open to internal contradictions. Further drawing from the work of Talheimer, who in the 1920s developed the idea of 'antagonistic cooperation', Marini stressed that imperialist integration of states results in conflict with the local working class and labour, which has 'the effect of obstructing the process of [imperialist] integration...[opening] fissures in the structure of the imperialist world, strongly favouring the forces bent on destroying the very bases of the [imperialist] structure: revolutionary movements in the underdeveloped countries' (ibid.). By describing the relationships between the Brazilian military dictatorship of the 1960s and its support for American capitalist expansion, Marini laid the foundation for the understanding of Brazil as a sub-imperial state in South America, although the term sub-imperialism only features once in his article.

In 1972 he used a more forceful application of the term sub-imperialism and developed some general observations about the behaviour of these states. He defines sub-imperialism as 'the form which dependent capitalism assumes upon reaching the stage of monopolies and finance capital' (Marini, 1972: 14). Elaborating on his economically-focused definition, he outlines three fundamental tenets of sub-imperialism: 'First, export of manufactured goods, durable as well as non-durable. Note that the expansion of exports requires the rising of the technological level, which in turn implies greater possibilities for the absorption of capital goods' (Marini, 1972: 16). In a similar

149

fashion, SA was able to secure the regional sub-system as a 'captive market' for its exports giving its industries a larger market to dominate.

Marini's second observation concerns an increase in state expenditure on infrastructure related to transportation and electrification, and the re-equipping of the armed forces. This expands the market for capital goods (ibid.). SA has also engaged in similar state-driven expenditure in key infra-structure areas related to natural resources or basic services. The primary in-tention of such expenditure was to support the main drivers of the economy – mining and manufacturing. As a result of sanctions imposed on apartheid SA, the country became an independent arms producer.

Marini's third observation relates to the formation of a 'consumer soci-ety' created through a transfer of income from the poorest strata to the mid-dle and upper strata, in order to secure the market for a high-technology in-dustry which is becoming increasingly removed from the 'real needs of the masses' (Marini, 1972: 20). In SA, there was an almost total wiping out of a self-sustained African peasantry and the formation of an urban African mid-dle class designed to fulfill the needs of labour and consumption. However, the state sought simultaneously to restrict the rights and privileges of this group and dictate where they could live, how much they could earn and what land they could own.

However insightful, Marini's use of sub-imperialism is highly context-specific and would clearly have benefited from further theoretical elabora-tion. Understanding of Brazilian sub-imperialism would also have been en-hanced, when viewed from other South American states, or through a de-tailed description of Brazil's spatial expansion into the region. Nonetheless, his work is insightful in its penetrating understanding of the class formations driving these processes and in highlighting the processes of resistance to sub-imperialism.

In the 1970s, the term sub-imperialism had spread in academic circles and appeared in the context of Iran (Ahmed, 1973) and SA (Bienefeld and Innes, 1976). It also featured in the work of Marxist theorist Amin (1974; 1977), and in the work of developmental economist, Frank (1979). The po-litical scientist, Shaw (1978; 1979), drew links between the global semi-periphery, semi-industrialised states and sub-imperialism. He applied what was understood of sub-imperialism in Latin America to the African political economy. However, in the mid-1970s an essay by Väyrynen and Herrera (1975) consolidated much of what was understood on the topic at the time. They sought to develop a structural framework for sub-imperialism and a greater understanding of the internal and external dynamics.

Drawing from Galtung's (1971) 'go-between relations', Väyrynen and Herrera note: 'In Galtung's view Western Europe, for example, *goes between* the United States and Eastern Europe; Japan between the United States and

South East Asia; Mexico between the United States and Central America...'
(1975: 167). They add that Galtung's viewpoint is akin to understanding the
international system as composed of a number of 'dependence chains' within
the capitalist and socialist worlds which operate as a link between them, as
well as between them and the third world countries (ibid.). In much the same
way, SA played an important role in bridging the gap between the developed
countries and the rest of southern Africa.

In developing a structural framework for sub-imperialism, Väyrynen and
Herrera state that there are 'three levels of dependence chains; [the] imperialist centre, sub-imperialist agents and dominated periphery countries' (1975:
168). The notion of inter-linked global capitalist processes is similar to
Wallerstein's (1987) world-systems analysis (see also Taylor, 1985 and more
recently Flint and Taylor, 2007). The imperialist centre, according to Väyrynen and Herrera, comprised America, countries from Europe and Japan.
They discuss Brazil, SA and Iran as examples of sub-imperial states. Drawing from Galtung, they further accentuate the importance of trade and technology in maintaining these relationships of dependence (1975: 168). European technology linked to mining gave SA an advantage over its neighbours.
This followed by more general technical, managerial and administrative
skills and technologies turning SA into a modern capitalist economy. One of
the consequences is that SA has a highly skewed trade relationship with the
region. Väyrynen and Herrera also emphasize the role played by the state,
transnational corporations and elite members in these processes. They contend that the alliance between state and business elite members forms 'a coherent interest alliance' which serves as 'a *precondition* for (sub)imperialist
policy' (1975: 170). There is some evidence to suggest that such an 'interest
alliance' between state and business elite members exists in SA.

According to Väyrynen and Herrera (1975: 171-172), the internal dynamics of sub-imperialism include the sub-imperial state moving from a system of colonial dependence to post-colonial subordination because of exploitation by the dominant imperialist power. Favourable conditions for such exploitation include a strong, often military state (such as the apartheid state),
which is able to denationalise industry (a policy pursued by the post-
apartheid government), monopolise raw materials, has a massive indebted-
ness to international financial institutions, and is able to exploit labour whilst
depriving the marginalised population of any real profits.

In describing the external dynamics of sub-imperialism, Väyrynen and
Herrera highlight how the sub-imperial states and the periphery states are
manipulated by the core imperialist powers, typically through corporations,
in the pursuit of 'economic expansion...under auspices of transnational capital' (1975: 173). In this connection and from an historical perspective, the
role played by British multi-national corporations (MNCs) in using SA as a

151

'gateway' into the region, is instructive. Väyrynen and Herrera further note that *economic integration* and its rhetoric in the Third World often serves sub-imperialist purposes, and that *expansion* by the sub-imperial state is not only restricted to the economic sphere but includes political, military and ideological institutions and initiatives (1975: 173-174). Väyrynen and Herrera highlight military intervention as the 'ultimate strategy of preserving the dominance structure, as well as of preventing any autonomous, independent development in the peripheral countries' (1975: 175). The role of the military in maintaining SA's regional economic dominance has been well documented.

Analysis of the concept sub-imperialism appears to have stagnated after the 1970s, appearing loosely in the literature as a feature of historical imperialism (Warhurst, 1984). However, once the Cold War ended and American-driven neo-liberalism had gathered momentum globally, a re-examination of sub-imperialism in the 'new' neo-liberal world order was certainly needed. This occurred belatedly. Only in the first decade of the 21st century did the concept appear regularly in the work of Patrick Bond in the context of democratic SA's re-emergence globally and as a leading power on the African continent (Bond, 2004; 2006a; 2006b). SA attained democracy in 1994, just in time to capitalise on the neo-liberal induced round of expanded accumulation. Many would argue that by the late 1990s, SA's 'new' elite members carried the mantle of sub-imperial power very comfortably by providing the necessary 'linkages' for Western capitalism in southern Africa (for a similar argument from a historical perspective see Atmore and Marks, 1974).

Bond typically analyses the African National Congress (ANC) government's relationship with America through the prism of sub-imperialism describing how the SA government is notorious for '"talking left but walking right", insofar as [the SA government attempts to] veil the underlying dynamics of accumulation, class struggle and geopolitics' (2004: 219). Bond describes how 'modern imperialism...in Africa combines an accumulation strategy based on neoliberalism and the extraction of ever cheaper minerals and cash crops, with increasing subservience to US-led, indirect, neocolonial rule' (2004: 220). He goes on to describe how 'imperialism is facilitated in Africa by the Pretoria-Johannesburg state-capitalist nexus, in part through Mbeki's New Partnership for Africa's Development (NEPAD) and in part through the logic of private capital' (ibid.).

In line with Bond's analysis, this paper uses the concept 'sub-imperialism' to encapsulate the idea that SA is subject to broader systemic rounds of capital accumulation driven by neo-liberalism and American interests. These interests are secured globally through the influence of Wall Street, the IMF and the World Bank. The term 'sub' is also used as a means to delineate a 'mini' or smaller form of imperialism that is regionally located.

Given SA's centrality to the concept of sub-imperialism, it was really only a matter of time until the link between BRICS and sub-imperialism was made. Bond (2013) has made this connection referring to SA's deputy sheriff role within the BRICS alliance. Building on Marini's observations, he proposes that a sub-imperial state would typically meet the following criteria: '[R]egional economic extraction, export of capital (always associated with subsequent imperial politics) and internal corporate monopolisation and financialisation' (2013: 266). He outlines a further two characteristics of a sub-imperial state: '[E]nsuring regional geopolitical stability [and]...advancing the broader agenda of neoliberalism, so as to legitimate deepening market access...' (ibid.). Referring to Yeros and Moyo (2011: 20), Bond further notes that the forms of BRICS sub-imperialism are diverse (2013: 267):

Some are driven by private blocs of capital with strong state support (Brazil, India); others, like China, include the direct participation of state-owned enterprises; while in the case of South Africa it is increasingly difficult to speak of an autonomous domestic bourgeoisie, given the extreme degree of de-nationalisation of its economy in the post-apartheid era. The degree of participation in the Western military project is also different from one case to the next although, one might say, there is a schizophrenia to all this, typical of sub-imperialism.

SA's centrality to the sub-imperial debate is significant and has been well argued by Bond. It is no surprise then that SA would make a good entry point into theorising the possible sub-imperial inclinations of the BRICS states. The late and somewhat confusing inclusion of SA into the BRICS alliance, given its relative diminutive status, does perhaps signal the intentions of the alliance – especially concerning Africa. The stated desire to include a representative from Africa within the alliance should be treated sceptically. It seems that the geopolitical calculation to include SA into the alliance was primarily for reasons of securing the interests of the BRICS state and business elite members in Africa, hence the phrase, BRICS as the new NEPAD. From this perspective, BRICS is merely the latest in a long line of international interests playing out in the southern African sub-region, and using SA as an intermediary to capital accumulation within the region. SA has a track record of getting swept away with such 'big ideas' and 'big projects' whilst neglecting the growing domestic unemployment and inequality, and the many problems in its immediate region. Perhaps it is pertinent to ask at this fairly early stage: will anyone even use the term BRICS in ten years' time? The rhetoric of the BRICS states dovetails closely with initiatives such as the African Renaissance and SA's broader multilateralism on the continent. However, in contrast to NEPAD, BRICS clearly signals a widening of SA's 'spatial fix' beyond Africa to include the global South and emerging markets

153

more generally. SA's state and corporate elite members have progressively looked to expand their operations and influence beyond the continent and SA's inclusion into the BRICS alliance provided the necessary launching pad. The affective labour for SA's inclusion into the alliance was really laid down by ex-President Thabo Mbeki, namely, his involvement with the Non-Alignment Movement and G77, and especially his founding of the India, Brazil and SA (IBSA) trilateral initiative.

Academics such as Miller, Saunders and Oloyede (2008), Taylor (2011) and Sampson (2009) concur broadly with the understanding of SA as a sub-imperial state. Others refer to SA's 'imperialism' more directly, as if SA were some form of 'primary' imperial power itself (Lesufi, 2004; 2006). However, none of these authors has attempted to develop a geographical theory of sub-imperialism, let alone any coherent theory on the phenomenon, despite a clear acknowledgement of a gap in the literature.

Regionally dominant States and Sub-Imperialism

The literature on regionally dominant powers can be confusing because of the terminology used. The two main terms are 'regional powers' (De-stradi, 2010; Flemes, 2007a; Kappel, 2010; Nolte, 2010; Nel and Nolte, 2010) and 'regional hegemony' (Mares, 1988; Nabers, 2010). Theoretically, these two terms are distinct. However, in practice they are often used loosely and interchangeably. Generally, 'regional powers' are believed to be states which have a clear advantage in terms of economic and political resources compared with the states based within their sub-system, region or continent. Regional hegemons – are states, which are not only able to define the norms and values of the region, but are able to get other states to follow those rules. Regional hegemons typically operate on the same scale as regional powers. Other scholars refer to 'pivot states' (Habib, 2003; Landsberg, 2004). A 'pivot state' is an important state, but *not* a dominant state. There is also a debate within the international relations literature distinguishing between 'middle powers' (Efstathopoulos, 2011; Mares, 1988), and 'emergent middle powers' (Flemes, 2007b; Jordaan, 2003; Schoeman, 2003; Van der Westhuizen, 1998). Middle powers tend to be states, which are traditionally powerful within their regions and play a significant role in international multilateral fora. Emergent middle powers are those states, which are yet to fully realise their middle power status.

Yet, despite the rather obvious link between sub-imperialism and the general growth of studies focusing on the regional scale, none of these studies engage seriously with the matter of sub-imperialism. Although some of the regional literature clearly locates regions within broader patterns of contemporary American imperialism and the pressures exerted by neo-liberalism

(Allen and Allan, 2007; Bracking, 2003; Destradi, 2010; Hentz, 2005; Nel and Nolte, 2010; Prys, 2010), no sustained and explicit theoretical link has been made in the regional literature between regionally dominant powers and sub-imperialism, particularly in the context of the 'new wave' of emergent non-Western countries.

Since the end of the Cold War and the winning over of neo-liberalism globally, a prosperous cycle of expanded rounds of accumulation has given rise to new poles of accumulation outside of the West amidst a relative decline in American power, leading to the prospect of a distinctly more multi-polar world. This shift in the global power relations is reflected in the recent regional literature which has mostly focused on the rise of non-Western regionally dominant powers (in the broadest of senses), such as: China (Harris, 2005; Roy, 1994; Shambaugh, 2004); India (Gupta, 2010; Pardesi, 2005; Stewart-Ingersoll and Frazier, 2010); Brazil (Bandiera, 2006; Bethel, 2010; De Lima and Hirst, 2006); a resurgent Russia (Kokoshin, 2002); South Africa (Ahwireng and McGowan, 1998a, 1998b; Alden and Le Pere, 2009; Alden and Soko, 2005; Kagwanja, 2009; Flemes, 2007a, 2009; Prys, 2009); and to a lesser extent, Iran (Rubin, 2006); Turkey (Erickson, 2004); Nigeria (Bach, 2007; Souare, 2005); Egypt (Breytenbach, 1997); Uzbekistan (Bohr, 2004); Ethopia (Iyob, 1993); and, Indonesia and Vietnam (Emmers, 2005).

The focus on non-Western regional powers was given further impetus by the new wave of studies focusing on the BRIC nations, after the now famous Goldman Sachs report which coined the term in 2001. Since the founding of the formal grouping of BRIC in 2006 (it became BRICS in 2010 when SA joined), a body of literature has developed surmising the prospects of a 'new wave' or 'second tier' of imperial powers. This literature generally focuses on the prospects of such powers to engage in expanded rounds of accumulation regionally and then to spread to other continents as they develop into what is called a major or superpower (Armijo and Burges, 2010; Dellios, 2003; Roberts, 2010; Sinha and Dorschner, 2010; Wadhva, 2006). This literature highlights the fact that the BRIC nations are estimated to outstrip the G7 in terms of economic size by 2027. Another strand within this literature suggests that the BRICS states will alter the global balance of power through their influence over political and economic global institutions. They argue that this is likely to result in a restructuring of the world order (Kurečić and Bandov, 2011; Pisani-Ferry, 2005; Renard, 2009; Roberts, 2011; Shaw, Cooper and Antkiewicz, 2007; Shaw, Cooper and Chin, 2009). Others are more cautious about these claims believing that it is just another multilateral body which faces the same limitations as any other (Glosny, 2010; Martynov, 2011). The India, Brazil and SA (IBSA) trilateral initiative adds to the prominence of these emergent powers on the global stage (Alden and Viera, 2005; Taylor, 2009). Implicit in much of this literature is the assumption that

155

in a post-recessionary global environment, these countries are less trusting of Western-led globalisation and neo-liberalism, and that their immediate regions have become more important. The assumption is that regional cooperation has been enhanced by the financial crisis due to uncertainties in the global macro-economy. The recession has had an impact on the direction of industrial development and industrial inputs at the regional scale, and the role played by dominant powers in these processes. Even before the 2008 global financial crisis, Harvey asked the question: 'Are we seeing the disintegration of US hegemony within the global system, and the rise of a "new regionalism" in political-economic power even as we see the United States acting as if it's the sole superpower to be obeyed?' (2005: 31). Is it time for a 'type' of regionalism centred on these rising powers to dominate global geo-political discourse?

Therefore, as global capitalism enters a period of deep uncertainty, it appears that the time is right for a critical re-assessment of the role of sub-imperial states, grounded within their regions, to be understood as independent actors directly seeking to devise their own form of '(sub)imperialism'. The term 'new imperialism' has been applied to a few historical imperial epochs (Gilmartin, 2009: 115; Hudson, 1977) and was recently used to refer to a resurgence of American imperialism (Harvey, 2005). However, it appears that 'new' imperialism might be the wave of non-western powers whose rise will most likely shape the 21st century. Surprisingly, despite the obvious rise of this 'new wave' of imperial powers the link with sub-imperialism has not been reflected in the literature.

Conclusion

SA's inclusion into the BRIC alliance as a 'regionally-mandated BRICS state' bears clear reference to its 'go-between relationship' in processes of global capital accumulation, suggesting that its inclusion into the BRICS alliance presents an opportune moment to reassess its relationship with the region using the sub-imperial concept. Such an investigation should be focused on the realities of historical and geographical processes of capital accumulation, and should ask critically whether SA's inclusion into the BRICS alliance runs the risk of further exacerbating regional inequalities and domestic crises.

But the rise of the BRICS alliance does not only suggest an opportunity to reflect on SA's relationship with the region. More broadly, the rise of the alliance presents an opportunity to theorise the concept of sub-imperialism itself. The proliferation of analyses centered on non-Western rising powers within the regional literature is indicative of this and brings the regional component of sub-imperialism into focus. The concept of sub-imperialism

156

has an explicit, yet strangely, under-theorised regional component. Of particular importance is the understanding that these sub-imperial states would seek to take advantage of uneven geographical conditions or asymmetries, which inevitably arise out of spatial exchange. How these rising powers insert themselves into regional spatial exchanges in support of an already existing neoliberal global framework, is of key importance.

References

Ahmed, F. (1973) 'Iran: Subimperialism in action'. *Pakistan Forum*, 3(6/7) pp. 10-18+20.

Ahwireng-Obeng, F. and McGowan, P. J. (1998a) 'Partner or hegemon? South Africa in Africa'. *Journal of Contemporary African Studies*, 16(1) pp. 5-38.

Ahwireng-Obeng, F and McGowan, P.J. (1998b) 'Partner or hegemon? South Africa in Africa'. *Journal of Contemporary African Studies*, 16(2) pp. 165-195.

Alden, C. and Le Pere, G. (2009) 'South Africa in Africa: Bound to lead?'. *Politikon*, 36(1) pp. 145-169.

Alden, C. and Soko, M. (2005) 'South Africa's economic relations with Africa: Hegemony and its discontents'. *Journal of Modern African Studies*, 43(3) pp. 367-392.

Alden, C. and Viera, M. (2005) 'The new diplomacy of the South: South Africa, Brazil, India and trilateralism'. *Third World Quarterly*, 26(7) pp. 1077-1095.

Allen, J. and Allan, C. (2007) 'Beyond the territorial fix: Regional assemblages, politics and power'. *Regional Studies*, 41(9) pp. 1161-1175.

Amin, S. (1974) 'Accumulation and development: A theoretical model'. *Review of African Political Economy*, 1(1) pp. 22-23.

Amin, S. (1977) *Imperialism and underdevelopment*. New York and London: Monthly Review Press.

Armijo, L. and Burges, S. (2010) 'Brazil, the entrepreneurial and democratic BRIC'. *Polity*, 42(1) pp. 14-37.

Atmore, A. and Marks, S. (1974) 'The imperial factor in South Africa in the nineteenth century: Towards a reassessment'. *The Journal of Imperial and Commonwealth History*, 3(1) pp. 105-139.

Bach, D. (2007) 'Nigeria's "manifest destiny" in West Africa: Dominance without power'. *Africa Spectrum*, 42(2) pp. 301-321.

Bandeira, L. (2006) 'Brazil as a regional power and its relations with the United States'. *Latin American Perspectives*, 33(3) pp. 12-27.

Berg, L., Evans, M., Fuller, D. and The Okanagan Urban Aboriginal Health Research Collective Canada (2007) 'Ethics, hegemonic whiteness, and the contested imagination of 'aboriginal community' in social science research in Canada'. *ACME: An international E-Journal for Critical Geographies*, 6(3) pp. 395-410. Available at: http://www.acme-journal.org/vol6/LDBetal.pdf Accessed on: 5 January 2008.

Bethell, L. (2010) 'Brazil as regional power in Latin America or South America'. *Policy Briefing 13*. Johannesburg: South African Institute for International Affairs.

157

Bienefeld, M. and Innes, D. (1976) 'Capital accumulation and South Africa'. *Review of African Political Economy*, 1(7) pp. 31-55.

Bohr, A. (2004) 'Regionalism in Central Asia: New geopolitics, old regional order'. *International Affairs (Royal Institute of International Affairs 1944-)*, 80(3) pp. 485-502.

Bond, P. (2004) 'US Empire and South African subimperialism' in Pantich, L. and Leys, C. (eds) *Socialist register 2005: The empire reloaded*. London/Merlin and New York: Monthly Review Press, pp. 125-144.

Bond, P. (2006a) *Looting Africa: The economies of exploitation*. London: Zeb Books.

Bond, P. (2006b) 'South African subimperial accumulation' in Bond, P., Chitonge, H. and Hopfmann, A. (eds) *The accumulation of capital in southern Africa*. Rosa Luxemburg Political Education Seminar, pp. 90-106.

Bond, P. (2013) Sub-imperialism as Lubricant of Neoliberalism: South African 'deputy sheriff' duty within BRICS. *Third World Quarterly*, 34(2) pp. 251-270.

Bracking, S. (2003) 'Regulating capital in accumulation: Negotiating the imperial "frontier"'. *Review of African Political Economy*, 30(95) pp. 11-32.

Breytenbach, W. (1997) 'South Africa and Egypt: The foreign policies of regional powers in search of African security'. *Africa Insight*, 27(4) pp. 274-278.

De Lima, M. and Hirst, M. (2006) 'Brazil as an intermediate state and regional power: Action, choice and responsibilities'. *International Affairs (Royal Institute of International Affairs 1944-)*, 82(1) pp. 21-40.

Dellios, R. (2003) 'China and India: New *mandalas* of power in 21st century geopolitics'. *Small and mid-great powers in southern hemisphere and their relationship with northern neighbours*. Conference Paper. University of Western Australia, Perth. 20-21 November 2000.

Destradi, S. (2010) 'Regional powers and their strategies: Empire, hegemony and leadership'. *Review of International Studies*, 36(4) pp. 903-930.

De Zengotita, T. (2003) 'The romance of empire and the politics of self-love'. *Harpers*. July.

Efstathopoulos, C. (2011) 'Reinterpreting India's rise through the middle power prism'. *Asian Journal of Political Science*, 19(1) pp. 74-95.

Emmers, R. (2005) 'Regional hegemonies and the exercise of power in Southeast Asia: A study of Indonesia and Vietnam'. *Asian Survey*, 45(4) pp. 645-665.

Erickson, E. (2004) 'Turkey as regional hegemon – 2014: Strategic implications for the United States'. *Turkish Studies*, 5(3) pp. 25-45.

Fanon, F. (1965) *A dying colonialism*. New York: Grove.

Flemes, D. (2007a) 'Conceptualising regional power in international relations: Lessons from the South African case'. GIGA Working Papers. Research Programme: Power, Violence and Security. 53.

Flemes, D. (2007b) '"Emerging middle powers" soft balancing strategy: State and perspectives of the IBSA Dialogue Forum'. GIGA Research Programme: Violence, Power and Security. 57.

Flemes, D. (2009) 'Regional power South Africa: Co-operative hegemony constrained by historical legacy'. *Journal of Contemporary African Studies*, 27(2) pp. 135-157.

Flint, C. and Taylor, P.J. (2007) *Political geography: World-economy, nation-state and locality*. Fifth edition. Harlow: Pearson/Prentice Hall.

Frank, A. G. (1979) 'Unequal accumulation: Intermediate, semi-peripheral, and sub-imperialist economies'. *Review* (Fernand Braudel Center), 2(3) pp. 281-350.

Galtung, J. (1971) 'A structural theory of imperialism'. *Journal of Peace Research*, 2(1) pp. 104-105.

Gilmartin, M. (2009) 'Colonialism/imperialism' in Gallagher, C., Dahlman, C., Gilmartin, M., Mountz, A. and Shirlow, P. (eds) *Key concepts in political geography*. Key Concepts in Human Geography Series. London: SAGE, pp. 115-123.

Glosny, M. (2010) China and the BRICs: A real (but limited) partnership in a unipolar world'. *Polity*, 42(1) pp. 100-129.

Gregory, D. (2004) *The colonial present*. Oxford: Blackwell.

Gupta, B. (2010) 'Waiting for India: India's role as a regional power'. *Journal of International Affairs*, 29(2) pp. 171-185.

Habib, A. (2003) 'Hegemon or pivot?: Debating South Africa's role in Africa'. *Public Debate*. Centre for Policy Studies, in conjunction with the Open Society Foundation of South Africa. August.

Hardt, M. and Negri, A. (2001) *Empire*. Cambridge, MA: Harvard University Press.

Harris, S. (2005) 'China's regional policies: How much hegemony?' *Australian Journal of International Affairs*, 59(4) pp. 481-492.

Harvey, D. (2005) *The new imperialism*. New York: Oxford University Press.

Hentz, J. (2005) 'South Africa and the political economy of regional cooperation in southern Africa'. *The Journal of Modern African Studies*, 43(1) pp. 21-51.

Hitler, A. (1942) *Mein kampf*. Boston: Houghton Mifflin.

Hudson, B. (1977) 'The new geography and the new imperialism: 1870-1918'. *Antipode*, 9(2) pp. 12-19.

Iyob, R. (1993) 'Regional hegemony: Domination and resistance in the horn of Africa'. *The Journal of Modern African Studies*, 31(2) pp. 257-276.

Jordaan, E. (2003) 'The concept of a middle power in international relations: Distinguishing between emerging and traditional middle powers'. *Politikon*, 30(1) pp. 165-181.

Kagwanja, P. (2009) 'An encumbered regional power? The capacity gap in South Africa's peace diplomacy in Africa' in Kondolo, K. (ed) Democracy and Governance Research Programme Occasional Paper. 6. pp. 1-36.

Kappel, R. (2010) 'On the economics of regional powers: Comparing China, India, Brazil, and South Africa'. GIGA Working Papers. Research Programme: Power, Norms and Governance in International Relations. 145.

Kokoshin, A. (2002) 'What is Russia? A superpower, a great power or a regional power?' *International Affairs: A Russian Journal of World Politics, Diplomacy and International Relations*, 48(6) pp. 100-125.

Kurečić, P. and Bandov, G. (2011) 'The contemporary role and perspectives of the BRIC states in the world-order'. *Electronic Journal of Political Science Studies*, 2(2) pp. 13-32.

Landsberg, C. (2004) 'South Africa: A pivotal state in Africa'. *Centre for Policy Studies Quarterly Governance Review*, 7(1) pp. 1-3.

Lesufi, I. (2004) 'South Africa and the rest of the continent: Towards a critique of the political economy of NEPAD'. *Current Sociology*, 52(5) pp. 809-829.

Lesufi, I. (2006) *Nepad and South African imperialism*. Johannesburg: Jubilee South Africa.

Mackinder, H. (1904) 'The geographical pivot of history'. *The Geographical Journal*, 23(4) pp. 421-437.

Mares, D. (1988) 'Middle Powers under regional hegemony: To challenge or acquiesce in hegemonic enforcement'. *International Studies Quarterly*, 32(1) pp. 453-471.

Marini, R. (1965) 'Brazilian "interdependence" and imperialist integration'. *Monthly Review*, 17(7) pp. 10-29.

Marini. R. (1972) 'Brazilian subimperialism'. *Monthly Review*, 23(9) pp. 14-24.

Martynov, B. (2011) 'BRICS: Dawn of a new era, or business as usual?' *Security Index: A Russian Journal on International Security*, 17(3) pp. 73-79.

Mercer, C. Mohan, G. and Power, M. (2003) 'Towards a critical political geography of African development'. *Geoforum*, 34 pp. 419–436.

Miller, D., Saunders, R. and Oloyede, O. (2008) 'South African corporations and post-apartheid expansion in Africa – Creating a new regional space'. *African Sociological Review*, 12(1) pp. 1-19.

Mohan, G. and Power, M. (2008) 'New African Choices? The Politics of Chinese Engagement'. *Review of African Political Economy*, 35(115) pp. 23-42.

Mohan, G. and Power, M. (2009) 'Africa, China and the 'new' economic geography of development'. *Singapore Journal of Tropical Geography*, 30 pp. 24-28.

Nabers, D. (2010) 'Power, leadership, and hegemony in international politics: The case of East Asia'. *Review of International Studies*, 36(4) pp. 931-949.

Nel, P. and Nolte, D. (2010) 'Introduction: Special section on regional powers in a changing global order'. *Review of International Studies*, 36(4) pp. 877-879.

Nolte, D. (2010) 'How to compare regional powers: Analytical concepts and research topics'. *Review of International Studies*, 36(4) pp. 881-901.

Ó Tuathail, G. (1996) *Critical geopolitics: The politics of writing global space*. Minneapolis: University of Minnesota Press.

Ó Tuathail, G. (2006) 'Introduction to part one' in Ó Tuathail, G., Dalby. S and Routledge, P. (eds) *The Geopolitics Reader*. Second edition. London: Routledge, pp. 17-32.

Ó Tuathail, G. and Agnew, J. (1992) 'Geopolitics and discourse: Practical geopolitical reasoning in American foreign policy'. *Political Geography Quarterly*, 11(2) pp. 151-166.

Ó Tuathail, G. and Dalby, S. (1998) *Rethinking geopolitics*. Routledge: London.

Pardesi, M. (2005) 'Deducing India's grand strategy for regional hegemony from historical and conceptual perspectives'. Institute of Defence and Strategic Studies. Singapore. 76.

Peters, E. J. (1997) 'Challenging the geographies of "Indianess": the Batchewana case'. *Urban Geography*, 18(1) pp. 56-62.

Peters, E. J. (1998) 'Subversive space: First nations women and the city in Canada'. *Environment and Planning D: Society and Space*, 16(6) pp. 665-686.

160

Pisani-Ferry, J. (2005) 'Can multilateralism survive the rise of the BRICs?'. Cercle des economists. Aix-en-Provence Economic Forum 2005. Introductory note for roundtable 7. 8-10 July.

Power, M. (2010) 'Geopolitics and "Development": An Introduction'. *Geopolitics*, 15(3) pp. 433-440.

Prys, M. (2009) 'Regional hegemon or regional bystander: South Africa's Zimbabwe policy 2000–2005'. *Politikon*, 36(2) pp. 193-218.

Prys, M. (2010) 'Hegemony, domination, detachment: Differences in regional powerhood'. *International Studies Review*, 12(4) pp. 479-504.

Renard, T. (2009) 'A BRIC in the world: Emerging powers, Europe, and the coming order'. Egmont Paper 31. The Royal Institute for International Relations. October.

Roberts, C. (2010) 'Challengers or stakeholders? BRICs and the liberal world order, introduction'. *Polity*, 42(1) pp. 1-13.

Roberts, C. (2011) 'Building the new world order BRIC by BRIC'. *European Financial Review*. February-March.

Roy, D. (1994) 'Hegemon on the horizon? China's threat to east Asian security'. *International Security*, 19(1) pp. 149-168.

Rubin, B. (2006) 'Iran: The rise of regional power'. *The Middle East Review of International Affairs*. September.

Said, E. (1978) *Orientalism*. New York: Vintage.

Sampson, M. (2009) '(Sub)imperial South Africa? Reframing the debate'. *Review of African Political Economy*, 1(119) pp. 93-113.

Schoeman, M. (2003), 'South Africa as an emerging middle power: 1994–2003' in Daniel, J., Habib, A. and Southall, R. (eds) *State of the Nation: South Africa, 2003–2004*. Cape Town: HSRC Press, pp. 349-367.

Scholvin, S. (2010) 'Emerging non-OECD countries: Global shifts in power and geopolitical regionalization'. *GIGA working papers*, No. 128.

Shambaugh, D. (2004) 'China engages Asia: Reshaping the regional order'. *International Security*, 29(3) pp. 64-99.

Shaw, T. (1978) 'Inequalities and interdependence in Africa and Latin America: Sub-imperialism and semi-industrialisation in the semi-periphery'. *Cultures et development*, 10(2) pp. 231-263.

Shaw, T. (1979) 'The semi-periphery in Africa and Latin America: Sub-imperialism and semi-industrialism'. *Review of Black Political Economy*, 9(4) pp. 341-358.

Shaw, T., Cooper. A and Antkiewicz, A. (2007) 'Global and/or regional development at the start of the 21st century? China, India and (South) Africa'. *Third World Quarterly*, 28(7) pp. 1255-1270.

Shaw, T., Cooper. A and Chin, G. (2009) 'Emerging powers and Africa: Implications for/from global governance?'. *Politikon*, 36(1) pp. 27-44.

Sidaway, J. (1992) 'In other worlds: On the politics of research by "first world" geographers in the "third world"'. *Area*, 24(4) pp. 403-408.

Sidaway, J. (2000) 'Postcolonial geographies: An exploratory essay'. *Progress in Human Geography*, 24(4) pp. 591-612.

Sidaway, J. (2012) 'Geographies of development: New maps, new visions?' *The Professional Geographer*, 64(1) pp. 49-62.

Sidaway, J. and Bryson, J. (2002) 'Constructing knowledges of "emerging markets": UK-based investment managers and their overseas connections'. *Environment and Planning A*, 34 pp. 401-416.

Sidaway, J. and Pryke, M. (2000) 'The strange geographies of 'emerging markets'. *Transactions of the Institute of British Geographers*, 25(2) pp. 187-201.

Sinha, A. and Dorschner, J. (2010) 'India: Rising power or a mere revolution of rising expectations?'. *Polity*, 42(1) pp. 74-99.

Slater, D. (2004) *Geopolitics and the post-colonial*. Oxford: Blackwell Publishing.

Souare, I. (2005) 'Is Nigeria a regional hegemon to be feared'. *African Renaissance*, 2(2) pp. 59-67.

Stewart-Ingersoll, R. and Frazier, D. (2010) 'India as a regional power: Identifying the impact of roles and foreign policy orientation on the south Asian security order'. *Asian Security*, 6(1) pp. 51-73.

Taylor, I. (2009) '"The South will rise again"? New alliances and global governance: The India–Brazil–South Africa dialogue forum'. *Politikon*, 36(1) pp. 45-58.

Taylor, I. (2011) 'South African "imperialism" in a region lacking regionalism: A critique'. *Third World Quarterly*, 32(7) pp. 1233-1253.

Taylor, P. J. (1985) *Political geography: World-economy, nation-state and locality*. London: Longman.

Van der Westhuizen, J. (1998) 'South Africa's emergence as a middle power'. *Third World Quarterly*, 19(3) pp. 435-455.

Väyrynen, R. and Herrera, L. (1975) 'Subimperialism: From dependence to subordination'. *Instant Research on Peace and Violence*, 5(3) pp. 165-177.

Wadhva, C. (2006) 'Management of rising power by China and India in the 21st century: Scope for strategic partnership'. *Vikalpa: Perspectives*, 31(3) pp. 1-12.

Wallerstein, I. (1987) 'World-systems analysis' in Giddens, A. and Turner. J. (eds) *Social theory today*. Stanford: Stanford University Press, pp. 309-324.

Warhurst, P. R. (1984) 'Smuts and Africa: A study in sub-imperialism'. *South African Historical Journal*, 16(1) pp. 82-100.

Yeros, P. and Moyo, S. (2011) 'Rethinking the theory of primitive accumulation'. Paper presented to the 2nd IIPPE conference, 20-22 May, Istanbul.

Sehlare Makgetlaneng, PhD[1]
Africa Institute of South Africa
Pretoria, South Africa

THE THEORETICAL MARGINALISATION OF SOUTH AFRICA'S MEMBERSHIP TO BRICS BY SOME SOUTH AFRICAN SCHOLARS: KEY ISSUES

Abstract

This chapter provides a critical analysis of the theoretical marginalisation of South Africa's membership to BRICS by some South African scholars. It also provides key reasons behind this theoretical marginalisation of its membership to BRICS. These reasons are political, economic and ideological issues which are useful in understanding why some South African scholars theoretically marginalise their country's membership to BRICS and key reasons behind their task.

South Africa's place within regional, continental and global affairs

The starting point in the contribution towards the concrete understanding that some South African scholars theoretically marginalise South Africa's membership to BRICS and key reasons behind their task is the provision of its place in Southern Africa, Africa and globally beyond the African continent. South Africa is a Southern African regional power and the African continental power consolidating its regional and continental status and striving to be an international power, a major force within the Group of 20 countries and BRICS and an important actor within the United Nations as a permanent member of its Security Council. The success of this programme of action is through the creation, maintenance and sustenance of a more conducive regional, continental and global environment for the effective advancement of its regional, continental and global interests. South Africa's regional, continental and global status characterised by its position in a hierarchy of political, economic, financial, trade, human resources development, technological and military international power relations that extends from the United States of America at the centre of capitalism to the African continent at the periphery of capitalism is such that its membership to BRICS was inevitable.

The theoretical marginalisation of South Africa's membership
to BRICS by some South African scholars: Key issues

Mills Soko and Mzukisi Qobo in their 2013 article represent a clear theoretical marginalisation of South Africa's membership to BRICS. They regard South Arica's acceptance of the invitation to be its member as the task of creating more walls than bricks in the advancement of its strategic interests on the global scale. They regard the organisation as "the amorphous entity" and South Africa's invitation to join it and its acceptance as "an affront to the country's foreign policy."[2] Why should Africans of South Africa have a problem with South Africa being a member of BRICS and hide their problem with the language they used in their work? This language is obvious in their statement: "The specter of South Africa rejoicing being invited to join an amorphous entity such as the BRICS is plainly degrading and it is an affront to our national pride." They are opposed not only to South Africa being invited to be a member of BRICS, but also to the very existence of the organisation itself. They maintain, that "the notion of BRIC as an analytical category is problematic and has outlived its usefulness." They register their confusion which they regard as misunderstanding by those they think do not understand Russia's role in international relations and cooperation when they state: "How, for example, does one justify the inclusion of the failing Russian state in the group?" The reality, that Russia is one of the key actors in international relations and cooperation, which has continued successfully frustrating the efforts of the Western imperialist powers in their agenda against the interests of developing countries, particularly within the United Nations Security Council, is not regarded as of strategic importance in the restructuring and transformation of the multilateral institutions, controlled by these powers. The position that the Russian state is "the failing" formation is not supported by role as a dominant actor in global affairs. Its role in global affairs rejects this position. Russia has been successful in its opposition against the regime change agenda of the West. It has successfully proposed a workable alternative to sanctions against Iran. This proposed solution is best reflected in a plan used in dealing with the Iranian nuclear programme. Thanks to Russia's leadership on this issue, the United States is making some serious efforts to normalise its relations with Iran. Russia has successfully opposed any United Nations Security Council resolution aiming at authorising and legitimising the Western military intervention in Syria. It has been successful as the permanent member of the United Nations Security Council in defending the global system of checks and balances which is critical to international peace and security.

Mills and Qobo regard South Africa's acceptance to be a member of BRICS as a crisis of identity in its foreign policy. Whose political practice is served by their theoretical position as South Africa confronts the present situation internally and externally in the advancement of its long-term strategic interests in regionally in Southern Africa, continentally in Africa and globally beyond the continent? Why should those responsible for formulation and implementation of South Africa's foreign policy be an integral part of what is "an affront" to the very same policy raises the fundamental question as to what Mills and Qobo are up to and whose interests are they defending? Central to their argument is the position that they understand what is best for South Africa than its policy-makers and diplomats. The advocacy and articulation of theoretical positions on key issues and the call for the abandonment of a particular programme of action are tasks specified by political practice as the present internal and external situation is confronted. Theory as the issue emerging out of practice and in turn serving practice is "always for someone and for some purpose."[3]

Contrary to the position of Soko and Qobo, South Africa's engagement with its BRICS partners will continue being informed by its national demands, needs and interests foreign policy being first and foremost a reflection and an extension of a domestic policy. South Africa's domestic policy, like that of other countries, is a mirror of the socio-political and economic structures underlying the relationship between different and antagonistic social forces constituted by its socio-economic fabric. Foreign policy as a process fundamentally and structurally shaped by national politics and internal interests serves particular internal interests over other internal interests. South Africa's foreign policy and its strategic interests externally predate the formation of BRIC and BRICS. They are more important than BRICS. Their advancement does not and will not depend on BRICS. BRICS provides South Africa with means and opportunities in the advancement of its interests globally.

South Africa, as a member of BRICS, will continue championing multilateral efforts to resolve global problems, providing practical progressive ideas on key global governance and democracy issues, demonstrating its leadership in conflict resolution, peace and security, reconstruction and development in deserving parts of Africa particularly as a donor country. Its membership to BRICS is a substantial and welcome addition to its weapons in its contribution towards the transformation of global socio-political and economic environment including the North-South relations. One of the fundamental and frightening weaknesses of their work is that it is largely economistic informed by narrow imperatives of trade and investment relations. Political economy is helpful in providing analysis and contributing towards a concrete understanding of the issue they are discussing in their work. Contrary to their position and their view of BRIC as if it is a static, not dynamic organisation, the fact that South Africa is a member of BRICS is the

forward movement towards a coherent alliance characterised by strong negotiating positions within multilateral institutions and forums.

Gerrit Olivier and Maxi Schoeman provide analysis of South Africa's
BRICS membership, which views South Africa as a field of action acted
upon by its BRICS partners. South Africa, in this perspective, is not an actor
advancing its strategic and tactical interests internally within itself and externally outside itself. Using their discussion with Russian diplomats and academics during their visit to Moscow in 2011 in hiding their position, they
maintain that it "became clear" that as "an early sponsor" of South Africa's
BRICS membership, "Russia expects South Africa to tow the BRICS foreign
policy line on crucial issues which means that the stronger partners will determine the diplomatic agenda."[4] They continue pointing out that what their
Russian "interlocutors particularly question is South Africa's lack of a clear
perception of its role as a new BRICS member, doubting whether the country
is a reliable partner in this powerful configuration". There is nowhere in their
work they propose a programme of action South Africa should embark upon
as a member of BRICS which will either satisfy or not satisfy its BRICS
partners. There is nowhere in their work where they explain what they have
told their "interlocutors". Did they agree or disagree with them on their position on South Africa as BRICS member? Did they agree or disagree with
them when they told them that they doubt whether South Africa is a reliable
BRICS partner? Do they agree or disagree with the position that South Africa will remain independent in its formulation and implementation of its foreign policy even within the United Nations, and that it will not be dictated to
on this issue by its BRICS partners?

In a typical South African eurocentric perspective which views South
Africa as a servant of the interests of "powerful" or "dominant" countries – a
servant advancing their causes and following their leadership and agenda,
Olivier and Schoeman appoint themselves as representatives of Russia and
China in their view of South Africa. In their words: As the weakest member,
but carrying symbolic importance as an African state, South Africa is regarded by Russia and China in particular as a pivotal diplomatic partner for
advancing their causes and following their leadership and agenda.[5]

Their manufactured position of Russia and China on South Africa regards South Africa as their "pawn" or tool in advancing their strategic and
tactical interests. They use this position in justifying their intention to serve
as South Africa's advisers on BRICS. Maintaining this manufactured position, the way is paved for them to belittle and ridicule South Africa and tell it
what it should do and should not do in their work. This theoretical exercise
articulated as follows: It is unclear whether the rest of the BRICS members,
particularly Russia, see South Africa as a pawn in their tactical game to challenge the western dominance of the global agenda. For South Africa, this

implies a clear choice, a specific mode of identification and alignment in world politics. In other words, South Africa must choose either collective foreign policy making, particularly where BRICS and western interests are at odds, or take an independent stance.[6]

South Africa under the leadership of the African National Congress (ANC) has been articulating its "challenge" to "the western dominance of the global agenda" since 1994. The ANC has been articulating its challenge or opposition to imperialism and programmes embarked upon by imperialist countries particularly in supporting oppressive regimes throughout the world many years before 1994.

Olivier and Schoeman maintain that the issue of South Africa being an integral part of "a deliberate effort to change the prevailing global power–political paradigm and pecking order, to affect the nature of global competition, wrestling control from the West to determine, orchestrate and run the global agenda in a way that would advance the interests of emerging states (as defined by BRICS) on key issues" should not pose problems for it. The reason, why at "first sight" this ""western-sceptic" foreign policy posture should not pose problems for post-apartheid South Africa", is because: Since 1994, a new South African identity, and with it a new global alignment, emerged, reflecting South Africa's new international personality and role perception: particularly its essential Afrocentric character and purpose; its role and destiny as a leading nation in Africa; a primary role-player in South-South, nonaligned and multilateral diplomacy. This posture also signaled a refusal to kowtow to western political and cultural hegemony and a resolve to join the developing world to resist and reduce this hegemony by way of trying to reset the global agenda, and promoting structural and policy changes in global politics.[7]

The key issue for Olivier and Schoeman is the question as to "whether South Africa has the capacity and determination to follow this foreign policy" posture "through to its logical consequences."[8]

South Africa's "identity" and "global alignment" have earned it a severe criticism from a considerable number of South Africans. The reason why is because, as Olivier and Schoeman maintain, since "1994, South Africa has indeed moved away from the West." This movement is viewed by some South African critics of its foreign policy as a process not only being closer to the rest of Africa and the South, but also being a servant of Russia and China "advancing" their "causes" and "following their leadership and their agenda." In other words, South Africa is not its own. It is an extension of Russia and China. There is essentially the same position which is not directly stated that Africans are not their own and that they are extensions of other people particularly Europeans. Currently, as a result of the increased expansion of China and India into Africa, the position is that if they are not careful,

Africans run a danger of becoming extensions of Asians. African countries as colonies were regarded by the Western powers and their organic intellectuals as their extensions. They had no interests of their own to advance. As their achievement of political independence did not end their economic, financial, trade and technological domination, this view has continued in their post-colonial era.

Olivier is bitter that the post-apartheid South Africa is not an ally of the Western powers. He articulates his bitterness as follows: A contrived anti-western skepticism, special relations with antidemocractic governments and human-rights violators, the idealisation of China and the "global South" and a questionable theory of imminent western decline characterise South Africa's external identification. South Africa's voting pattern in the United nations Security Council, its stance on international issues, its uneasy relationship with the European Union and the bias against "Eurocentrism" form a consistent pattern hampering good business.[9]

He hides and camouflages his bitterness through a provision of his patronising advice that this does not mean South Africa "should embrace the West or retreat from its efforts to redress the iniquities in the existing global financial and political order and from maximizing its African agenda" and that "rejection of the West on ideological premises cannot be a wise policy and is definitely not in the national interests."[10] Has the South African state ever rejected the West? Has any serious person or organisation rejected imperialism and the policies of the Western imperialist powers only on the "ideological premises?"

Foreign policy of the Western powers towards Africa combines the importance of maintaining, defending and expanding their strategic interests with fear either to lose them to China, for them to be fundamentally affected as a result of structural changes in African countries or for them to decrease and articulate their importance to themselves by using concerns about Africa's security and development which camouflage or hide issues of greed and pity. As China increases its intensified expansion into Africa, they maintain that it poses a threat to the continent's security and development. Africans cannot be themselves in deciding who are their allies, friends and enemies and in advancing their interests through partnership not only with China, but also with Brazil, Russia and India.

Olivier has continued raising issues, which constitute the theoretical marginalisation of South Africa's membership to BRICS. He maintains critics, whose names he does provide "suggest" that given its "small size" and its "inferior global status in relation to other members" of BRICS, South Africa does not qualify to be its member and that countries, such as "South Korea, Indonesia, Mexico, Turkey and possibly Nigeria, are better qualified for membership of the power club",[11] than South Africa. This raises the question: what is the position of these countries on issues which constitute objectives of BRICS and which unite its members. These countries have not been vocal on these issues. It is not clear as to what is their position on these issues? Why are they more or better "qualified for membership" to BRICS than South Africa? Why they were not invited to be its members? Why have they not expressed an interest in becoming its members? He hides the settler colonial nature of the apartheid South Africa and distorts its reality as an African social formation by maintaining that it has replaced its "European/Western identity with an African identity" and that this became "the ruling ANC coalition's priority."[12] What he regards as South Africa's "European/Western identity", which he argues was replaced with "an African identity", is basically the settler colonial and racist rule and its nature in the country. This was one of the key issues, the ANC was struggling to end. It does not make sense theoretically for a scholar to maintain that the priority of the ruling party of an African country became that of the replacing "European/Western identity with an African identity." One as a scholar can maintain this position, provided one has a problem with the position that a country has been an African country not "European/Western" formation. The notion of South Africa's "essential Afro-centric character and purpose"[13] is an issue camouflaging and hiding key issues some South African scholars do not want to raise in public. Any African country particularly in the sub-Saharan Africa is a social formation of African-centric character and purpose in its internal and external relations. He repeats this position in his work dealing with South Africa's policy towards the North when he maintains that its "new" foreign policy, which "first and foremost, reflected its African personality; its essential Afrocentric character and purpose." Its "intellectual, ideological and strategic foundations" were laid by Thabo Mbeki[14] under whose "watch, replacing South Africa's European identity with an African identity became an ANC and government priority."[15]

Olivier maintains that benefit, which South Africa could obtain from its membership to BRICS, would not be significant: if it fails to get wider African support and allows itself to be manipulated into becoming a malleable tool or captive ally of Chinese and Russian political power play, it is bound to perform a secondary satellite function in the BRICS configuration, losing credibility, not being taken seriously as a role player and generally sacrificing its foreign policy thrust and independence in global policy.[16]

Central to this position, which is articulated in the form of advice and proposal, is the thesis that South Africa as a member of BRICS is used by China and Russia for their strategic and tactical interests particularly in Africa. In other words, South Africa is their tool and extension. It has no movement of its own within BRICS. This is an integral part of the thesis that Africa has no movement of its own in the world and it is an extension of other countries. The possibility, that South Africa can use China and Russia as well as India and Brazil for its own strategic and tactical interests and those of Africa, does not arise in this fallacious and degrading perspective. The point is that South Africa, as Olivier maintains, compared to its BRICS partners is "a minnow."[17]

Olivier appoints himself as a representative of Africa on South Africa's role in African affairs when he maintains that South Africa, firstly, did not lobby the continent for its support to be a member of BRICS. Secondly, it "simply" assumed that Africa accept its membership. Thirdly, it "vaingloriously preferred to go it solo, claiming the honour to itself."[18] He concludes, that had African countries particularly the African Union and "several" regional economic communities been concluded and lobbied, before South Africa became a member of BRICS for them to make "a joint effort" under its "leadership, more substance and legitimacy would no doubt have accrued to its membership" and that this "display of assertive unilateralism runs counter to traditional African multi-lateral diplomacy."[19] This conclusion raises the question as to why Brazil, India and China did not do what Olivier is saying in the case of regional orgranisations, of which they are members, and countries, which are their members, before they became members of BRICS. Are there African leaders who agree with Olivier on this position? Should South Africa have acted in line with Olivier's proposal before it became a member of the regional, continental and global organisations and institutions?

There are other key issues behind the theoretical marginalisation of South Africa's membership to BRICS. There is a considerable number of South Africans who identify themselves racially, historically and in terms of interests with the West. They see not only their interests and future, but also those of the country lying with the West. Any serious policy measure by South Africa to crucially identify itself with and work together with countries opposed to the Western dominance of the global system and its multilateral institutions is viewed as the threat posed to their interests and future and that of the country. According to them, South Africa's international relations and cooperation and foreign policy should be supportive of those of the Western powers for them to be acceptable and be viewed as credible and legitimate. This is the case particularly given the fact that South Africa is viewed as central to the continued Western dominance in the region and the continent. Some of these South Africans never supported the national liberation movement. They either supported or served the apartheid regime. This can best be understood, if one comes to grips with the reality, that the apartheid South Africa was "a part of the West in the post-Second World War period, attractive as an economic partner, a place to invest in, trade in and emigrate to, despite the opprobrium, in which its system of race discrimination was avowedly held by all concerned", and that it "derived its ability to assert its inter-

170

est in the world from the very fact of its dependence on the West, a relationship which it accepted wholeheartedly and even sought to augment."[20]

Sam C. Nolutshungu provided some of the features chracteristing relations between the apartheid South Africa and the West as some of the issues the post-apartheid South Africa was going to experience. According to him: all of South Africa's success in the field of foreign policy owed a great deal to the fact that it was a white state, that was being defended for which, independently of ideology or any precise calculation of economic advantages, publics in the dominant countries had a great deal of sympathy. A government of dark skinned people is not likely to attract either as much investor confidence or popular sympathy in the West where, despite the anti-apartheid campaigns, the silent majorities remained deeply sympathetic to white South Africa. Indeed, all the negative presumptions with which the emergence of black governments has been met elsewhere will be applied here, also.[21]

The fact that Nolutshungu did point out that the post-apartheid state will not enjoy "a popular sympathy" from some South Africans does not mean that he was not aware of this reality.

The very reality that South Africa is an African country is opposed to and disputed by some South African scholars. Greg Mills is one of those representing these South African scholars when he maintains that South Africa bears "the African burden" because of its "geographic location and perception as part of Africa."[22] This position views the interests and future of South Africa lying with the West not with Africa and the rest of the South. It dismisses the strategic importance of the rest of Africa to South Africa. It is against South Africa's working with other countries of Africa and the rest of the South particularly as the tactical means to liberate itself from the Western dominance and to contribute towards the restructuring and transformation of the global system and its institutions. Terence Corrigan articulates his opposition to the reality that South Africa is an African country in his review essay of four books.[23] For him, South Africa is "African, European and Asian" country.[24] This unbecoming position is based on another incorrect position that "its identity" should not be "defined through the lens of a particular cultural nationalism" and that to do so will be to include only that of "the African majority" and exclude that of its "minorities."[25]

Attempting to justify the position that South Africa is not an African country and provide its evidence, he maintains that: South Africa needs to lay its race problems to rest. This is a sensitive issue and needs to be dealt with carefully. Striving a sense of common citizenship is the task of all. Looking back, [Thabo] Mbeki's stress on defining South Africa as an African country may have been a serious mistake, whatever applause he received at the time. [RW] Johnson reminds the reader of Albert Camus, critic of co-

171

lonialism, but also of Algeria's liberation movement which saw that country's future in terms of purely of Muslim or Arab culture. This betrayed Algeria's history as a cultural crossroads. South Africa is likewise a country sewn up from different experiences: African, European and Asian, with considerable variety within each. To demand that its identity be defined through the lens of a particular cultural nationalism is to repeat the mistakes of South Africa's own history. Just as, Johnson cautions, the country could not succeed by excluding the African majority, so it cannot succeed by excluding the country's minorities.[26]

One of the key features characterizing the theoretical marginalisation of South Africa's membership to BRICS is the economistic view of the organisation. The economistic view of BRICS is in favour of the narrow profit interests of the South African private companies and being for the status quo in South Africa, Southern Africa and Africa. According to this view, South Africa's contribution towards the achievement of regional and continental integration and development and progress is primarily economic and trade not political process. It is basically against equitable integration and development and progress. Thus, the way the country's African agenda is viewed is largely economistic informed by narrow imperatives of trade relations of the South African private companies. This position is supportive of the dominant fraction of the South African private capital in its economic and trade relations with other African countries. Criticising this perspective, Nolutshungu pointed out that: Foreign policy would be ill-served by an insistence that obedience to the dictates of the world economy, or the need for national unity, cast a veil of silence over the problems that concern the people the most, and in which, after all, the rest of the world has its share of responsibility.[27]

Conclusion and Recommendations

Given the theoretical marginalisation of South Africa's membership to BRICS, it is important to defeat this task by raising some pertinent questions. How will South Africa as BRICS member affect its citizens? Which members of the South African society will benefit more and which will benefit less from its membership of BRICS? Are there members of its society who will not benefit from its membership? How will it benefit the South African capital and labour? Whose interests will be more served by South Africa playing increased role within BRICS and within the multilateral institutions as a result of it being BRICS member? Will South Africa's BRICS membership be in line with or against the interests of advanced capitalist countries or African countries, the International Monetary Fund, the World Bank, the World Trade Organisation, the North Atlantic Treaty Organisation or those of the Southern African Development Community, other African regional economic communities and the African Union?

If some of South African scholars, who theoretically marginalise South Africa's membership to BRICS, are in practice for South Africa's right to its national self-determination and the free, independent exercise of its sovereignty and foreign policy and if they are for the popular African continental change and development and progress, why do they articulate fears of those, who are self-appointed world gendarmes with self-appointed world mission, who in practice do not respect the right of African countries to their national self-determination and the free, independent exercise of their sovereignty and foreign policy? Why do they worry about those who "have lost all sense of the noble idea of human solidarity?" Those who what 'seems to predominate' in their relations with African countries and the South in general is "the question" raised, "in its narrowest and most naked meaning – what is in it for me! – and all this with absolutely no apology and sense of shame?"[28].

The primacy of politics over economics in internal and external relations and the fact that BRICS is primarily a political formation not economic and trade formation are against the theoretical marginalisation of South Africa on the basis that it is small particularly in terms of its economy and population. To the extent that the objectives of BRICS are primarily political and that obstacles to the restructuring and transformation of the global governance and its multilateral institutions is political successfully challenge the obsession with economic and trade factors in the analysis of South Africa's membership to BRICS.

The deployment of economic and trade issues by South African scholars in their theoretical marginalisation of South Africa's members were rejected in advance many years back before they wrote their works by Nolutshungu. He criticised this task in calling upon South Africa to determine and control its limitations and programmes of action in international relations and cooperation and foreign policy. To achieve this objective, it is essential to recognise that: Whatever may be the constraints imposed by the international system and by the internal economic weakness and social problems of the state, foreign policy can only be based on the assumption of choice and initiative: there are alternatives. It is very effective when it is rooted in clearly perceived needs and backed by a broad consensus on domestic politics. Effectiveness and power are based not on the attributes of military strength or even economic power, as on strategic efficacy and purposefulness.[29]

This strategic perspective is a key to a successful foreign policy. Moeletsi Mbeki is short to the point on this issue. According to him: "A country's foreign policy is credible and therefore has a greater chance of achieving its goals if it addresses important concerns of its domestic constituencies, not because of what foreigners, friends or foes, think of it or want it to be."[30]

[1] Dr. Sehlare Makgetlaneng is a Chief Research Specialist and Governance and Security Programme leader at the Africa Institute of South Africa, Human Sciences Research Council in Pretoria, South Africa.

[2] Mills Soko and Mzukisi Qobo, "Creating more walls than BRICs", Mail & Guardian (Johannesburg), 7 to 13 January 2011, p. 25.

[3] Robert W. Cox, "Social forces, state and world order: Beyond international relations theory," in Robert O. Keohane (editor), Neorealism and its Critics, New York: Columbia University Press, 1986, p. 207.

[4] Gerrit Olivier and Maxi Schoeman, "South Africa needs diplomatic finesse to make its mark in BRICS", Business Day (Johannesburg), 12 July 2011, p. 9.

[5] Ibid.

[6] Ibid.

[7] Ibid.

[8] Ibid.

[9] Gerrit Olivier, "South Africa is not the 'influential global player' it thinks it is," Business Day (Johannesburg), 12 June 2013, p. 11.

[10] Ibid.

[11] Gerrit Olivier, "South Africa in BRICS: Substance or Piggybacking?" in Francis A. Kornegay and Narnia Bohler-Muller (editors), Laying the BRICS of a New Global Order: From Yekaterinburg 2009 to eThekwini 2013, Pretoria: Africa Institute of South Africa, 2013, p. 400.

[12] Ibid., p. 401.

[13] Ibid.

[14] Gerrit Olivier, "South Africa's foreign policy towards the global North," in Chris Landsberg and Jo-Ansie van Wyk (editors), South African Foreign Policy Review, Vol. 1, Pretoria: Africa Institute of South Africa, 2012, p. 176.

[15] Ibid., p. 178.

[16] Olivier, "South Africa in BRICS: Substance or Piggybacking?" in Kornegay and (editors), Laying the BRICS of a New Global Order: From Yekaterinburg 2009 to Ethekwini 2013, p. 405.

[17] Ibid., p. 407.

[18] Ibid.

[19] Ibid.

[20] Sam C. Nolutshungu, "South Africa's Position in World Politics," in South Africa: The Challenge of Change, Vincent Maphai, (editor), Harare: SAPES Books, 1994, p. 128 and p. 132.

[21] Sam C. Nolutshungu, "South Africa's Position in the World," Southern African Political & Economic Monthly, Vol. 6, No. 6, 1993, p. 48.

[22] Greg Mills, "Waiting for the Fig Leaf to Drop," in Greg Mills, Alan. Berg and Anthoni van Nieuwkerk (editors), South African in the Global Economy, Johannesburg: South African Institute of International Affairs, 1995, p. 11.

[23] These three books are RW Johnson, South Africa's brave new world: The beloved country since the end of apartheid, London: Allan Lane, 2009, Brian Pottinger, The Mbeki Legacy, Cape Town: Zebra, 2008, Alec Russell, After Mandela: The battle for the soul of South Africa, London: Hutchinson, 2009, and Moeletsi Mbeki, Architects of poverty; why African capitalism needs changing, Johannesburg: Picador Africa, 2009.

[24] Terence Corrigan, South Africa's strange case of modernity: Book Review Essay," South African Journal of International Affairs, Vol. 16, No. 3, December 2009, p. 395.

[25] Ibid.

[26] Ibid.

[27] Sam C. Nolutshungu, "Foreign Policy and Domestic Politics after Apartheid, South Africa and the World," Johannesburg: South African Institute of International Affairs, 1992), pp. 47-48.

[28] Speech of the President of South Africa, Thabo Mbeki, at the Launch of the African Renaissance Institute, Pretoria, 11 October 1999.

[29] Sam C. Nolutshungu, "South Africa's Position on the World", Southern African Political & Political Monthly, Vol. 6, No. 6, 1993, p. 48.

[30] Moeletsi Mbeki, "Towards a More Productive South African Foreign Policy", in Elizabeth Sidiropoulos (editor), South African Yearbook of International Affairs 2002/03, Johannesburg: South African Institute of International Affairs, 2003, p. 54.

IV. CHINA IN AFRICA: STRENGTHENING THE PARTNERSHIP

Tatiana Deych, Dr.Sc.
Institute for African Studies
Russian Academy of Sciences

CHINA'S ROLE IN AFRICA IN THE 21st CENTURY

China has a long involvement with African countries, going back to the early days of the independence movement. At that time, its intentions were primarily political. The main goal was to counter recognition of Taiwan as the representative of China. The important goal was to compete with Western influence, and during the Chinese-Soviet conflict – with the USSR. Now the level and intentions of China's involvement have changed. The new Millennium sees sharp intensification of China's activity in Africa. Chinese economy's demands for raw materials, primarily oil, continue to grow, prompting Beijing to engage in fierce competition with other global actors. Now China, the second economy in the world, is viewing Africa as a place to exploit its resources and to gain access to the vast African market.

But what has changed in XXI century is not only China's growing need in African resources, but its emergence as a significant world player on African scene. Africa has taken a central place in China's strategy of building a 'Southern block' of states as a mechanism meets the challenges of globalization.

Today China has diplomatic relations with the most African countries – 50 out of 54. Only four African states – Gambia, Burkina Faso, Swaziland and San-Tome – have diplomatic relations with Taipei. In 2012, the new African state – the Republic of South Sudan – has made a choice in use of China, by establishing official relations with Beijing. The evidences of China's deep interest in Africa are frequent visits of the Chinese leaders' to the African continent. Coming to power, the new Chinese president Xi Jinping in March 2013 paid visits to South Africa, the Republic of Congo and Tanzania. A year after in May 2014 Chinese premier Li Keqiang with 129-members delegation visited Ethiopia, Nigeria, Angola and Kenya. Li delivered a speech in new convention centre of the African Union, met with the current chairperson of the AU, Mohamed Ould Abdel Aziz, and took part in

176

the World Economic Forum on Africa in Abuja (Nigeria)[1]. It became a tradition for Chinese foreign ministers to begin the every new year with a tour to African countries.

'Soft power' is long and reliable means of Chinese African policy. In struggle for Africa, China always used multiple 'soft power' tools. Diplomatic support and cultural ties, loans and credit lines, development aid and investment help China to win favor with African governments. The more impressive Chinese tool is Forum on China-Africa Cooperation (FOCAC) – a consultative and dialogue mechanism launched by China in 2000. On FOCAC summits and ministerial conferences, the new initiatives of the Chinese government and the new aid programs announced. On the Fifth Ministerial Conference of the FOCAC in July 2012 Beijing Action Plan for 2013-2015 was adopted. In his address to this Conference, UN Secretary-General Ban Ki-moon called Forum as a successful example of South-South cooperation[2]

The African continent has become an important oil source for rapidly growing China's economy. In 2012, China was the second oil importer in the world after the USA. In September 2013, it imported more oil than USA and became as a result of the month the main oil importer[3]. The International Energy Agency projects that in 2035 its net oil imports will jump to 13.1 million barrels per day (b/d)[4].

At the end of 2011African oil reserves estimated as 17.6bn tons, or 132.4bn barrels (8 percent of the world reserves)[5]. More than 60% of this oil came to three countries: Nigeria, Angola and Algeria[6]. In 2012 China imported 64.7 million metric tons of crude oil from Africa, accounting for 24% of the country's total crude imports, according to official figures[7]. China was the second importer of African oil after the USA. In 2010 USA imported 2 million b/d of African oil, but in the first four months of 2014 American import of African oil declined to 170000 b/d. At the same time, China imported at this period 1.2 mln b/d of oil from the African continent. Therefore, China took the place of the main importer of African oil[8].

China's biggest oil suppliers in Africa are Angola, Sudan and South Sudan, the Republic of Congo, Equatorial Guinea. It has also sought supplies from Nigeria, Algeria, Chad and Gabon. In 2006 Angola has become the biggest oil supplier to China (18, 2%), temporarily outgoing Saudi Arabia (16, 2%). Now Angola is the second oil supplier to China after Saudi Arabia with crude deliveries of 10, 66 million tons in the first quarter of 2014.

The important oil supplier to China is Sudan. China National Petroleum Corporation (CNPC) has been producing oil and natural gas in this country since 1996 and invested $5bn in the country. CNPC, the largest investor in Sudan, is the largest stakeholder (40 percent controlling stake) in Sudan's main oil producing consortium – the Greater Nile Petroleum Operating

Company. CNPC now dominates oil exploration in both Sudan and the new state of South Sudan. The two states host CNPC's largest foreign operations that produce 250.000 b/d and form lion' share of revenue for South Sudan. CNPC and China National Offshore Oil Corporation (CNOOC) are very active in Nigeria, the largest oil producer in Africa.

China is also the world largest consumer of copper and imports a substantial part of its needs from Africa. It depends increasingly on African ferrochrome, platinum, cobalt, iron, gold, silver and timber. China is engaged in copper mining in Zambia, cobalt and copper extracting in the Democratic Republic of the Congo, manganese and gold in Côte d'Ivoire. After the years of France dominance in the field of uranium mining in Niger, Chinese companies invaded a country.

Today, China is Africa's largest trading partner. China' trade with African countries increased from $11bn in 2000 to $106.8bn in 2008, $91bn in 2009 (the crisis year), $126.9 bn in 2010, $166.3bn in 2011, $198.49 bn in 2012[9] and to $210.2 bn in 2013[10]. Standard Bank has projected that China-Africa trade volume may reach $280 bn in 2015[11]. As Jeremy Stevens, Standard Bank Group Beijing-based economist says, African markets matter more to China than ever before. China's exports to Africa have grown at a pace five percentage points faster than in any other region in 2012, while China's import from Africa have increased by 26%, which is twice the speed of China's imports from any other region. Africa's export to China is growing faster than import from China. China's trade deficit reached $24.6 bn in 2013[12]. Today China accounts for 20% of Africa's trade. Africa is China's fastest-growing export destination and trade partner"[13]. While China maintains broad trade relations with 50 African countries, the bulk of trade between China and Africa is concentrated in a few countries. Angola, South Africa, Sudan, and the Republic of Congo – all export raw materials to China, and make up 70 percent of African exports to China.

The first China-Africa trade expo – "The Africa-China Commodities, Technology and Services Exposition" took place in December 2013 in Addis Ababa, Ethiopia. This expo demonstrated growing demand for Chinese business in Africa. More than 150 companies from across China participated in the event, including major Chinese firms such as Huawei, Sinosteel Corporation and others[14].

China's investment in manufacturing intended to take advantage of the African Growth and Opportunity Act (AGOA). The third-country fabric provision, which expired on 30 September 2012, extended until 30 September 2015. This provision allows 27 of 41 African countries South of Sahara eligible for AGOA to source raw materials from the third countries for making clothing that exported duty free to the U.S. market. These countries could therefore source clothing inputs from China and can be competitive in the

178

U.S. market[15]. Ethiopian president Mulatu Teshome said, that Chinese companies can set up in Ethiopia, sell to the US and European Union and avoid the import duties they would face if they were based in their own country. "Once they are fully integrated into Ethiopian economy, what they make won't be called a Chinese product but Ethiopian"[16].

Beijing already became the important donor and investor in Africa. China provides aid to almost all African countries, although its financing activities are concentrated in resource-rich countries. China's foreign aid financing takes the form of grants, interest free loans and concession loans. The concession loans are China's main instrument of support. From 2010 to May 2012 China approved concession loans worth a total $11.3bn for 92 African projects. This includes preferential export buyer's credits and foreign aid concession loans. It is in fulfillment of the FOCAC-2009 pledge of $10bn over three years. In 2012 China declared the $20 billion credit to African countries for developing infrastructure and the African Talent Programme, which intended to train 30,000 Africans in various sectors[17].

China widely uses in Africa so-called 'Angola method', which includes a basic term: Chinese loans accompany by requirements that a high percentage of contracts goes to Chinese companies. Firstly, this method has been used in Angola. In 2004 Chinese loan to Angola 70 percent of contracts were reserved for Chinese firms. In 2010, at least 50 Chinese contractors were in Angola and the Angolan government admitted in 2011 that more than 258.000 work visas issued to people from China[18]. Now the 'Angola method' can considered a most typical case study in Chinese policy in Africa.

China's state-owned Export-Import Bank of China (Exim-Bank) has become the world's largest export credit agency with significant and expanding operations in Africa". In March 2013, China Morning Post Newspaper reported that the state-owned China Development Bank had overtaken the World Bank and Asian Development Bank as the world largest financial institution for overseas loans. Ethiopian president Mulatu Teshome highly appreciates the participation of Chinese Exim-Bank and China Development Bank in building African infrastructure. "These institutes are playing a very significant role in Africa's economic development,"– he said[19].

The China Development Bank oversees government equity support for Chinese corporations in their commercial activities in Africa, as a major part of China's economic cooperation[20]. China's African Development Fund (CADF), a subsidiary of China Development Bank, announced during the third FOCAC summit, launched in June 2007 with $1 billion fund to encourage and support Chinese business operating in Africa. Now CADF uses its capital of $5 bn to support private Chinese investors in Africa. In 2013 at the conference in Gabon Wang Yong, the executive vice president of China-

Africa Development Fund, said, that this Fund in the past six years has already committed $2.4bn in 64 projects in more than 30 African countries[21].

The cumulative stock of Chinese investment in Africa grew according to "China Analyst" from less, than $9.3bn in 2009 to $21.2bn in 2012[22]. At the end of 2012, the African Development Bank estimated that Chinese investment in Africa totaled $20 billion[23]. Figures from China's FID Statistic Bulletin for the year to September 2013 show that it has increased its outbound FID spending to a record $87.8 billion, up to 17 percent over 2012–2013, in sharp contrast to global foreign investments, which have declined by the same amount[24]. China is one of the top investing countries in Least Developed Countries (LDC), such as Sudan and Zambia. Speaking at Africa Investment Summit in Hong Kong in November 2013, Zhao Changhui of Exim-Bank said that China has pledged to provide $1 trillion in financing to Africa in the years to 2025 to be invested in various sectors of African infrastructure, industry and agriculture.

China widely practices the principle – "raw materials in exchange for infrastructure", striking series of billion dollar minerals-for-infrastructure deals. China has been more involved in African infrastructure than Western countries; it accounts for more than 30% of the total value of infrastructure projects in Africa, pouring billions dollars into rails, roads, power and housing projects on the continent. Only in few African state capitals, China has not built a national sports stadium, a new presidential palace, or other public building. The biggest Chinese project – International convention centre for the African Union – built in Addis-Ababa (Ethiopia) free of charge and opened in January 2012. Africans call the new headquarters of the African Union a "China's gift to Africa'. China also donated or assisted in building hospitals in Luanda, Angola, a road from Lusaka, Zambia, to Chirundu in the southeast of the country, stadiums in Sierra Leone and Benin, a sugar mill and sugar cane farm in Mali, a water supply project in Mauritania. In July 2012, Chinese president Hu Jintao said about 100 schools, 30 hospitals, 30 anti-malaria centers and 20 agricultural technology demonstration centers built with China's aid in Africa[25]. During a state visit to Tanzania in March 2013 Chinese President Xi Jinping and President of Tanzania Jakaja Kikwete signed at least 19 agreements worth more than $6 billion. The major component is the construction of a port at Bagamoyo, northwest of Dar Es-Salaam, which will be able to handle 20 times more cargo than Dar Es-Salaam[26].

Some 2500 China's firms are operating on the continent now. Chinese companies have become the most confident investors in Africa. The diversity of Chinese companies is considerable, ranging from major multi-billion dollar SOE to small business run by individuals[27]. In September 2012 China Railway Construction Corporation (CRC) signed a $1.5 billion contract to modernize a railway system in western Nigeria. China South Locomotive and Rolling Stock Corporation signed a $400 million deal to supply locomotives to a South African firm Transnet. In February 2012, CRC announced projects in Nigeria, Djibouti and Ethiopia worth about $1.5bn. in total[28].

China realizes Special Economic Zones (SEZ) projects in six African countries. (The successful model of SEZ, employed in China, transplanted into Africa now). A SEZ project launched in 2009 generated a massive spurt of Chinese FID. The zones will house high-value technology industries and will generate jobs and foreign exchange. However, some experts consider that when the SEZ become operational fully, they will have few positive effects on African economies, because they will use mainly Chinese workers and repatriate export proceeds to China[29].

In recent years, China is modifying its African policy. During the 5th FOCAC Ministerial Conference in July 2012 Hu Jintao declared that China will focus on 5 areas: 1) supporting African sustainable development rather than scout for natural resources; 2) benefiting African people; 3) enhancing African overall development capacity; 4) enhancing the foundation of public support for China-Africa relationship; 5) promoting African peace and stability. "China will expand cooperation in investment and financing to support sustainable development in Africa and support the African integration process and help Africa enhance capacity for overall development, including supports to the Millennium Development Goals (MDGs), The Comprehensive African Agricultural Development Programme (CAADP), the Programme for Insfrastructure Development in Africa and the Presidential Infrastructure Championing Initiative", – Hu Juntao said[30].

Now China is shifting development assistance for Africa from 'hard' infrastructure assistance to 'soft' one[31]. If Summits FOCAC 2006 and 2009 paid main attention to measures for promoting support for "hard" infrastructure (roads, rails., conference centers and so on), by contrast 5th Conference in 2012 attached greater importance to 'soft' ones, like education, people-to-people exchange, joint researches, etc. China is adding a 'soft power' component to its economic links with Africa. Chinese efforts include 18.000 African students with scholarships to Chinese universities, embassies established in all but three of Africa's countries, a growing number of Chinese cultural centers and dispatch of 1,500 of health professionals. It is setting up more than 40 Confucius Institutes as a means of ensuring that Chinese culture and language spread the 'Black continent'[32]. «All this illustrates that China's involvement on the continent is more diverse than it is given credit for», – Ethiopian Foreign minister Adhanom Tedros told in interview to Al Jazeera on July 2013[33].

China attaches greater importance to security problems. It launches China-Africa Cooperative Partnership Initiative for the sake of peace and security. The outbreak of so-called 'Arab spring' highlighted the importance of protecting China's overseas economic interests and national citizens. To protect 'overseas Chinese' and economic interests was proclaimed as one of the top priorities of China's policy in Africa[34].

China plays a significant role in peacekeeping operations in Africa. Chinese 'blue helmets' served in Western Sahara, Burundi, Cote d'Ivoire, DRC, Ethiopia and Eritrea, Mozambique, Liberia, Sierra-Leone and Sudan. They served mainly as non-combatant troops in medical and engineering roles. At the end of 2012, Chinese experts and police personnel assigned to six of Africa's seven UN peacekeeping operations. In August 2014 there were 2192 Chinese peacekeepers in 'hot tops' of the world, mostly in Africa[35]. The South Sudan crisis pointed China's emergent peacekeeping role. The team of 331 officers and soldiers made a vital contribution to the conflict-ridden country. The UN mission to Mali in 2013 was the first where the Chinese had combat mandate[36]. The West African country was struggling to recover from a jihadist rebellion – and it remained volatile and dangerous. China bolstered the UN mission there by sending in troops.

China's advancement in Africa has received condemnations from Africa's traditional donors. "Chinese menace" is a popular cliché in Western media. Some politics and scholars call China 'resource hunter' and Chinese policy in Africa 'neocolonial'. They say that China helps some African governments to avoid criticism of bad governance, corruption or human rights violation. They point to in particular China's alleged lack of respect for human rights and reluctance to fight corruption in Africa[37]. Others are worried about the fact Beijing cooperates with some regimes denounced by the international community[38].

China's rise as a significant global economic power and its expansion in Africa is widely discussed. It is said, for example, that the deep interest for oil pushes China to close eyes on genocide in Darfur. The West condemns China for Al-Bashir protection in Sudan and R. Mugabe in Zimbabwe from international pressure.

Of course, there are problems in China-Africa relations. Not everything in Chinese policy suits Africans. They fear the pressure with which China operates in Africa; they do not like the growing presence of Chinese people on the continent. In 2013, there were more than one million Chinese in Africa. In June 2014 answering the questions about the growing presence of Chinese in Africa, China's Special Representative to Africa Zhong Jianhua said, that the one million Chinese people in African countries is not a very big proportion of the entire Chinese population. Ninety nine percent of Chinese would never leave China and move to Africa. Those who leave will return to China, because according to Chinese traditions, one should die at home near one's ancestors. Additionally, there is a lot of prestige when returning to Chinese villages from Africa. While many Chinese people remained in Africa, the majority of them returned after finishing their contracts. Zhong Jianhua also admitted problems with Chinese in Africa. For example, he told that China's Foreign Ministry had to work with the Ministry of Public Security to resolve issues pertaining to the Chinese mafia in Angola. A special police force sent to the country, and the government worked with the Angolan police to persecute the culprits. He stressed that there are many challenges for the Chinese government, businesspersons and scholars when going abroad, and there are constantly new problems that require solving[39].

Africans view the influx of cheap Chinese goods to their markets as a threat. Many African business people cannot compete with Chinese traders who take their supplies directly and cheaply from China. In Angola, Chinese street sellers have put out of business thousands of local sellers who have been there for generations. Chinese competition forced 28% of Ethiopian producers into bankruptcy and 32% to downsize. About 30000 textile jobs were lost in South Africa after China became a member of World Trade Organization (WTO) with rights to free trade. South African trade unions protested the inflow of low-cost Chinese goods, particularly textiles. Chinese companies have been accused in poor labor conditions, lack of attention to the social and environmental regulation and so on. During his visit to Africa in May 2014, Chinese premier Li Keqiang urged Chinese companies in Africa to abide by local laws and regulations and take responsibility to protect the interests of local communities and the environment[40].

Nevertheless, is China's policy a real 'neocolonial' menace to Africa? Is China really Africa's new colonial master? Is it sucking away African resources offering little in return? Chinese leaders try to reject such accusations and to dispel fears that the growing Beijing presence in Africa conceals a new form of colonialism. During his visit to Africa in May 2014 Chinese premier Li Keqiang in interview to African press called the frequent references by international media to "Chinese neo-colonialism in Africa" false accusations, which do not reflect the reality of a friendly cooperation on an equal footing with mutual benefits"[41].

Loro Horta from the School of International Relations of Technological University in Singapore pays attention on opposite views dominated in debates on China's involvement in Africa. One tends to see China's presence on the continent as negative and generating a lot of resentment among Africans. The second view is inclined to see the Chinese presence as largely beneficial, providing African states with generous aid in the form of soft loans, major infrastructure programs but, above all, providing a balance to traditional European and American dominance of the region. As Loro Horta considers, both views are wrong and right, depending on to what region of Africa and to which group of Africans is referring. African elites in general seem to welcome China's newfound enthusiasm for the continent. China provides the African governments with large loans, allowing them to develop infrastructure, expand agriculture, and strengthen their security apparatus. China's so-called non-interference policy and its no-strings-attached approach to aid have gained it support among African elites. Perhaps most attractive of all, Beijing asks no questions, nor imposes any conditionality on its investments[42].

In 2012, a Report of the Carnegie Endowment for International Peace dismissed the misconception that China was just a 'resource hunter'. "Chinese investment covers a wide range of sectors including infrastructure, education and information technology. These investments benefit Africa". The report showed that a much higher percentage of US direct investment in Africa was in mining than that from China[43].

When Western companies are often afraid of high investment risk in Africa, China fills up the vacuum. China-Africa cooperation based on win-win approach is attractive for the Black continent. Aid packages, which include investments not only in raw materials, but also in African infrastructure, benefit African economies. Chinese aid, trade and investments give African countries new opportunities. In recent years, Africa demonstrated an average growth of 5.5 percent, partly thanks to Chinese investments. China's success in Africa is largely due to its key principle of non-interference in the internal affairs of other states. Africans suit that China's 'does not link business with politics'.

China not only changes traditional trade and investment relations of African states, but also creates opportunities for African economies. Africans appreciate the advantages, which China aid and cooperation gives them. For many years, they adopted a Western aid and followed Western models of development, but never managed to put an end to underdevelopment. In their view, countries such as China, can bring something new within the scope of cooperation with Africa and help them to solve some problems of development. Moreover, many African rulers look upon China's model of a strong government and its focus on economic growth as an example to follow. After the Cold War, the West has reduced attention to Africa; China has forced developed countries to refocus attention on the problems of the African continent.

---

[1] China seeks to improve image in Africa//SME Times. 05 April 2014.

[2] Ministers adopt Beijing Action Plan for 2013-2015.UN Press Release Conference Website. 5th Ministerial Conference of the FOCAC. Bejing Action Plan. 20 July 2012.

[3] http://www.bbc.co.uk/russian/business/2013/10/131010china_oil_imports russia. shtml

[4] World Energy Outlook. 2011. International Energy Agency. Paris, OECD/IEA. Paris. 2011.P. 9557.

[5] BP Statisrical Review of World Energy. 2012 bp statistical review.com

[6] British Petroleum – http://j-times.ru/biznes/mirovye-zapasy-i-proizvodstvo-nefti-po-dannym-britis-petroleum; Top 10 газовых империй мира. 03/ 272012/194; British Petroleum Statistical Review of World Energy 2012.

[7] Du Juan. Got backs energy mining investment in Africa//China Daily. June 16.2013. Updated 2013-04-11 – http://www.chinadaily. com.cn/business/2013-04-11/content_16392202_2.htm

[8] U.S. crude import from Africa declines by 90% – EIA. Energy Mix Report. June 10, 2014. African News. Oil and Gas Industry news htm

[9] China-Africa Economic and Trade Cooperation (2013). Information Office of the State Council The People's Republic of China. Beijing. August 2013.

[10] China-Africa trade topped $210 bln in 2013. Xinhua 2014-04-23 – www.ecns.cn/business/2014/04-23/110674 shtml.

[11] Premier Li Kequang Visits Africa.// News Plus. 2014-05-04.

[12] Vines Alex. China's Priorities in Africa: Enhancing Engagements. London, Chattam House. Africa Programme Summary. 13 June 2014.

[13] Africa: China-Africa Ties Deepen. Standard Bank, Johannesburg //Business Africa. March 2013, P. 19.

[14] China's Continued Quest for Natural Resources // The China Analyst. Regional Focus: China-Africa. Apr.2014.

[15] Africa-BRICS cooperation. Implications for growth, employment and structural transformation in Africa. United Nations Economic Commission for Africa. Addis-Ababa, 2013. P. 15.

[16] Investment from China beneficial to Africa // China Daily. 2014-01-27. http://www.ecns.cn/business/2014/01-27/98750.shtml

[17] Kingsley Ighobor. China in the heart of Africa// Africa Renewal, January 2013 – http://www.un.org/africarenewal/magazine/january-2013/china-heart-africa

[18] Vines Alex. Africa. Premier Li Keqiang in Africa – the importance of Angola for China. London Chattam House. 6 May 2014.

[19] Investment from China beneficial to Africa // China Daily. 2014-01-27. http://www.ecns.cn/business/2014/01-27/98750.shtml

[20] Alden Chris, Large Daniel and Ricardo Soares De Oliveira.(eds). China Returns to Africa. L., 2008. P.14-15.

[21] Symbiotic China-Africa relationship expected to grow. CNV. 2014-01-29. – http://www.ecns.c/2014/01-29/00328.shtml

[22] China's Continued Quest for Natural Resources // The China Analyst. Regional Focus: China-Africa. Apr.2014.

[23] Symbiotic China-Africa relationship expected to grow. CNV. 2014-01-29. – http://www.ecns.c/2014/01-29/00328.shtml

[24] Patlansky Lauren. No reason to fear Chinese investment in Africa. 30.01. 2014 http://www.bdlive.co.za/opinion/2014/01/30/no-reason-to-fear-chinese-investment-in-africa

[25] Kingsley Ighobor. China in the heart of Africa// Africa Renewal, January 2013 – http://www.un.org/africarenewal/magazine/january-2013/china-heart-africa

[26] China drops anchor in Tanzania // Mail and Guardian. 4 Oct. 2013 http://mg.co.za/print/2013-10-04-00-china-drops-anchor-in-tanzania

[27] Alden Chris, Large Daniel and Ricardo Soares De Oliveira.(eds). China Returns to Africa. L., 2008. P.16.

[28] Kingsley Ighobor. China in the heart of Africa// Africa Renewal, January 2013 – http://www.un.org/africarenewal/magazine/january-2013/china-heart-africa

[29] Ancheraz Venaye and Nowbutsing Baboo. The Impact of China-Africa Investment Relations: the Case of Mauritius // Policy Brief. Africa Economic Research Consotrium. Nairobi, 2011.

[30] Hu Jintao. Open up New Prospects for a New Type of China-Africa Strategic Partnership. Speech at the Opening Ceremony of the Fifth Ministerial Conference of the Forum on China-Africa Cooperation. Beijing, 19 July 2012.

[31] Zhand Chun. A Promising Partnership between BRICS and Africa. A Chinese Perspective // China Monitor. BRICS. Special Edition. March 2013. Center for Chinese Studies. Stellenbosch University. Stellenbosch, March 2013. P. 33.

[32] Haebiger Marcus M. China's soft power in Afrika. Neue Zuricher Zeitung, 4 Jan. 2013.

[33] Measuring China's motivations in Africa. AlJazeera, 01 July 2013. http://www.aljazeera.com/indepth/features/2013/07/201371102586

[34] Zhan Chun. Prepare to future on Symmetrical Ties// China Daily (Africa Weekly). Jan. 25, 2013.

[35] United Nations peacekeeping troops and police contributors. Monthly Summary of military and police contributions to the United Nations operations as of 31 August 2014 – www.un.org/en/peacekeeping/resources/statictics/ contributors.shtml

[36] China's peacekeeping mission in Africa. CCTV Africa. March 13, 2014 cctvafrica.cctv-news. net/ chinas-peacekeeping-mission-in-africa

[37] Alessi C. And Hanson S. Expanding China-Africa Oil Ties. Council on foreign relations. 2012.

[38] Van Dijk. The New Presence of China in Africa. Amsterdam Univ. Press. 2009. P. 13.

[39] Vines Alex. China's Priorities in Africa: Enhancing Engagements. London, Chattam House. Africa Programme Summary. 13 June 2014.

[40] Vines Alex. Africa. Premier Li Keqiang in Africa – the importance of Angola for China. London, Chattam House. 6 May 2014.

[41] China seeks to improve image in Africa//SME Nimes. 05 April 2014.

[42] Horta Loro. China-Africa: Development partner or neo-colonizer? Special Global Edition. Issue: 0042. 29 November 2009.

[43] Chen Weihua. China has potential to play a positive role// China Daily. June 13, 2013. Updated: 2013-03-25. – chinadaily.com.cn

David Shinn, Dr., Prof.
Elliott School
of International Affairs
George Washington University

ETHIOPIA AND CHINA: TWO FORMER EMPIRES CONNECT IN THE 20th CENTURY

Introduction

Ethiopia was never colonized and along with China has a long imperial history. China's imperial period came to end with the fall of the Qing dynasty and formation of the Republic of China as a constitutional republic in 1912. The overthrow of Emperor Haile Selassie in 1974 by a left-wing military junta ended Ethiopia's empire. In 1970, four years before the end of Ethiopia's empire, the People's Republic of China established formal diplomatic relations with Haile Selassie's imperial government.

Although China and Ethiopia have imperial backgrounds, they only became well acquainted after both of them became republics. In the early years, this relationship grew modestly and only began to surge in the mid-1990s when the government of Prime Minister Meles Zenawi encouraged closer ties with China to tap into its financial resources and balance close ties with Western countries, particularly the United States. Today, China is arguably Ethiopia's most important bilateral economic partner.

While Ethiopia now exports few natural resources of strategic interest to China, it is important for other reasons. With a population of about 90 million people, Ethiopia is the second most populous country in Africa after Nigeria. It serves as the headquarters for the African Union. China provided $200 million in grant assistance and built the new African Union conference center, which came complete with a traditional Chinese-style garden. The New Partnership for Africa's Development, which China supports, has moved to Addis Ababa and the UN Economic Commission for Africa has its headquarters there. Ethiopia has one of the strongest militaries in Africa and, although landlocked, serves as a regional center for the Horn of Africa.

Ethiopia Eventually Recognizes China

The Republic of China's (ROC) Chiang Kai-shek government publicly supported Emperor Haile Selassie during the 1936-1941 invasion of

Ethiopia by fascist Italy. The ROC was one of the few countries that did not recognize the Italian occupation.[1] Although Ethiopia never recognized the ROC, it appreciated this support and was reluctant to recognize the People's Republic of China (PRC) following the 1949 victory on the mainland by Mao Zedong. A close ally of the United States in the years following the end of World War II, Haile Selassie sent troops to Korea in the early 1950s. Ethiopian and American forces fought side-by-side with South Korea against Chinese troops who entered the war on the side of North Korea.[2]

As Mao Zedong solidified control over China and the importance of the PRC became increasingly apparent, Ethiopia pursued an ambiguous policy on diplomatic recognition. It accepted agricultural assistance from Taiwan while a PRC cultural mission visited in 1956. The PRC and Ethiopia established trade relations the following year. Ethiopia supported Taiwan in the United Nations from 1950 to 1958, abstained in 1959 and supported Beijing thereafter. Ethiopia sent a cultural delegation to the PRC in 1961, signed an agreement to exchange journalists in 1962 and permitted China's official news agency, Xinhua, to open an office in Addis Ababa. Premier Zhou Enlai visited Ethiopia in 1964, when China mistakenly thought Haile Selassie was prepared to recognize the PRC.[3]

China's support for the Eritrean Liberation Front (ELF), which beginning in the early 1960s agitated for independence from Ethiopia, complicated Beijing's effort to obtain Ethiopian recognition. China provided the Eritrean insurgents covertly with weapons. Ethiopia and China had different policies on a rebel insurgency in neighboring Sudan. Ethiopia supported the southern insurgents while China backed the Arab government in Khartoum, which allowed the ELF to operate from its territory against Ethiopia. Ethiopia also suspected that the PRC backed Somali insurgents in efforts to take control of Somali-inhabited territory in southeastern Ethiopia. When Ethiopia finally recognized the PRC in 1970, it extracted a promise that Beijing would terminate support for the ELF.[4]

Haile Selassie Visits China

In 1971, less than a year after recognizing Beijing, Haile Selassie visited Beijing where he praised both the progress being made in China and Chairman Mao's "outstanding achievements." They signed trade, economic, and technical cooperation agreements. China granted Ethiopia an interest-free loan of $84 million and sent several teams to help with Ethiopia's development.[5] Mengistu Haile Mariam led a left-wing military coup in 1974 that toppled the Haile Selassie monarchy. This development complicated China's goal to strengthen relations with Ethiopia because the Soviet Union, seeing an opening after

Ethiopian relations worsened with the United States, switched its support from neighboring Somalia to Ethiopia. This occurred at the height of the Sino-Soviet conflict; the Soviets promised the Mengistu regime more than China could offer. China made clear that it was ready to give moral support to Ethiopia's new revolutionary government, but it was not prepared to compete with the Soviets in providing arms and financing.[6]

Problems Develop during the Sino-Soviet Split

China began to criticize Soviet involvement in Ethiopia while Ethiopia's new military leaders accused China of cooperating with the reactionary West and Ethiopia's enemies in Somalia. In 1979, Ethiopia expelled the Xinhua representatives. By 1984, Ethiopia was heavily under Soviet influence and when prompted by Moscow, Mengistu would excoriate China.[7] Nevertheless, China-Ethiopia economic development cooperation continued. In 1978, China completed construction of a diesel power station at Bonga.[8] Between 1975 and 1982, it constructed a 185-mile highway between Weldiya and Werota that to this day is known as the China Road.

During the Mengistu government, no senior Ethiopian official visited China until the Sino-Soviet conflict came to an end in the mid-1980s. Ethiopia's foreign minister visited in 1987 followed by Mengistu in 1989 and 1991. These visits occurred as the Mengistu government was under increasing pressure from Eritrean, Tigrayan, and other opposition groups and reflected the declining power of the Soviets in Ethiopia and the desperation of Mengistu for outside support. There were no senior visitors from China to Ethiopia until the vice premier/foreign minister came in 1989 and again in 1991. Throughout the Mengistu regime, however, China and Ethiopia maintained diplomatic and trade relations. China continued to send medical teams to Ethiopia, a program begun in 1974, and offered ten scholarships annually beginning in 1988. Mengistu fell in 1991, opening the door for a return of more cordial Ethiopia-China relations.[9]

The EPRDF Strengthens Ties with China

The coalition that overturned Mengistu, the Ethiopian People's Revolutionary Democratic Front (EPRDF), revived interaction with China soon after it took power. Following mid-level visits, Ethiopia's chief of the general staff went to Beijing in 1994. Prime Minister Meles Zenawi made his first visit to Beijing in 1995. President Jiang Zemin visited six African countries, including Ethiopia, in 1996. The two countries signed a series of new agreements, including an important one on trade, economic and technical cooperation. Premier Wen Jiabao visited Ethiopia in 1996 and 2003.

189

Xinhua signed a news exchange agreement with the Ethiopian News Agency. During the 1998–2000 Eritrean-Ethiopian conflict, China sold Ethiopia (and Eritrea) significant quantities of arms and ammunition. This led to an increase in high level military exchanges on a regular basis.[10] Meles returned to Beijing in 2004, when he signed additional cooperation agreements and, in 2006, he co-chaired the Forum on China-Africa Cooperation in Beijing.

Loans and Government Contracts Highlight China's Engagement

By 2005, China's embassy in Addis Ababa hosted more high-level visits, than any Western mission and Chinese companies had become a dominant force building highways and bridges, dams and power stations, cell phone networks, schools, and pharmaceutical factories. Ethiopia's trade minister said, that "China has become our most reliable partner."[11] China became involved in nearly every aspect of Ethiopia's economy. One agreement in 2006 with three Chinese companies is valued at $1.5 billion in commercial suppliers' credit at Libor (interbank lending rate) plus 1.5 percent to develop cellular and 3G services across Ethiopia.[12]

Chinese companies built and largely financed the $365 million dam on the Tekeze River in northern Ethiopia.[13] The Industrial and Commercial Bank of China is funding the Dongfang Electric Machinery Company to supply electrical equipment and turbines for the Gibe III dam on the Omo River. Environmental groups have expressed concern about potential damage to communities along the river and its impact on Lake Turkana in neighboring Kenya. Another Chinese company with Export Import Bank financing agreed to build a high-tension line for supplying electricity to Addis Ababa. These large loans contain a grant component, although the terms are not always transparent. The grace period for the two hydro projects is three years and the loans mature at the end of ten years. The interest rate is Libor plus 1.8 percent to 2.35 percent. China does not offer grant budgetary assistance to Ethiopia.[14] China also won the contract for building power transmission lines from the Grand Renaissance Dam on the Blue Nile River.

In 2010, the China Road and Bridge Corporation signed a $67 million contract to expand the Addis Ababa airport.[15] Chinese companies are building about 70 percent of the roads in Ethiopia, including the highly visible Addis Ababa Ring Road. Chinese soft loans often provide financing for bids below cost and sometimes with no bidding process. Chinese companies have largely displaced those from South Korea and Japan that had previously been important in road construction. Because these projects are seen and used by so many Ethiopians, they tend to create considerable good will.[16]

In 2010, China and Ethiopia announced loans to cover the cost of a light rail system in Addis Ababa, the purchase of nine vessels for Ethiopian Shipping Lines, and the construction of 200 buildings for the Ethiopian Housing Corporation.[17] The following year, the China Railway Group and Ethiopian Railway Corporation signed a $1.1 billion agreement for construction of the first phase of the Ethio-Djibouti railway project. By 2013, loans from China for this project reached about $3 billion. The two countries also signed a $100 million loan for the construction of deep water wells and $300 million memorandum of understanding for support of projects in Ethiopia's master plan. By the end of 2011, China's Export-Import Bank lending to Ethiopia had reached $1.8 billion.[18] Ethiopia has become one of the largest recipients in Africa for credit lines from the Export-Import Bank.

Foreign Direct Investment

A Chinese investment group is providing $713 million to construct the first industrial zone in Ethiopia.[19] Still under development, the Eastern Industrial Zone in Dukem anticipates an investment of $2 billion over the next ten years. China's Huajian Group, which specializes in shoe production, is one of the principal investors.[20] China is a major buyer of Ethiopian leather and is looking to expand its investment for the manufacture of shoes and leather goods in Ethiopia.[21] President Mulatu Teshome inaugurated in May 2014 a Lifan Motors assembly plant in the economic zone for production of the Dukem 500 automobile.[22]

A number of large Chinese companies are engaged in Ethiopia. They include ZTE Telecom, Huawei, China Construction Corporation, China Aviation Technology Exports and Imports Company, China Water Conservancy and Hydropower Engineering Corporation, and Sinohydro. Most of these companies are more interested, however, in winning contracts, which often result from Chinese government loans, than they are in investment.

China's share of foreign direct investment (FDI) in Ethiopia, while still modest, has increased from only 1.5 percent of total FDI in 2000 to 16 percent in 2007. Total Chinese FDI in 2009 was $74 million and in 2010 $58.5 million. By 2012, China's cumulative FDI reached more than $345 million according to its ambassador to Ethiopia.[23] This placed Chinese companies as the third largest foreign investor in Ethiopia after Saudi Arabia and India.[24] In 2013, China invested more in Ethiopia than any other country followed by Turkey.[25] Cumulative Chinese investment in Ethiopia as of 2013 reportedly reached $1.1 billion.[26]

China opened a branch office in Addis Ababa of the China-Africa Development Fund. The two countries have signed agreements on investment promotion and reciprocal protection as well as avoidance of double taxation.

Some 316 Chinese investment projects are fully or semi-operational and more than 900 projects are in the pre-implementation phase.[27]

Chinese Foreign Aid Is Modest but Growing

While the loan component of the relationship and commercial interaction has been intense in recent years, China's foreign aid to Ethiopia has been modest. Compared to other donor countries, it was almost non-existent in 2006, when it constituted about $1 million or 0.14 percent of Ethiopia's total aid.[28] It has increased significantly since then. China provided $12 million to fund a technical and vocational education and training program that resulted in the assignment of about ninety Chinese teachers throughout Ethiopia as of 2007. The same year, China increased its annual scholarship program for Ethiopians to forty annually. There were twenty-two Chinese vocational education teachers in the country as of the end of 2009.[29] In 2011, China provided $55 million in emergency food aid for Ethiopia and other drought affected countries in the region.[30] It also donated a fleet of 90 vehicles to the government.[31]

Ethiopia was the first African country to receive young Chinese volunteers, a program similar to the U.S. Peace Corps. Twelve volunteers arrived in 2005. The following year, China sent fifty volunteers to Ethiopia, the largest group ever sent to a foreign country. China provides training for up to several hundred Ethiopian professionals each year.[32] From the beginning of its medical cooperation program and until 2012, China sent sixteen medical teams comprising 255 personnel to Ethiopia. In 2012, China opened a $13 million hospital at Akaki, located south of Addis Ababa.[33] China also built malaria prevention and agricultural demonstration centers.[34]

In 2009, the Addis Ababa Confucius Institute (AACI) began teaching Mandarin at the Ethio-China Polytechnic College in cooperation with Tianjin University of Technology and Education. AACI also offers courses on Chinese culture, provides training for Ethiopian diplomats in the Ministry of Foreign Affairs and in 2011 signed agreements with Addis Ababa, Hawassa, and Mekelle universities to establish Chinese language learning centers.[35]

Ethiopia Has a Significant Trade Deficit with China

In recent years, Ethiopia has consistently experienced a major, albeit declining, trade deficit with China. In 2004, Ethiopia imported $291 million in goods from China and exported only $16 million in value to China. Ethiopia imported eighteen times more Chinese goods than it exported. In 2011, according to International Monetary Fund statistics, Ethiopia imported $987 million in goods from China and exported $265 million in value to China. In

2011, Ethiopia imported almost three times more Chinese goods than it exported to China. The range during the intervening years was between five and seventeen times more imports from China than exports to China. In 2006, China became Ethiopia's largest trading partner, passing Saudi Arabia, and has maintained that rank ever since.[36]

Ethiopia's major exports to China are sesame, coffee, cut flowers, textiles, and leather products. Its principal imports from China are transport and electronic equipment, consumer goods, and chemical products. In order to rectify the trade imbalance, China began in 2005 to accept up to 192 products duty free. In 2007, it expanded the list of duty free imports to 442.[37] While the trade gap has narrowed, it continues to be an issue of concern. There have also been occasional trade disputes. In 2012, Huawei Technologies illegally imported $13 million of telecom equipment in the name of state-owned Ethio Telecom without the knowledge of the Ethiopian company. Ethiopia demanded that Huawei return the equipment to China, which Huawei did in 2014.[38]

While Ethiopian consumers generally welcome Chinese products, some business persons have raised concerns about the entry of sub-standard merchandise, dumping by Chinese suppliers, unfair competition and displacement of small Ethiopian businesses.[39] In one case, ZTE communications equipment sat in a warehouse because no government entity wanted it. The more common reaction, however, is a belief that although Chinese products are not the best they are adequate and much cheaper than their competition.[40] There have also been issues concerning Chinese labor displacing Ethiopians, resulting in occasional complaints from members of Parliament. The Chinese embassy has acknowledged there are more than 10,000 Chinese working in Ethiopia. Other estimates put the number much higher. After a 2010 wage dispute at a cement factory in Mekelle, China sent home more than 300 Chinese employees.[41]

While there are still relatively few Chinese tourists visiting Ethiopia, the air connections reflect the sharp increase in economic interaction. Ethiopian Airlines began flying between Addis Ababa and Beijing in 1973; it was the first African airline that connected China and Africa. Ethiopia now operates direct flights to five cities in China. This includes daily non-stop service to Beijing and Shanghai, ten flights a week to Guangzhou, five flights weekly to Hong Kong, and four to Hangzhou. It has code share agreements with Air China and a joint venture with Hainan Air and the China-Africa Development Fund to build a five-star hotel near the Addis Ababa airport.[42]

Strong Ethiopia-China Political Ties

Although the strength of the Ethiopia-China relationship is in the economic area, political ties are also flourishing. In 2006, for example, the

Ethiopian Parliament passed a resolution in support of China's Anti-Secession Law. In 2007, Ethiopia joined other African countries in preventing a resolution in the UN Human Rights Commission that censored China's human rights practices.[43] In 2008, Prime Minister Meles said Tibet is an internal affair and external powers have no right to interfere. He added: "Ethiopia strongly opposes any external force's attempts to destroy China's national unity and create hatred among Chinese nationalities."[44] China's ambassador to Ethiopia praised Addis Ababa's "strong support" for China's position on Taiwan and Tibet.[45] For its part, China never criticizes Ethiopia's human rights policies or comments publicly on internal conflicts.

Ethiopia not only has an embassy in Beijing, but it has a consulate general in Guangzhou, Chongqing, and Shanghai. To underscore the importance of its relationship with China, Ethiopia sent its sitting foreign minister and former EPRDF insider, Seyoum Mesfin, at the beginning of 2011 as its ambassador in Beijing. Mulatu Teshome, Ethiopia's president beginning in late 2013 earned his PhD in international law at Peking University in the 1970s and subsequently served as Ethiopia's ambassador to China.[46] He speaks Mandarin.

The EPRDF has developed close ties with the Chinese Communist Party (CPC). In 2000, Dai Bingguo, then director of the CPC International Liaison Department, visited Ethiopia. In 2002, Kassu Ilala, who became a senior figure in the EPRDF, visited the CPC.[47] China sent a delegation to the EPRDF's Seventh Organizational Conference in 2008 and the Eighth Congress in 2010. The CPC International Department Vice Minister, Ai Ping, led a goodwill delegation to Ethiopia in 2010 when he signed a memorandum of understanding on Exchange and Cooperation between the CPC and EPRDF.[48] During a visit to China by an EPRDF delegation, a senior CPC official said that growing ties between the two organizations "have helped form a solid foundation for the development of relations between China and Ethiopia."[49] There are also close links between Ethiopia's Parliament and the China National People's Congress. The two organizations have established a China-Ethiopia friendship group.[50]

China's deep commitment to Ethiopia has not been free of controversy. Chinese companies have a reputation for taking greater risks and occasionally putting their personnel in jeopardy. In spite of warnings to stay out of the disputed Ogaden region of Ethiopia by the Ogaden National Liberation Front (ONLF), which seeks self-determination for the area, China went in anyway. The Ogaden is rich in gas reserves and may have oil. Zhongyuan Petroleum Exploration Bureau, a subsidiary of Sinopec, operated an exploration base in the Ogaden that was heavily protected by Ethiopian soldiers. In 2007, the ONLF attacked the base, killing nine Chinese employees and sixty-five Ethiopian soldiers. After the attack, the ONLF announced that it would not

194

allow resources from the region to be exploited by the Ethiopian government or "any other firm that enters into an illegal contract."[51]

China subsequently pulled its team out of the Ogaden. In 2011, Hong Kong-based PetroTrans Company announced that it had agreed to invest \$4 billion over twenty-five years to develop oil and gas reserves in the Ogaden and build oil and gas pipelines to Somaliland's port of Berbera.[52] Days later the ONLF announced, that these deals constitute an act of war against the Ogaden people and vowed to take all necessary measures to prevent their implementation.[53] PetroTrans failed to carry out its commitments and Ethiopia's Ministry of Mines said in 2013 that it had awarded the concessions to another unnamed Chinese company.[54] There has been no visible movement on this project in the Ogaden.

Premier Li Keqiang's 2014 Visit to Ethiopia

Chinese Premier Li Keqiang visited Ethiopia in May 2014. On this occasion, senior Chinese officials and company executives signed 16 economic and development agreements with their Ethiopian counterparts. They included a comprehensive framework agreement for the period 2015-2024 and a loan release for the Addis Ababa-Djibouti railway project. China extended the \$1.4 billion loan for the project and agreed to provide financial assistance for the Dire Dawa-Dewalle highway as well as the Welkait sugar development project in Tigray Region.[55]

Ethiopia signed a memorandum of understanding with the China Civil Engineering Construction Corporation, China Railway Engineering Corporation, China Communications Construction Company, and China to Overseas Construction Group Company to develop special economic zones in Kombolcha, Hawassa, Dire Dawa, and Addis Ababa. Following a feasibility study, Ethiopia will sign a contract for construction of the zones. Ethiopia has prepared land for the zones at Kombolcha, Hawassa and Dire Dawa.[56]

During the visit to Ethiopia by Premier Li Keqiang, Prime Minister Hailemariam Desalegn said that the "best days of vibrant partnership with China" lie ahead.[57] There should be no doubt about the importance of the China-Ethiopia relationship.

Conclusion

China and Ethiopia are strategic partners. China provides technical assistance and jamming equipment to help Ethiopia's Information Security Network block signals from anti-government radio stations and, from time to time, the Amharic-language programs of the Voice of America and Deutsche Welle.[58] The two countries have established a Joint Ministerial Commission.

China supplies artillery, light armored vehicles, and troop transport vehicles to Ethiopia's army. Each year it trains a small number of Ethiopian officers. There are routine high-level exchange military visits. China's embassy in Ethiopia is one of a small number in African capitals that has a resident military attaché.[59]

Prime Minister Meles Zenawi, who died in 2012, commented, that "China has been playing an irreplaceable role in our economy. It has unparalleled contribution towards funding infrastructure activities."[60] In 2010, *The Economist* reported that Hailemariam Desalegn, at the time deputy prime minister and foreign minister, was urging Ethiopia to follow China's model.[61] Following Meles' death, Hailemariam replaced him as prime minister.

A senior official in the Ministry of Foreign Affairs commented that China has become "critical" to Ethiopia for economic reasons. Ethiopia understands, however, that China has its own interests in the country and close relations with China will not make relations with the West "redundant."[62] Then Deputy Prime Minister Hailemariam Desalegn emphasized that China is supporting with substantial loans Ethiopia's growth program. He added that Chinese loans are preferable: "We like the Chinese way of doing things, because they don't say 'do this, don't do that'—there are no preconditions."[63]

Ethiopia-China relations are strong and likely to get stronger. Increasingly, Ethiopia sees China as an alternative to the West and, especially, Western political conditionality. At the same time, as China's presence and influence grow in Ethiopia it will become subject to many of the same suspicions that countries such as the United States and the former Soviet Union experienced in past decades.

---

[1] Richard Greenfield, *Ethiopia: A New Political History*. New York: Frederick A. Praeger, 1965, 249.

[2] Kimon Skordiles, *Kagnew: The Story of the Ethiopian Fighters in Korea*. Tokyo: Radiopress, 1954, 100-104.

[3] Wei Liang-Tsai, *Peking versus Taipei in Africa 1960-1978*. Taipei: The Asia and World Institute, 1982, 229, 387; Alaba Ogunsanwo, *China's Policy in Africa, 1958-1971*. London: Cambridge University Press, 1974, 9, 37, 242; CIA, "Chinese Communist Activities in Africa," declassified study dated 30 April 1965, 14.

[4] Liang-Tsai, 230-234; Bruce Larkin, *China and Africa 1949-1970*. Berkeley: University of California Press, 1971, 177-178; Eugene K. Lawson, "China's Policy in Ethiopia and Angola," in *Chinese and Soviet Aid to African Nations*, ed. Warren Weinstein and Thomas H. Henriksen. New York: Praeger, 1980, 168-169; Alan Hutchison, *China's African Revolution*. London: Hutchinson of London, 1975, 119-120, 166.

[5] Liang-Tsai, 235-236.
[6] David A. Korn, *Ethiopia the United States and the Soviet Union*. Carbondale: Southern Illinois University Press, 1986, 18-19.
[7] Kinfe Abraham, *Ethiopia from Empire to Federation*. Addis Ababa: EIIPD Press, 2001, 408-409; Korn, 100.
[8] Kim Woodard, *The International Energy Relations of China*. Stanford: Stanford University Press, 1980, 45.
[9] China Ministry of Foreign Affairs, "Bilateral Relations: Ethiopia," 12 October 2003; Addis Dilnesa, *China Comes to Africa*. Addis Ababa: EIIPD, 2005, 245.
[10] China Ministry of Foreign Affairs, "Bilateral Relations: Ethiopia,"; Ethiopia Ministry of Foreign Affairs, "An Overview of the Bilateral Relations between the Federal Democratic Republic of Ethiopia and the People's Republic of China," September 2006.
[11] Karby Leggett, "Staking a Claim: China Flexes Economic Muscle throughout Burgeoning Africa," *Wall Street Journal*, 29 March 2005.
[12] Deborah Bräutigam, "Ethiopia's Partnership with China," *The Guardian*, 30 December 2011.
[13] Sonal Patel, "Ethiopia Completes Construction of Africa's Tallest Dam," *Power Magazine*, 1 July 2009.
[14] Toh Han Shih, "Ethiopia Dam Blot on China's Record," *South China Morning Post*, 7 June 2010. Jean-Pierre Cabestan, "China and Ethiopia: Authoritarian Affinities and Economic Cooperation," *China Perspectives*, no. 2012/4, 55.
[15] "Chinese Company Signs Agreement to Expand Airport in Ethiopia," *Walta Information*, 15 December 2010.
[16] Author's meeting in Addis Ababa on 5 July 2007 with Zaid Wolde Gebriel, Director General, Ethiopian Roads Authority. Peter H. Gebre, "China in Ethiopia: Just-in-Time," in *China, Africa, and the African Diaspora: Perspectives*, ed. Sharon T. Freeman (Washington: AASBEA, 2009), 169-172.
[17] Tamrat G. Giorgis, "China to Finance $293.5m of ESL's Nine Vessels," *Fortune*, 16 January 2011.
[18] "Ethiopia, China Sign Ethio-Djibouti Railway Construction Agreement," *Ethiopian News Agency*, 26 October, 2011; "China to Lend Ethiopia $100 Mln," *Reuters*, 17 November 2011; "China, Ethiopia Sign Loan Agreement," *Xinhua*, 5 December 2011.
[19] Deborah Bräutigam and Tang Xiaoyang, "African Shenzhen: China's Special Economic Zones in Africa," *Journal of Modern African Studies*, vol. 49, no. 2 (2011), 32.
[20] William Davison, "Huajian of China's Ethiopian Export Zone May Generate $4 Billion," *Bloomberg*, 22 March 2012. Li Wenfang, "Putting Best Foot Forward in Africa," *China Daily*, 16 December 2013.
[21] Mahlet Mesfin, "Gov't Pulls All Stops to Court Chinese Delegates," *Fortune*, 18 September 2011.
[22] Advertisement in *Fortune*, 18 May 2014, 38.
[23] Alemayehu Geda, "Scoping Study on the Chinese Relation with Sub-Saharan Africa: The Case of Ethiopia," March 2008, 5-6. "Chinese Investment in Ethiopia

Reached Over $345 Million: Ambassador," *Ethiopia Radio and Television Agency*, 19 January 2012. The World Bank, *Chinese FDI in Ethiopia: A World Bank Survey*, Washington: Africa Region, November 2012, 3.

[24] Christine Hackenesch, "Competing for Development? The European Union and China in Ethiopia," Centre for Chinese Studies, Stellenbosch University, November 2011, 20.

[25] Author's meeting on 21 May 2014 with Ethiopian President Mulatu Teshome.

[26] "A Friend in Need, Indeed," *Ethiopian Business Review*, no. 15 (16 May-15 June 2014), 34.

[27] Remarks by Ethiopian Ambassador to China, Seyoum Mesfin, on 27 April 2011 in Shijiazhuang, Hebei.

[28] Alemayehu Geda, 11.

[29] China Ministry of Commerce, "China-Ethiopia Bilateral Relations," 17 April 2011; Chinese embassy website in Addis Ababa, "China, Ethiopia Sign Technical, Vocational Cooperation Accord," 16 April 2007.

[30] "Prime Minister Meles on an Official Visit to China," *A Week in the Horn*, 19 August 2011.

[31] "China to Lend Ethiopia $100 Mln."

[32] August 2008 *Walta Information* interview with China's Ambassador to Ethiopia, Gu Xiaojie, in Addis Ababa.

[33] CCTV, "Ethiopia-China Aid/Hospital," 5 March 2012.

[34] Hackenesch, 19.

[35] "Confucius Institute Signs Agreement with two Ethiopian Universities to Establish Chinese Language Centers," *Xinhua*, 11 November 2011. "Addis Ababa Confucius Institute," see http://english.hanban.org/confuciusinstitu-tes/node_10957.htm.

[36] International Monetary Fund, *Direction of Trade Statistics Yearbook 2011*, 218; IMF, *Direction of Trade Statistics Yearbook 2012*, 219. Statistics from the National Bank of Ethiopia show a larger trade deficit with China than the IMF numbers. See "A Friend in Need, Indeed," 32.

[37] Cabestan, 57. Interview with Gu Xiaojie.

[38] Yonas Abiye and Wudineh Zenebe, "Imported Telecom Equipment Create Disarray," *The Reporter*, 17 May 2014.

[39] Gebre, 176-180. Alemayehu Geda, 10-11 and 13. Cabestan, 61.

[40] Author's meetings in Addis Ababa on 29 June 2007 with senior government official and another on 5 July 2007 with the managing editor of a leading private newspaper. For a brief case study of ZTE's entry into Ethiopia, see Gebre, 173-175.

[41] Voice of America Horn of Africa service, 16 February 2010. Cabestan, 61.

[42] "Ethiopian to Launch Daily Non-stop Flights to Beijing," *Ethiopian News Agency*, 22 March 2011; "Ethiopian Airlines, Air China to Build Five-Star Hotel," *Reporter*, 12 March 2011. Forum on China Africa Cooperation, "Ethiopian Airlines Launches Nonstop Flight to Shanghai," 31 March 2014.

[43] Hackenesch, 21.

[44] "Ethiopia Objects to Politicizing Olympics: PM," *Xinhua*, 26 April 2008.

[45] 19 August 2008 *Walta Information* interview with Gu Xiaojie.

[46] "Ethiopian President Talks about His Stay in China," *CCTV.com*, 4 May 2014.

[47] Cabestan, 55.

[48] China Ministry of Foreign Affairs website, "Bilateral Relations."

[49] "Senior Communist Party of China Leader Vows to Boost Partnership with Ethiopia," *Xinhua*, 23 February 2011.

[50] Gu Xiaojie interview.

[51] Jeffrey Gettleman, "Ethiopian Rebels Kill 70 at Chinese-Run Oil Field," *New York Times*, 25 April 2007; Tsegaye Tadesse, "Petronas and Sinopec in Ethiopia Exploration Talks," *Reuters*, 10, December 2007.

[52] "Ethiopia, Somaliland, China to Sign Agreements on Gas, Oil, Logistic Deals," Ethiopian Ministry of Foreign Affairs website, 15 August 2011.

[53] "Unholy Tri-partite Deal between China, Ethiopia and Hargeisa Administration," ONLF press release, 24 August 2011; Peter Heinlein, "Ethiopian Forces, Rebels Clash in Ogaden Oil Exploration Region," *VOA*, 2 September 2011.

[54] Kaleyesus Bekele, "Gas Fields' Development Awarded to Chinese Company," *The Reporter*, 23 November 2013.

[55] "A Friend in Need, Indeed," 32.

[56] Fasika Tadesse, "China Agrees to Construct Flagship Special Economic Zones," *Fortune*, 11 May 2014.

[57] Fasika Tadesse, "China-Africa: The Great Renewal," *Fortune*, 11 May 2014.

[58] Michael Malakata, "China Accused of Jamming TV, Websites in Ethiopia," *Computerworld*, 29 June 2011.

[59] Cabestan, 55.

[60] 19 February 2011 interview with *Walta Information*.

[61] "Ethiopia and China: Looking East," *The Economist*, 21 October 2010.

[62] Comment made to author in Addis Ababa on 30 July 2010.

[63] 7 November 2010 interview with *Capital* newspaper.

Mamoudou Gazibo
Professeur titulaire/Professor
Université de Montréal,
Département de science politique

CAN AFRICA BENEFIT FROM ITS BOOMING COOPERATION WITH CHINA? THE STATE CAPACITY FACTOR IN COMPARATIVE PERSPECTIVE

Abstract

Over the last decade China has become one of Africa's most important political and economic partners. Whether in trade or oil exploitation, the construction of infrastructure or diplomatic exchanges, it is difficult to list all the sectors in which China and Africa cooperate. Most of the research produced on this relation can be classified in two main competing camps. The first group of analysts interprets China's presence in Africa as a threat, a view that has been recently stressed by the Nigerian Federal Reserve chief who warned that China is harming Africa's industrialization prospects. The second group sees China as a helpful and "win-win" partner. These analyses generally lack precision and nuance. Rather than analyzing the relationship in general terms or focusing solely on China's activities in Africa, the purpose of this paper is to identify the domestic factors – African state capacity – that determine whether China's presence is a benefit or a threat

Introduction

Over the last decade, China has become one of Africa's most important political and economic partners. Whether in trade or oil exploitation, the construction of infrastructure or diplomatic exchanges, it is difficult to list all the sectors in which they cooperate. The volume of trade between the two sides, for example, has culminated to (in American dollar) more than 200 billion in 2103, compared to only 10 billion in 2000. China is now Africa's primary commercial partner.

This rapid development of China-Africa relations has raised questions as to whether China's enhanced role on the continent has improved or undermined the prospects for African countries to achieve economic development and foster democracy. There are two main competing arguments about the political and economic implications of China's presence in Africa. In a *Financial Times* op-ed, the then-President of Senegal, Abdoulaye Wade, vigorously re-

200

buked Western criticism of Chinese aid and investment programs, saying "China's approach to our needs is simply better adapted than the slow and sometimes patronizing post-colonial approach of European investors, donor organizations and non-governmental organizations"[1]. More skeptical, Papa Kwesi Nduom, former Minister of Public Sector Reform in Ghana, worries "that some governments in Africa may use Chinese money in the wrong way to avoid pressure from the West for good governance"[2]. In a similar vein, in December 2006, South African former President Thabo Mbeki warned fellow African leaders to "guard against sinking into a 'colonial relationship' with China as Beijing expands its push for raw materials across the continent"[3]. The real question, however, is whether there are grounds for such assertions or whether there is an alternative interpretation of China's engagement in Africa.

Some authors have tried to escape this dichotomous view. Chris Alden notes for example that in a continent of over fifty countries and deeply diverse societies, the complexity of assessing how Africans respond to China's dramatic arrival is obvious. In order to establish some common features of African responses, suggests Alden, it is best to look at the nature of individual countries. He identifies three types of regimes: pariah partnerships; illiberal regimes or weak democracies with commodity-based economies; and democracies with diversified economies. Alden argues that a discernible set of patterned responses to China's new engagement can be identified, according to each of these three models[4].

This brief paper is part of a broader project that attempts to follow the above-mentioned call for a "nuanced look" at China's engagement in Africa. But it goes further with two sets of arguments. First, I assume that the outcomes of China's engagement in Africa may vary from one country to another, and from one specific economic sector to another. Second, I argue that three variables make almost all the difference: 1) state capacity and the nature of political institutions; 2) leadership style and 3) the presence or absence of a strong civil society. Together or individually, they largely determine whether African states may benefit from China's presence or be harmed by it. Because I lack space in this brief paper however, only the state capacity variable is explored through the comparison of two countries, South Africa and Sudan. The countries themselves are analyzed by looking at the specific sector in which China's presence is the most important in each country. This paper is thus an exploratory introduction to a broader project that attempts to build a universalizing comparison.

Why state capacity counts

Three decades ago, Jackson and Rosberg emphasized the weakness of African states and even questioned how they still persist[5]. State capacity is a fuzzy concept. It has been conceptualized in several ways by practitioners and sub-disciplines, ranging from civil conflicts specialists to public administration or democratization studies[6]. Rice and Patrick measure states' capacity "according to their relative performance in four critical spheres: economic, political, security, and social welfare". The concept does not refer to the capacity of a state leader to dominate its people. Rather, "a state's strength or weakness is a function of its effectiveness, responsiveness, and legitimacy across a range of government activities"[7]. I propose in the same line to conceptualize state capacity here by emphasizing state bureaucratic capacity and state regulations regarding interstate cooperation[8], and on the institutional nature (authoritarian or pluralistic) of the state (see Freedom House or Polity rankings). These characteristics are seen as the crucial ingredients without which it is difficult for an African country to deal advantageously with China in crucial cooperation domains.

State capacity counts for at least three reasons. First, it allows the adoption of a contextual-institutional approach, which offers a relatively new insight on a topic (cooperation) generally analyzed through the lenses of grand theories like developmentalism and dependency theory. Second, it emphasizes on the internal structures and dynamics of African countries rather than on the external aspects of cooperation. This is challenging because, given Africa's weak and externally oriented economies, external variables are usually considered as more decisive in explaining the outcomes of Africa's international relations. Third, state capacity counts because of the asymmetric nature of China-Africa relations. The Chinese population is one and half times that of the population of the entire African continent. Chinese metropolises like Beijing or Shanghai have larger populations than many mid-size African states like Niger, Mali or Chad. In the same vein, China's economy (around US 10 thousand billion) is twenty times that of Africa's biggest economy, Nigeria (US 500 billion). Africa itself is characterized by huge discrepancies: Nigeria has 150 million people while Seychelles has only a population of one hundred thousand. Also, as estimated by the World Bank, Nigeria and South Africa, Africa's biggest economies, earn more than 50% of Africa's total GDP. Therefore, these asymmetries force us to ask whether African countries (all tiny compared to China but at the same time different in size and strength) have the necessary capacity, institutions and social control mechanisms to deal with China in a win-win way.

Because China prefers to deal with governments, the degree of pluralism in the African state has huge consequences on the nature of the relationship, especially given that African states are among the weakest in the developing world[9] and are virtually all neopatrimonial[10]. As we know, in a weak neopatrimonial state, the absence of pluralist institutions is generally related to corrupt political behavior.

The State Capacity Factor: Diverging Cooperation Patterns with China in South Africa and Sudan

Until 2014, South Africa was Africa's leading economy. According to Rice and Stewart (2008), South Africa has also the fifth strongest state on the continent (the others are Tunisia before the 2011 uprising and tiny states like the Seychelles, Mauritius, and Cape-Verde) [11]. Nonetheless, South Africa has been often cited as having several problems with the Chinese presence in sectors such as textile manufacturing. However as shown below, the state has managed to mitigate the problems more successfully than other states, especially Sudan.

During the mid-1990s, up to 80 percent of the t-shirts imported into South Africa came from China [12]. During the same period, employment in the textile industry was reported to have declined steadily. According to Rupp, the situation was so critical that, by 2002, at least 75,000 jobs in South Africa's apparel industry had been cut, beginning what was then considered a steep and steady slide in Africa's textile and manufacturing industries in South Africa, and several other countries including Lesotho, Swaziland, Madagascar, Mauritius, Ghana, and Kenya. Indeed, with the end of the Multi-Fiber Agreement in 2005, the stringent and long-standing U.S. quota limiting the import of Chinese textiles and apparel was lifted. As a consequence of this, and buoyed by the preferential terms of trade established by the African Growth and Opportunity Act, African producers that had established burgeoning industries in textiles and apparel were rapidly swamped by Chinese competition. "African factories have closed and employees have been laid off, affecting tens of thousands of workers and hundreds of thousands of individuals in families and communities that were supported by workers' wages. In tiny, landlocked Lesotho, six textile factories closed in 2005 alone and over 10,000 workers lost their jobs, affecting tens of thousands of these workers' dependents" [13].

When the government of South Africa expressed its concerns about the imbalances in economic competitiveness and the subsequent displacement of the South African textile industry, analysts observed that the Chinese state initially reacted defensively. For instance, China's economic and commercial counselor in South Africa, Ling Guiru, expressed China's frustration with cries of foul play by African states and protectionism for African industries. He stressed that "China's success in expanding its textile industries was based on its positive response and timely readjustment in the face of difficulties, instead of flinching and resorting to self-protection. . . . This (effort) entailed the readjustment of the industrial policy, renovation and restructuring of the textile and clothing sector, as well as the optimization of sectoral structure. Thanks to the arduous efforts over the years, the Chinese textiles and clothing industry managed to sharpen its international competitive edge and gained the comparative advantages it now enjoys. . . . [U]nfair and discriminative restrictions will never be accepted by China''[14].

However, after several months of further negotiations, China voluntarily agreed to restrict its apparel exports to the South African market in order to give South African businesses time to reorganize and revive after their precipitous collapse. While visiting South Africa in 2006, Wen Jiabao signed an agreement covering a temporary stop on Chinese textile exports to the country, mining of uranium, development of peaceful nuclear reactors, and exchange of personnel in the nuclear field[15]. The same year, President Mbeki represented South Africa at the Beijing FOCAC. He urged that Africa seek "a fair and equitable global trading system that is characterized by transparency, good corporate governance, predictability and poverty alleviation and eradication". In late 2006, Mbeki commented that African states run the risk of getting stuck "in an unequal relationship" with Beijing as had developed with colonial powers.[16]

In 2007, he backed away from this criticism but gently warned China not to repeat the mistakes of the colonial relationship with Africa. He called on China to participate in Africa's development and not use it just as a source of raw materials. While visiting South Africa in 2007, Hu Jintao said that China is concerned by its trade surplus and, to please his counterparts on this issue, signed several agreements in the mining, energy, and agricultural sectors[17]. During President Hu Jintao's speech in Pretoria in February 2007, he assured his audience that China would create new balances in trade relations as one demonstration of its sensitivity to African interests and opinion[18].

This willingness to find middle ground with their African counterparts, indeed making concessions to support African industries that compete directly with Chinese investments, marks a significant departure from classic relations of dependency. But it came after a fierce commercial and diplomatic battle conducted by South Africa.

However, as Rupp among several authors observe ironically, as soon as China systematically withdrew its imports from the South African textile and apparel markets, the void was filled not by rejuvenated South African products, but by cheap imports from Bangladesh and Vietnam, suggesting that in the twenty-first century Africa is being buffeted by the broader challenges of globalization, rather than by specific competition from China[19].

The way in which strong and democratic South Africa manages its relations with China stands in sharp contrast with that of authoritarian Sudan. The domestic political context of Sudan, ranked by Rice and Patrick as the fourth weakest state in Africa (only after Somalia, DRC and Burundi) and the sixth weakest state out of 141 countries in the world[20] is clearly important here.

The relations between China and Sudan were officially established in 1959, but before 1989 and the coup that brought Omar al-Bashir to power, "China's economic relations with Sudan featured forms of barter trade, concessionary loans, arms transfers and medical assistance as well as assorted infrastructure construction projects, including the Khartoum Friendship Hall. However, even during the 1970s, when relations were comparatively good, China's links with Sudan did not involve a significant, lasting Chinese social presence within Sudan"[21].

Trends in diversification of selected African countries, 1998–2002

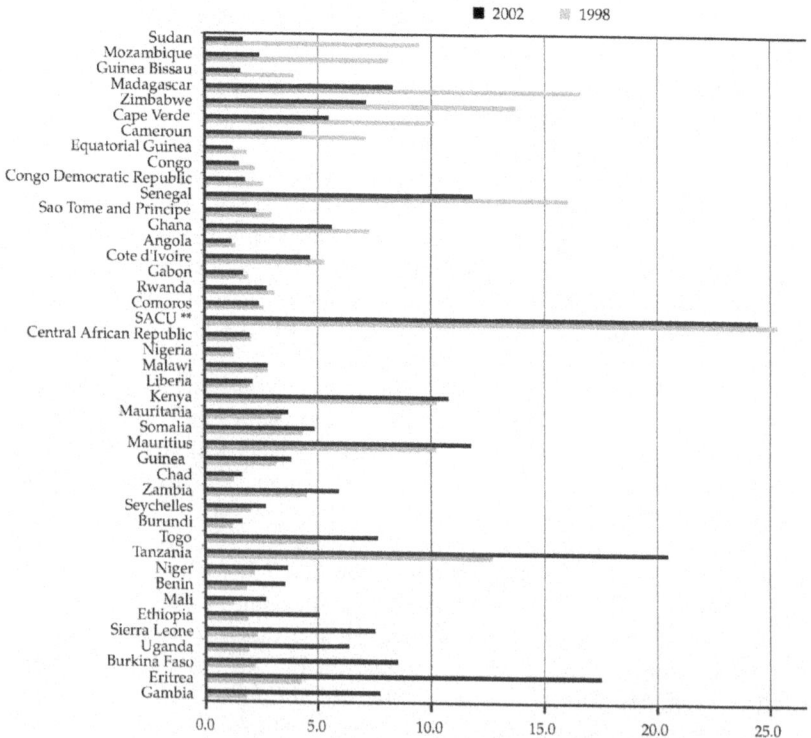

Source: Goldstein and Helmut 2006, 52

Sudan and China tightened their relations via the oil sector thanks to the deteriorating relation between Khartoum and Washington. Chevron's departure in 1992 signaled to other western companies that Sudan was now "off limits"[22]. This disengagement represented an investment opportunity for Chinese firms that were not subject to the same pressures from their government and human rights advocacy groups.

China's involvement in the Sudanese oil sector via the China National Petroleum Corporation (CNPC) led to a rapid increase in their trade[23]. Exports grew from 0 in 1998 to 276 millions of US$ in 1999 and 3,097 billion in 2004. Indeed, they represented at that time up to 81% of all exports[24]. Since then Sudan has, however, been replaced by Angola as the first oil exporter to China[25] and, due to the partition of the country, Sudan's position as an oil producer has considerably decreased, as 80% of the oil fields are located in the South.

Thanks to China, real GDP in Sudan grew by some 11.8% in 2006[26]. The oil-fueled economic boom enabled Sudan to sustain double-digit GDP growth for a few years, making it one of the fastest growing economies in Africa[27]. The rise of oil prices on the international market also contributed to this trend. Sudan is now considered a lower middle income country by the World Bank after having long been considered to be one of the least developed, poor low income and highly indebted countries[28].

However, there are at least two problems to note regarding this relation. First, because of the authoritarian and pariah status of the regime, Sudan has been prevented from taking advantage of the leeway given to many African countries in this era of the "new Scramble for Africa". The result is that Sudan rapidly became one of the less (if not the least) diversified economies in Africa. According to Nour, "the share of China in total loans and grants offered to Sudan greatly increased from 17% in 1999 to 73% in 2007 out of total loans and grants offered to Sudan"[29]. China's input has replaced the funds allocated by western donors, the IMF and the World Bank that had been drastically reduced following the establishment of the Islamist regime. China's input decreased however between 2007 and 2009, probably as a consequence of the global economic crisis.

Conclusion

China's engagement in Africa in many ways follows the patterns that were previously set by traditional, Western partners insofar as it emphasizes local elites, is founded on resource-backed loans and subscribes to a clear profit motive. This point has been well documented by Alden and Alves who, at the same time, recognize that China has proved to be sensitive to African and international pressures and has repeatedly introduced changes in its policies towards the continent[30]. Thus, even though the Chinese seek in Africa, as any country, to maximize their national interests, they are also probably more flexible and accommodative than many of the traditional bilateral (Western countries) and multilateral (IMF, World Bank) partners. This flexibility has something to do with the Chinese way of doing things in the international arena labeled as "soft power" by many authors. But it is also explainable by the fact that, unlike the Western countries such as France and the US, China has virtually no military or political leverage on African countries. This means that, depending on their policy choices, their awareness of the issues at stake and their capacity to negotiate, African countries have a window of opportunity to shape their cooperation with China and other partners in a way that is more beneficial to their people. In this respect, state capacity, along with the other variables – civil society and leadership strategies (not discussed here) – play a crucial role in determining African states' ability to shape their relationship with Chinese investors for the development of their countries.

---

[1] Wade, Abdoulaye. 2008. Time for the West to Practice What It Preaches. // Financial Times, 23 January.

[2] Swann, Christopher and William McQuillen. 2006. "China to Surpass World Bank as Tope Lender to Africa," Bloomberg News 3.

[3] Mbeki, Thabo. 2006. Speech Delivered at the Fourteenth National Congress of the South African Students Congress (9–14 December).

[4] Alden, Chris. 2007. China in Africa. London/New York: Zed Books, p. 59-60.

[5] Jackson H. Robert and Carl G. Rosberg. 1982. Why Africa's Weak States Persist: The Empirical and the Juridical in Statehood // World Politics 35 (1): 1-24.

[6] Rice, Susan E. and Stewart Patrick. 2008. Index of State Weakness in the Developing World, The Brookings Institution

[7] Ibid., p. 3.

[8] See Hendrix, Cullen S. 2010. Measuring State Capacity: Theoretical and Empirical Implications for the Study of Civil Conflict // Journal of Peace Research 47: 273-285.

[9] Rice, Susan E. and Stewart Patrick, p. 39-42.

[10] Bach, Daniel and Mamoudou Gazibo. 2012. Neopatrimonialism in Africa and Beyond, Routledge

[11] Rice, Susan E. and Stewart Patrick, p. 41.

[12] Safo, Amos. 2005. South Africa: The Textile Saga: Workers Turn the Heat on Government. // Public Agenda (27 June 2005), available at allafrica.com/stories/200506271442.html (accessed 21 February 2008).

[13] Rupp, Stephanie. 2008. frica and China: Engaging Postcolonial Interdependencies in Robert I. Rotberg (ed.), China into Africa: Trade, Aid, and Influence (Cambridge: World Peace Foundation, p. 70-71

[14] Ibid, p. 71.

[15] Xinhua. 2009. Nigeria, China Sign Pact to Replace Faulty Satellite by 2011, 25 March.

[16] Mbeki, Thabo. 2006. Speech Delivered at the Fourteenth National Congress of the South African Students Congress (9–14 December)

[17] Shinn, David H. and Joshua Eisenman. 2012. China in Africa: A Century of Engagement. Pennsylvania: University of Pennsylvania Press, 2012, p. 247-8.

[18] Hu, Jintao. 2007. China Faces Charges of Colonialism //International Herald Tribune (28 January 2007), available at http://www.nytimes.com/2007/01/28/world/asia/28iht-sudan.4374692.html and "Enhance China-Africa Unity and Cooperation to Build a Harmonious World," speech by Chinese President Hu Jintao at University of Pretoria, 7 February.

[19] Rupp, Stephanie, p. 70-71.

[20] Rice, Susan E. and Stewart Patrick, p. 39.

[21] Large, Daniel. 2008. China & the Contradictions of 'Non-Interference' in Sudan // Review of African Political Economy 35 (115), p. 94–95.

[22] Patey, Luke Anthony. 2007. State Rules: Oil Companies and Armed Conflict in Sudan // Third World Quarterly 28(5), p. 1005.

[23] Jakobson, Linda, and Zha Daojiong. 2006. China and the Worldwide Search for Oil Security // Asia-Pacific Review 13(2), p. 66.

[24] Abbadi, Karrar AB, and Adam Elhag Ahmed. 2006. Brief Overview of Sudan Economy and Future Prospects for Agricultural Development. Food Aid Forum. Khartoum, p. 3.

[25] Foster, Vivien, William Butterfield, Chuan Chen, and Nataliya Pushak. 2009. Building Bridges: China's Growing Role as Infrastructure Financier for Sub-Saharan Africa. World Bank Publications, p. 39; Vines, Alex. 2007. China in Africa: A Mixed Blessing? // Current History 106, p .214.

[26] Large, Daniel, p. 94.

[27] Nour, Samia Satti Osman Mohamed. 2011. Assessment of Effectiveness of Chinese Aid in Financing Development in Sudan. United Nations University Working Paper, p. 2.

[28] Ibid, p. 1-2.

[29] Ibid, p. 2.

[30] Alden, Chris and Ana Christina Alves. 2009. China and Africa's Natural Resources: The Challenges and Implications for Development and Governance. South African Institute for International Affairs, Occasional Paper no 41, p. 21.

Alice Nicole Sindzingre, PhD,
National Centre for Scientific Research
(CNRS, France);
Research Centre EconomiX-University
Paris-West

CHINA'S RELATIONSHIPS WITH SUB-SAHARAN AFRICA: DESPITE CONVERGENCE WITH INDUSTRIALISED COUNTRIES, DRIVERS OF STRUCTURAL TRANSFORMATION?

Abstract

China has become a major trading and investment partner of Sub-Saharan African economies since the early-2000s. It is argued, that China's trade and investment patterns converge with those of developed countries, but also that they may foster structural transformation. Sub-Saharan African growth rates since the early-2000s are indeed driven by China's demand for goods produced in Sub-Saharan Africa and its contribution to high commodity prices. Yet these growth rates stem from distorted export structures (based on primary commodities), and they may strengthen commodity-dependence with its negative effects. Against these views, the paper argues that Sub-Saharan African countries' growth rates as well as commodity prices may stay high, as China's growth expected to remain sustained, and a long period of high growth rates and improved fiscal room for manoeuvre may foster structural transformation. Also China is not exposed to the negative effects of conditional aid, and it increasingly invests in Sub-Saharan African infrastructure and industrial sectors, both being key determinants of structural transformation.

1. Introduction

China has become a major trading and investment partner of Sub-Saharan African (SSA) economies since the early-2000s. The paper shows the complexity of the impacts of these trade and investment relationships, as well as their convergence with those of developed countries vis-à-vis SSA. It argues that these relationships may foster the structural transformation of SSA economies, i.e. a break with pre-existing structures, industrialisation and productivity growth. SSA economies have indeed exhibited spectacular growth rates since the early-2000s, which have mainly been driven by China, via several direct and indirect transmission channels, notably China's demand for goods produced in SSA and its contribution to high international commodity prices (e.g., for metals, oil), SSA export structures being characterised by a high proportion of primary commodities.

Different views could suggest that there are uncertainties, in particular that SSA growth rates stem from distorted export structures, i.e., based on primary commodities with low value-added, and that these growth rates may not imply any change of commodity-based export structures. These growth rates may even strengthen commodity-dependence, as high growth rates and high prices are incentives to continue the status quo and may lock SSA economies into the exporting of primary commodities, with its negative effects (vulnerability to volatile prices and external shocks, 'Dutch disease'). These processes may threaten SSA economies' prospects for industrialisation and they may be compound by the weakening of SSA industrial sectors by cheaper manufactured products from China.

Against these views, however, the paper argues that SSA countries' growth rates may stay at high levels, as China's growth (and that of other emerging countries') expected to remain sustained in the medium term, and as the price of some commodities may stay high. A long period of high growth rates, together with an improved fiscal room for manoeuvre, may therefore constitute a genuine opportunity for structural transformation for SSA economies. Equally, commodities may create linkages towards industrialisation. In addition, China's cooperation is not exposed to the negative effects of conditional aid, and increasingly invests in infrastructure and industrial sectors, both being key determinants of structural transformation.

Therefore, the paper firstly examines the trade relationships between China and SSA and shows their convergence with industrialised countries as well as their ambivalent effects: for both industrialised countries and China, the detrimental effects of commodity-based trade patterns and positive effects of investment. Secondly, the paper examines the specificities of China's impact: apart from differences in the matter of conditional aid, China's specific growth path may contribute to SSA industrialisation and long-term growth.

2. China trade and investment policies: convergence with developed countries

2.1. The pattern of trade between Sub-Saharan Africa countries and China: China's convergence with developed countries

A similar trade pattern: trading commodities. All SSA countries export a lower share of their products to their 'traditional partners' (the United States and the EU countries) than in 1990, and a greater share to emerging countries, in particular China (figure 1). The sustained demand for SSA commodities by China represents a diversification of partners. A key point is that regarding its trade pattern with SSA, China does not exhibits any 'exceptionalism' (in contrast with its claims of distinctiveness in terms of international relations, Alden and Large, 2011): China's trade pattern converges with the secular pattern of developed countries with SSA, which trade commodities with SSA since the colonial period. China imports primary commodities ('hard' commodities, notably oil or metals, and 'soft' commodities, such as agricultural raw materials) from SSA and exports industrial products to the continent (Ye, 2010) (figures 2).

Indeed, SSA is characterised by a commodity-based structure for its exports to all countries, developed and emerging. For example, in 10 SSA countries, commodities exports represent more 75% of total exports (World Bank, 2012). It is this distorted structure that has been the main driver of growth in the 2000s (figure 3). China continues this pattern via two channels: Chinese demand for SSA products and China's contribution to high international commodity prices (Akyüz, 2012). China has indeed become the first importing country in the world, and notably of primary commodities[1]: China is now the dominant importer of metals (aluminium, copper, iron) and agricultural raw materials (Roache, 2012), and the first energy consumer in the world (IMF, 2011a). High commodity prices represent a positive gain for SSA exporters, as they imply an enhanced fiscal space, hence more space for investment, which is a key determinant of long-term growth. Yet they strengthen SSA exporters' incentives to remain commodity producers (Sindzingre, 2013). Driven by high commodity prices and Chinese demand, SSA economies have enjoyed high growth since the early-2000s – 4.9% in 2013 (IMF, 2014) (figure 4).

The negative economic effects of a commodity-based export structure. Yet this trade pattern that maintains commodity dependence has notorious negative effects. A key point is that here the contribution of China does not exhibit any specificity vis-à-vis SSA 'traditional' partners, i.e. developed countries.

Commodity dependence generates vulnerabilities (Sindzingre, 2012a; Robinson and Sindzingre, 2012). Beyond Dutch disease, the inherent volatility of commodity prices spawns volatility in fiscal receipts and therefore resources for investment, and may generate unsustainable debt. In oil-rich countries government revenues from natural resources represented 60% of total government revenues in 2011 (World Bank, 2012). Price volatility has a negative impact on GDP growth rates for commodity-dependent countries not only because prices may decline, but also because repeated price shocks are detrimental to long-term growth. Here domestic policies have little effect on growth rates: growth may just stem from 'good luck' (East-

211

erly et al., 1993). Commodity-dependent countries' growth rates depend on the fluctuations of prices, which are determined by external forces, on the growth and demand of other countries (the United States, EU countries, China) and on the latter' domestic policies. Equally, the incentives created by high commodity prices induce disincentives for industrial projects, though they are the best routes towards growth.

Another key negative effect is the low value added of primary commodities: the exports of commodities make a contribution to a country's wealth that is lower than manufactured products. In addition, most commodity sectors are characterised by low productivity, which has a detrimental impact on growth. A definition of long-term sustained growth may indeed be growth that is based on structural transformation: i.e., for a given economy the shift from a regime of low-productivity – usually agricultural and more generally unprocessed products – to a regime of high productivity – usually manufactured products. Growth divergence across countries stems from differences in factors productivity and total factor productivity (technology, knowledge). The difference in the productivity levels between high-income countries and SSA – the 'convergence gap' – remains large (Rodrik, 2011). This distorted export structure explains the diminution of the share of SSA in global exports, as other countries trade goods with more value-added, despite the increase of SSA exports in absolute value (figure 5). Likewise, when SSA growth performances are put in a longer-term perspective, the broad picture is that of a divergence vis-à-vis other regions (figure 6).

Similarly, regarding its exports to SSA, the key point is that China follows the same trade pattern as industrialised countries (EU countries, the United States), i.e. it exports industrial products. Be it driven by industrialised countries or by China, this export pattern may have negative effects for local SSA industries, and therefore on the possibility of structural transformation: it may strengthen SSA specialisation in the export of commodities (Kaplinsky and Morris, 2008).

Chinese exports are more situated in the low-end than those from developed countries: China's trade is indeed driven by its comparative advantage in labour-intensive production and economies of scale in its shipping and light manufacturing sectors (Eisenman, 2012). Yet China exports medium technology machinery to SSA, which can be particularly helpful in filling bottlenecks that affects SSA manufacturing sectors, and be a key route towards sustained growth (Poon, 2014).

2.2. Investment in Sub-Saharan Africa by Chinese firms

The convergence in the determinants of foreign direct investment in SSA by industrialised countries and China. Chinese foreign direct investment (FDI) is very difficult to compute, in particular due to the use of tax heavens and 'roundtripping' (Pairault, 2013a, b; Milelli and Sindzingre, 2013). Chinese FDI to SSA as a share of total FDI to the region climbed from less than 1% in 2003 to 16% by 2008 (IMF, 2011b). Investment in SSA countries exhibit wide variations: e.g., in South Africa, China was in 2010 only the 6th largest investor, with 3.7% of FDI stock (90% being a single investment, in Standard Bank of South Africa) (Gelb, 2013).

According to the criteria developed by Dunning (2000), the motives of FDI may be market-seeking, efficiency-seeking, resource-seeking and strategic-asset-seeking. Using this framework, Milelli and Sindzingre (2013) demonstrate the convergence of the determinants of Chinese FDI in developed countries (in particular Europe) and SSA: while the determinants of Chinese FDI in developed countries were initially access to their markets, these now include efficiency-seeking motives and assets-seeking motives – asset-seeking motives remaining a contrast with developing countries. Chinese FDI in developing countries, notably SSA, is mostly driven by resource-seeking motives (strategic inputs for China's growth). Resource-seeking FDI, however, characterises Chinese and non-Chinese FDI in developed countries when these countries are resource-rich (Australia, Canada). Moreover, as shown by the many Chinese small and medium private enterprises that invest in SSA, market access has increasingly become a determinant of Chinese FDI, together with efficiency– and assets-seeking motives – rising labour costs in China being incentives for relocating abroad in labour-intensive sectors where competitiveness is driven by prices (table 1).

Indeed, a great share of all FDI in SSA is directed towards primary resources, in particular oil. For example, in Angola, the United States is the leading investor in the oil sector (GAO, 2013), and as with FDI in SSA from the rest of the world, Chinese FDI is also driven by resource-seeking motives, these resources being strategic for China's own growth (Kragelund, 2009), Chinese FDI being therefore driven by countries' endowments in natural resources (Biggeri and Sanfilippo, 2009; Deych, 2013). Chinese FDI, however, appears to be increasingly driven by the 'linkage', 'leverage' and 'learning' drivers (the LLL' framework, Mathews, 2006): firms invest in order to augment their competences by learning from their overseas investments ('leveraging' FDI, Kaplinsky and Morris, 2009b). Equally, Chinese FDI in commodity and infrastructure sectors is driven by large state-backed enterprises (Pairault, 2013a, b) which represent the largest share of FDI in value (77% of China's FDI in SSA, Xu, 2014; in oil, copper, iron ore, Alves, 2013a), while Chinese small and medium enterprises, which target local and regional markets, dominate in numbers. Large state-backed Western firms also invest in SSA. Finally, as Western multinational firms, Chinese firms have harnessed trade agreements (e.g., unilateral trade preferences). Some

US investors have come to SSA thanks to the AGOA[2], and some China's firms invested in SSA in order to use the AGOA for exporting to US markets (Kaplinsky and Morris, 2009a).

The positive spillover effects of 'resource-for-infrastructure' contracts. The so-called 'resource-for-infrastructure' contracts may be used by large Chinese firms and could constitute a difference with the pattern of FDI of Western countries, i.e. barter deals in which infrastructures are exchanged for primary 'hard' commodities (oil, minerals – the so-called 'Angola model') (Alden and Alves, 2009; Corkin, 2008, 2011a). These 'commodity-for infrastructure' deals imply a risk of lock-in SSA structure in the exporting of commodities – indeed, such investments are conditioned to a stream of export of commodities over several years (Foster et al., 2009; Alves (2013b) -, and may stem from China's direct and indirect securing of the provision of inputs for its growth.

Many of these contracts, however, are used for infrastructure projects. SSA is characterised by very low levels and quality of infrastructure, which generate huge transaction costs and impede trade. The possible negative impact of 'resource-for-infrastructure' contracts compared to FDI from Western countries may be counterbalanced by the positive impacts of the improvement in infrastructure on SSA growth (Calderon and Serven, 2010; Foster and Briceño-Garmendia, 2010). The China's White Paper (The People's Republic of China, 2013) thus underscores that Chinese government encourages Chinese firms' participation in SSA infrastructure construction via concessional and commercial loans (e.g., the Addis Ababa-Adama Expressway of Ethiopia, or the Kribi Deep-water Port of Cameroon).

In fine, SSA countries cannot be viewed as passive entities both vis-à-vis developed countries and China. They have a capacity for 'agency' whatever the constraints analysed above (Mohan and Lampert, 2013; for Angola, Corkin, 2011c; 2012; 2013; Alves, 2013c).

3. A specific contribution of China to Sub-Saharan African economies?

3.1. A channel of relationships that contrasts China vis-à-vis Western countries: aid

The contrast between Chinese and Western aid. Some SSA countries are excessively dependent on aid, e.g., for budgets, investment, maintenance, infrastructure, health, education. Net official development assistance (ODA) to SSA represented in 2011 4% of GNI, 18.7% of gross capital formation and 8.8% of imports of goods, services and income (World Bank Development Indicators, 2013). Despite important variations within SSA, besides the small island economies of Oceania, SSA is the region of the world that is the most dependent on aid, and much above the average of low-income– and middle-income countries (figure 7). Aid dependence induce well-known negative effects (Easterly, 2009), e.g. Dutch disease (Harrigan, 2007), intrinsic negative effects of volatility (Bulir and Hamann, 2008), and the undermining of institutions, in particular tax institutions (Moss et al., 2006).

China's aid refers to an old tradition of cooperation, which began in the 1960s (Brautigam, 2009; 2010). Chinese aid flows are notoriously difficult to compute: loans are difficult to distinguish from export credits, and Chinese statistics do not use the OECD Development Assistance Committee (DAC) criteria that define ODA[3]. The OECD, however, computes 'ODA-like' flows, i.e. concessional financing for development, for 'non-traditional' donors such as China: Chinese flows are still limited compared with major donors such as the United States or Japan (OECD, 2013; figure 8). A substantial part of Chinese aid consists in the abovementioned contracts associating aid, trade and investment, and includes subsidising infrastructure, direct finance to Chinese firms and resource-backed infrastructure loans (Davies, 2008). According to the Government of China's White Paper (Chinese Government, 2011), China's financial resources provided for aid fall into three types: grants, interest-free loans and concessional loans. The first two types come from China's state finances, while concessional loans are provided by the EximBank. For Brautigam (2009), Chinese aid to SSA is much less important than EximBank export credits, but nevertheless exhibits a clear increase (Mlachila and Takebe, 2011).

Chinese aid flows display important variations across countries. In Ghana for example, US grant commitments exceeded China's during the period 2006-2010, while the US government committed smaller amounts of loans than China – China's loans being primarily for infrastructure construction, their repayment being sometimes tied to commodities (oil, cocoa) (GAO, 2013). In Kenya, China has become one of the top donors since 2009, primarily providing highly concessional loans (GAO, 2013).

China's cooperation displays many characteristics that contrast with developed countries' aid. Chinese financing is largely focused on infrastructure investments; part of export credits are linked to extraction of natural resources through 'infrastructure for natural resources' deals, and such financing is less concessional than ODA. China's aid differs from 'traditional' donors by its close ties with the state banks and state enterprises, often involved in the implementation of China's foreign policy vis-à-vis SSA (Christensen, 2010). China's model of 'economic cooperation' has in fact followed the one practised by Japan in Asia, linking aid, investment and trade (Nissanke and Söderberg, 2011). There are other differences: e.g., Chinese aid has not suffered from volatility in amounts, paradigms and fads that have characterised Western aid (Brautigam, 2009; Sindzingre, 2012b).

215

Chinese aid: avoiding the detrimental effects of conditionalities? A key point is that this Chinese development cooperation – a nexus of aid, trade and investment – does not include (economic or political) conditionalities on particular policies. This is a major difference with Western aid, multilateral (such as the international financial institutions/IFIs, the IMF and the World Bank, or the European Commission) or bilateral. Whether it is made of loans or grants, the ODA of OECD-DAC countries, of IFIs or of a major donor such as the European Commission is conditional to economic, and often, political reforms (e.g. 'good governance').

In contrast, China's aid is more a development cooperation driven by diplomatic and political economy relationships, which go back to the period of independence of SSA countries in the late 1950s-early 1960s and Cold War context, and its motives are broader than strictly economic ones, as they explicitly include the support of Chinese firms (Brautigam, 2009; Rotberg, 2008; Shinn and Eisenman, 2012; Taylor, 2009). China's claims non-interference with recipient countries domestic affairs and its cooperation therefore deals with all regimes, be they illiberal democracies, dictatorships or even 'pariah' regimes (Alden, 2007; Samy, 2010; on Zimbabwe, Hodzi et al., 2012).

This lack of conditionality is in sharp contrast with the conditionalities attached by major Western donors. Cooperation between SSA governments and the Chinese government – with its various agencies (e.g., the EximBank, the MOFCOM, the China-Africa Development Fund) – involves conditions, e.g. on the contracts established between the African and the Chinese contractor. Such conditions radically differ from conditionalities, however: for example, from IFI conditionalities that involve for recipient countries both extensive and deep policy reforms, which encompass the entire economy, as is the case with the conditionalities attached by the IFIs to their programmes. These conditionalities, which are extended to all aspects of a country's economy, may even be supplemented by political conditionalities ('good governance), as in the case of European aid, the EU Generalised System of Preferences/GSP (which also includes conditions related to labour and environment), bilateral mechanisms such as the US AGOA[4] or the Millennium Challenge Corporation[5].

The absence of wide and deep conditionalities, as is the case of China, may have positive effects on SSA economies. It has been argued that with this 'non-interference' stance, China has been able to import more from SSA countries that exhibit a lower governance standing: thus filling a gap left open by the other major world economies, China contributes positively to SSA development (De Grauwe et al., 2012). Moreover, and as is shown by a large literature, Western agencies' 'exchange' of finance for deep policy reform has had many detrimental effects on recipient countries' economies. Conditionalities (e.g. fiscal, monetary), may be very intrusive and prescribe drastic changes in recipient countries economic and political equilibria, and given the asymmetry of the 'donor'-'recipient' relationship – aid-dependent low-income countries have a limited room for manoeuvre.

There is no doubt that the absence of conditionality may induce many problems, e.g., the support of undemocratic political regimes, opaque deals and corruption. It may be argued, however, that conditional aid as practiced by developed countries' agencies – multilateral or bilateral -, also includes these problems, in addition to the negative effects that are inherent to conditionality itself. For both developed countries and China, cooperation is driven by interests, and aid has always been a dimension of the foreign policy of developed economies (Alesina and Dollar, 2000). Aid delivered by developed countries' donors has also allowed for the maintenance in power of autocratic and corrupt regimes (Alesina and Weder, 2002), which use aid as a rent and for redistribution to clienteles, manipulate donors' conditions as instruments for the implementation of their own domestic politics, or use donors as 'scapegoats' (Vreeland, 1999). The share of OECD-DAC countries' aid going to corrupt countries has actually increased since the early 1990s, despite conditionalities and the rhetoric of 'good governance' (Easterly and Pfutze, 2008), and aid to autocracies and mixed regimes of autocracies and democracies has not diminished (Easterly, 2013).

Moreover, key detrimental aspects are inherent to the mechanism of conditionality itself -making aid conditional on reform. They have long been demonstrated since the first programmes of policy-based lending prescribed to SSA governments by the IFIs from the 1980s onwards (as performance did not improve in the 1980s and 1990s – the 'lost decades' -, the IFIs reacted in augmenting their conditionalities, which became increasingly structural and extended to non-economic issues). Conditionalities by definition express tensions, imply a limitation of sovereignty, induce policy reversals (stemming from the 'buying of reform') and pave the way of the 'aid game'. The persistent failure of conditional IMF stabilisation programmes has led, on the donors side, to a repetition of lending since the 1980s onwards, and on the recipients side, to the continuation of dependence on donor lending, which has been acknowledged by the IMF (the 'prolonged users', IMF-IEO, 2002). IFIs also added 'selectivity' to conditionality, where donors lend to governments that already have 'good policies' (Thomas, 2004) – conditionalities thus being tautologically effective in countries that wish to reform.

Attempts to reform conditionality have met with mixed success and cannot change its intrinsic asymmetry, i.e. between the one who has the power to give money and therefore impose conditions, and the one who needs it. These divergences in interests and objectives, which are inherent to conditionality, entail negative effects, e.g., the 'Samaritan dilemma' (Gibson et al., 2005): if the recipient government knows that donors condition their aid on a reduction of poverty, it has little incentives to exert high effort toward this objective, as in doing so it will receive less aid in the future – which is aggravated by moral hazard: the donor can never know if a poor outcome is the result of low effort ('bad policies') or 'bad luck' (Svensson, 2005). Conditional aid indeed inherently exhibits important coordination failures (including information problems on other donors' aid). On their side, donors did not enforce conditions, due to their own institutional incentives to lend. Loans may also be given to enable old aid loans to be repaid: conditionality has therefore contributed to the erosion of the credibility of the IFIs vis-à-vis borrowing countries (Svensson, 2000; Marchesi and Sabani, 2007).

In being non-conditional, not prescribing economy-wide policy reforms, China's aid avoids these pitfalls and may therefore be more effective. China's cooperation thus displays a significant contrast with developed countries' development assistance. This difference, however, may diminish over time and a convergence with developed countries donors may emerge. As shown by Grimm (2014), the discourse attached by the Chinese government to its cooperation with SSA, which underscores 'mutual benefits' and 'non interference', may be challenged by the mixed success of this cooperation over time in terms of development: the Chinese government may also be confronted with the necessity for SSA countries to implement policy reform.

3.2. China's contribution in industrialisation of Sub-Saharan Africa: a driver of structural transformation?

China's investment in Sub-Saharan Africa industrial and manufacturing sectors. Besides oil and mining, Chinese firms invest in industrial sectors of SSA – manufacturing, construction, finance, agriculture and services sectors (IMF, 2011b; Shen, 2013; Gu, 2009). Large state-backed firms tend to focus on resources and infrastructure, whereas private firms tend to concentrate on manufacturing and service industries. Chinese FDI has also been oriented towards resource-poor countries (Mali, Ethiopia, Uganda) (The People's Republic of China, 2013). In addition, large Chinese state-owned enterprises may be associated with smaller firms (e.g., sub-contractors in the construction sector) (Xu, 2014): this may create positive spillover effects and Hirschmanian backward and forward linkages within SSA economies (Hirschman, 1958). In some SSA countries Chinese FDI is more concentrated in the manufacturing sector than in primary commodities. An example is Ethiopia, where one of the largest Chinese shoes exporters has started an important investment in 2013[6] (IMF, 2011b; Lin and Wang, 2014a).

The contribution of China to Sub-Saharan Africa's structural transformation. Growth is expected to stay high in the medium term (Felipe et al., 2013), despite the uncertainties associated with China reorientation of its growth

218

towards domestic consumption. China's contribution to high growth rates in SSA, via its demand for SSA exports, and via its contribution to high international commodity prices, is therefore likely to continue. This contribution to growth gives an additional fiscal room for manoeuvre to SSA countries' policy choices, e.g., industrial policies focusing on structural transformation, as did the Asian 'developmental states' at the time of their 'catch-up' (Japan, Korea, Taiwan, Amsden, 1989; Wade, 1990). In addition, the growth of China implies increasing wages and costs, hence opportunities for SSA countries where Chinese firms can outsource activities of the low-end segments of production networks. The sector of labour-intensive, little sophisticated, manufactured products is often viewed as a first step towards industrialisation and China may be here a factor of structural change. Equally, Chinese manufacturers increasingly invest in SSA in order to benefit from preferential trade tariffs (Dinh et al., 2012).

The diffusion of the benefits of growth, however, may be difficult for commodity-dependent countries (Macmillan and Rodrik, 2013), due to the 'lock in' effects and trapping mechanisms that are generated by the incentives provided by commodities prices (Sindzingre, 2012). It depends on the characteristics of SSA countries, notably on whether they have the institutions that can channel the benefits of these growth rates (and not 'extractive' institutions, Acemoglu and Robinson, 2012). Countries may also lack the capabilities and knowhow that are necessary to transform the benefits of growth into foundations for long-term growth via the diffusion of technology and higher total factor productivity (Arthur, 2009; Hausmann, 2014). Yet even trade and investment in the commodity sector may contribute via spillover effects to the industrialisation of SSA countries, and create linkages in Hirschman's sense with other sectors that exhibit higher productivity and diffusion of knowledge and technology (Morris et al., 2011; 2012) – SSA countries, however, differ, e.g., China's investment in Angola's oil sector generated little spillovers (Corkin, 2011b).

China may thus contribute to SSA structural transformation in two ways: China-financed infrastructure projects address SSA infrastructure bottlenecks, and China's industrial upgrading and its FDI foster labour-intensive light-manufacturing sectors (Lin and Wang, 2014b). China established several Special Economic Zones in SSA with the aim of promoting manufacturing, and, as argued by Brautigam and Tang (2014), they may foster SSA structural transformation. *In fine*, China may contribute to SSA growth since industrialisation is a key determinant of long-term growth (Rodrik, 2009).

4. Conclusion

Firstly, the paper has shown that the effects of China on SSA depend on the channels – trade, investment, aid – and time horizons. While China's cooperation is less affected by the detrimental effects of Western conditional aid, China's demand for primary commodities may perpetuate the negative effects of SSA commodity-based export structure. Yet China may foster structural transformation via multiple channels: high commodity prices and the associated fiscal space, demand for SSA products, investment and infrastructure. Secondly, China's trade and investment patterns increasingly converge with those of Western countries. An important difference, i.e. a development cooperation that for China is not based on economy-wide policy-conditionality, may also converge with that of other donors.

Vis-à-vis China and industrialised countries, SSA governments and societies have a capacity of agency: outcomes result from combinations of elements, external forces are always transformed by internal features, and there is room for manoeuvre for domestic policies. Domestic political economy creates the difference between countries that will be able to harness Chinese investors' demand when China's production costs will become too high, and countries that will remain in the production of primary commodities with its vulnerabilities. Path dependence may prevail, but, as shown by Arthur (1994) and David (2000), small bifurcations may always occur and produce unexpected effects.

Bibliography

Acemoglu, Daron and James Robinson. 2012. Why Nations Fail: The Origins of Power, Prosperity, and Poverty, New York, Crown Business.

Akyüz, Yılmaz. 2012. The Staggering Rise of the South?, Geneva, South Centre, research paper 44.

Alden, Chris. 2007. China in Africa, London, Zed Books.

Alden, Chris and Ana Cristina Alves. 2009. China and Africa's Natural Resources: the Challenges and Implications for Development and Governance, Johannesburg, South African Institute of International Affairs, SAIIA occasional paper 41: http://www.saiia.org.za/images/stories/pubs/occasional_papers/saia_sop_41_alden_alves_20090917.pdf

Alden, Chris and Daniel Large. 2011. China's Exceptionalism and the Challenges of Delivering Difference in Africa, Journal of Contemporary China, vol. 20, n°68, January, pp. 21-38.

Alesina, Alberto and David Dollar. 2000. Who Gives Foreign Aid to Whom and Why?, Journal of Economic Growth, vol. 5, n°1, March, pp. 33-63.

Alesina, Alberto and Beatrice Weder. 2002. Do Corrupt Governments Receive Less Foreign Aid?, American Economic Review, vol. 92, n°4, September, pp. 1126-1137.

Alves, Ana Cristina. 2013a. Chinese Economic Statecraft: A Comparative Study of China's Oil-backed Loans in Angola and Brazil, Journal of Current Chinese Affairs, vol. 42, n°1, pp. 99-130.

Alves, Ana Cristina. 2013b. China's Economic Statecraft and African Mineral Resources: Changing Modes of Engagement, Johannesburg, SAIIA occasional paper 131, January.

Alves, Ana Cristina. 2013. China's 'Win-Win' Cooperation: Unpacking the Impact of Infrastructure-For-Resources Deals in Africa, South African Journal of International Affairs, vol. 20, n°2, pp. 207-226.

Amsden, Alice. 1989. Asia's Next Giant, Oxford, Oxford University Press.

Arthur, W. Brian. 1994. Increasing Returns and Path Dependence in the Economy, Ann Arbor, University of Michigan Press.

Arthur, W. Brian. 2009. The Nature of Technology: What It Is and How It Evolves, New York, Free Press.

Biggeri, Mario and Marco Sanfilippo. 2009. Understanding China's Move into Africa: an Empirical Analysis, Journal of Chinese Economic and Business Studies, vol. 7, n°1, February, pp. 31-54.

Brautigam, Deborah. 2009. The Dragon's Gift: the Real Story of China in Africa, Oxford, Oxford University Press.

Brautigam, Deborah. 2010. China, Africa, and the International Aid Architecture, Tunis, African Development Bank, working paper 107.

Brautigam, Deborah and Xiaoyang Tang. 2014. "GoingGlobal in Groups": Structural Transformation and China's Special Economic Zones Overseas, World Development, forthcoming.

Bulir, Ales and Javier Hamann. 2008. Volatility of Development Aid: From the Frying Pan into the Fire?, World Development, vol. 36, n°10, pp. 2048-2066.

Calderon, Cesar and Luis Servén. 2010. Infrastructure and Economic Development in Sub-Saharan Africa, Journal of African Economies, vol. 19, AERC Supplement 1, pp. 13-87.

Chinese Government's Official Web Portal. 2011. White Paper on Foreign Aid Activities, Information Office of the State Council, The People's Republic of China, April. http://www.gov.cn/english/2011-04/21/con-tent_1849764.htm

Christensen, Benedicte Vibe. 2010. China in Africa: a Macroeconomic Perspective, Washington D. C., Center for Global Development, working paper 230.

Corkin, Lucy. 2011a. China and Angola: Strategic Partnership or Marriage of Convenience?, Bergen, Chr. Michelsen Institute, Angola Brief, vol. 1, n°1, January.

Corkin, Lucy. 2011b. Chinese Construction Companies in Angola: a Local Linkages Perspective, Cape Town, University of Cape Town and Open University, Making the Most of Commodities Programme (MMCP), MMCP discussion paper 2.

Corkin, Lucy. 2011c. Uneasy Allies: China's Evolving Relations with Angola, Journal of Contemporary African Studies, vol. 29, n°2, April, pp. 169-180.

Corkin, Lucy. 2012. L'Exim Bank à Luanda : modèle angolais ?, Outre Terre, n° 30, pp. 227-239.

Corkin, Lucy. 2013. Uncovering African Agency: Angola's Management of China's Credit Lines, Farnham, Ashgate.

Corkin, Lucy et al. 2008. China's Role in the Development of Africa's Infrastructure, Washington D. C., Johns Hopkins University, SAIS working paper in African Studies 04-08.

221

David, Paul A. 2000. Path Dependence, its Critics and the Quest for 'Historical Economics', mimeo, Oxford, All Souls College (in Pierre Garrouste and Stavros Ioannides eds., Evolution and Path Dependence in Economic Ideas, Cheltenham, Edward Elgar, 2001).

Davies, Martin, with Hannah Edinger, Nastasya Tay and Sanusha Naidu. 2008. How China Delivers Development Assistance to Africa, Stellenbosch, University of Stellenbosch, Center for Chinese Studies.

De Grauwe, Paul, Romain Houssa and Giulia Piccillo. 2012. African Trade Dynamics: Is China a Different Trading Partner?, Journal of Chinese Economic and Business Studies, vol. 10, n°1, February, pp. 15–45.

Deych, Tatiana. 2013. Chinese Companies on African Raw Materials Markets, Lisbon, 5th European Conference on African Studies (ECAS) 'African dynamics in a multipolar world', 27-29 June.

Dinh, Hinh T., Vincent Palmade, Vandana Chandra and Frances Cossar. 2012. Light Manufacturing in Africa: Targeted Policies to Enhance Private Investment and Create Jobs, Washington D. C., the World Bank and Agence Française de Développement.

Dunning, John H. 2000. The Eclectic Paradigm as an Envelope for Economic and Business Theories of MNE Activity, International Business Review, vol. 9, pp. 163–190.

Easterly, William. 2009. Can the West Save Africa?, Journal of Economic Literature, vol. 47, n°2, June, pp. 373–447.

Easterly, William, Michael Kremer, Lant Pritchett and Lawrence Summers. 1993. Good Policy or Good Luck? Country Growth Performance and Temporary Shocks, Journal of Monetary Economics, vol. 32, pp. 459–483.

Easterly, William and Tobias Pfutze. 2008., Where Does the Money Go? Best and Worst Practices in Foreign Aid, Journal of Economic Perspectives, vol. 22, n°2, Spring, pp. 29-52.

Easterly, William. 2013. The Tyranny of Experts: Economists, Dictators, and the Forgotten Rights of the Poor, New York, Basic Books.

Eisenman, Joshua. 2012. China–Africa Trade Patterns: Causes and Consequences, Journal of Contemporary China, vol. 21, n°77, September, pp. 793–810.

Felipe, Jesus, Utsav Kumar, Norio Usui and Arnelyn Abdon. 2013. Why Has China Succeeded? And Why It Will Continue To Do So, Cambridge Journal of Economics, vol. 37, pp. 791–818.

Foster, Vivien, William Butterfield, Chuan Chen and Nataliya Pushak 2009. Building Bridges: China's Growing Role as Infrastructure Financier for Sub-Saharan Africa, Washington D.C., the World Bank and PPIAF, Trends and Policy Options 5.

Foster, Vivien and Cecilia Briceño-Garmendia. 2010. Africa's Infrastructure: A Time for Transformation, Washington D. C., the World Bank, Africa Development Forum series, AICD (Africa Infrastructure Country Diagnostic).

Gelb, Stephen. 2013. Chinese Brown Goods Manufacturers in South Africa, Milan, COST Conference on the Impact of Emerging Multinationals on Global Development, May.

Gibson, Clark C., Krister Andersson, Elinor Ostrom and Sujai Shivakumar. 2005. The Samaritan's Dilemma: The Political Economy of Development Aid, Oxford, Oxford University Press.

Government Accountability Office (GAO). 2013. Sub-Saharan Africa: Case Studies of U.S and Chinese Economic Engagement in Angola, Ghana, and Kenya; a Supplement to GAO-13-199, Washington D. C., Government Accountability Office.

Grimm, Sven. 2014. China–Africa Cooperation: Promises, Practice and Prospects, Journal of Contemporary China, forthcoming.

Gu, Jing. 2009. China's Private Enterprises in Africa and the Implications for African Development, European Journal of Development Research, vol. 21, n°4, September, pp. 570-587.

Harrigan, Jane. 2007. The Doubling of Aid to Sub-Saharan Africa: Promises and Problems, Journal of Contemporary African Studies, vol. 25, n°3, September, pp. 369-389.

Hausmann, Ricardo. 2014. The Mismeasure of Technology, Project Syndicate, 29 April. https://www.project-syndicate.org/commentary/ricardo-hausmann-explains-why-technological-diffusion-does-not-occur-according-to-economic-theory

Hirschman, Albert O. 1958. The Strategy of Economic Development, New Haven, Yale University Press.

Hodzi, Obert, Leon Hartwell and Nicola de Jager. 2012. Unconditional Aid': Assessing the Impact of China's Development Assistance to Zimbabwe, South African Journal of International Affairs, vol. 19, n°1, April, pp. 79-103.

International Monetary Fund. 2011a. World Economic Outlook, Washington D.C., International Monetary Fund, April.

International Monetary Fund. 2011b. Regional Economic Outlook: Sub-Saharan Africa: Sustaining the Expansion, Washington D. C., International Monetary Fund, October.

International Monetary Fund. 2014. Regional Economic Outlook: Sub-Saharan Africa: Fostering Durable and Inclusive Growth, Washington D. C., International Monetary Fund, April.

International Monetary Fund-Independent Evaluation Office (IEO). 2002. Evaluation of Prolonged Use of IMF Resources, Washington D. C., International Monetary Fund.

Kaplinsky, Raphael and Mike Morris. 2008. Do the Asian Drivers Undermine Export-Oriented Industrialisation in SSA?, World Development, vol. 36, n°2, pp. 254–273.

Kaplinsky, Raphael and Mike Morris. 2009a. The Asian Drivers and SSA: Is There a Future for Export-oriented African Industrialisation?, World Economy, vol. 32, n° 11, pp 1638-1655.

Kaplinsky, Raphael and Mike Morris. 2009b. Chinese FDI in Sub-Saharan Africa: Engaging with Large Dragons, European Journal of Development Research, vol. 21, n°4, September, pp. 551–569.

Kragelund, Peter. 2009. Part of the Disease or Part of the Cure? Chinese Investments in the Zambian Mining and Construction Sectors, European Journal of Development Research, vol. 21, n°4, September, pp. 644-661.

223

Lin, Justin Yifu and Yan Wang. 2014a. Africa's Low-Hanging Fruits: the Right Intervention, at the Right Time, and Right Place, Helsinki, UNU-WIDER Angle newsletter, 23 April: http://www.wider.unu.edu/ publications/newsletter/articles-2014/en_GB/04-2014_1_JL

Lin, Justin Yifu and Yan Wang. 2014b. China-Africa Co-Operation in Structural Transformation: Ideas, Opportunities, and Finances, Helsinki, United Nations University, WIDER working paper 2014/046.

Marchesi, Sylvia and Laura Sabani. 2007. IMF Concern for Reputation and Conditional Lending Failure: Theory and Empirics, Journal of Development Economics, vol. 84, n°2, November, pp. 640-666.

Mathews, John A. 2006. Dragon Multinationals: New Players in the 21st Century Globalization, Asia Pacific Journal of Management, vol. 23, pp. 5-27.

Mcmillan, Margaret, Dani Rodrik and Inigo Verduzco-Gallo. 2013. Globalization, Structural Change, and Productivity Growth, with an Update on Africa, World Development, forthcoming.

Milelli, Christian and Alice Sindzingre. 2013. Chinese Outward Foreign Direct Investment in Developed and Developing Countries: Converging Characteristics?, Paris, University Paris-West-Nanterre, EconomiX, working paper 2013-34.

Mlachila, Montfort and Misa Takebe. 2011. FDI from BRICs to LICs: Emerging Growth Driver?, Washington D. C., International Monetary Fund, working paper WP/11/178.

Mohan, Giles and Ben Lampert. 2013. Negotiating China: Reinserting African Agency into China-Africa Relations, African Affairs, vol. 112, n°446, January, pp. 92-110.

Morris, Mike, Raphael Kaplinsky and David Kaplan. 2011. 'One Thing Leads to Another': Commodities, Linkages and Industrial Development: A Conceptual Overview, Cape Town, University of Cape Town and Open University, MMCP discussion paper 12 (revised).

Morris, Mike, Raphael Kaplinsky and David Kaplan. 2012. One Thing Leads To Another: Promoting Industrialisation by Making the Most of the Commodity Boom in Sub-Saharan Africa, Milton Keynes, the Open University and Cape Town, University of Cape Town, Making the Most of Commodities Programme.

Moss, Todd, Gunilla Pettersson and Nicolas van de Walle. 2006. An Aid-Institutions Paradox? A Review Essay on Aid Dependency and State Building in Sub-Saharan Africa, Washington D. C., Center for Global Development, working paper 74.

Nissanke, Machiko and Marie Söderberg. 2011. The Changing Landscape in Aid Relationships in Africa: Can China's Engagement Make A Difference to African Development?, Stockholm, Swedish Institute of International Affairs (UI), UI paper 2011-2.

OECD-DAC. 2013. Development Cooperation Report 2013, Paris, OECD.

Pairault, Thierry. 2013a. Les entreprises chinoises sous la tutelle directe du gouvernement illustrées par leur investissement en Afrique, Revue de la régulation, vol. 13, 1er semester, Spring, http://regulation.revues.org/10195

Pairault, Thierry. 2013b. Chinese Direct Investment in Africa: A State Strategy?, Région et Développement, n° 37-2013, Note et Document.

Poon, Daniel. 2014. China and South-South "Self-Sustaining Growth": An Opening for Industrial Policy and Catch-Up Development, Geneva, UNCTAD, discussion paper, forthcoming.

Roache, Shaun K. 2012. China's Impact on World Commodity Markets, Washington D. C., International Monetary Fund, working paper WP/12/115.

Robinson, Lee and Alice N. Sindzingre. 2012. China's Ambiguous Impacts on Commodity-Dependent Countries: the Example of Sub-Saharan Africa (with a Focus on Zambia), Paris, University Paris West-La Défense, EconomiX, working paper 2012-39. http://economix.fr/pdf/dt/2012/ WP_EcoX_2012-39.pdf

Rodrik, Dani. 2009. Growth after the Crisis, London, CEPR discussion paper DP7480.

Rodrik, Dani. 2011. The Future of Economic Convergence, Cambridge MA, NBER working paper 17400.

Rotberg, Robert I. ed. 2008. China into Africa: Trade, Aid and Influence, Washington D.C., Brookings Institution Press.

Samy, Yiagadeesen. 2010. China's Aid Policies in Africa: Opportunities and Challenges, The Round Table: The Commonwealth Journal of International Affairs, vol. 99, n°406, February, pp. 75-90.

Shen, Xiaofang. 2013. Private Chinese Investment in Africa: Myths and Realities, Washington D. C., the World Bank, policy research working paper 6311.

Shinn, David H. and Joshua Eisenman. 2012. China and Africa: A Century of Engagement, Philadelphia, University of Pennsylvania Press.

Sindzingre, Alice Nicole. 2012a. The Impact of the 2008–2009 Crisis on Commodity-Dependent Low-Income African Countries: Confirming the Relevance of the Concept of Poverty Trap?, Journal of International Development, vol. 24, n°8, November, pp. 989–1007.

Sindzingre, Alice Nicole. 2012b. Theoretical Criticisms and Policy Optimism: Assessing the Debates on Foreign Aid, Vienna, University of Vienna, Department of Development Studies, working paper n°1. http://ie-workingpaper.univie.ac.at/ fileadmin/user_upload/proj_int_entwicklung/IE-Working-Papers/IE-WP-1-2012_Sindzingre.pdf

Sindzingre, Alice Nicole. 2013. The Ambivalent Impact of Commodities: Structural Change or Status Quo in Sub-Saharan Africa? South African Journal of International Affairs, vol. 20, n°1, pp. 23-55.

Svensson, Jakob. 2000. When is Aid Policy Credible? Aid Dependence and Conditionality, Journal of Development Economics, vol. 61, pp 61-84.

Svensson, Jakob. 2005. Absorption Capacity and Disbursement Constraints, Paris, Agence Française de Développement, AFD-EUDN Conference.

Taylor, Ian. 2009. China's New Role in Africa, Boulder, Lynne Rienner.

The People's Republic of China, Information Office of the State Council. 2013. China-Africa Economic and Trade Cooperation (China-Africa White Paper), Beijing, August. http://news.xinhuanet.com/english/china/2013-08/29/c_132673093.htm

Thomas, M.A. 2004. Can the World Bank Enforce its own conditions?, Development and Change, vol. 35, n°3, pp 485-497.

Wade, Robert. 1990. Governing the Market: Economic Theory and the Role of Government in East Asian Industrialisation, Princeton, Princeton University Press.

225

World Bank. 2012. Africa Pulse, vol. 6.

Xu Yi-Chong (2014): Chinese State-owned Enterprises in Africa: Ambassadors or, Freebooters?, Journal of Contemporary China, forthcoming.

Ye, Xiao. 2010. A Path to Mutual Prosperity? The Trade and Investment between China and Africa, Tunis, African Development Bank, AEC Conference.

Appendixes

Figure 1: Sub-Saharan Africa: total exports and percentage of exports by partner

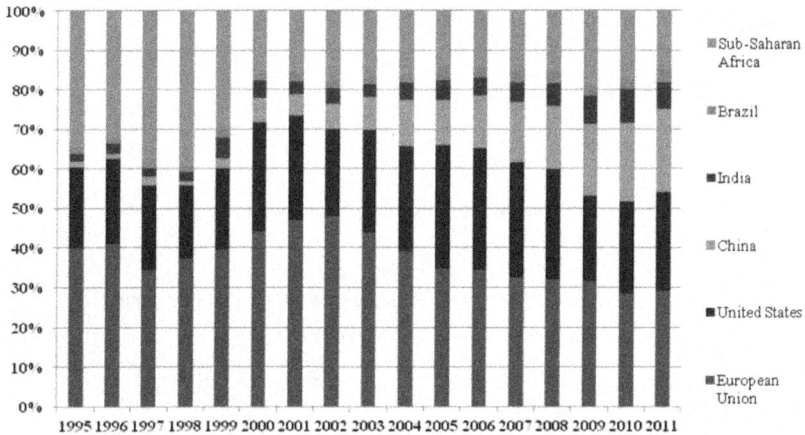

Source: http://unctadstat.unctad.org, author's calculations.

Figure 2a: Sub-Saharan Africa exports to China by key product groups, 1995–2011

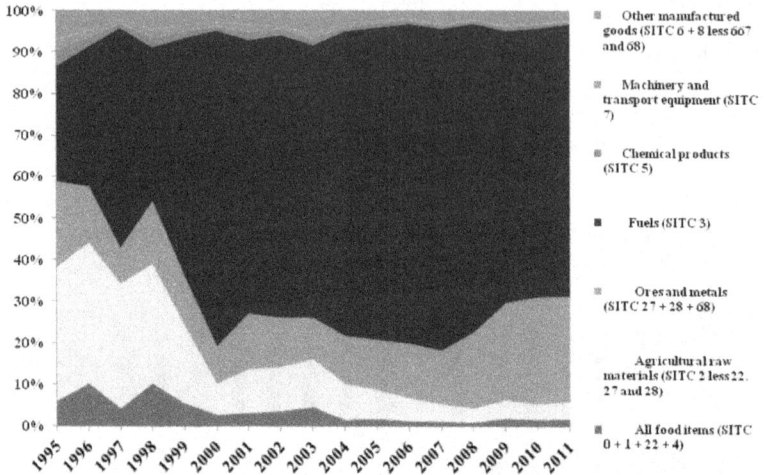

Source: UNCTAD Statistics: http://unctadstat.unctad.org; author's calculations.

Figure 2b: Sub-Saharan Africa exports to G8 countries by key product groups, 1995–2011

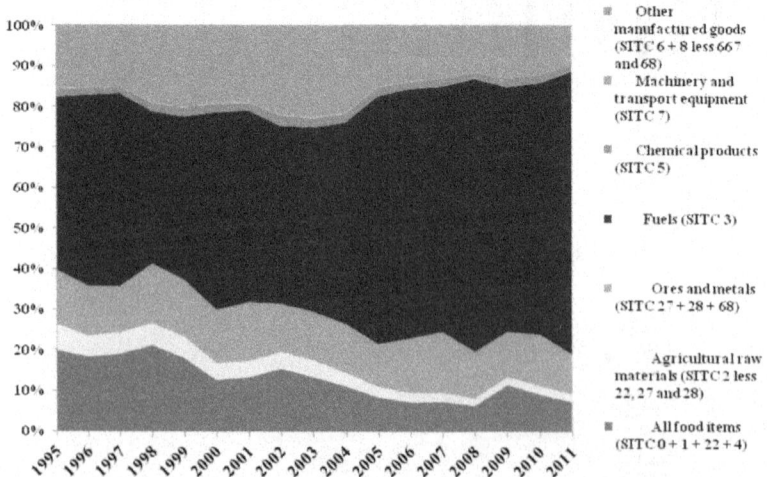

Source: UNCTAD Statistics: http://unctadstat.unctad.org; author's calculations.

Figure 3: Sub-Saharan Africa: GDP growth rate (right scale) and commodity prices (annual price indices, 2000=100, left scale), 1960–2013

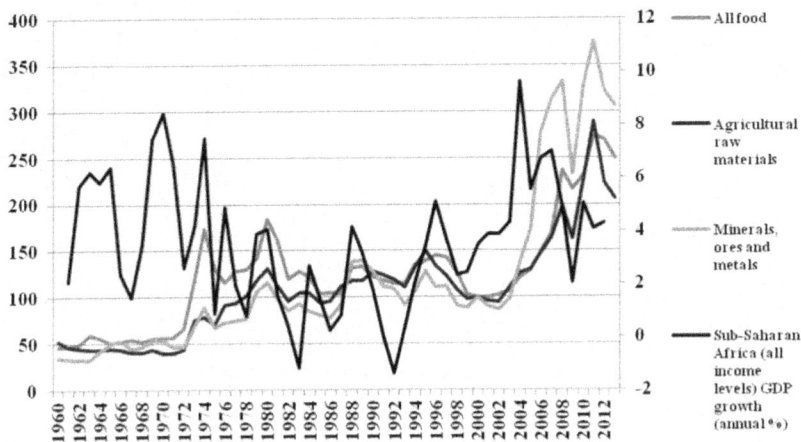

Source: UNCTAD Statistics and World Bank World Development Indicators, May 2014.

Figure 4: Sub-Saharan Africa: GDP growth and GDP per capita growth, 1960–2012

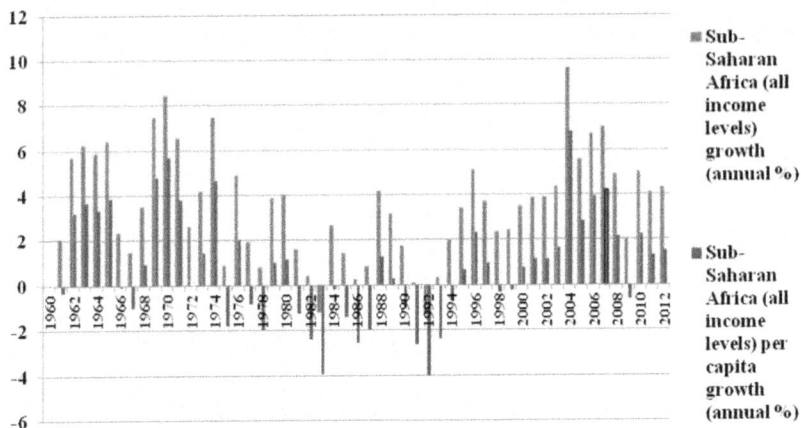

Source: World Bank World Development Indicators, May 2014.

228

Figure 5: Sub-Saharan Africa's exports: percentage of world exports (right axis) and value (left axis), 1948–2013 (USD billions)

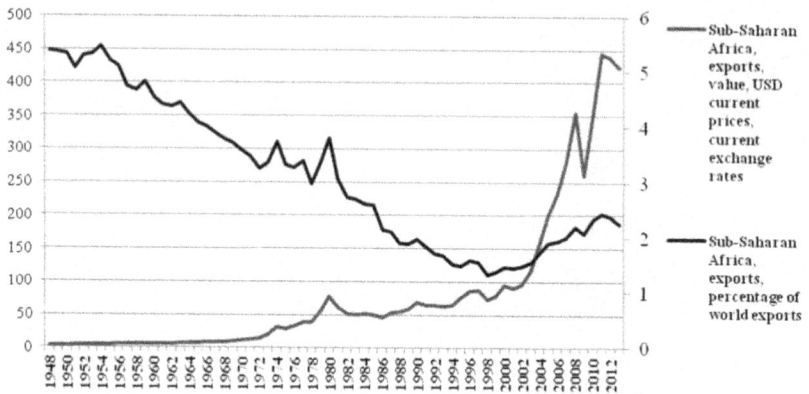

Source: UNCTAD Statistics: http://unctadstat.unctad.org, May 2014.

Figure 6: GDP per capita, Sub-Saharan Africa vs. the world, 1960–2012 (constant 2005 USD)

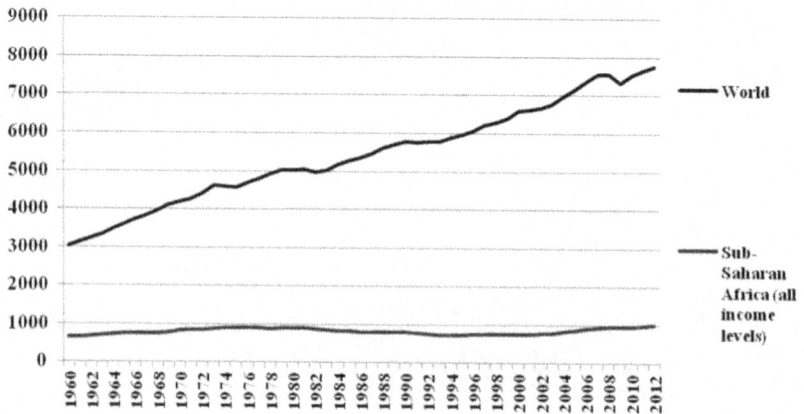

Source: World Bank World Development Indicators, May 2014.

229

Figure 7: Net Official Development Assistance received, in percentage of Gross National Income, 1960–2012

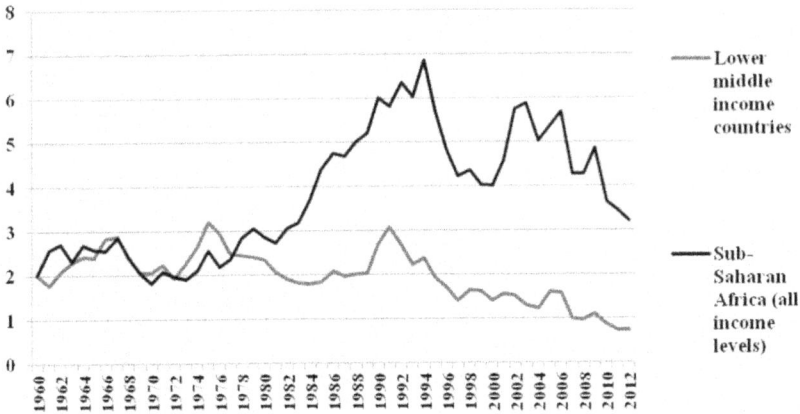

Source: World Bank World Development Indicators, May 2014.

Figure 8: Concessional financing for development ("ODA-like" flows), 2011 (billions USD)

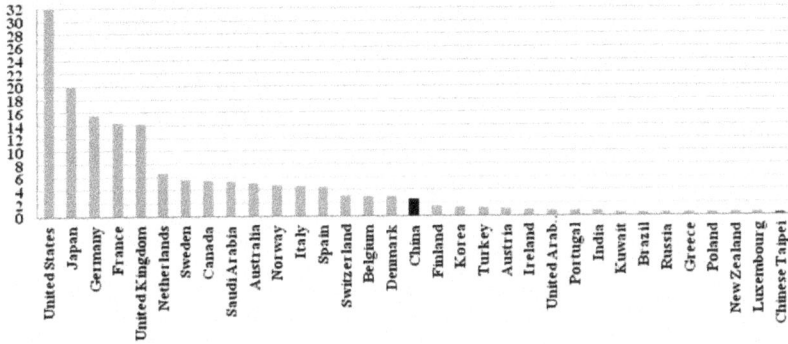

Source: OECD (2013).

Table 1a: Motives of Chinese FDI: Europe versus Sub-Saharan Africa

Motive	Europe	Sub-Saharan Africa
Resource-seeking		Main motive due to abundant natural resources
Market-seeking	First motive	New motive but expanding in order to supply local markets
Asset-seeking	Motive expanding	
Efficiency-seeking	New motive, in order to acquire skilled workforce and regionally streamline organisational structures	Relocation of Chinese firms, particularly SMEs, in low technology and labour-intensive industries

Source: Milelli and Sindzingre (2013), using Dunning' (2000) conceptual framework.

Table 1b: Processes underlying Chinese FDI: Europe versus Sub-Saharan Africa

Process	Europe	Sub-Saharan Africa
Linkage		Linkages across Chinese communities and financial institutions, and SSA private sectors
Leverage	Large financial resources (state-owned enterprises, state banks, sovereign wealth funds)	Large financial inflows
Learning	Learning from previous partnerships in China with Western firms; learning from Chinese difficulties encountered in Europe	

Source: Milelli and Sindzingre (2013), using Mathews' (2006) conceptual framework.

231

¹ Jamil Anderlini and Lucy Hornby, China overtakes US as world's largest goods trader, *Financial Times*, 10 January 2014: http://www.ft.com/intl/cms/ s/0/7c2dbd70-79a6-11e3-b381-00144feabdc0.html#axzz32aXUvTX5

² African Growth and Opportunity Act, a unilateral system of trade preferences granted by the US to a group of SSA countries that meet specific conditions.

³ See also Brautigam's very informative and relevant blog: http://www.china-africarealstory.com

⁴ http://trade.gov/agoa/eligibility/index.asp

⁵ http://www.mcc.gov/pages/selection

⁶ William Wallis, China plans multimillion Ethiopia investment, *Financial Times*, 3 June 2013.

Yuri Smertin, Dr.Sc.
Kuban State University,
Krasnodar, Russia

CHINA AND AFRICA: MUTUAL INTEREST

In the last decade, China has managed to strengthen seriously its influence in Africa. The Chinese government and business are interested in African oil (1/3 of Chinese imports of hydrocarbons), ores, non-ferrous and rare metals. To ensure its food security China is building its agricultural enterprises on the rented or purchased lands of the continent. Africa is becoming an important market for the goods exported from China. At 2012, the trade turnover between China and the African countries reached $198.49 billion, and in 2015 it should reach $300 billion. The volume of Chinese investments in Africa increased to $21.23 billion.

China is present, politically and economically, in 50 countries of the continent. To achieve its goals in Africa, Beijing uses different strategies, which arranged in a precise system.

First, it appeals to the history, focusing on general distant and not-too-distant common past with the African nations. The brilliant episode, which draws attention, was when in 1415 an Imperial fleet led by Admiral Zheng He visited the East African coast. It is emphasized, that he had not attempted to colonize the region: his purpose was the establishing friendly relatioThe Chinese influence in Africa began in the 60 – 70s of the 20th century when China was involved in the liberation wars on the continent and in the construction projects in independent countries. But the scale of this presence was limited by the USSR and the West rivalry in Africa. The African countries, for the sake of receiving the economic help, were guided generally by one of the two superpowers, and with both the People's Republic of China had hostile relations. After the end of the Cold war and the actual withdrawal of Russia from Africa, China could stabilize its positions as an important actor on the continent.

When the present Chinese leaders speak of their relations with Africa, they always refer to the historical context. Beijing puts emphasis on common past, in which China and African countries were the victims of the Western imperialism[1].

This historical discourse must convince the African leaders that China, having become a great nation, is committed to the interests of developing countries.

Secondly, China uses offensive policy in the field of education and culture. China provides scholarships for African students (6 000 in 2012) for

233

prepare technical, military and medical specialists. The majority of students study in Chinese. Thus the elite, loyal to Beijing, is forming. Moreover, the increasing presence of Africans in China offers the Chinese a wonderful opportunity to show their hospitality, which presents as an important tradition in African culture. Beijng opens Confucius Institutes, which are the tools of promoting Chinese language, culture, and Chinese visions of history, in many African countries. The first one opened in Nairobi in 2005. To date, 45 such Institutes established in 30 African countries[2].

Thirdly, an important element of Chinese influence in Africa has become diplomacy, which takes into account the interests of the African countries, marginalized in the international arena. In 2006 the Chinese authorities published "The White Paper", in which the fundamentals of its new African policy were declared. Beijing has emphasized: "China seeks to establish and to develop new type of strategic partnership with Africa, characterized by equality and mutual confidence in political affairs, mutually beneficial cooperation in the economic realm, and the strengthening of exchanges in cultural affairs"[3].

China offers Africa to fight together for the democratization of international relations, including the reform of the WTO and the UN, and for strengthening the positions of the African countries in them. All African countries have associated themselves with a Beijing's offer to provide the developing countries with two seats of non-permanent members of the Council. Beijing is promoting the concept of a multipolar world, in which the major powers balance their influence and collaborate with each other.

The Chinese leadership enhances South-South cooperation with the aim to improve the position of developing countries in the international arena. Frequent state visits also help to strengthen the positions of China on the continent. This allows establishing personal contacts between the leaders of China and the African countries. The frequency of official visits, particularly intensified since the early 1990s. Four Presidents of the People's Republic of China: Li Xiannian, Yang Shangkun, Jiang Zemin, Hu Jintao visited Africa. The latter made six visits to Africa: two as the vice-president and four as the president. The current President, Xi Jin-ping, committed his first overseas tour to Africa, visiting Tanzania, South Africa and the Republic of Congo. For their part, the heads of African states and governments also often visit China. During mutual visits exchange China announces its new assistance initiatives, signs a multi million-dollar contracts[4].

China has diplomatic relations with 50 countries of Africa. Only 3 states – Burkina Faso, Swaziland and São Tomé and Príncipe – continue to maintain diplomatic relations with Taiwan. Since 1991, each new Minister of Foreign Affairs of China has made his first official visit to an African country. Every year groups of young diplomats from different African countries, upon the invitation of the Chinese side, spend a month in China, and get acquaintance with the Chinese model of development[5]. The People's Republic of China uses also so-called symbolical diplomacy. In January 2012 China constructed the headquarters of the African Union in Addis Ababa.

China is also attractive for Africa for many reasons, one of which is its powerful economic boom carried according to the non-Western recipes. After decades of policies with an eye to the West, now Africans are looking for the new models of development. Africans willingly cooperate with China that is not following the neo-liberal prescriptions of the international financial institutions.

It's not by chance that the China begun its diplomatic offensive in Africa with such countries as Angola, Sudan and Zimbabwe. All these countries had valuable economic assets, and, more importantly, were in a difficult relationship with the World Bank and other international financial institutions because of charges of corruption and human rights violations. Representing itself as a commercial and diplomatic partner outside the structures of the OECD, China has been able to access some attractive projects on favorable terms, such as oil production in Angola and Sudan. Chinese does not associate their assistance with human rights defense, democracy, eradicating corruption, etc. For many Africans, tired from Western politicians' lectures, whose moral mandates were not always faultless, it became a breath of fresh air. Africans are willing to be the partners with China, which looks as a generous coach, but not as a mentor. In general, Africans are very receptive to China's politics, which aimed on establishing strategic partnership based on equality and mutual benefit.

An important instrument for the development of relations between China and the African countries is the Forum on China-Africa Co-operation (at the ministerial level), which has been held every 3 years since 2000. At Forum the cooperation programs concerning social and economic development are accepted, and concrete figures are defined. The 4th Forum conference took place In November 2009 in Egypt (Sharm el-Sheikh). The results of cooperation during the last decade were summed up there, and also further plans of the Chinese investments into the African economies were announced. Beijing promised to allocate $10 billion credits, to create a fund with authorized capital in $1 billion for lending to medium-sized and small African companies. Besides, the People's Republic of China promised to introduce a zero duty for 95% of goods from the poorest countries of Africa, as well as to write off the debts to the most hopeless debtors. The humanitarian program of cooperation assumed granting the medical equipment worth $73 million to 30 hospitals, building of 50 schools and construction of 100 projects on the production of "clean" energy from renewable sources in Africa. This program fulfilled completely[6].

According to the 2010 State Council White Paper, it will be composed of $3 billion in preferential loans, $2 billion in preferential export buyer's credits, and $5 billion will go toward the establishment of the China-Africa Development Fund, which is designed to encourage and support the Chinese companies investing in projects in Africa. The White Paper also indicated that China would provide credits of up to $1 billion toward Chinese financial institutions for the development of small and medium enterprises in Africa[7]

The 5th Forum took place in 2012 in Beijing, where the document "The Plan of Action for 2013-2015" was accepted. Some basic provisions of it were in speech of Chinese President Hu Jintao at Forum opening[8]. Five main areas of strategic partnership between China and Africa called. First, cooperation should be expanded in the spheres of investments and money accumulation for the purpose to assist Africa in moving towards sustainable development. Secondly, further increase in the help to Africa in order to ensure that all African people could use the results of development. Thirdly, support of integration processes in Africa and rendering help to it to increase the general ability to develop. Fourthly, to strengthen the friendship of the China and Africa peoples, to lay the strong social basis for their joint development. Fifthly, to struggle for peace and stability in Africa, to create the safe environment for the African development.

China's interest in Africa, the results of cooperation urge the developed countries to invest in Africa. The Chinese-African cooperation not only helped to integrate the African continent into the globalization process, but also forced the global community to reconsider its ways of assistance to Africa, for the sake of keeping the access to its resources. Europe and the USA don't perceive Africa as "patient" any more, but rather consider it as a partner.

Certainly, Africa's cooperation with China is not free from the problems. China adheres to the principle of non-interference into internal affairs of the African countries and respects their sovereignty. However, here Beijing is also acting out of pragmatic interests. Technocratic management of China realizes that absence of the effective and legitimate state institutes in some African countries creates problems for modern business. China refused large investments in Zimbabwe, understanding that after Robert Mugabe's death the country can plunge into chaos. The Chinese government was deeply shocked by the crash of their Libyan ally, M. Gaddafi, in 2011, and by the need to rescue 30 000 Chinese citizens from disorders after that. Keeping rhetoric of respect for the African sovereignty, China joins the international efforts on establishing order in the African problem countries. It actively participates in peacekeeping missions in Africa. Thereby it exploits existing international architecture in its own interests. Besides, Beijing creates the image of the great power, capable to assume the responsibilities that go with that status.

Certain discontent of Africans is caused by lack of China's interest in the creation of the enterprises of manufacturing industry. The rare exception is

Sudan, where the industry of oil refining and production of cheap and simple products from plastic is developing with the Chinese aid. Africans criticize the weak attraction of local labor force to work for the Chinese companies in Africa in the conditions of mass unemployment. Many construction projects are realised with the minimum attraction of local labour; even drivers and unskilled workers brought from China. Periodically there are disputes, concerning the wage level for attracted local people. The question of the negative impact of some Chinese industrial projects for local ecology is also raises.

One million Chinese lives in Africa. Some of them remained in the African countries after the end of joint projects. This tendency amplified after the Chinese emigration laws became less strict in 1985. The majority of them are small business owners, many of which are engaged in trade. In many African countries, there are shops in which the Chinese who are tolerably speaking local languages, trade in cheap goods of mass consumption made in China. Moreover, some Chinese manufacturers illicitly copy African designs, such as wax print textiles, and then produce them more cheaply in order to export back to Africa. Sometimes it considered unfair competition and causes public indignation, as it was in Senegal and Malawi[9].

Some Chinese traders use the false companies to import from Africa illegally everything from timber, diamonds to prized body parts of wild animals which RE under the threat of total extermination. The traders from Hong Kong moved into Africa as well. Recent years the Triads demonstrated their activity in Africa. They are engaged in stripping of the southern African coast of abolone (another name of these mollusks is "sea ears"), in shark fin and rhino horn trade, and in people trafficking[10].

All this has an adverse effect on the image of the Chinese in Africa. In some countries, there were anti-Chinese demonstrations. In Zambia the oppositional leader Michael Sata won presidential election in 2011 largely due to his anti-Chinese rhetoric. However, these negative moments of the Chinese-African interaction compensated by benefits for Africa. And not only material ones. The Chinese presence in Africa also influences African countries' relations with other partners. China paves the path for the countries trying to find their own ways and means for the development, wanting to assert themselves on the international arena, while maintaining their independence and protecting their way of life in a world dominated by the West.

[1] Alden C., Alves C. History and Identity in the Construction of China's Africa Policy // Review of African Political Economy. Vol. 35, № 115. 2008. P. 43-58.
[2] Confucius Institute Online // http: www.confuciusinstitute.net/

[3] The People's Republic of China. White Paper on China's African Policy. Beijing, 2008.

[4] Alden C. China and Africa. L.: International African Institute, 2007. P. 32.

[5] Gazibo M. How China Seduces Africa // The Newsletter. № 60. 2012. P. 25.

[6] Full text of Wen's speech at 4th Ministerial conference of FOCAC – www.china.org.cn/world/2009-11/09/content_18849890.html

7 White Paper on China-African Economic and Trade Co-operation. People's Republic of China (PRC). Information Office of State Council. December 1, 2010.

[8] Chinese President Hu Jintao addresses the opening ceremony of the Fifth Ministerial Conference of the Forum of China-Africa cooperation (FOCAC) in Beijing, capital of China, July 19, 2012 – www.cntv.cn/20120719/112038.shtml

[9] Brown D.E. Hidden Dragon, Crouching Lion: How China's Advance in Africa is Underestimated and Africa's Potential Underappreciated. Strategic Studies Institute. 2013. P. 4 – www. StrategicStudiesInstitute.army.mil/

[10] Ibid. P. 118.

V. RUSSIA-AFRICA RELATIONS IN PAST AND PRESENT

Evgeny Korendyasov, PhD (Economy)
Institute for African Studies
Russian Academy of Sciences

RUSSIA RETURNS TO AFRICA

In recent years, the dynamics of Russian-African relations notably improved. Investment activity has become more brisk, foreign trade turnover has somewhat increased. Russia has written-off $20 billion debts of African countries that practically eliminated the Soviet loans debt issue from the agenda of Russian-African relations. Russian overseas development aid in 2004-2012 reached the point of about $ 400 million.

However, the existing considerable potential of Russian-African relations is clearly untapped in full. These relations, today, are clearly lacking in scale, ambition, institutional equipment, and implementation tools.

Meanwhile, the role and importance of Africa in the world politics and economy is growing. The economy's growth rate accelerated. In the period from 2005 to 2012 it was on average 5.4% per year (in 2013 – 6,4%)[1]. African natural resources became more important for maintaining the stable supply of mineral raw materials to the world economy. FDI inflows expanded. In the last five years, it averaged 50-60 billion dollars a year, the stock investment in 1990-2013 exceeded $ 689 billion[2]. More than 40 African TNCs operate in Africa, and they are not inferior to the Western ones in competitiveness. There appeared also the first dozen of African billionaires, of which the wealthiest is a cement magnate, Nigerian Aliko Dangote whose fortune is $ 25 billion[3].

The shapes of the "African lions" (by analogy with the "Asian tigers") are already visible on the horizon. Africa at the turn of the XXI century has become an indispensable link in the global political and economic networks.

The nineties of last century were "failed years" in the history of Russian-African relations. The idea that since the end of the Cold War, Russia's national interests in Africa also ceased to exist is quite widely spread among certain Russian political and business circles, in the academic and expert community.

239

Russian diplomacy had to make considerable efforts to minimize damage to Russian-African relations caused by the replacement of the principles, forms and conditions of cooperation, which previously based on the logic of the bipolar confrontation and on the dogmas of the cold war.

In general, Russia managed to keep friendly climate in its relations with Africa. Favorable conditions for expanding the fruitful interaction between the two sides retain and expand.

Political and diplomatic relations

Presently a political and diplomatic sphere of Russian-African partnership is the main and the most productive one. In all likelihood, it will retain that position for many years ahead.

The proximity of positions of Russia and African countries on the new world order expands the objective possibilities of Russian-African cooperation in various fields. However, to improve Russia's African policy it is necessary to make timely adjustments to reflect the rapidly changing realities in the international arena.

The principles of respect for national sovereignty and non-interference in internal affairs, upon which the UN Charter is based, have ceased to be immutable. The exceptions to these principles were legitimized as well as the right to preventive intervention, in order to eliminate the terrorist threat, crimes against humanity, threats of genocide, and mass killings of civilians... The Africans have approved in principle, these exceptions, although retain high sensitivity and irritability in cases of their practical application.

It is especially relevant, considering that in practice the right to a humanitarian, preventive intervention began to be interpreted as the right to "force democracy", undertake a regime change.

So where is the compromise between the rule of non-interference in internal affairs and the right to a humanitarian intervention?

Search for it turned out to be difficult for Russia and Africa. Moreover, both of them sometimes find themselves on the opposite sides of the barricades. It happened in Libya, and it is happening now in Syria.

"Forcing democracy", proclaimed the legitimate grounds of armed intervention in the conflict. Meanwhile, such interference in the complex problem of determining the ways and the pace of modernization of African societies often drives this problem into the mainstream of tough confrontation between the preservation of identity and Westernization.

The purpose of peacemaking thus becomes not the reconciliation of the parties at the negotiating table on a mutually acceptable basis, but a strong support for one of them as the most democratically oriented.

The principal approaches of compromise between preserving the sovereignty and the right to a humanitarian intervention are in line with the observance of certain rules and regulations. Among them:

– Encouraging and promoting the peaceful settlement of the conflict, preventing the events from development along the confrontational scenario;

– Wide involvement of the African Union and sub-regional organizations of the continent in the peacekeeping efforts;

– Unacceptability of external interference with the expectation of "regime change" by force and pressure, as well as interference with the goal of "forcing democracy". Nobody can claim a monopoly in determining the optimal model of socioeconomic and democratic development. With all the universality of democratic values, they implemented in different ways, depending on the historical experience of development, the peculiarities of national culture and mentality. Viable democratic institutions, as global practice shows, formed on their own, national basis.

Under these conditions, today Russia should behave cautiously on what concerns international intervention in the internal affairs of the conflicting parties. Russia should also expand its cooperation in this area with the African Union, sub-regional organizations, taking into account the interests of the countries involved in the conflict.

Topical problems of trade and economic partnership

The turnover of the Russian-African trade and economic cooperation remains quite modest. Foreign trade turnover does not exceed $13 billion. Russian assets in Africa are estimated at 8-10 $ billion. As a rule, 950 state scholarships are annually offered by Russia to the students from African countries.

Foreign trade turnover in 2013 amounted to $9 billion dollars, of which the share of North African countries accounted for more than 70%. Among the countries of Sub-Saharan Africa, there were only seven countries, with which the trade turnover reached $ 100 million, with 9 countries – from 10 to 50 million, with 11 Sub-Saharan countries the turnover of foreign trade is less than 1 million dollars. Trade is not balanced: exports from Russia to Africa are 2 times more than its imports[4].

At the expense of trade with Africa, Russia covers from 50 to 60% of the needs of its aluminum industry in bauxites and much of the imports of cocoa and citrus fruits.

Russian assets in African countries are estimated at $ 8-10 billion.

In this context, the view that Russia has finally lost its "African chance" becomes more widespread. Such assertions seem hasty. It is enough just to look at the intensification of Russian business in the development of African mineral resources.

Russia has rich natural resources. Meanwhile, domestic capabilities to meet the industry's requirement in quality raw materials at competitive prices declined. Profitably exploited deposits are depleted or on the verge of exhaustion. A substantial deficiency of a number of important minerals emerged, which covered by imports, including manganese by almost 100%, chromium – 80%, bauxites – up to 60%, etc[5]. New Russian deposits are located mainly in the northern latitudes, and their development is associated with large investments and long lead times to commissioning and development, as well as with great environmental damage.

Africa accounts for approximately 30% of the planet's natural resources. The development of partnership with Africa in their exploration provides opportunities to overcome the difficulties Russia has faced. Table 1 quite convincingly demonstrates the potential of cooperation and the degree of complementarity in the field of mineral raw materials between Russia and Africa.

Table 1. **The Russia's deficit of mineral resources and potential of the mining sector in Africa**

Minerals	Russia		Africa	
	Extraction	The deficiency, %	Reserves[2] (*)	Extraction[2]
Manganese in ores	17 thousand tons 0.05%	97.0	1 326.0 million tons (22.1%)**	10.63 million tons (31.5%)**
Uranium in ores	3.6 thousand tons (9.2%)**	82.0	433.2 thousand tons (16.7%)**	6.0 thousand tons (15.4%)**
Tin in ores and concentrates	814 tons (0.3%)**	61.7	415 thousand tons (7.5%)**	15 thousand tons (4.8%)**
Chrome in ores	733 thousand tons (3.0%)**	60.3	1,839,200.0 thousand tons (48.4%)**	10,470.5 thousand tons (43.4%) **
Titanium concentrates	82.0 thousand tons (0.7%)**	59.2	435.8 (44.6%) **	2.389 (20.0%)**

242

Minerals	Russia		Africa	
	Extraction	The deficiency, %	Reserves^2 (*)	Extraction^2
Aluminium in bauxites	5.3 million tons 2.6%	50.0	7464.0 million tons (42.6%)**	20.9 million tons (10.5%)**
Zinc ores and concentrates	337.5 thousand tons 2.9%	27.8	17,040.0 thousand tons (7.1%)**	284.4 thousand tons (2.4%)**
Molybdenum ores and concentrates	5.4 thousand tons (2.4%)**	19.5	19.0 (0.1%)**	0.0
1	2	3	4	5
Tungsten ores and concentrates	4220.0 tons (7.5%)**	4.3	6000.0 tons (0.2%)**	160.0 tons (0.3%)**
Niobium (only produced at Solikamsk factory)		70		

Sources:
[1] State report «On the state and use of mineral resources of the Russian Federation in 2008", Ministry of Natural Resources, Moscow, 2009
[2] Statistical Handbook "Mineral Resources of the World," Information and Analytical Centre "Mineral", Moscow, 2009
* Table 2 shows only proved reserves by category ABC $_1$.
** As a percentage of the relevant international statistical data.

Africa produces 600 times more manganese than Russia, 20-fold more tin, 15 times more chromium, almost 30 times more tantalum, and 7 times more bauxites. The attractiveness of African ores also lies in more favorable conditions of their occurrence, in a high concentration of useful components in ore, and therefore in their lower cost price.

The access to the African hydrocarbon deposits is particularly important for our country. Africa is rapidly promoted to the role of a strategic player in the energy sector.

Proved oil reserves in Africa – 15.6 billion tons, or 9.8% of world reserves[6]. According to the estimations of the experts from JSC

"VNIIZARUBEZHGEOLOGIA", oil resources of the continent reach 40 billion tons, accounting for 7.2% of the world's resources[7].

It is predicted that the proven oil reserves in Africa could increase over the next two decades to 22.9 billion tons, in the optimistic perspective – to 29.2 billion tons[8].

Oil production in Africa has increased 4.5 times since 1965 to reach 490–500 million tons (12.5% of world production). Particularly high growth rates are observed in Angola (8%), Sudan (5%), and Equatorial Guinea (4%)[9]. The oil production in Africa is expected to increase in the next 10-15 years to 975 million tons (in the moderate variant), and up to 1.3 billion tons (in the optimistic variant). Export opportunities of the continent will increase respectively to 0.8 – 1.0 billion tons per year[10].

As for gas, its resources are estimated at 31 trillion cubic meters, while proven reserves – 14-15 trillion cubic meters (7.8% of world reserves). Production of gas (commodity) is 190 billion cubic meters (6.5% of world production), exports – 104 billion cubic meters[11].

African hydrocarbons play an increasingly prominent role in world markets. Thirty-two percent of African oil exports go to European countries, the same percentage – to the U.S. and 12% – to China. West African countries supply 40% of its exports to the U.S. market and 32% – to China, North African countries supply 56% of their hydrocarbon exports to Europe and 24% to the U.S[12]. At the expense of African sources the U.S. cover 15% of its oil imports, China – 20%[13]. Europe imports nearly 80% of African gas[14]. Gas resources' flows from Africa to Europe are growing particularly intensively (table number 2).The inflow of gas and oil resources from Africa to Europe begins to affect the interests of Russian companies.

Natural gas supplies from Russia to the countries of West, North, South and Central Europe declined from 148.44 billion cubic meters in 2004 to 132.8 billion cubic meters in 2009 (i.e. by 16 billion cubic meters), and from Africa increased from 68.7 to 78 billion cubic meters respectively (i.e., by 10 billion cubic meters).

In recent years, Russian companies have made significant efforts to expand their positions in the development of natural resources in Africa. Eighteen largest Russian companies implement 40 projects. The most significant of them are: diamond mining in Angola (Alrosa), construction of the pipeline Nigeria – Algeria (Gazprom), production of nickel in Botswana (Nornickel), field development of oil deposits in the coastal zone of Côte d'Ivoire, Ghana and Sierra Leone (Lukoil), the extraction of manganese and vanadium in South Africa (Renova, Evraz), oil production in Equatorial Guinea (Gazpromneftegaz), extraction of niobium in the DRC, gold in Burkina Faso, iron ore in Liberia (Severstal), etc. Most projects are still underway.

An important condition for the successful promotion of the interests of Russian mining companies in Africa is to achieve an optimum combination of business interests of Russian and African partners. Africa (as well as Russia), sits tightly on the "resource dependence" needle. Mining complex over the coming decades will continue to be the most important, for many African countries – the only source of revenue and the only way to attract investment resources. In this regard, Africans consistently seek to organize the most thorough possible processing of mined ore on the spot, up to the making of the final product. They continuously insist on the observance of the established international standards for corporate social responsibility.

In the face of difficulties and obstacles to the activities of Russian business in Africa, the latter needs systematical support from the state.

In this regard, it is particularly important to form an integrated system of promotion and support of Russian business' investment activity in partnership with African countries.

$$* * *$$

Both Russia and Africa declare intentions to seek the qualitative improvement of their cooperation, recognize the great role this co-operation could play in solving national problems in economic development and international affairs. However, the declared intentions are not being adequately reflected in the practical affairs. In Russia it prevented by its limited material and financial resources, Russian businesspersons' lack of sufficient information and experience, high political and commercial risks. In Africa – by the care to maintain cooperative relations with the Western economies, uncertainty in business-quality and reliability of Russian companies. However, the importance of cooperation with Africa will grow alongside with structural and technological modernization of Russian and African economies.

---

[1] FMI. African Economic Outlook. 2014. Basic Indicators.

[2] UNCTAD. World Investment Report 2013. N.Y – Genève, 2014. Annex. Table 2. P. 209.

[3] La fortune d'Aliko Dangote a crû de 4.2 milliards de dollars en 2013 // Jeune Afrique. 4 Mars 2014 – http://economie.jeuneafrique.com/regions/ afrique-subsaharienne/21557-la-fortune-daliko-dangote-a-cru-de-42-milliards-de-dollars-en-2013.html

[4] Customs statistics of Russia on the continent.

[5] Centre "Mineral" FGUNPP "Aerogeology". On the status and use of mineral resources of the Russian Federation in 2009. M. 2010.

[6] EIA. World Energy Review 2008. Oil of Russia. M., 2009. № 1. Pp.7-10; M., 2008. № 12, Pp. 7-10.

[7] Proceedings of the scientific and practical conference "Hydrocarbon and solid mineral resources in Africa". M., 2008. Pp. 24-44.

[8] Ibid. Pp. 93 -95.

[9] Oil of Russia. M., 2009. № 1. Pp. 93-95.

[10] Proceedings of the scientific and practical conference "Hydrocarbon and solid mineral resources in Africa". M., 2008. Pp. 26-27.

[11] Ibidem.

[12] Electronic resource: http://minerals.usgs.gov/minerals/rubs/country/2007/mybs3-3um-2007-africa.

[13] EIA. World Energy Review, 2009.

[14] Global Trends 2025: A Transformed World. US National Intelligence Council. Washington, 2008. P. 45-51.

Galina Smirnova, PhD (Economy)
Institute for Oriental Studies,
Russian Academy of Sciences

RUSSIA'S TRADE AND ECONOMIC COOPERATION WITH SUDAN AND SOUTH SUDAN: STATUS QUO AND PROSPECTS

On 9 July 2011, two new independent states appeared on the world map – the Republic of Sudan and the Republic of South Sudan (RSS). Both states are facing numerous difficulties and need to make important decisions while choosing models of political, social and economic development. Russia, which has accumulated vast experience in this regard and written a long history of cooperation with African countries, may help the two Sudan Republics in the solution of their numerous problems.

Before the global financial crisis of 2008, the economy of 'bigger' Sudan had developed in a very dynamic way. The real growth of GDP in some years reached 10% and more (11.3% in 2006 and 10.2% in 2007). The oil production, which started at the end of 1990s, drove most of Sudan's growth. However, at the turn of the centuries, the growth began to slow down and in 2010 the real growth of GDP was only 3.5% (2.8% in 2011). The latest International Monetary Fund (IMF) estimates indicate that the economy contracted by 4.4% in 2012. The IMF forecast for the growth of Sudan's real GDP in 2014 was 2.6%, in the event that oil exploration from South Sudan continues unabated, which, due to recent developments, is now deemed highly unlikely[1]. Inflation comprised 15% in 2011 and remained high thereafter. According to the Sudan Central Bureau of Statistics, consumer price index (CPI) inflation in May 2013 reached 37.3%. The current account deficit was 7.6% of GDP in 2011 and estimated at 10.2% of GDP in 2012 and 8.9% in 2013. Mostly a sharp drop in exports caused this. The unemployment rate estimated at 15.9% in 2011[2]. The IMF has warned of a "permanent shock" to the economy. Foreign exchange reserves are extremely low, hindering international trade; subsidies for oil and sugar have been cut, prompting a number of protests; and cuts that are more painful are coming. At the same time, the regime acknowledges has need for much higher taxes. Relevant finance ministry officials acknowledge there will be a 37% decline in oil revenue ($2 bn – $3bn annually) once the full effect of southern secession[3].

The American sanctions of 2007 and strained internal policy (the conflict in Darfur, South Kordofan and in the other parts of the country) also affected on the deterioration of the economic situation in Sudan. After the conclusion of the Comprehensive peace agreement (CPA) in 2005 and separation of South Sudan in 2011the economic situation in the Republic of Sudan deteriorated dramatically because the country lost the most part of their income from the export of oil. In such conditions, the Government of the Republic of Sudan was forced to look for the new sources of incomes. The President of Sudan, Hassan Omar Al-Bashir announced that the development of agriculture will be the main direction of Sudan's economic policy. This means that the country is going to return to the economic model, which existed before the start of oil production, when cotton export was the main source of hard currency. Thus, it is necessary to keep a balance between technical and food crops since the significant part of Sudan's food needs satisfied by imports. However, for the realization of these goals the Government of Sudan must extend the land under cultivation and modernize the country's irrigation system, which serves the main areas of cotton growing. Russia (as the successor of the USSR) has considerable experience in carrying out such works – an experience that Sudan may benefit from.

Sudan's Five-Year Strategic Plan 2012-2017 aimed at enhancing economic growth and development in a situation when the country has lost significant sources of income. The target is to achieve a growth rate of 6% by 2016 paying particular attention to private sector development. The plan targets to enhance youth employment and build capacity through training programs and development of micro-finance projects. The plan also includes a Three-Year Emergency Program that stipulates reforms required for macroeconomic stability. Besides, Sudanese authorities have extended the Green Revolution Plan 2008-2011 aimed at diversifying economic activities in agriculture, as part of the Five-Year Strategic Plan. The Green Revolution Plan envisages diversifying means and directions of economic growth beyond oil production. A key focus is to enhance agricultural production to meet domestic consumption needs, especially for wheat and cooking oil, and to expand export of cotton and animal products[4]. It is important to underline that, in July 2013, Sudan has become the 32nd African country to sign the Comprehensive Africa Agriculture Development Program (CAADP) Compact. This document defines priority areas for investment in the agricultural sector agreed upon by stakeholders and addresses national priorities of each state-party[5]. This step points out to the fact that the Government of Sudan has long-term plans in respect of the agricultural sector.

Another prospective field of cooperation is mining industry. North Sudan has many deposits of different minerals: iron ore, copper, zinc, gold, silver, uranium, gypsum, etc. According to the Government of Sudan, a top priority lies with the development of commercial gold production. The recent opening of a gold refinery in Khartoum should improve the quality of Sudanese gold delivered to the international market. Production of gold in Sudan was 26.3 tons in 2010. In the first half of 2011, it amounted to 36 tons, whereas, according to an independent consulting agency GFMS Ltd., in 2010 Sudan produced just 10.1 tons of gold. In 2011, Sudan planned, according to President al-Bashir, to increase revenues from exports of gold and other minerals to $3 billion (compared with $1.4 billion in 2010)[6]. The Republic of Sudan plans to increase the share of raw materials other than oil in the structure of its exports. In early 2000 this was only 4.5% of the total value of exports from Sudan.

As most of Sudan's oil deposits discovered before July 2011 are now in South Sudan, present-day Sudan needs to intensify oil and gas exploration within its new borders. The target is to increase oil production by developing new deposits and by using contemporary technologies. Russia can help Sudan do geological surveys for oil and gas. In 1996, Russia's *Mintopenergo* and the Ministry of Energy and Mining of Sudan signed a cooperation agreement in the fields of oil and energy production. In October 2013, Sudan's minister of oil Avad Ahmed discussed with Russia's minister of energy A. Novak the prospects of Russian companies' participation in tenders for the development of oil fields in Sudan. In February 2013, Sudan received a delegation of the Ministry of Natural Resources and Ecology of the Russian Federation. The parties discussed prospects of cooperation for the exploration of hydrocarbons. Large deposits of natural gas were discovered in the northern region of Sudan and the Sudanese authorities plan to attract Russian investments to develop these deposits[7].

Another potentially lucrative area of Sudan's economic development is power engineering. Sudan is planning to construct a number of dams and hydropower plants on the Nile and its tributaries. Despite the huge hydropower potential of the Nile, there are few hydropower plants in Sudan. After separation of South Sudan, the country will be forced to develop hydropower due to the lack of fuel for geothermal stations. The largest project in this area is a hydropower plant at Merowe. The then Soviet engineering institute Hydroproject conducted hydrogeological studies for this project long ago. Three out of 4 contracts for this project went to Chinese companies, which offered more favorable terms. During the construction, no structural changes introduced to the initial schemes, which remained fully based on the Soviet documentation. In 2009, the first stage of the power station at Merowe was completed. Representatives of Hydroproject attended an opening ceremony. Sudan's minister of State Usama Al-Hasan expressed hope that *Hydroproject* will participate in another project on the Sudanese territory, such as the design and construction of power generating facilities at Kazbara, Shereik and Sabaloka[8]. It should be emphasized, that Russia will not only take part in designing but also in the construction of power plants, which may include supplies of equipment.

On its turn, the Republic of South Sudan vests its major hope in the development of the oil industry. After several decades of war, this young country lacks basic infrastructure and, therefore, faces considerable difficulties in terms of developing its economy. The oil revenue gives South Sudan an opportunity to invest in social, agricultural and industrial development. As stated by the Government of South Sudan itself, the main goals of its economic policy are to overcome the country's backwardness and to create a modern national economy. Other important directions of South Sudan's policy, as defined in the country's Development Plan 2011–2013, include the development of agriculture, infrastructure, eeducation, health, social and human development, conflict prevention and security. The Plan places focus on "agriculture, animal resources, roads, transport and infrastructure development' that will provide opportunities in isolated regions and create a national market, and on providing social infrastructure development, including particularly water resources management and sanitation services"[9]. Two new countries need a lot of financial investment for the solution of their problems and heavily depend on trade and economic cooperation with developed industrial countries.

Among the BRICS countries, Sudan, before its partition in 2011, mostly cooperated with China, India and Russia. Its biggest partner in the BRICS group was China, which, after the partition, managed to keep leading positions in the raw materials' markets of Sudan and South Sudan. So far, China has invested $5 billion in the oil production of the 'bigger' Sudan (Sudan and South Sudan). China also helps the present-day Sudan to build large-scale hydropower plant Merowe on the Nile and many other enterprises, including infrastructure for oil production and transportation. Up to July 2011, China used to import annually about 60% of crude oil produced by the 'bigger' Sudan. India has also cooperated with Sudan in the oil industry. India's state-owned *Oil and Natural Gas Corporation* has acquired a stake in Sudan's largest oil consortium, the Greater Nile Petroleum Operating Company. Its ONGC Videsh subsidiary has invested $1200 million to build an oil-refinery at Port Sudan[10]. India has also imported oil from the 'bigger' Sudan.

Russia (the USSR) has experience of fruitful cooperation with Sudan since 1970 when it helped build a number of enterprises in the manufacturing and food industries. Soviet specialists carried out geological and geophysical studies in the country and actually discovered deposits of iron ore, copper, zinc, lead, silver and other minerals. Around 1990, cooperation between the two countries was curtailed. Only in the second half of 1990s the governments of Russia and Sudan and private entrepreneurs on both sides began to show interest in revival of trade and economic cooperation between the two countries. In January 1998, an agreement on trade, economic and technical cooperation between the governments of Russia and Sudan was concluded.

This laid the ground to bilateral business cooperation and created several regulatory mechanisms in terms of legal procedures and payments. A special board, a Russian-Sudanese Business Committee, was set up. Foreign trade turnover between Russia and Sudan increased from $6.5 million in 2000 to $93 million in 2009. In 2012, the trade turnover between Russia and Sudan was $153.5 million[11]. In 2004, Russia's Stroytransgaz won a tender to construct a pipeline from a field of Melut to Port Sudan on the Red Sea. The pipeline was commissioned into operation in 2008[12].

In 2013, Sudan granted six licenses to develop deposits of gold and polymetal ores to Russian companies from the *GAZPROM* group, to *Zarubezhgeologia* and to a joint Russian-Sudanese venture *African Minerals*. The Government of Sudan invited *Russian railways* to take part in the construction of a transcontinental railway in Africa from Dakar in the west to Port Sudan and Djibouti in the east. Inside Sudan, *Russian railways are already* constructing and modernizing parts of the country's railway network. Another Russian company *Lianozovsky mechanical plant* received an order to reconstruct a railway district Port Sudan – Khartoum, which is part of a modernization program for 2007–2026.

As stated by the Ambassador of the Republic of Sudan in Russia Omer Dahab Mohammed in July 2013, Russia's high technological and intellectual potential gives it considerable competitive advantages on the Sudanese market[13]. He also added that the relations between the two countries have a big potential for development and that Sudan makes efforts to create a favorable climate for direct foreign investments. After separation of South Sudan in 2013, a Russian-Sudanese business forum took place in Moscow. Fifteen large Russian companies participated in this forum, including *Gazprom*, *Russian railways*, *Zarubezgeologia*, *Rushydro*, *InterRao* and others. The Republic of Sudan offered 25 business projects to Russia with a total value of 6 $ billion. These include construction of an industrial zone in the Red Sea state ($3 billion), construction of a nuclear research center ($350 million), modernization and development of the city economy of Khartoum ($211 million), the launch of a *Sputnik* satellite ($200 million) *et al.*[14] Other spheres of cooperation may include manufacturing industry, energy production, agriculture, telecommunications, education, and public health.

Russia is also interested in establishing trade and economic cooperation with Africa's youngest state – the Republic of South Sudan. Special representative of the Russian Federation in Africa M. Margelov declared that new country possesses oil, water and agricultural resources and is ready to buy weapons. The new country needs to develop infrastructure, build governmental institutions, national army, transport and communications networks. According to Margelov, Russia must enter the market of South Sudan as soon as possible and with serious intentions."[15]

South Sudan does have a rich potential as for natural resources. The most important ones are oil, fertile land, timber, water, metals and other resources. At the same time, South Sudan has almost no industrial and social infrastructure. The country has no more than 100 km of paved roads. Railways are also practically absent. South Sudan needs to build its own railways, roads, power plants. It needs to develop domestic industrial production. Decades of civil war destroyed commercial agriculture, so in the near future the country will not be able to provide its population with domestically produced food. According to FAO, 4.7 million people in South Sudan were short of food in 2012. The country's health care system remains at a very low level. Public sanitation control does not exist as a system. To say the least, the vast majority of South Sudan's population has little access to clean water. According to the UN, more than 3 million people in South Sudan are infected with HIV. More than 10 million children suffer from lack of medical services and medicine. Infant and maternal mortality rates remain very high. Most residents of South Sudan are illiterate. There is an acute shortage of skilled workers, professionals and managers. The country also needs to build governmental institutions, basic sectors of the economy, infrastructure, health care, education system, national army and more.

According to M. Margelov, Russia is ready to assist South Sudan in addressing the challenges of its economic, social and political development.[16] Russia could offer in particular, to set up joint assembly plants for the production of *Ural* and *Kamaz* trucks. Russia may also establish a joint venture to produce agricultural machinery. Besides, South Sudan is in need of fertilizers, chemicals, insecticides, which Russia could also supply. It is impossible to solve the country's educational problems without enhancing education and training. Russia could contribute to it as well. However, in order to do this, the Government of Russia needs to provide students from South Sudan with more scholarships to enter Russian universities and colleges.

On May 2013, a Russian business delegation visited South Sudan. This included members of large Russian industrial companies: *Kontsern Traktorniye zavody* (Tractor Plants concern), *KAMAZ* Trade House, *Kontsern Sozvezdiye* and others. The delegation included experts in business consulting from the Institute for African Studies of the Russian Academy of Sciences. A Memorandum on cooperation between the Chambers of Trade and Commerce of Russia and South Sudan was signed. The parties agreed to develop mutually beneficial bilateral relations in different spheres. The document also listed proposals for business cooperation and joint business projects[17]. In May 2014, South Sudan's foreign minister and minister of international cooperation Marial Benjamin Barnaba visited Moscow and made a presentation on economic and investment opportunities of his country. He stressed that South Sudan is rich in various kinds of natural resources, not only hydrocarbons. However, the level of natural resources development in South Sudan is extremely low. There is a need to develop agriculture. Russia could supply fertilizers to South Sudan. Russian companies may also be interested in planting fruit and coffee, developing food processing and fishery. The Republic of South Sudan aims at developing its road network and, therefore, particularly welcomes investments in transport infrastructure. Eco-tourism is another promising branch. Representatives of a number of Russian companies, such as *Tekhnopromexport, VTB Bank, Tractor plants* and *LUKOIL overseas*, were present at the meeting with the governmental delegation from South Sudan. The parties agreed to develop further the productive dialogue between the two countries[18].

The internal political situation in South Sudan remains tense. The country remains on the brink of civil war. The ruling Sudan People's Liberation Movement (SPLM) has been experiencing the most serious internal crisis since 2005, the year when the Comprehensive Peace Agreement with the Government of Sudan was signed. Inter-ethnic and inter-tribal clashes periodically occur. On December 2013, 10 members of the government were arrested on accusations of attempted coup d'état. The government accused former Vice President Riek Machar of staging the plot. He was removed from office in July 2013 which marked intensification of an open struggle between two major factions in the SPLM. After the failed coup of 15 December 2013, the fighting between supporters of incumbent President and the former Vice President broke out. UN officials say that the level of violence is alarming. Incumbent President hails from the largest ethnic group, the Dinka, and Vice President comes from the second largest group, the Nuer. Most of the Nuer backed the coup. Hundreds of people were killed during the first weeks of fighting. The US and Britain were forced to evacuate the staff of their embassies. On April 2014, five members of the Russian *Safinat* company were wounded in clashes between government forces and guerrilla groups in South Sudan's Unity State[19].

In April 2014, the United States intended to impose sanctions on South Sudan, blaming its government for fueling inter-tribal fighting in the country. Because of fighting, South Sudan is approaching a food disaster. Millions of people are in urgent need of food aid.

The relations between the two Sudans remain troubled too, which is caused, in particular, by territorial disputes over oil-producing areas Abyei and Heglig. In 2012, this provoked cross-border clashes between armed forces of the two states. Hostilities were suspended only after direct engagement from the United Nations[20]. Some experts believe that the partition of Sudan into two states answered the interests of the U.S. more than any other interested party. The introduction of U.S. sanctions against Sudan in 1997 means that no American company is allowed to invest in Sudan's mineral resources. Meanwhile, South Sudan has long attracted the attention of American oil producers. Some of these companies, such as *ExxonMobil, which* is currently constructing a pipeline from Chad to the Atlantic coast of Cameron, may be willing to enter the market of South Sudan in the future. Separation of South Sudan, where the main oil fields are situated, has enabled American companies to access these resources regardless of the state of affairs in Washington's relations with the Government of Sudan.

China, on its turn, is trying to keep a balance between Sudan and South Sudan and, at the same time, to secure its leading position in the oil industry of South Sudan. Chinese authorities have called on their companies to invest in the economic development of South Sudan, especially in the oil industry. The Chinese Government has also played a role in promoting the dialog between Sudan and South Sudan on their unresolved issues.

Thus, the resource wealth of the two Sudan Republics remains in focus of other powerful countries' attention. The Government of the Russian Federation needs to consider this while planning its policy towards this region of Africa. From the beginning of the 20th century, Russian companies and entrepreneurs tend to be more active in Africa. Russia's interest in cooperation with the continent is clearly on the rise. Russia should, in particular, intensify economic and trade cooperation with the two newly formed states, the more so because they are interested in cooperation. In order to develop business cooperation between Russia and the both Sudans, it is necessary to create a new comprehensive program for trade and investment, develop new regulatory mechanisms, conclude new intergovernmental agreements on economic and technical cooperation in each of the branches in question, move on to cooperation in the social sphere, etc.

There are certain risks as well. The internal political situation in both countries remains very complicated, as is their relationship with neighbors and leading powers in the world arena. These countries have not worked out long-term programs of socioeconomic development. In these circumstances, the Russian entrepreneurs need to study carefully the risks and opportunities of doing business with the Sudan Republics. The state should support this.. This should also be accompanied by the business-oriented academic research about the present-day economic, political and social life in the two states.

At the same time, these countries are rich in valuable natural resources. It is a strategic asset, which, if properly capitalized on, should help them build capacity for sustainable economic and social development. The Sudan and South Sudan need foreign expertise and investment to overcome their difficulties and find ways to move forward.

[1] International Monetary Fund (IMF). Attachment (II). Sudan. Nemorandum of Economic and Financial Policies. June 18, 2009, p.17; IMF Staff Report for 2012. Sudan. Article IV Consultation. September 7, 2012, p.30; www.kpmg.com/Africa/en/kpmg-in Africa

[2] Sudan Economy 2011–2012, CIA World Factbook; www.kpmg.com/Africa/en/kpmg-inAfrica; http://www.sudantribune.com; rea.au.int/en/states/default/

[3] International Monetary Fund. Staff Report for 2012. Sudan.Article IV, p. 4.

[4] International Monetary Fund. Staff Report for 2012. Sudan.Article IV , p. 4.

[5] *Sudan signs the national CAADP Compact, July 30, 2013, By Brenda Zulu. http://www.scoop.it/t/nepad-caadp?page 6. from www.youtube.com-July 30, 2013.*

[6] Africa South of the Sahara, 2009. Sudan. 38th Edition.Taylor and Francis Group. London and New York, p. 1132.

[7] Алексей Андреев. Надо использовать шансы российских компаний. Эксклюзивное интервью министра нефти Судана Авада Ахмеда Эль-Джаза. 16.10.2013.Aleksey Andreev. Nado – ispolzovat shansi rossiiski kompanii.Exklusivnoe interviuy ministra nefti Sudana /www.inforos.ru/ru/ ?module=news&action=view&id=35851; inforofor.ru/news/29179568

[8] Судан. Электроэнергетика. Sudan/Electroenergetica.EnergyLand.info//rusara bbc.com (3 апреля 2009 № 186575) Polpred.com/?c nt=&ns=&sector=19; Rus-Cable.Ru.03.04.2009

[9] Government of the Republic of South Sudan. South Sudan Development plan 2011-2013. Juba, August 2011, p. 42

[10] Africa South of the Sahara 2009, Sudan. 38th Ed. Routledge Tailor & Francis Group. London and New York. 2009, p.1133.

[11] Савенков А. В ТПП РФ прошла встреча членов делегации Республики Судан с российскими деловыми кругами. – Торгово-промышленная палата Российской Федерации. 21 мая 2013. Savenkov A.V. V torgovo-promishlennoi palate proshla vstrecha chlenov delegazii Respubliki Sudan s rossiiskimi delovimi krugami Torgovo-promishlennaya palata Rossiiskoy Federazii/ 21.05.2013 – http://old.tpprf.ru/ ru/news/about/index.php?id_12=42119&from_12=47

[12] Российско-суданские экономические отношения. rossiisko-sudanskiye economicheskije otnosheniya. Dosie. 13.12.2013. Itar-tass.Com/info/832066

[13] News. Mail.ru/global 2902 html

[14] Mnr.gov.ru/news/detail.php? ID=132073;

[15] Topneftegas.ru/неиs/view/9929

[16] Topneftegas.ru/news/view/99298

[17] Харитонова Е.В. Стратегия российского бизнеса в Африке. О визите делегации РФ в Республику Южный Судан (12-15 мая 2013 г.) и Республику Уганда (15–18 мая 2013 г.) Haritonova E.V. Strategija rossijskogo biznesa v Afrike. O vizite delegazii RF v Respubliku Uyznii Sudan (12-15.05.2013) i v respubliku Uganda (15-18.05.2013). inafran.ru>node/541

[18] 26 мая 2014 г. в Торгово-промышленной палате Российской Федерации состоялась встреча Вице-президента ТПП России Г.Г.Петрова с Министром иностранных дел и международного сотрудничества Республики Судан Барнабой Мариалом Бенджамином. 26 maya 2014 v torgovo-promishlennoy palate Ros-

siiskoy Federazii sostoaylas vstrecha vice-presidenta torgovo-promishlennoy palati Rossii G/G /Petrova s ministrom inostrannih del I mezhdunarodnogo sotrudnichestva Reshubliki Uyzhnii Sudan Barnaboi Marialom Bendjaminom tpprf. ru>ruttpp/Отчет 26-30 мая 2014.Doc; www.tpprf.ru/145061

[19] www.africom.ru/news/1084; РИАновости

[20] www.geopolitics.ru/2014/01/

Mohamed Hamchi, PhD Candidate
Samia Rebiai, PhD Candidate
Department of Political Science
University of Oum El Bouaghi,
Algeria

RUSSIAN-ALGERIAN RELATIONS IN MULTIPOLARIZING WORLD

Abstract

Russian-Algerian bilateral relations have recently gained more signifi-cance for both states. For Russia, as a (re)emerging global actor following the Soviet era decline, Algeria continues to be an indispensable partner to any global actor's strategy seeking more engagement *in* Africa. Regarding Russia-Africa complex, in which Algeria's component-ness is – and will continue to be central, Russia has never been a newcomer to the continent if compared with other BRICS (Brazil, India, China and South Africa). Both countries should do their utmost to take advantage of their *exceptional* his-tory. This *exceptional*ness traces back to the hard times of the Algerian War of Independence (1954–62); USSR then generously provided Algerian revo-lutionaries with political, military as well as financial assistance. Therefore, diplomatic relations have been established between USSR and Algeria early on March 1962, just after Algeria proclaimed its independence. Accordingly, it is no wonder that Algeria has eventually become the first Arab country to sign recently a strategic partnership agreement with Russia (2001). Consider-ing the multidimensionality of such partnership, this paper offers three en-deavors. First, it describes recent history of Russian-Algerian relations focus-ing on the *renaissance* in such relations during the last decade. Second, it analyzes the *very* interrelatedness between Russia's – more crucially than the other BRICS' – re-emergence as a revisionist global actor and how it matters to Russian-Algerian relations. Third, it debates the realities and challenges of Russian-Algerian relations, particularly in the three main fields of bilateral interaction, military, energy and political.

Introduction

Russia has recently re-emerged as a global actor following the Soviet era decline. On the other hand, Algeria tends to become a new regional actor within its very neighborhood, regarding its economic resurgence during the

257

last decade, and regarding the many aspects of threatening, both political and security, turbulence in the Maghreb and Sahel region.

For Russia, as a (re)emerging global actor, Algeria continues to be an indispensable partner to its strategy seeking more engagement *in* Africa, even if Russia has never been a newcomer to the continent if compared with the other BRICS. Doubtlessly, Algeria's increasing role in North Africa, in the aftermath of state collapse in Libya and the war in northern Mali as well, has asserted its centrality in any global actors' strategy in Africa.

The paper, assuming that the history of Russian-Algerian relations, which traces back to the Soviet era, has been undoubtedly *exceptional*, argues that both countries should do their utmost to take advantage of such *exceptional*ness. Russian-Algerian relations trace back to the hard times of the Algerian War of Independence (1954-62); USSR then generously provided Algerian revolutionaries with political, military as well as financial assistance. Therefore, diplomatic relations between USSR and Algeria have been established in March 1962, just after Algeria proclaimed its independence. Accordingly, it is no wonder that Algeria has eventually become the first Arab country to sign recently a strategic partnership agreement with Russia (2001).

Considering the multidimensionality of such partnership, this paper offers three endeavors. First, it describes the main fields of cooperation/coordination between Russia and Algeria. Second, it analyzes the *very* interrelatedness between Russia's – more crucially than the other BRICS' – approach(es) to reconstructing the current global governance system, with particular focus on the international system mutlipolarization question, on one hand, and maintaining a high level of thinking and acting strategically in terms of its relations with Algeria, and with Africa broadly speaking, on the other hand. Third, it reflects prospectively on the future(s) of Russian-Algerian bilateral relations; it attempts to do so through paying special attention to the potentials to develop more friendship-based relations that promise equal benefits for both countries. Such potentials do rely heavily on the *exceptional* heritage of Russian-Algerian relations history.

The paper is divided into three main sections. The first section briefly examines the history of recent Russian-Algerian relations. The second section attempts at dealing with the issue of Russia's re-emerging as an ambitious global actor, particularly after the re-election of President Vladimir Putin (2008). The third section addresses more closely the challenges the Russian-Algerian Partnership faces in what may be analytically as well as empirically considered as a new global context, a context that is characterized not only by global governance's increasing complexities, but also by local governance's new challenges for both states.

1. Russian-Algerian Relations. Recent History

Why is history important to the Russian-Algerian case? In fact, it is context more than history itself. The context in which Algeria decolonized and gained its independence and what role the Soviet Union – the ancestor of Russia – played in the process, both during and just after the revolutionary war of independence (1954-1962), help to understand even the future trends. The Soviet Union was the first state in the world that established diplomatic relations with independent Algeria on March 23rd, 1962, and they have kept expanding from then on. In return, Algeria internationally recognized the Russian Federation on December 26th, 1991 after the dissolution of the former Soviet Union. What follows offers a survey of the main official visits exchanged among Russian and Algerian highest statesmen during the last two decades.

Official mutual visits during the last decade[1].

April 3rd–6th, 2001: Algerian President, Abdelaziz Bouteflika, visited Moscow and gave a new quality to Russian-Algerian bilateral relations. This has become a major milestone in the expansion of Russian-Algerian relations. During the visit, both parties signed a declaration on *strategic partnership* and an intergovernmental agreement on cooperation in culture, science, education, sports, tourism and archives.

March 10th, 2006: Russian President, Vladimir Putin, visited Algiers. It was the first top-level Russian Leader to visit Algeria since Soviet President Nikolai Podgorny in 1969. Intergovernmental various agreements were signed on trade, economic and financial relations and the settlement of the Algerian debts to the Russian Federation on earlier loans, in addition to the Convention on the avoidance of double taxation and the Agreement on encouragement and reciprocal protection of investments.

February 18th–19th, 2008: President Bouteflika visited Moscow. A bilateral agreement on air traffic between the two countries was signed. President Bouteflika was accompanied by Chakib Khalil, who was then both the president of the Organization of Petroleum Exporting Countries (OPEC) and Algerian minister of energy and mines. The visit was an occasion to discuss the possibility of creating an organization on the model of OPEC for gas producers, including a prospected energy deal between Russian Gazprom and Algerian Sonatrach.

October 6th, 2010: President Medvedev visited Algiers and held talks with President Bouteflika. They addressed the development of industrial cooperation, investment projects, and military and technical cooperation. A number of documents aimed at promoting interaction in the economic, energy, and sea transport sectors, in standardization and conformity assessment, and the humanitarian sector were signed in the presence of both presidents.

Algeria has been among the only eight African countries Russian presidents have visited over the past two decades[2]. Certainly, the choice of countries visited reflects Russia's geographical priorities on the continent. This is an important aspect of the Russian-Algerian relations processing. However, it seems that both sides think of their bilateral relations interdependently. As the paper argues, for Russia, as a (re)emerging global actor following the Soviet era decline, Algeria continues to be a crucial partner to any global actor's strategy seeking more engagement in Africa. Besides, for Algeria as for a developing country in a recently turbulent environment, the Arab Spring mainly speaking, Russia has represented a political partner, sharing the same attitudes towards the political developments not only in its neighborhood (North Africa and the Middle East), but also in the broader international relations system (global terrorism, international intervention, state sovereignty among other issues).

Regarding Russia's activeness in Africa, Arkhangelskaya and Shubin[3] argue that what prompt[s] Moscow to become active in Africa is not only the superpower rivalry of the Cold War legacy. They argue, that "the Soviets never regarded the independent African countries and political bodies as 'proxies'. On the contrary, the constitution of the Soviet Union cited the support for the struggle of peoples for national liberation and social progress as one of the aims of its foreign policy."

However, "the changes in the political situation near the threshold of the 1990s and the dissolution of the Soviet Union in 1991 in particular largely wasted this political capital. The deterioration of relations with Africa reflected a negative trend in Russia's foreign policy, although it suffered more than other vector in that period. Apart from the demise of Russia's economy due to the IMF-proposed (or rather, imposed) reforms, other factors, both political and psychological, contributed to this deterioration. The new rulers and the 'pro Western' media often automatically held negative attitudes toward the friends of the former Soviet Union."[4]

It is important to notice that the particular context both inside and outside Russia has unsurprisingly caused Russian foreign policy in this period to largely abandon the global South in general and Africa in particular. Russia decreased its diplomatic presence in Africa as it closed nine embassies, three consulates, most of its trade missions and 13 of its 20 cultural centers. It also terminated most of its development projects, such as a multi-million steel plant in Ajaokuta, Nigeria that had neared 98 percent completion, which proved even more damaging. [5] Even for Algeria, the internal security instability during the 1990's – to which Algerians refer as the 'Black Decade' – led Algerian foreign policy to a stagnation period until the end of 1990s and President Bouteflika's arrival to presidency in 1999. Interestingly, even in the case of Russia, many attribute the changes in foreign policy to the replacement of Boris Yeltsin by Vladimir Putin in 2000. In fact, however, change has begun several years earlier in 1996 when Evgeny Primakov became foreign minister. "The rise of the Russian economy and accumulation of huge currency and gold reserves also placed it in a position to conduct independent policy on major international issues such as Africa. Russia's admission to the G8 in 1998 encouraged further attention to Africa as the continent regularly appeared on G8 summit agendas; it also meant that it had effectively joined the 'club' of those who historically colonized and exploited Africa. Nevertheless, Russia's G8 membership lost its significant as the world economic crisis highlighted the G8's growing inefficiency and obsolete nature."[6]

For the case of the paper's theme, it is widely assumed that Russia-Algeria exceptional history, including the Soviet Era, is a "crucial asset in reinforcing their bilateral relations in a fruitfully prospective way. As a non-colonial state in Africa in general and due to its global-socialist tendency during the Soviet era, Russia "made essential contributions to Africa's decolonization." First, Russia supported Ethiopia's (then called Abyssinia) sovereignty and provided practical assistance in its struggle against Italian aggression in late 19th Century. It did so not only because of its geostrategic interests, but also because of the proximity between the Russian and Ethiopian Orthodox churches. At about the same time, more than 200 Russian volunteers supported the Boers in their war with the UK. In both cases, Russia gave support to those seen as the victims. 'Old' Russia also maintained several diplomatic missions in Africa and re-established relations with Egypt, Ethiopia and South Africa during World War II."[7]

2. Russia as a Re-emerging Global Actor

Russia in contemporary global politics has been always imagined as a revisionist actor, but at the same time seeking to restore the USSR great power position within the post-cold war international system; as Varol put it, "seeking to encourage the emergence of a countervailing coalition of the rest versus the West or the transformation of the unipolar structure into a Multipolar power structure."[8] Even the West, in Varol's terminology, has always suspicious about Russia's intentions and objectives regarding playing globally. The question of Russia's integration in the international economy has never been a concern for the West, particularly after it has become a member of WTO. The West, however, has been increasingly much concerned about how Russia conceives of international system governance, particularly security and energy issues. It was stated in a recent 2013 report, written by Sean Roberts, that "despite the *positive* development of continuing integration in the international system, there is a clear parallel trend that sees Russia challenging the international consensus on a range of important issues. These issues have ramifications for global governance as their resolution is increasingly demanding a concerted, international effort and agreement among states."[9]

Addressing the question of Russia's re-emergence as a global actor is to be done through dealing with a set of analytical questions such as, which world order is emerging after the Cold War and which one is the most preferable for Russia; how are the state, its sovereignty, and national interests affected in the new era of globalization; what kind of foreign policy strategy should Russia adopt to adequately respond to the new world's challenges and conditions?

What makes Russia an ambitiously re-emergent global actor? It seems that historical heritage of the USSR is not the only explanation. Russia is considered an important actor on the global stage, conditioned in no small part by its seat on the UN Security Council, which often provides a decisive voice in some of the most pressing issues facing the international community. Furthermore, Russia is becoming more integrated in intergovernmental organizations, evident by Russia's ascendancy to the World Trade Organization in 2012 and its recent efforts to join the Organization for Economic Cooperation and Development (OECD).

Russia has remained conservative and consensual in its approach, pushing for economic growth as the global economy continues its recovery, although there are signs that Russia is ready to play a greater role in the global financial system. Russia made an important financial intervention in restructuring Cypriot loans in April 2013, in what was a difficult period for EU-Russia relations. Russia is also supporting efforts to create a multilateral banking system along with Brazil, India, China and South Africa, to provide an alternative source of investment to pre-existing development banks, with the idea of a BRICS bank agreed in principle at the 2013 BRICS summit held in Durban, South Africa, in March 2013.[10]

There are several documents that have outlined Russia's foreign policy during its re-emergence era. The most important is the Foreign Policy Concept of the Russian Federation[11] (FPCRF), which President Putin approved in 2013 replacing an earlier version signed by President Medvedev in 2008; the new version reflects a "rapid acceleration of the global processes in the first decade of the 21st century, strengthening of the new processes in the world development" that requires a reassessment of the priorities of Russia's foreign policy. It also speaks proudly of Russia's "increased responsibility for the formation of the international agenda and fundamentals of the international system."[12]

Moreover, the FPCRF Concept cites the "deployment of a broad and non-discriminatory international cooperation, promoting the emergence of flexible network alliances that transcend blocs" as one of the main aims of Russia's foreign policy. It is worth-noting that G8 is mentioned as third (after G20 and BRICS) in the list of "formats" where Russia "will make itself more fully engaged," rather than as the first as five years earlier. The Concept essentially repeated previous promises by declaring that "Russia will expand its multipronged interaction with African States at the bilateral and bilateral basis with a focus on, improved policy dialogue and promotion of mutually beneficial trade and economic cooperation, and facilitate the settlement and the prevention of regional conflicts and crisis situations in Africa. An important part of this line is the development of partnerships with the African Union and sub-regional organizations." In contrast, the document gives extensive coverage to developments in "the Middle East and North Africa."[13] Such a tendency should be considered as a shortcoming in Russia-Africa complex.

A further important document is Russia's National Security Strategy (RNSS)[14], adopted in 2010 and valid until 2020. It states that "Russia will increase its interaction with multilateral forums such as the G8, G20, RIC (Russia, India, and China), BRICS, and will likewise capitalize on the potential of other informal international institutions." RNSS document, similarly to the FPCRF Concept, almost completely neglects Africa as it mentions it only once in the following statement: "the situation in a number of African countries will continue to exert a negative influence on the international situation."[15] This is a further shortcoming that should not be overlooked.

It can be argued that Russia's limited structural engagement in Africa undermines its strategic tendency to play a more global role in world politics. Africa is not only the world's *reservoir* of natural resources which makes it indispensable for any global actor's strategy but also a historical space for competition over influence, particularly through its continuing ties with the former colonial states. The recent Sahel crisis serves as an analytically evident case.

3. Russian-Algeria Relations in a New Global Context: realities and challenges

Russian-Algerian relations underwent a period of recession at the 1990s due to distinctive factors for both parties. For Russia, it was due to the transition from the former Soviet Union to the new Russian Federation after the disintegration of the USSR, followed by structural political and then economic crisis. For Algeria, on the other hand, it was due to the security destabilization during the decade following the cancelation of 1991 legislative elections. Both factors served as constraining obstacles to deepening bilateral relations.

However, changes in both national environments by the end of the 1990s have prompted both political elites to restore the momentum of their past bilateral rapprochement and initiate a new era of cooperation. Many reasons can be stated to account for such a *renaissance*. For Algeria, renewing its relations with Russia was part of President Abdelaziz Bouteflika's[16] endeavors to revive Algerian diplomatic relations and foreign policy in general after a decade of international isolation due to the 1990s' security instability. In this respect, history matters again. For Algeria, Reestablishing fluid relations with Russia "could mean the recovery of some of the highly-positive results it gained from its cooperation with the former Soviet Union." Moreover, as a developing country looking forward a distinct position in a competitive neighborhood, it seemed very crucial for Algeria to keep constructive relations with a great state which shared the same environment and the same attitude as well. However, Russia constituted – and most probably still constitutes – a "source of modern weapons at reasonable prices, and is also the most important agent for the repair and maintenance of the large quantity of Soviet armament in Algeria. Both aspects would contribute to increasing Algeria's regional power role, which is one of the country's aspirations."[17]

For Russia, on the other hand, geostrategic implications are of great importance. Antonio Sánchez Andrés[18] considers four reasons for Russia to revive its relations with Algeria by the end of the 1990s: first, because Algeria constitutes an essential link in North African regional dynamics; second, because it could have a considerable impact on the Arab world politics; third, because of its proximity and relations with the European Union; and fourth, because it is an internationally important producer of hydrocarbons, particularly gas, sharing markets with Russia and having relations which are of relevance to Russia's foreign energy strategy. In this regard, it should be brought in mind that Algeria is indispensable for Russia's ambition to create an association of gas producing countries.

It should be emphasized that a characteristic feature of Russia-Algeria relations in the 21st century is the perceptible stepping up of both investment cooperation in the energy sphere and the intensification of cooperation in military field. The first feature has been due both to the strong position of the two countries in the world energy markets and the intensified competition over energy on a global scale. The second one, however, has been due to the needs of the two countries to play an independent role in the regional/international politics. Moreover, both countries have maintained a high level of political cooperation and coordination due in large part to the historical legacy of relations between the two countries. Therefore, Russian-Algerian relations have been distinguishingly concentrated in three major fields: armament and weapons trade, energy cooperation and political attitudes' convergence. However, we suppose that the three sectors are highly interlinked which eventually constitute one aspect – among others – of the necessity to diversify and re-frame the bilateral relations among Russia and Algeria.

First, Armament and Weapons Trade

The term 'weapons trade' might be misleading at a first quick glance. Algeria, since the first years after it gained its independence, has been a prominent and constant customer of Soviet/Russian weapons. During the period 1962-1989, the Soviet Union delivered armament to Algeria to the value of around $11 billion, consisting of aircrafts (MiG-21, MiG-23 and Su-24), tanks (T-55 and T-72), armoured vehicles and several ships (corvettes, frigates, patrol boats and submarines), as well as light weapons and munitions.[19]

The 'Trends in International Arms Transfers, 2012' report[20] points out that the volume of global arms deliveries to Algeria increased by 277 per cent between 2003–2007 and 2008–12 and it rose from 22nd to 6th largest recipient. Although Algeria in 2011–12 turned to Germany for 2 MEKO-A200 frigates and for a first batch of 54 of a planned 1200 Fuchs armoured personnel carriers and to China for 3 F-22A frigates, Russia remained its biggest exporter. It (Russia) supplied 93 per cent of Algerian arms imports, including 44 Su-30MKA combat aircraft, 2 Project-636 submarines, an estimated 3 S-300PMU-2 (SA-20B) long-range surface-to-air missile (SAM) systems and 185 T-90S tanks.

Many analysts argue that arms exportation has been to a large extent a foreign policy tool for the Soviet Union formerly and for Russian currently. Moreover, it seems that such issue "will remain an important instrument used to strengthen Russia's position on the international stage [...], even though one should not expect an increase in its volume. This is due, on the one hand, to the technological aging of the Russian arms industry and weapons, which could prove unattractive to some of Russia's traditional clients (such as China and India) and, on the other, to the high probability of increased domestic purchases."[21]

The question of armament relations between Russia and Algeria was associated with another issue, Algeria's debt reimbursement to Russia and how both parties agreed on its settlement during the mid 2000s. During the second half of the 1990s, they initiated bilateral talks to reach an agreement concerning how Algeria should reimburse its debt to Russia. The debt was inherited from loans granted by the former USSR. Some observers argue that the debt issue did constitute an obstacle in the development of relations between the two countries. However, during the 2005 Russian Minister of Foreign Affairs' visit to Algeria, both parties agreed that $1 billion of the $4.7 billion "would be returned in cash and the rest compensated by the purchase of Russian armament. Specifically, each quantity of cash allocated toward the pur-

265

chase of Russian armament would redeem the same volume of debt."[22] Therefore, the settlement of the debt issue, in this way, was associated with a significant armament transaction. Furthermore, the deal did not consist only of armament sanctions, but also of more Russian petroleum companies' access to Algerian energy sector.

Claires Spencer (2012) stated, that "for reasons partly associated with the rising instability on its southern flank, Algeria has been increasing defense expenditure in recent years, with the defense budget increased by 22 percent in July 2011, at the height of the Libyan crisis, to an estimated $9.5 billion by year's end. This is in addition and complementary to an extensive upgrade of military equipment launched in 2006, when a $7.5 billion military modernization and training program was concuded with Russia. This is believed to include 40 MiG-29 fighters, 20 Sukoi-30 fighters and 16 Yak-130 training planes, together with 8 S-300 PMU-2 Favorit rocket systems and up to 40 T-90 tanks. In 2008, 15 of the MiG planes were returned to Russia on the grounds that they contained faulty components[23], but despite reports that Algeria might exchange these for French Rafale aircraft or seek more equipment sales from the U.S., the Russian deal has remained on track. One reason for this was reported to have been the inclusion in the original agreement of a debt write-off component of $4.7 billion owed by Algeria to the Soviet Union. Another may be the laissez-faire approach that has developed between senior Algerian military officers and their Russian counterparts, which would be hard to replace by the more demanding end-use requirements of French or U.S. military trainers."[24]

Second, Energy Cooperation

Russia is today's top natural gas exporter in the world, followed by Norway, Canada, Algeria and Qatar[25]. However, in fact, "the Soviet legacy has dominated Russia's transition to a more open market economy. Largely as an inheritance from its Soviet past, Russia has little to export other than arms and raw materials. Russia can no longer afford to transfer arms freely as did the Soviet Union for many years. Sales now are driven by profits more than by ideological interests. [...] Russia possesses a vast repository of energy reserves, and oil was the principal factor for the economic recovery of the last few years."[26] Moreover, it can be noticed that energy sector has not only replaced military sector in importance for Russia, but it has also dominated the external aspects of the contemporary Russian economy.

While Russia cannot much influence the prices of oil, since the world market is relatively free and transports mainly go by tankers, the gas prices are more linked to pipeline transport and regulated in bilateral agreements. In order to divide the markets and maximize prices Russia has in recent years tried to form a gas export cartel with Qatar, Iran and Algeria, and Gazprom is making investments in e.g. the Algerian energy sector.[27]

In Algeria, Russia has advantage over its rival competitors like United States or France, as Russia is an energy exporting country while the others are in need for energy resources. Thus, Russia can become a powerful player in nuclear energy sector. In gas sector, the Russian Company, Gazprom, is willing to establish $10 billion gas pipeline between Nigeria and Algeria[28]. "On August 4, 2006, Algerian Gas Company, Sonatrach, and Gazprom signed a memorandum on cooperation in natural gas prospecting and production. Russia rewarded Algeria because of this progress and President Putin cancelled nearly $5 bil by Algerian debt saying that 'trade' with Algeria is more beneficial than debt repayment. Considering that Algeria is the third gas supplier to Europe after Russia, if Gazprom would achieve to control the Algerian gas sector, Russia would surround Europe from East, North and South." [29] Also Algerian gas was mentioned as an alternative of that of Russia which considered to supply Europe countries.

However, EU needs Russian oil and gas and it is impossible to – their large-scale replacement is impossible: dependence could be reduced only partially using other sources of hydrocarbon supply, as well as nuclear and renewable energy.[30] Gazprom is supplying one quarter of EU gas supplies or 40 percent of its imports and 50% of the gas imported in Europe comes from the Russian gas pipelines.

Although the most recent partnership agreement between Sonatrach and Gazprom expired in 2007 and was not renewed, due to a lack of common projects on the horizon, but with the announcement in June 2012 of a tentative agreement between Sonatrach and Gazprom to conduct a 'swap exchange,' a system of regular financial flows that will allow each country to optimize sales in the other's key markets, may serve as a basis for future collaboration between the two national operators Under the agreement, Sonatrach will distribute liquefied natural gas (LNG) to Gazprom's European clients using its network, and Gazprom will supply Sonatrach's clients in Asia. The partnership with Gazprom should significantly increase Sonatrach's access to clients in the growing Asian market.[31]

Gas producers should increase cooperation within the framework of the Forum of Gas Exporting Countries (GECF). The two gas exporters are well aware of the fact that the international context, marked by strong demand, and the utmost tension concerning other major producing countries, (Iran, Venezuela), enables them to guarantee the energy security sought by the Western world. Within this framework, the idea of a cartel on the model of the OPEC is often mentioned by both countries in the aim to defend the interests of the producing countries while taking into account those of the consumers. It is obvious that increased energy cooperation between Russia and

Algeria, the two largest suppliers of natural gas to Europe, is causing some Europeans to fear that the two could form a gas cartel to control prices.

Nonetheless, there have been plans to transform the 'Gas Exporting Countries Forum' from just a 'debating forum' into an effective international cartel that could exert tangible influence the price-formation mechanism in the market for natural gas. Such plans have been, to a large degree, promoted by some of the members of the organization, including Russia and Algeria. These two countries share an interest in maintaining the oil price at sufficiently high levels, and they both hope to regulate competition in the gas market. But it seems that the path to a gas 'OPEC' is not that easy.

Third, Political Attitudes Convergence

Two prominent examples can be emphasized as to Russian-Algerian political convergence, attitudes towards the Arab Spring and the global war on terror, in order to highlight the shape and type of political 'coordination' between the two countries.

Russia has tried to take advantage of the dramatic shifts in the Arab world's landscape to reinsert itself as a key player in Syrian conflict, in addition to copious arms deliveries[32], and other direct support, Russian diplomacy skillfully helped avert possible U.S. military intervention in Syria by working out a deal to eliminate Syria's chemical arsenal by other means. Russia and China as well often cooperate in the UN Security Council, where Russia has cast several double vetoes against Western-proposed sanctions on Syria[33]. This statement of Russian foreign minister Lavrov concluded the Russian basis approach toward the Arab spring: "We stressed the need for the supremacy of law, the central role of the UN and its Security Council and the commitment to settle conflicts with political and diplomatic efforts without interference in sovereign countries' internal affairs."[34]

So, the Arab revolutions have helped fuel contradictions between Russia and the West, but Algeria's stand is closer to that of Russia, particularly its attitude toward the Libyan conflict and even more so in the Syrian conflict. Algeria, as a well-known resistant to outside pressure, was critical of NATO's role in regime change in Libya which they viewed as contributing to regional instability. The fallout from Libya has also colored Algeria's approach to the Syrian crisis, where, like its strategic partner, Russia, Algiers is on its guard against allowing UN Security Council resolutions to be used to justify Western-led mission creep. The diplomatic consultations between Moscow and Algiers to discuss developments increased in early 2012. It is not surprising that Algerian position should converge with those who, like Russia and China, are opposed to an international or regional drift toward regime change in Syria.

Concerning the war on terror, Russia never suspected Algeria of aiding transnational jihadist networks fighting in Chechnya[35], as Qatar, UAE, and Saudi Arabia did. Moscow views this resource-rich Persian Gulf states as a source of funding for Islamic extremists and as a security threat to Russia. This ties in to Moscow's attempt to highlight the potential of a domino effect of Islamic extremism that links conflicts in the Middle East and North Africa to domestic concerns with militant Islam in Russia's southern regions.[36]

Russia has also trained Algerian Special Forces in counterterrorism techniques[37]. Moreover, a memorandum of cooperation between the Algerian Ministry of Religious Affairs and Endowments and the Council of Muftis of the Russian Federation signed on 18 November 2009. Russia wants to mitigate the risks of "potential alienation of Muslims from the Russian state which has shed communist atheism and made the Orthodox Church a political institution."[38]

4. Conclusion

A strategic partnership is a long-term interaction between two countries and there are three main fields of interaction that discern the content and the purpose of strategic partnership between Algeria and Russia.

In military field, the Algerian army, considered pro– Russian, whereas 80% of its material is Russian, was willing, with its greater financial resources, to rearm itself via Russia and it continues to use Russia as its main arms supplier. Russia also has its pragmatic goals aim at improving the country's economy and security by increasing arms transfers.

In economic field, Algeria and Russia continue their coordinate policy on natural gas exports to Europe. For Russia, considering its importance in the EU's gas supply system, Algeria has become a country to tip the balance in Gazprom's strategy[39], in order to increase EU dependence and at the same time, raise profits for both countries. Due to their assets in natural resources, the two countries could have controlled some 40% of the EU's gas supply. Although, Algeria is the second largest importer of Russian goods in Africa and the fifth largest in the Middle East[40]; however, both countries need to diversify their economic/trade relations, which currently rely heavily on Europe. The two countries need to search of new forms of cooperation which meet their interest.

In political field, insofar as a strategic partner with Algeria, Russia offers its strategic cooperation free from any political restrictions in contrast to other major powers. In addition, there is much more convergence in attitudes towards critical issues such as the so-called Arab Spring, or the global war on terror. However, there is more need for cooperation in so many issues such as the situation in the Sahara Sahel region, in the Middle East and North Africa, to ensure adequate reaction to new challenges and threats.

References

Abramova, Irina O. and Fituni, Leonid L. (2011) "Russia, BRICS and Africa: Relations of Partnership and Competition," www.transnational-studies.org/.../ russia%20brics.pdf

Andrés, Antonio Sánchez (2006) "Political-Economic Relations between Russia and North Africa." Real Insituto Elcano, WP 22/2006, November 2006.

Anders, Åslun, (2009) The Russian Economy: More than Just Energy?, Peterson Institute for International Economics Testimony for the Committee on Foreign Affairs of the European Parliament.

Arkhangelskaya, Alexandra and Shubin, Vladimir (2013) "Russia's Africa Policy." Occasional Paper No. 157, September 2013, South African Institute of International Affairs, African perspectives. Global insights.

Arkhangelskaya, Alexandra and Shubin, Vladimir (without a publication year) "Is Russia Back? Realities of Russian Engagement in Africa." downloadable from <www.lse.ac.uk>

Aymen, khalil,(2012) Algeria: Diversifying economic ties with Brazil, Russia, India and China, http://www.safpi.org)http://www.safpi.org/ news/article/2012/ algeria-diversifying-economic-ties-brazil-russia-india-and-china.

Daği, Zeynep (2007) "Russia: Back to the Middle East?" Perceptions. Spring 2007, 123-141.

Darbouche, Hakim and Dennison, Susi (2011) "A 'Reset' with Algeria: The Russia to the EU's South." ECFR/46 December 2011, www.ecfr.eu.

Darbouche, Hakim (2007) "Russian-Algerian Cooperation and the 'Gas OPEC': What's in the Pipeline?" CEPS Policy Briefs. No. 123, March 2007.

De Haas, Marcel (2010) Russia's Foreign Security Policy in the 21st Century: Putin, Medvedev and beyond. New York: Routledge.

Fidan, Hakan and Aras, Bülent (2010) "The Return of Russia-Africa Relations." Bilig. Winter/2010, Number 52: 47-68

Katz, Mark N. (2007) "Russia and Algeria: Partners or Competitors?" Journal Compilation 2007, Middle East Policy Council.

Kemp, Geoffrey and Saunders, Paul (2003) "America, Russia, and the Greater Middle East: Challenges and Opportunities." Paper Series, The Nixon Center, Washington Dc., November 2003.

Khan, Muslim. "Russia-Africa Relations in the Era of Globalization," International Journal of Research in Engineering, IT and Social Sciences, Volume 2, Issue 1, www.indusedu.org.

Kristin Linke, Kristine and vietor, Marcel (eds) (2010), Prospects of a Triangular Relationship? Energy Relations between the EU, Russia and Turkey, library.fes.de/pdf-files/id/07150.pdf

Malashenko, Alexey (2013) "Russia and the Arab Spring!" an October 2013 Paper, Carnegie Moscow Center.

Martinez, Luis (2010) Algeria's Position Regarding Mediterranean Integration, Panorama, Med2010.

Oldberg, Ingmar (2010) "Russia's Great Power Strategy under Putin and Medvedev." Occasional Paper No. 1/2010, Swedish Institute of International Affairs, Sweeden.

Rivlin, Paul (2005) "The Russian Economy and Arms Exports to the Middle East." *Memorandum* No. 79, November 2005.

Roberts, Sean P. (2013) "Russia as an International Actor: The View from Europe and the US." FIIA Report 37/FIIA Occasional Report 2, Finnish Institute of International Affairs, Finland.

Sherlock, Thomas (2007) *Historical Narratives in the Soviet Union and Post-Soviet Russia: Destroying the Settled Past, Creating an Uncertain Future.* New York: Palgrave Macmillan.

Schneider, Brett (2013) "Russian Pragmatism in the Middle East: Success in Algeria," http://muftah.org/tag/brett-schneider/

Spencer, Claires (2012) "Strategic Posture Review: Algeria," worldpoliticsreview.com.

Varol, Tugce (2013) *The Russian Foreign Energy Policy.* Egalite: European Scientific Institute Publishing.

Weitz, Richard (2014) "Strategic Posture Review: Russia," worldpoliticsreview.com.

World Economic Forum (2013) "Scenarios for the Russian Federation." World Scenario Series, January 2013.

---

[1] Based on the official websites of both Algeria and Russia's foreign ministries and a number of news agencies websites.

[2] President Putin went to Egypt, Algeria, South Africa, Morocco and Libya, and President Medvedev went to Nigeria, Angola, Namibia, Egypt and Algeria.

[3] Alexandra Arkhangelskaya and Vladimir Shubin, "Is Russia Back? Realities of Russian Engagement in Africa," downloadable from www.lse.ac.uk, p. 21.

[4] Ibidem.

[5] Ibidem.

[6] Ibid., p. 22.

[7] Ibid. p. 19.

[8] Tugce Varol, (2013) *The Russian Foreign Energy Policy.* Egalite: European Scientific Institute Publishing, p. 23.

[9] Sean P. Roberts, (2013) "Russia as an International Actor: The View from Europe and the US." FIIA Report 37/FIIA Occasional Report 2, Finnish Institute of International Affairs, Finland, p. 18. [emphasis is added]

[10] Ibid., p. 17.

[11] 'Concept of the Foreign Policy of the Russian Federation,' downloadable from, http://news.kremlin.ru/media/events/files/41d447a0ce9f5a96bd c3.pdf

[12] Alexandra Arkhangelskaya and Vladimir Shubin, op. cit., p. 22.

[13] Ibid., p. 22.

[14] 'Russia's National Security Strategy to 2020,' http://rustrans.wikidot.com/russia-s-national-security-strategy-to-2020

271

[15] Alexandra Arkhangelskaya and Vladimir Shubin, op. cit., p. 22.

[16] It might not be considered coincidental that Russian-Algerian relations *renaissance* started with the coming of both Algerian President Abdelaziz Bouteflika (1999) and Russian President Vladimir Putin (2000–2008 and 2012) to power in both countries.

[17] Antonio Sánchez Andrés, (2006) "Political-Economic Relations between Russia and North Africa," Real Insituto Elcano, WP 22/2006, November 2006, p. 2.

[18] Ibid., p. 2.

[19] Ibid., p. 5.

[20] Paul Holtom et al. (2013) "Trends in International Arms Transfers, 2012," SIPRI Fact Sheet, March 2012, pp. 4-5.

[21] Śmigielski draws attention to some difficulties with the Russian arm industry which have been "reflected in the problems that have emerged with certain contracts—with Algeria (MiG-29SMT), China (Il-76MD and Il-78) and India (the Admiral Gorshkov aircraft carrier). Moreover, the Russian arms industry's decreasing capabilities mean that, for the first time since 1945, Russia is forced to seek modern weapons abroad, evidence of which can be seen in the talks with Israel about supplies of unmanned planes and with France about the sale of Mistral class amphibious assault ship." See Robert Śmigielski, (2010) "The Role of Arms Exports in the Foreign Policy of the Russian Federation," Polish Institute of International Affairs, Bulletin No. 54 (130), April 9, 2010, p. 249.

[22] Antonio Sánchez Andrés, op. cit., pp. 2-3.

[23] When the Algerian military earlier in 2008 returned 15 MIG fighter jets to it's the Russian supplier, complaining that they were substandard, some observers thought that this incident was part of a gradual shift in Algerian economic and diplomatic alliances. However, such conclusion has later proved to be incorrect.

[24] Claires Spencer (2012) "Strategic Posture Review: Algeria," worldpoliticsreview.com, p. 8.

[25] Tugce Varol (2013) *The Russian Foreign Energy Policy,* Egalite: European Scientific Institute Publishing, p. 119.

[26] Rivlin, Paul (2005) "The Russian Economy and Arms Exports to the Middle East." *Memorandum* No. 79 November 2005.

[27] Ingmar Oldberg (2010) "Russia's Great Power Strategy under Putin and Medvedev," Occasional Paper No. 1/2010, Swedish Institute of International Affairs, Sweeden, p. 20.

[28] When the trans-Saharan gas pipeline goes into operation, Nigerian gas will start going to Southern Europe through Algeria. Russia is encountering resistance from the EU in its attempts to expand cooperation with the African countries in the oil and gas sphere. The matter concerns, for example, resistance to the implementation of Russian-Algerian and Russian-Nigerian energy projects and attempts to block Russia's participation in exploiting the trans-Saharan gas pipeline. See, Irina O. Abramova and Leonid L. Fituni, (2011) "Russia, BRICS and Africa: Relations of Partnership and Competition," Institute for Transnational Studies, Landshut, Germany.

[29] Tugce Varol (2013) *The Russian Foreign Energy Policy,* Egalite: European Scientific Institute Publishing, pp. 231-232.

[30] Tatiana Mitrova (2010) "New Approaches in Russia's Foreign Energy Policy – East and West," in Kristin Linke and Marcel Viëtor (eds), *Prospects of a Triangular Relationship? Energy Relations between the EU, Russia and Turkey*, April 2010

[31] SAFPI (2012) "Algeria: Diversifying economic ties with Brazil, Russia, India and China,"; *http://www.safpi.org/news/article/2012/algeria-diversifying-economic-ties-brazil-russia-india-and-china*

[32] Though the Russian navy might receive expanded basing opportunities on Syria's Mediterranean coast.

[33] Alexey Malashenko, (2013) "Russia and the Arab Spring," an October 2013 Paper, Carnegie Moscow Center.

[34] Lavrov during its visit to Algeria on February 2013, voice of Russia.

[35] For over a decade, Chechen militant separatism and terrorism had been the major real danger to Russia's national security.

[36] Sean P. Roberts, (2013) "Russia as an International Actor: The View from Europe and the US." FIIA Report 37/FIIA Occasional Report 2, Finnish Institute of International Affairs, Finland, p. 20.

[37] Brett Schneider (2014) "Russian Pragmatism in the Middle East: Success in Algeria," http://muftah.org/tag/brett-schneider/

[38] Richard Weitz (2014) "strategic posture review: Russia," www.worldpoliticsreview.com

[39] Among the ten countries with the largest proven natural gas reserves, only Algeria is positioned to undermine Russia's monopoly in Eastern Europe

[40] There has been in recent years a significant evolution in trade exchange between Algeria and Russia from $ 157 million in 2001 to more than $ 2 billion in 2010 (http://www.algerianembassy.ru/Ambassade.htm#RelationsBL).

VI. OTHER EMERGING POWERS' INTERESTS IN AFRICA

Viacheslav Usov, PhD
Institute for African Studies
Russian Academy of Sciences

AFRICAN POLICY OF INDIA AND INDIAN DIASPORA: RISK ASSESSMENT

Historically, the dispersion of people from India and the formation of Indian diaspora communities are the result of different waves of migration over hundreds of years driven by a number of reasons. Nowadays, from 20 to 25 million Indians live across 130 countries and constitute the second largest diaspora in the world today after the Chinese. In Africa, the total number of People of Indian Origin (PIO) and Non-Resident Indians (NRI) in Africa may be as high as 2.4 million.

Since the Indians that settled in Africa migrated for different reasons and since their backgrounds were very different, a number of various Indian communities have emerged in Africa, which, roughly speaking, may be divided into two main groups, known as the 'old diaspora' and the 'new diaspora'. The main distinction between them is a different level of their engagement with their 'mother country'. 'Old diaspora' consists of descendants of Indians that arrived in the colonialism era, mostly as workers and traders, and who are now the fourth or fifth generations of Indians living in Africa. Many of these people have lost or are often losing their links to India and are officially called PIOs. The 'new diaspora' comprises the skilled Indian immigrants who started to come to African countries in the 1970s, most often to work as IT professionals, teachers, doctors, lawyers, etc. or to found their private business.[1] This group mostly includes the Indian citizens who maintain regular contacts with their relatives in India and are officially referred to as NRIs.

Only one third of the Indian migrants living abroad have Indian passports, and most of them live in developed countries of Europe and North America. But the majority of members of the Indian diaspora live in developing countries.[2] Many years India hardly had any consistent policy towards its diaspora. The policy of independent India envisioned and implemented by

274

Jawaharlal Nehru, who gave the Indian diaspora little recognition, except for the advice that they should be best citizens of the countries of their adoption. Global political changes, liberal economic reforms and a burst of new technologies around the globe highlighted a new role of diaspora. The diaspora emerged as a valuable contribution to the development of national economies and important factor in promoting economic ties with the countries of diaspora accommodation. Chinese government has been especially successful in engaging with the diaspora to set up joint ventures and other industries. This policy has proven successful, and has bee emulated by some other governments, including the Indian one.

The first means to engage with the Indian overseas diaspora were to introduce legal and tax incentives for attracting diaspora's financial resources in the wake of the economic liberalization. Other measures include the usage of PIO's card, created in 1999. It is a long-term visa (20 years), which allows PIOs to have property or access the educational system in India. However, most important changes were brought about in the beginning of 2000s when the High Level Committee on Indian Diaspora (HLC) was established. In 2001, the HLC issued a Report that defined the framework of a new Indian policy in relation to its overseas diaspora. It also set the priorities for this policy.

Some of the measures suggested by the Committee led to controversies, such as a recommendation to introduce dual citizenship, which faced a serious criticism by a number of Indians in Africa. In 2004, a new Indian government established the Ministry of Overseas Indian Affairs (MOIA).[3] The Ministry transformed the idea of 'dual citizenship' into the Overseas Citizenship of India Scheme.[4] The Ministry also continued organizing the Pravasi Bharatiya Divas and since then 12 PBD have taken place in India not only in New Delhi but also in Mumbai (2005), Hyderabad (2006), Chennai (2009), Jaipur (2012), Kochi (2013).

In response to a strong and persistent demand for holding such events, some mini- or regional PBDs were organized in 2007 to reach out to a vast majority of diaspora communities that, for various reasons, are unable to attend the main event in India and benefit from its deliberations. The fourth one in the series, called 'PBD Africa', was held in Durban, South Africa on 1st-2nd October 2010 to commemorate the anniversary of Mahatma Gandhi on (2nd October) and marked the 150th anniversary of the arrival of indentured Indians in the country[5].

The Annual Report for 2012–2013 released by the Ministry appraised the achievements of the MOIA including the establishments of the Prime Minister's Global Advisory Council, the Indian Council of Overseas Employment, the Overseas Indian Facilitation Centre, the India Development Foundation, the Global Indian Network of Knowledge, and Overseas Indian Centers (at the Indian Missions in Washington and Abu Dhabi)[6].

Most of these and other steps announced by the MOIA were aimed primarily at the NRIs in the developed countries and at the Indian workers in the oil-rich Persian Gulf countries. Only some of the new initiatives such as the establishment of PIO University or Know India Programme might have had direct implications for the Indian diaspora in Africa.[7]

For many years, the Indian government was blamed for pro-Western bias in its diaspora policy. There are important reasons for that. A great number of ethnic Indians are holding high governmental positions or operating in major business offices in the USA and the UK. The role of American Indian diaspora in brokering the US-Indian Nuclear Agreement in 2008 is also well-known. All these factors seem to support the idea that Indian communities in the developed countries should be in the focus of the Indian diaspora policy[8].

At the same time, Indian participation in IBSA, BRICS and other South-South initiatives, its active involvement in Africa makes India seek diversification of its diaspora policy. The "Indian Diaspora Engagement Meet" was held in Nairobi, Kenya, in April 2012. The meeting was attended by delegates, representing primarily senior and influential diaspora community members, and small and mid-sized investors of Indian origin, residing in East African countries. The main emphasis during the discussions was on the willingness and potential of the Indian diaspora in facilitating the economic cooperation of their countries of adoption with India and creating synergy between the two countries[9].

The Indian government also took some other measures. They decided to unite the Overseas Citizenship of India and PIO Card Scheme and to give the NRIs some voting rights[10]. This decision was strongly appraised by many Indians abroad. Responses such as *"we are very happy"* or *"Indian government has finally fulfilled its promise to Indian expatriates"* have been very common[11].

However, despite of all these efforts and some real results (for example a steady increase in remittances from US$ 15.8 billion in 2001-02 to US$ 70 billion in 2011-12[12]), the Indian diaspora policy has recently faced a lot of criticism in India and abroad. Ambassador J. C. Sharma, who has undertaken serious analysis of the Indian diaspora policy, says, *"after 10 PBDs, it would be useful to review its organization and content to ensure its relevance for both India and the diaspora"*[13]. The Ambassador also regretted the fact that India's policy approach towards the Indian diaspora so far has remained largely inconsistent and a victim of poor implementation.

Among other issues, he feels that the Ministry of External Affairs and the Ministry of Overseas Indian Affairs have not agreed on a clear division of duties to be done in order to address the issues of interest to the overseas Indians. Without proper representation from the Ministry of External Affairs, the MOIA is significantly missing valuable inputs[14].

There are also critics among the experts, businessmen and media who blame the Indian government for not taking necessary measures to attract more investment from the diaspora. Nimisha Madhvani, the Ugandan high commissioner to India, who belongs to a family that owns and runs one of the biggest business conglomerates in East Africa, stated: *"The Indian government has not really focused on the Indians in Africa, which is why many of the big Indian business groups of Indian origin in that continent do not look at putting their money in India but instead tap business opportunities in Europe and America. However, if certain restrictions were eased and some steps taken by the government, India could attract a lot of investment from this segment"*[15].

Not only Indian but also some African experts see clear shortcomings in the current Indian policy related to the Indian diaspora in Africa. Phillip O. Nyinguro, Professor of University of Nairobi, Kenya, has assured that the economic and political positions that Indians occupy in South Africa and East Africa, have put them at vantage points in influencing policy in their host countries. Their entrepreneurship and wealth are sources of leverage they can use to bargain with governments. It is an open secret that many politicians, especially those from the ruling parties in South Africa, Uganda, Kenya and Tanzania, have always received substantial donations for their election campaigns from Indian businesspersons. The Indian government and Indian businesspersons could benefit by maintaining strong links to their diasporas in these countries, for they could influence governments of their host countries to adopt more friendly policy towards India[16].

While some critics think that the Indian government is too modest in its efforts to attract diaspora, others see it as too active and sometimes even provocative.

According to a Portuguese scholar, Constatntino Xavier, in order to demand more rights from New Delhi, NRIs and PIOs from across the globe have started lobbying the central and state governments, pressuring MPs and MLAs, and even petitioning courts. Trying to meet the demands of the diaspora the Indian government has been involved in a larger set of cultural and religious agendas, such as the turban controversy in France, the Hindu Americans' efforts to pressure US states to make changes to school textbooks[17] or building crematoriums in UAE for Indian expats living in the Gulf[18].

Some prominent Indian scholars, for example Ruchita Beri, doubt that the current approach to Indian diaspora could work in Africa. *"People of Indian origin [in Africa] are a totally different ball game because they settled there centuries back... They are South Africans, Tanzanians, or Ghanians. They have a totally different kind of identity now"*, she said[19].

Beri's opinion is echoed by that of Gerard McCann from the University of York, who concluded that while India's dynamic diasporic transitions do

277

provide potential for India and overseas Indians, diaspora's -cultural linkages will not be able to automatically provide India with advantages in its over-seas activities. The post-colonial history of India-diaspora relations, as well as the controversial place of overseas Indian communities within certain African societies, has produced complex situations that need negotiated collectively by India, overseas Indians and the 'host' nations with which India hopes to make contacts through its 'children' abroad[20].

The director of the South African Association for International Affairs, Elizabeth Sidiropoulos also said, that more than anything else, the very longevity of many of Africa's Indian-origin citizens, some of whom belong to sixth generation, could make hard for them to lobby or promote trade ties by the same way as the Indian-Americans, many of whom were just a generation or two old. However, in her opinion, recent arrivals from China and India, because of new investments, are creating a corps of people, equally familiar with Asia and Africa, and they could take on playing a stronger role in fostering relations[21].

A number of Indian experts on the Indian diaspora suppose that India should emulate the Chinese approach to diaspora affairs and believe that, if all the hurdles have gone away, "India has the potential to gain more than what China did from its diaspora"[22].

To sum up these opinions, one can say that a trajectory of Indian diaspora policy and especially its future development is still a rather divided topic. The overseas Indian communities are as diverse as the very ideas of how to deal with the diaspora. However, there is a major difference between those, who would like to utilize the diaspora resources for the aims of India development and feel that India should emulate the Chinese approach, and those, who see the diaspora mostly from the Nehruvian point of view.

Supporters of the idea that India should follow the Chinese way, usually say China is much more successful than India in attracting the diaspora investments because of the policies adopted by China. It is interesting, however, however that the same people do not usually speak a lot about the measures that China has applied to its diaspora to make it more governable.

Experts in China's diaspora policies think that China's current strategy relies on two pillars: influencing overseas Chinese organizations and creating a homogeneous diasporic identity. To begin with, China is now involved in the supervision of Chinese overseas associations. These associations turn out to be very standardized worldwide with the Mandarin, instead of regional dialects, being used by these associations, thus fostering their standardization. China also aims at fostering a uniform overseas Chinese identity. As a result, it first seeks to promote interactions between different migrant communities through the organization of business fairs around the world or the merging of different overseas associations.

278

China also creates dedicated organizations such as the China Overseas Friendship Association, whose goal is officially "to promote the unity of the sons and daughters of China and for the unification of the motherland". Such initiatives are especially important to fill the gap that might exist between the old overseas communities and the new migrants. Moreover, an important propaganda apparatus such as TV channels, state-sponsored websites and newspapers are involved in the policy aimed at influencing the overseas Chinese. These media are used to create a 'correct' and uniform overseas identity[23].

The current India's strategy was designed to be quite similar to that of China. The Indian government set up an institutional apparatus to cope with overseas Indians, created incentives for them to invest, and conducted a rhetorical strategy to bind them emotionally to India. The government's discourse glorified the diaspora as the "umbilical cord" connecting the "motherland" to its "lost children", the media started to actively cover diaspora affairs. Overseas Indians naturally felt proud of belonging to the "emerging Asian superpower"[24]. The years of economic growth have undoubtedly resulted in growing patriotic and national feelings in the country and led to the appearance of the ideas to promote a uniform diaspora identity among overseas Indians, especially Hindu, which to some extent echoes the Chinese case. Creating self-regulated emigrants, which would act in accordance with India's objectives, investing in the motherland, can be seen as the aim of this strategy.

However, not everyone agrees that Indian diaspora unified. According to Gijsbert Oonk, there is no such thing as one united Indian diaspora, but a number of Indian communities or diasporas.[25] They are as diverse as India itself and one can hardly expect all of them to speak Hindi. From Nehruvian point of view, India's identity is "unity among diversity", it is not based on ethnicity or religion but on territorial and cultural grounds. In addition, India is a democracy and its political parties and forces have different ideas about how to treat the diaspora.

People of Indian origin in Africa are in a position to help India improve its relations with the many countries that they have settled in. They have domain knowledge about local business conditions and customs, and many of them are successful businesspersons themselves. Apart from business, there are teachers and professionals of Indian origin in virtually every African country. While many PIOs are not so enthusiastic to follow the policy projected for them by the Indian government, NRIs can effectively act as "unofficial ambassadors" and "Indian cultural informants" amongst local population. In Ethiopia, for instance, the word 'teacher' is almost synonymous with 'Indian'.

The BJP's (and this is the party that once envisioned the contemporary Indian diaspora policy) victory in the recent elections in India can give a new impulse to the Indian Diaspora policy and revitalize it. The new government will also obviously have to draw the thin line between using Indians living abroad as a diplomatic tool and not letting them become an obstacle that impedes the achievement of important goals in the country's international relations.

[1] Modi Renu. Indian communities in Africa. Gateway House. Indian Council on Global Relations. 13 September 2012. http://www.gateway house.in/ publication/analysis-amp-background/backgrounders/ind..

[2] Foreign Policy of India with Special Reference to India's Africa policy. 21 November 2008. http://www.diplomacy.bg.ac.rs/pdf/lecture_Dubey _20081121.pdf

[3] "We will listen to Indians abroad". Interview with the Minister for Overseas Indians Jagdish Tytler. December 03, 2004. http://specials.rediff.com/news/2004/dec/03inter.htm.

[4] Dual Citizenship. http://www.indiaday.org/government_policy/dual_ citizenship.asp; Singh, Shubha. Taking India to overseas Indians. http://www.dailypioneer.com/columnist1.asp

[5] Ministry of Overseas Indians Affairs. Government of India. Pravasi Bharatiya Divas: Mini PBD. http://moia.gov.in/services.aspx?ID1=28&id=m1&idp=25&mainid=23; Krishnakumar, Lakshmi. Durban to host Africa diaspora conference. 5 августа 2010 г. http://www.thaindian.com/newsportal/uncategorized/durban-to-host-africa-diaspora-conference_1004074 66.html

[6] Ministry of Overseas Indians Affairs. Government of India. Annual Report 2011-2012. P. 13. http://moia.gov.in/writereaddata/pdf/Annual_Report _2012-2013.pdf

[7] The Diversity and Spread of Indian Diaspora. Ambassador J C Sharma. http://voiceof.india.com/7817-2

[8] Chandramohan, Balaji. The Diaspora can shape Foreign Policy. 13 February 2012. http://www.indiannewslink.co.nz/index.php/archives_2011/feb_15_ 2011/the-diaspora...

[9] Indian Diaspora Engagement Meet in East Africa, Nairobi, Kenya. Press Release. http://www.oifc.in/Uploads/MediaTypes/Documents/Kenya-Meet-Press-Release.pdf

[10] Ministry of Overseas Indians Affairs. Government of India. Annual Report 2011-2012. P. 40. http://moia.gov.in/writereaddata/pdf/Annual_Report_2011-2012. pdf

[11] Overseas Indians welcome right to vote. Jaipur, 9 January 2012. http://overseasindian.in/2012/jan/news/20120901-105420.shtml

[12] Ministry of Overseas Indians Affairs. Government of India. Annual Report 2011-2012. P. 13. http://moia.gov.in/writereaddata/pdf/Annual_Report_2012-2013. pdf

[13] The Diversity and Spread of Indian Diaspora. Ambassador J.S.Sharma. http://voiceof.india.com/7817-2

[14] The Role of Diaspora in India's Foreign Policy, National Security and Economic Development. 31 July 2012. Report prepared by Sanjay Kumar. http://www.vifindia.org/event/report/2012/08/04/the-role-of-diaspora-in-india-s-foreign-policy-national-security-and-economic-development

[15] Duttagupta, Ishani. Indian Diaspora in Africa. Finding friends for the safari. 31 January 2010. The Economic Times. http://www.peerpower.com/et/ 60/Indian-Diaspora-in-Africa-finding-friends-for-the-safari

[16] Nyinguro, Phillip O. The Role of Indian Diaspora in Indo-African Co-operation // India and Africa: Enhancing Mutual Engagement / Ed. by Ruchita Beri. Institute for Defence Studies and Analyses. New Delhi, 2014. P. 138. http://www.idsa.in/system/files/Book_IndiandAfrica_RuchitBeri.pdf

[17] Xavier, Constantino. Beyond borders: Governing the diaspora. 1 March 2010. Pragati. http://gatewayhouse.in/publication/gateway-house-affiliated/pragati/beyond-borders-governing-diaspora

[18] UAE Indian expat alert: NRI minister 'kills' Air India, 'opens' Sharjah cemetery. 13 November 2012. http://www.emirates247.com/news/emirates/ uae-indian-expat-alert-nri-minister-kills-a...

[19] Lahiri, Tripti. An African USINPAC? The Wall Street Journal. 24 May 2011. http://blogs.wsj.com/indiarealtime/2011/05/24/an-african-usinpac/tab...

[20] McCann, Gerard. Global India and its Diaspora. 1 June 2011. http://africanarguments.org/2011/06/01/global-ubdia-and-its-diaspora/

[21] Lahiri, Tripti. An African USINPAC? The Wall Street Journal. 24 May 2011. http://blogs.wsj.com/indiarealtime/2011/05/24/an-african-usinpac/tab...

[22] 'Craft India diaspora policies like China'. The Indian Express. 16 June 2011. http://www.indianexpress.com/news/craft-india-diaspora-policies-like-china/804669/0

[23] Chemouni, Benjamin. The Diaspora as an Economic Asset. How China and India use their Diaspora to support their economic development. Dissertation submitted for the obtention of the degree. MSc China in Comparative Perspective. London School of Economics and Political Science. P. 19. http://www2.lse.ac.uk/ economichistory/Research/CCPN/publications/Dissertations/DissertationsCCP/72190.pdf

[24] The Diversity and Spread of Indian Diaspora. Ambassador J.S.Sharma. http://voiceof.india.com/7817-2

[25] Global Indian Diasporas. Exploring Trajectories of Migration and Theory. Collection of essays. Edited by Gijsbert Oonk. IIAS / Amsterdam University Press, 2007.

Alla Borzova, Phd,
Peoples' Friendship University of Russia,
Moscow

BRAZIL'S COOPERATION WITH AFRICA
(Agricultural aspect)

At the World Economic Forum on Africa, (7-9 May 2014) it was pro-claimed, that Africa is on track to achieve 5.5% economic growth in 2014. To do this, Africa needs to create jobs, build vital infrastructure, foster intra-African trade, fund the agribusiness revolution and seek out new pockets of industrialization[1]. African leaders have defined an agenda for agricultural growth that is both sustainable and inclusive.

The problem of Food Security and Nutrition in Africa was resolving on different levels, including the creation of the Grow Africa Investment Forum, where discussed an opportunity for companies, farmers and governments to further accelerate sustainable agricultural growth in Africa. According to the recently published Grow Africa Annual Report, Grow Africa partners dou-bled their commitments for agriculture and food security to US$7.2bn in 2013; of this, US$970 million has already been invested, which has led to the creation of 33,000 new jobs and assistance to 2.6 million smallholder farmers throughout the continent[2].

For Brazil, the expanding of cooperation with Africa is one of the priori-ties of foreign policy. The course of Ex-President Lula da Silva was called "Preferential policy of Brazil according to Africa ". Brazil develops coopera-tion with African countries on several levels: South – South cooperation in the frames of intercontinental summit "South America-Africa" (ASA), and in line with the IBSA, which represents the association of leading developing countries, as well as through the Community of Portuguese-speaking coun-tries (CPLP). South Africa and Brazil have a leading role in the intensifica-tion of cooperation between regional integration and trade unions – Mercosur and the Southern Africa Customs Union (SACU), the Southern African De-velopment Community (SADC) and the Common Market for Eastern and Southern Africa (COMESA).

Brazil has rather deep cooperation with the African Union (AU), and both parts signed in 2007 the Agreement on technical cooperation and an agreement on the implementation of projects in the field of social develop-ment (2009), innovative projects for sustainable development, agriculture and livestock. Brazil and AU cooperate in solving the problems of food secu-rity and agricultural development in the framework of COMBASA (Joint Bilateral Commission on Agriculture and Food Security), which includes representatives from the AU and NEPAD. Brazil signed more than 50 agreements with 18 different African countries for technical cooperation in agricultural development, prepared a program for social policy, 53 agreements with 22 African states in the area of health care. Brazil is rapidly expanding scientific, technical and cultural cooperation with Africa. This country has 55 agreements with 20 African countries in order to cooperate in the field of education[3].

Brazil states that its development cooperation is guided by the following principles:

– joint diplomacy, based on solidarity;
– demand-driven action, as a response to demands from developing countries;
– acknowledgement of local experience and adaptation of Brazilian experience;
– no imposition of conditions;
– no association with commercial interests or profit;
– no interference in domestic issues of partner countries[4].

These principles demonstrate, that Brazilian cooperation differs from traditional forms of cooperation, they reflect the horizontal relationship between southern countries. Brazil prefers to describe its cooperation as a mutually beneficial relationship between partners. Technical cooperation consists of the transfer and adaptation of expertise, skills and technology for development mainly through training courses, workshops, consultancies, exchange programs, and the donation of equipment. Poverty reduction strategies (such as Zero Hunger) and cash transfer programs (such as Bolsa Familia) immediately caught the attention of several countries, such as Ghana, which was the first to request formally Brazilian support for similar social programs.

Now Brazil ranks third in the world in the export of agricultural products, which goes to almost 200 countries. The agriculture, which employs 37% of the population, accounted for 28% of GDP. Programs in the field of agriculture are of great importance, 21% of finance is precisely on scientific and technological development of this sector. On the program for the development of agriculture in 2009–2013 was allocated US\$ 252.6 million.

The great role in research and development in Brazilian agriculture plays a state-owned company EMBRAPA (Empresa Brasileira de Pesquisa Agropecuária (EMBRAPA) (Brazilian Enterprise for Agricultural Research).

EMBRAPA established in 1973 as part of the Ministry of Agriculture, Fisheries, and Food Supply. Its mission is "to provide feasible solutions for the sustainable development of Brazilian agribusiness through knowledge, technology generation and transfer in order to increase productivity and support agriculture in the Brazilian territory." The institution has generated and recommended more than 9,000 technologies for Brazilian agriculture, reduced production costs, and helped Brazil to increase food supply while observing natural resources and the environment and diminishing Brazil's dependence on external inputs[5]. With 38 research centers, 13 central divisions, and 3 service centers, EMBRAPA is present in almost every Brazilian state. It has 9,248 employees, including 2,215 researchers (74 percent with doctoral degrees, 18 percent with master's degrees, and 7 percent with postdoctoral degrees). It coordinates the Sistema Nacional de Pesquisa Agricola (National Agricultural Research System or SNPA), which includes universities and most public and private entities involved in agricultural research in the country. In 2010, its budget was US$1, 1 billion[6].

EMBRAPA is one of the world's leading tropical-agricultural research institutions. Its technological innovations initiated the transformation of the Brazilian savannah (cerrado), and it is now focusing on areas such as biotechnology and bioenergy. EMBRAPA has therefore strengthened its international connections – it has 78 technical cooperation agreements with 56 countries and 89 foreign institutions, consisting of research partnerships, as well as technology transfers (mainly in agricultural research), as well as 20 multilateral agreements with international organizations. Internationally, it has innovated virtual laboratories, placing researchers in well-known agricultural research institutions abroad to contribute to strategic areas for agricultural development.

- Precision in agriculture
- Environmental services in agricultural landscapes
- Alternative agroenergy
- Functional foods – adding value to health promoting foods important to Brazilian agribusiness
- Technologies for aquaculture
- BioSeg: biosafety on GM crops
- High quality beef
- Science and technology for organic agriculture
- Conserving the national genetic resources of Brazil
- Creating tools for plant protection
- Forests for energy production
- Measuring the environmental, social and economic impacts of beef industry
- Nanotechnology, the power of the quasi-invisible
- Sustainable production of sugarcane for energy purposes
- Genomics technologies for the development of water-use efficient plants
- Technologies for biodiesel production

– Genomics for the advancement of animal breeding and production
– Climatic risks zoning for small farming agriculture, bioenergy and pastures[7].

The main purpose of Embrapa in Africa is sharing scientific and technological knowledge to contribute to social and economic development, to food security and to combat hunger across the region. The activities emphasize specific demands of each partner country on projects focused on agricultural development. Embrapa develops actions of technical assistance and opportunities for training and development of human resources. Embrapa Africa's work platform covers the areas of agroenergy, tropical fruit production, and vegetables (production and processing), post-harvest technologies, animal beef/milk production and forests.

In 2010, Africa accounted for the largest regional increase in spending, having absorbed 57 percent of Brazil's overall technical cooperation budget. The five Portuguese-speaking African countries remain Brazil's main technical cooperation partners, with Mozambique as the single largest beneficiary. In 2010, these countries accounted for 74 percent of resources spent in technical cooperation in Africa.

Agriculture tops the list of priority fields of Brazilian technical cooperation. Between 2003 and 2010, it accounted for 22 percent of the country's technical cooperation portfolio worldwide. In Africa, the proportion of agriculture-related projects was even greater (at 26 percent, over the same period). EMBRAPA has increased its presence in Africa in 2006, when its office was opened in Accra, Ghana. EMBRAPA's collaboration with African countries is carried out mainly through three instruments: so-called structuring projects, technical training, and the Africa-Brazil Platform for Agricultural Innovation. The organization conducts technology transfers with markets in Africa: Ghana, Senegal, Mozambique and Mali.

In 2012, Embrapa established a partnership with the Forum for Agricultural Research in Africa (FARA) to share technologies that support cotton production.

The Cotton Four Project. This project was conceived in 2008 to support the development of the cotton industry in the "C-4 countries"—Benin, Burkina Faso, Chad, and Mali[8].

Technical Support to the Development of Agricultural Innovation in Mozambique. This project is the first structuring project implemented since 2010 in cooperation with the Agricultural Research Institute of Mozambique. The organization conducts technology transfers with markets in Africa (including Ghana, Senegal, Mozambique and Mali).

Rice-Culture Development Project. The EMBRAPA's third structuring project is in Senegal. Launched in 2010, the US$ 2.4 million project

285

jointly developed by the Senegalese Institute for Agricultural Research and EMBRAPA[9].

Technical training. The second instrument used by EMBRAPA to support other countries is a technical training through CECAT (Centre for Strategic Studies and Training on Tropical Agriculture). It offers courses: research in agriculture, forage production and pasture, good practices in agriculture, and livestock production; seed production; production systems for family-based agriculture, community based seed production, and water-resources conservation in small properties and farms; and soy production (ABC 2010). In October 2010 alone, 45 technicians and researchers from 20 African countries participated in CECAT training events. Continuing education is a central component of its programs and, between 2007 and 2010, it trained more than 21 million rural workers[10].

Africa-Brazil Platform for Agricultural Innovation. The third instrument is the Agricultural Innovation Marketplace, launched in 2010 to strengthen ties between EMBRAPA and African researchers.

The More Food Programme and the Food Acquisition Programme (Programa Mais Alimentos Africa) aims to increase agricultural productivity and food security in Africa by improving access to technology. It consists of a credit facility to support the acquisition of farm machinery and equipment supplied by Brazilian manufacturers, which have been intensively involved with the design of the programme, including in negotiations over pricing. It is directed at 'family farming' or the African equivalent, with lending complemented by specialized technical assistance.

The loan is provided on concessional terms, offering a 15 to 17 year repayment period, a 3 to 5 year grace period and an interest rate of 2 percent. A total of $640 million has been approved by the Brazilian Foreign Trade Chamber (CAMEX) for implementation of this programme in Africa in 2011–12. Credit lines have already been negotiated with Ghana, Zimbabwe, Mozambique, Senegal and Kenya. The programme draws on a similar programme implemented in Brazil by the Ministry of Social Development (MDS) and MDA. The Brazilian government has committed $2.4 million to support the programme's implementation in five African countries: Ethiopia, Malawi, Mozambique, Niger and Senegal[11].

Since then, the number of partner countries in Africa has increased to 38 (ABC 2011) for technical cooperation in agriculture). As Malawi and Niger, Mozambique and Senegal, will pilot the Africa version of the Food Acquisition Programme.

The Food Acquisition Programme (PAA) aims to address food insecurity and strengthen local food markets by procuring foodstuffs produced by small farmers, donating them to families facing food insecurity, supplying school feeding programmes and building up food stocks. Embrapa dominates

286

the portfolio of cooperation projects as the source of expertise for agriculture-related issues, particularly in areas such as strengthening developing countries' research capacity and adapting Brazilian technology to these countries' agro-ecological conditions. The Food Acquisition Programme is a trilateral cooperation partnership, between Brazil, FAO and WFP and five African countries.

ProSavana, currently the largest project in the agriculture, is the product of a trilateral cooperation agreement between Brazil, Japan and Mozambique, in the Nacala Development Corridor: 14 districts in the provinces of Niassa, Nampula and Zambezia, the square almost 14mln hectares[12].

Food Security Research Project in Mozambique, called ProAlimentos, researchers from specialist Embrapa centres in Brazil are working directly in the field (literally) with researchers from the Mozambican Agrarian Research Institute testing suitable horticulture varieties for the Maputo greenbelt

Energy Security. Brazil began to develop a partnership with various African governments for the development of the biofuels industry, which acted as the basis for the program in the "poverty reduction and mitigation of global warming. Brazilian company Odebrecht, concluded a major biofuel partnership with Mozambique, Nigeria and Angola. The need to use renewable energy sources could meet energy needs and contribute to poverty reduction in rural Africa[13].

A Brazilian company to manufacture alcohol and sugar cane, «Dedini», in 2007 opened a sugar processing plant in South Africa. Now Brazil is interested in buying agricultural land in South Africa to grow food for biofuels. The mining company Vale in 2008 signed an agreement on the development of the biofuels industry between Brazil and Mozambique on US $6 billion. For the development of the biofuel sector in Mozambique, which covers 83,000 hectares, about US$ 256 million was invested. One of the important treaties on the development of biofuels in Africa was signed between Brazil and Angola. It assumed a construction of the largest production facility of biofuels in Angola. The project, costing about $ 258 million was supposed to start in 2012. It includes 30,000 hectares of land for growing sugar cane, as well as the construction of a plant for processing into sugar and ethanol[14].

Reflecting the country's diplomatic and economic motivations, Brazilian cooperation has been spreading steadily across the continent. According to the latest official information, there are technical cooperation projects at either design or implementation stage in 38 countries[15].

Brazil in Africa does not pursue a strategy of export of raw materials, and its policy, along with the development of trade and economic relation, is aimed to change the social and humanitarian situation in Africa.

[1] World Economic Forum on Africa.Forging Inclusive Growth, Creating Jobs. Abuja, Nigeria 7-9 May 2014. http://www.weforum.org/reports/world-economic-forum-africa-forging-inclusive-growth-creating-jobs

[2] Investing in the future of African agriculture. 1st Annual Report on private-sector investment in support of country-led transformations in African agriculture. http://www3.weforum.org/docs/IP/ .../WEF_GrowAfrica_ AnnualReport 2014.pdf

[3] Борзова А.Ю. Бразилия-Африка: пример высокоэффективного и перспективного сотрудничества. // Азия и Африка сегодня, 2013, №9. Borzova A. Brazilia-Africa: primer visokoeffektivnogo sotrudnichestva// Azia i Afrika segodnija, 2013, No 9.

[4] ABC 2011. http://www.abc.gov.br/CooperacaoTecnica/OBrasileaCooperacao

[5] Brazilian Agricultural Research Corporation. (2012) Embrapa. 10 December. http://www.embrapa.br/english/embrapa

[6] Brazilian Agricultural Research Corporation (Embrapa) http://reports.weforum. org/manufacturing-growth/view/brazilian-agricultural-research-corporation-embrapa-brazil/

[7] de Alvarenga Neto, R, C, D and Vieira, J, L, G. "Building a Knowledge Management Model at Brazil's Embrapa (Brazilian Agricultural Research Corporation): Towards a Knowledge-Based View of Organizations" *The Electronic Journal of Knowledge Management Volume 9 Issue 2 (pp. 85-97), available online at* www.ejkm.com

[8] Africa and Brazil to Share Cotton Know-how, Théodore Kouadio, Summary posted by Meridian on 9/10/2012.http://www.merid.org/en/ Content/News_Services/ Food_Security_and_AgBiotech_News/Articles/2012/Sep 10/Brazil.aspx.

[9] ABC (updated) Coton 4: Programa brasileiro de apoio a iniciativa do algodro. Agencia Brasileira de Cooperacao, Ministerio das Relacoes Exteriores, Brasilia.

[10] ABC (2010b) A Cooperacao Tecnica do Brasil para aAfrica. Ajencia Brasileira de Cooperacao, Brasilia. http://www.abc.gov.br/CooperacaoTecnica/ OBrasileaCooperacao

[11] ABC (2011) Brazilian Technical Cooperation. Agencia Brasileira de Cooperacao, Brasilia. http://www.abc.gov.br/CooperacaoTecnica/OBrasilea Cooperacao

[12] Cabral L., Shankland A. Narratives of Brazil-Africa Cooperation for Agricultural Development: New Paradigms? March 2013. Working Paper 051 www.future-agricultures.org

[13] "First high-level biofuels seminar in Africa " // UNIDO http://www.unido.org/ fileadmin/import/70430_AfricaBiofuels_IISD_Highlights_DAY02.pdf

[14] "Brazilian senate approves biofuel partnership with Mozambique" // IPIM. http://www.ipim.gov.mo/worldwide_partner_detail.php?tid=11384&mode=print& lang=en-us

[15] ABC (2011) Brazilian Technical Cooperation. Agencia Brasileira de Cooperacao, Brasilia

Aya Abenova,
Kazakh Ablai-khan University
of International Relations and World Languages
Almaty, Kazakhstan

THE INTERNATIONAL COOPERATION FOR AFRICAN DEVELOPMENT: BRICS AND SOUTH AFRICA' ROLE

In the last decade, Africa has been mostly perceived as a continent of opportunities, whose voice has become louder in the international arena. In particular, one of the most developed African states, South Africa, nowadays drives the economic growth of the entire Southern African sub region.

For decades, African countries have repeatedly attempted to join forces in their fight against underdevelopment and poverty. They have committed themselves to integrate, which has paved the way to the formation of the African Union (2001). The idea of the African unity, which has been realized in the form of the AU, was paralleled by the development of an "African Renaissance" concept declared by the former South African President Thabo Mbeki. The African Union seeks to use the experience of the European model of integration, which includes the establishment of a continental parliament, courts, the central bank, the overall market as well as the formation of armed peacekeeping forces and police units. It is the most ambitious project of its kind in the world after the European Union. No other community in the developing world is so aimed at integration, as the African Union. The proponents of integration hope that it will significantly accelerate the democratization and economic development of Africa.

In particular, the African Union has paid particular attention to a large-scale development program to be implemented across the continent, namely the "New African Initiative", which was later transformed into "New Partnership for Africa's Development" (NEPAD). NEPAD has become the first development program designed and put forward by the Africans themselves. South Africa, on its turn, managed to help NEPAD by attracting the attention of the international community to this program. The analysis shows that NEPAD essentially incorporates key provisions of the "African Renaissance".[1]

NEPAD contains programs aimed at the economic development of Africa, which include a specific set of measures and require partnership at the global level for their implementation. These programs are based on common economic interests of African countries and, therefore, represent a most effective way to solve the numerous problems of Africa. However, the implementation and effectiveness of these programs depend upon overcoming disagreements between state-parties themselves. Another serious problem for the AU leadership is lack of financial resources. This makes them dependent on external funding, restricts the freedom of action and affects its ability to carry out peacekeeping missions.[2]

Major regional organizations for economic cooperation, including the SADC (Southern African Development Community) and the Common Market for Eastern and Southern Africa (COMESA), established on the continent with the participation of South Africa. SADC is the most promising African regional organization, which is now comprised of 14 countries. It is a major regional association, whose main objectives include regional peace, stability and economic integration. Its purposes in the economic integration sphere also include the creation of a free trade zone, customs union, common market, the central bank and monetary union and currency integration by 2018.

Africa has long been the most conflict-ridden region of the world. The root cause of its many conflicts is competition over mineral resources.

The AU has demonstrated its ability to act as a peacemaker in resolving African conflicts. Although the financial capacity of the AU is limited and its peacekeeping forces lack professionalism, with the assistance and support of the UN and Western donors, this organization will be able to gain experience and create opportunities for a more active participation in peace- and security-building in Africa. South Africa acts as a mediator in peace negotiations, aimed at conflicts resolving in Africa, and allocates forces for peacekeeping operations.[3]

South Africa has a multi-faceted approach in pursuit of its foreign policy in the world arena: on the one hand, it uses all the features of the existing system of international organizations, on the other – it actively contributes to the reform of this system.

South Africa finds it necessary to reform the existing structures in order to maintain international peace and security in the African continent. SA advocates for reform of the UN Security Council, IMF and WTO.

South Africa is an active participant in discussions and meetings of the Commonwealth Heads of States, where the most important issues of the world politics are discussed, such as counterterrorism, struggle against AIDS, debt relief and problems of the WTO.

Actively participating in the global processes of disarmament, as well as in the programs of non-proliferation of WMD, South Africa strengthens its position as a leader in the Southern African region and actively uses the institute of international peacekeeping.

In the context of growing global demand for natural resources, Africa has gained the status of a key player in the market of mineral raw materials.

So, in 2009–2010 Africa accounted for 82% of the world production of platinum, 43% of palladium, 42% of cobalt, etc. The export share of goods and services in South Africa's GDP rose from 20% in the 1990s to 44% in 2011[4].

South Africa's relationship with other countries of the continent remains a priority in its foreign policy. In particular, it is necessary to solve the problems associated with the influx of migrants from other African countries to the territory of the country.

South Africa cannot accept the role of a satellite of developed countries. It strongly favours equal representation of the Third World countries in all international institutions.

At the same time, South Africa is engaged in dialogue with the developed countries, especially when it comes to trade and other economic issues. Some leading experts believe that the total GDP of African countries will reach 2.6 trillion dollars by 2020, which will put the growth rate at 35%. Such dynamics further encourages the interaction between African countries[5]. According to the World Bank, by 2050 Africa's GDP will reach $19.3 trillion[6].

South Africa, like other countries in the region, sees strengthening regional integration, mutual support and solidarity between African countries as one of the main ways to protect its national interests in the contemporary world. South Africa is one of the leaders of the continent, which plays an important role in strengthening the inter-African cooperation and reducing the gap between the developed and developing countries. Its foreign policy is based on democratic principles and commitment to the development of all Africa.

South Africa's participation in the BRICS strengthened its political, economic and military cooperation with the countries of its region and all Africa, and increased its prestige in the world arena. Although South Africa's neighbors recognized the leading economic role of South Africa, it creates some controversy about the ability of South Africa to represent the continent in the world. Given the gap in the level of development between South Africa and poorer countries in the continent, it might be problematic for South Africa to effectively defend their needs. .

South Africa's representatives have actively participated in the fourth BRICS summit, held in New Delhi (March 29, 2012), in the sectoral meetings preceding it, as well as in the forum of research centers. Speaking after the meeting, South Africa's President Jacob Zuma said that the BRICS forum is a place where Africa is treated with respect. All the partners are equal[7]. In other words, South Africa seeks to use BRICS as an engine of its economic development, with an obvious desire to strengthen its position on the African continent[8].

A need to support the developing economies of Africa reflected in the theme of the 2013 BRICS Summit in South Africa. It was called "BRICS and Africa", and its focus was placed on the regional cooperation (between African countries), especially in the field of infrastructure development. The summit held a meeting called "Unlocking Africa's potential: BRICS and Africa Cooperation on Infrastructure" which also focused on Africa's development[9].

South Africa may also benefit from the BRICS countries' intention to use national currencies in their mutual trade. The first step in this direction already made. The central banks of the member-states signed an agreement on loans in their respectful currencies. An idea to create the BRICS Development Bank was discussed, which should be based on the World Bank model and serve to mobilize the resources needed for the implementation of infrastructure projects and for sustainable growth in Africa. BRICS leaders announced their intention to create the bank in March 2013 in Durban. At present, an agreement has been reached on the amount of authorized capital and the principle of decision-making. There were negotiations on the allocation of quotas among participants. Since March 2013, the distribution of the initial capital of $50 billion and the location of the headquarters were discussed, as all BRICS participants expressed great interest to host future Bank's headquarters in their countries. Some experts believe that, by 2015, the work will be completed. On the sidelines of the G20 Sydney meeting the respective document was discussed, and it was stated that the document is by 80% or even 90% ready[10].

Excellent infrastructure allows South Africa to play an active and influential role in the regional integration and in the solution of a broad range of pan-African issues. This contributes to the establishment of regular contacts between the Eurasian and African integration organizations, such as the Customs Union and the Southern African Customs Union and the Common Economic Space, in the long term – between the Eurasian Economic Union, the African Union and the Southern African Development Community. It enhances international cooperation in the struggle against terrorism, separatism, drug trafficking and other kinds of organized crime[11].

Another advantage of South Africa is that the country that got rid of the apartheid regime and created a truly democratic society has great moral authority around the world. But at the same time South Africa bears the additional burden resulting from expectations of African migrants, who believe that because of the history of fighting apartheid, South Africa is obliged to provide asylum to all economic and political refugees, and also should solve difficult problems of the whole continent.

In conclusion, it can be argued that South Africa historically serves as a link between cultures, countries and continents. The success of its foreign policy depends on the abilities of the country's leadership to use the combination of all its advantages. The South Africa's foreign policy is aimed at both protecting national interests, promoting economic development and defending the security of the country, as well as at strengthening the political and economic consolidation in Africa.

Participants of the Deauville summit in France (May 2011) referred to South Africa as "a new pole of the global development". All members of the "Big Eight" recognize that the importance of Africa in the world economy in XXI century will grow[12].

This is a clear indicator of the high level of international expectations of this country and the attractiveness of its economy for external actors. There is no doubt that South Africa has a large potential for further development, but it is also true that this potential depends on and needs to be backed up by pragmatic and wise foreign policy.

[1] Prokopenko L., Shubin V. Afrikanskiy renaissance. Afrika: poisk identichnosti. Moscow: Institute for African Studies, 2001 (in Russian)

[2] Organizaciya africanskogo edinstva. Istoriya sozdaniya I deyatel'nost'. Collection of documents. M., 1970 (in Russian)

[3] Belugina E. BRICS – Budushee mirovoi ekonomiki? // Rynok cennyh bumag» 2012, № 7 (424). (in Russian)

[4] BRICS I Afrika: partnerstvo I vzaimodeistvie. Otv. Red. T.L.Deych, E.N.Korendyasov. M., Institute for African Studies, 2013. p.51 (in Russian)

[5] Collection of information and analytical data by the theme of the BRICS Summit 2013 in SA: «BRICS i Africa: Partnerstvo dlya razvitiya, integracii, industrializacii». Industrial Innovation Club: http://www.unido.ru/eng/project/ industrial_club/ (in Russian)

[6] Korendyasov E.N. BRICS I Afrika: potencial partnerstva I vzaimodeistviya / E. N. Korendyasov // Diplomaticheskiy ezhegodnik, 2012 / [Dip. acad. MFA of Russia]. M., 2013. p. 156-188

[7] Kruger A. From BRIC to BRICS and South Africa's military. News on ISS Africa 2011, 27 May. – http://www.iss.co.za/iss_today.php?ID=1289 (last viewed 13 May 2013)

[8] Zuma taunts West, says Africa is treated with respect in BRICS. Thaindian News. 2012, 29 March. – http://www.thaindian.com/newsportal/uncategorized/zuma-taunts-west-says-africa-is-treated-with-respect-in-brics_100608068.html (last viewed 13 May 2013)

[9] Shubin V.G. Zachem Yuzhnoi Afrike BRICS i zachem BRICS Yuzhnaya Afrika http://www.pircenter.org/media/content/files/11/13730353600.pdf (in Russian)

[10] First Annual G20 Conference "Africa and the G20: A Critical Assessment" Wednesday, 19 December 2012 – http://www.gegafrica.org/g20-blog/first-annual-g20-conference-africa-and-the-g20-a-critical-assessment

[11] Vystuplenije V.Putina na vstreche s liderami afrikanskih gosudarstv 27.03. 2013. – http://kremlin.ru/transcripts/17759 (in Russian).

[12] Informatsionnij bulletin: Sammit "Gruppy vosmi v Dovile (Francija) 26-27 maja 2012.

AUTHORS

Abenova Aya, student, Kazakh Ablai Khan University of International Relations and World Languages, Almaty, Kazakhstan.

Borzova Alla, PhD (History), Senior Research Fellow, Peoples' Friendship University of Russia, Moscow.

Gazibo Mamoudou, Prof., University of Monreal.

Deych Tatiana, Dr.Sc. (History), Leading Research Fellow, Institute for African Studies RAS, Moscow.

Hamchi Mohamed, PhD candidate; assistant professor of International Relations at University of Oum El Bouaghi, Algeria.

Karpov Grigory, PhD (History), Research Fellow, Centre for Russian-African Relations and African Countries' Foreign Policies, Institute for African Studies RAS, Moscow.

Khazanov Anatoly, Dr.Sc., Prof., Institute for Oriental Studies RAS, Moscow.

Korendyasov Evgeny, PhD (Economy), Head of the Centre for Russian-African Relations and African Countries' Foreign Policies, Institute for African Studies RAS, Moscow.

Kochetov Dmitry, PhD candidate, Institute for African Studies RAS, Moscow.

Kostelyanets Sergey, PhD (Political Science), Research Fellow, Institute for African Studies RAS, Moscow.

Kulkova Olga, PhD (History), Senior Research Fellow, Centre for Russian-African Relations and African Countries' Foreign Policies, Institute for African Studies RAS, Moscow.

Lileev Ivan, PhD (Political Science), Senior Research Fellow, Institute for African Studies RAS, Moscow.

294

Makgetlaneng Sehlare, PhD (History), Africa Institute of South Africa, Human Sciences Research Council, Pretoria, South Africa.

Mularoni Claudia, CEO of Pragmata Institute (Dogana, Republic of San Marino), Member of Board of Directors of Cespi, Center for Studies in International Policies.

Poruchikov Sergey, PhD candidate, Tambov State University named after G.R. Derzhavin, Tambov.

Rebiai Samia, PhD candidate; assistant professor of International Relations at University of Oum El Bouaghi, Algeria.

Rodin Anton, PhD candidate, Institute for African Studies RAS, Moscow.

Scarpellini Piero, General Director of Pragmata Institute (Dogana, Republic of San Marino), Member of the Presidency Committee of Cespi, Center for Studies in International Policies, University of Bologna.
Sepeleva Natalia, PhD candidate, Research Fellow, Institute for African Studies, RAS, Moscow.

Seregichev Sergey. PhD (History), Russian State University for the Humanities.

Shamilov Murad, Master Degree S. Kazakh Ablai Khan University of International Relations and World Languages, Almaty, Kazakhstan.

Shinn David, Dr.Sc., Prof. Elliott School of International Affairs, George Washington University.

Sindzingre Alice Nicole, PhD (Economy), Research Fellow, National Centre for Scientific Research (CNRS, France), Research Centre Economix-University Paris-West.

Smertin Yury, Dr.Sc. Kuban State University, Krasnodar, Russia

Smirnova Galina, PhD (Economy), Senior Research Fellow, Institute for Oriental Studies, RAS, Moscow

Tsvetkova Nina, PhD (Economy), Senior Research Fellow, Institute for Oriental Studies, RAS, Moscow.

Urnov Andrey, Dr.Sc. (History), Leading Research Fellow, Institute for African Studies RAS, Moscow.

Usov Viacheslav, PhD (History), Senior Research Fellow, Institute for African Studies RAS, Moscow.

Van der Merve Justin, DPhil, Centre for Military Studies (CEMIS). Faculty of Military Science. Stellenbosch University, South Africa.*Yurtaev Vladimir,* Dr.Sc. (History), Prof., Director of the Scientific and Educational Centre for African Studies, Peoples' Friendship University of Russia, Moscow.

Yurtaev Vladimir, Dr.Sc. (History), Prof., Director of the Scientific and Educational Centre for African Studies, Peoples' Friendship University of Russia, Moscow.

AFRICA'S GROWING ROLE
IN WORLD POLITICS

Chief of Publishing Department
Natalya Ksenofontova

Design and desktop publishing
Gulzhamal Abisheva

Подписано к печати 25.11.14. Объем 23 п.л.
Тираж 500 экз. Заказ № 90.

Отпечатано в ПМЛ Института Африки РАН
123001, Москва, ул. Спиридоновка, 30/1